HTML and XHTML

Gary Rebholz

SAMS
201 W. 103rd Street
Indianapolis, Indiana 46290

How to Use HTML and XHTML

International Standard Book Number: 0-672-32031-2

Library of Congress Catalog Card Number: 00-105842

Printed in the United States of America

First Printing: June 2001

04 03 02 01 4 3 2 1

Trademarks

All terms mentioned in this book that are known to be trademarks or service marks have been appropriately capitalized. Sams Publishing cannot attest to the accuracy of this information. Use of a term in this book should not be regarded as affecting the validity of any trademark or service mark.

Warning and Disclaimer

Every effort has been made to make this book as complete and as accurate as possible, but no warranty or fitness is implied. The information provided is on an "as is" basis. The author and the publisher shall have neither liability nor responsibility to any person or entity with respect to any loss or damages arising from the information contained in this book.

Acquisitions Editor
Betsy Brown

Development Editor
Alice Martina Smith

Managing Editor
Charlotte Clapp

Project Editor
Carol Bowers

Copy Editor
Mike Henry

Indexer
Erika Millen

Proofreader
Matt Wynalda

Technical Editor
Sunil Hazari

Team Coordinator
Amy Patton

Interior Designer
Gary Adair

Cover Designer
Dan Armstrong

Illustrator
Stephen Adams

Layout Technician
Cheryl Lynch

Contents at a Glance

Contents

About the Author

Gary Rebholz has been working with HTML and Web technologies for the past five years. He is employed as a Training and Development Specialist for Sonic Foundry in Madison, Wisconsin, where he is involved in every aspect of creating training materials. These materials include books, videos, Web-based tutorials, computer-based training materials, and other multimedia presentation technologies.

He is involved in virtually every stage of the process of creating training from conceptualization through final production. This process includes research, writing, graphic design, programming, video editing, audio editing, narrating, teaching, and occasionally vacuuming his office rug. However, he can't be counted on to remember to water plants, so his office has none.

Gary has traveled from coast to coast in the United States, as well as in Canada, Mexico, and Europe to present Sonic Foundry products and to train users and Sonic Foundry employees. His experience teaching basic HTML classes has helped him form a unique vision of the challenges that face beginning HTML authors.

This is Gary's second book for Sams Publishing. His first (co-written with Denise Tyler) was *How to Use Macromedia Flash 5.* He is currently working on his third book for Sams (with Michael Bryant), *Sams Teach Yourself ACID 3.0 in 24 Hours.*

Gary lives among the cows and trolls in the rolling hills of southwestern Wisconsin with his wife Rebecca and their children Jake, Leah, and Kyrianna (with a fourth and fifth on the way). He also lives with the scars inflicted by viewing far too many Web pages with black background and white text.

Dedication

To Jack & Rose, and Rudolf & Rose

Acknowledgments

First I want to thank my family—Rebecca, Jake, Leah, and Kyri—who have forgotten what I look like without a laptop attached to the tips of my fingers. For months, you have put up with my preoccupation with this project. I'm thankful I've finished just as spring is awakening so that we can enjoy the warming days once again as a family.

Special gratitude goes to Rebecca who has handled everything around the house while I've buried my face in my computer. Thank you for worrying that I wasn't getting enough sleep, and for letting me sleep in on Saturday mornings instead of waking me up early as I asked you to!

Thanks to Rose and Rudolf, who have fed me at least one wonderful meal a week and have worried that I wasn't getting enough sleep—yet nonetheless called early enough on Saturday mornings so that I could still wake up and get some work done.

Thanks to Jack and Rose, who also feed me once a week, who don't seem to worry about my lack of sleep, and who never call on Saturday mornings.

I also owe a great deal of thanks to the folks at Sams Publishing who have helped me through this process. Thank you, Betsy Brown, my Acquisitions Editor, for giving me another chance to write. Thank you, Alice Martina Smith, my Development Editor, for your refreshing enthusiasm, compassionate support, and wonderfully creative ideas. Thanks also to Amy Patton, Mark Taber, Carol Bowers, Sunil Hazari, Mike Henry, and several other people unknown to me who have helped make this book possible. Special thanks to Stephen Adams and the other artists at Sams who did such a great job on the graphics for this book.

Tell Us What You Think!

As the reader of this book, *you* are our most important critic and commentator. We value your opinion and want to know what we're doing right, what we could do better, what areas you'd like to see us publish in, and any other words of wisdom you're willing to pass our way.

You can e-mail or write me directly to let me know what you did or didn't like about this book—as well as what we can do to make our books stronger.

Please note that I cannot help you with technical problems related to the topic of this book, and that because of the high volume of mail I receive, I might not be able to reply to every message.

When you write, please be sure to include this book's title and author as well as your name and phone or fax number. I will carefully review your comments and share them with the author and editors who worked on the book.

E-mail: **webdev@samspublishing.com**

Mail: Mark Taber
Associate Publisher
Sams Publishing
201 West 103rd Street
Indianapolis, IN 46290 USA

How to Use This Book

The Complete Visual Reference

Each part of this book is made up of a series of short, instructional tasks, designed to help you understand all the information you need to get the most out of writing HTML and XHTML code.

Click: Click the left mouse button once.

Double-click: Click the left mouse button twice in rapid succession.

Right-click: Click the right mouse button once.

Pointer Arrow: This highlights an item on the screen you need to point to or focus on in the step or task.

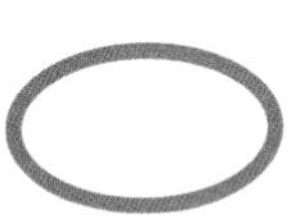

Selection: This circle highlights the area that is discussed in the step.

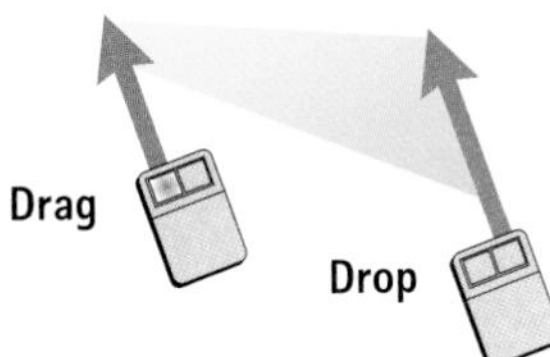

Drag and drop: Position the mouse pointer over the object, click and hold the left mouse button, drag the object to its new location, and release the mouse button.

Each task includes a series of easy-to-understand steps designed to guide you through the procedure.

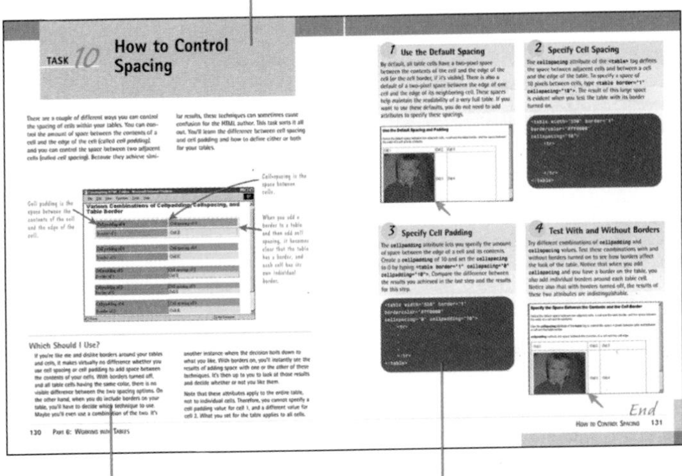

Extra hints that tell you how to accomplish a goal are provided in most tasks.

Each step is fully illustrated to show you how it looks onscreen.

Screen elements (such as menus, icons, windows, and so on), as well as things you enter or select, appear in **boldface** type.

If you see this symbol, it means that the task you're in continues on the next page.

Continues

Introduction

Don't let the recent reality check that's shaking up the "dot-com" and tech-stock whiz kids fool you. The Internet—and its most well-known facet, the World Wide Web—are here to stay. And the language of the Web is HTML. Learning HTML is much easier than you probably think. By following the tasks in this book, you'll be creating your own Web pages within the first couple of hours.

Even though this book presents HTML techniques in terms of how you can use them to create your own Web pages, you've made a wiser decision in deciding to learn how to write HTML than you might think. HTML is used for much more than creating Web pages. It is the basis of a growing number of help systems integrated into software packages; it can be used for presentations, training materials, and much more.

As you make your way through the easy-to-follow tasks in this book, I'll teach you how to code HTML and use related technologies. But I'll also give you some insight into doing your part to make sure that the pages you add to the millions already out there communicate effectively and...well...look nice.

What is HTML, and how does it work? The *HT* stands for hypertext. *Hypertext* is a system of linking documents together with hyperlinks that the reader can click to navigate from one document (or page) to another. These links are what make the Web so useful.

Each of these links points to a Uniform Resource Locator (URL), which provides the direction for how to get from one page to another. The URL of a page is its address on the Web. The URL includes all the information that the user's *browser* (a software application made specifically for viewing Web pages) needs to find the page or other resources such as graphics, multimedia files, and so on.

The *ML* in *HTML* stands for *markup language*. A *markup language* is a collection of symbols—often called *tags*—that are inserted within a document to define the way that document should look when printed or displayed. For example, one tag makes text print bold. Another tag makes an image appear on the page. The key to learning HTML is learning the tags used to mark up, or build, the structure of your pages. You'll learn that and more in this book.

Unfortunately, there is no standards organization that oversees the development and implementation of HTML, or that issues standards to which developers must adhere. An organization called the World Wide Web Consortium (W3C) attempts to bring structure to the chaotic development of the Web; the W3C has issued specifications for the implementation of HTML (the current implementation is HTML 4.0).

Even more unfortunately, browser manufacturers have not gained a reputation for adhering strictly to the specifications issued by the W3C. That makes your job as an HTML author more difficult. The good news is that growing pressure from authors like you and me is causing the major browser manufacturers to sit up and take notice of the fact that people are getting fed up with browsers that do things their own way.

Because of the inconsistency that exists between how major browsers handle the same HTML code, I've purposely left some things out of this book. I want to make sure that you come away knowing how to create pages that are supported by all the major browsers, so I try not to waste your time explaining tags that work with one browser but not another.

Another thing I don't do in this book is worry about whether or not a tag has been *deprecated* (that is, designated as obsolete) by the W3C in favor of a new technology called Cascading Style Sheets (CSS). I think it's important for you to learn the basics of straight HTML and how to use it to create a complete page. In Part 10 of the book, I'll teach you how to create CSS.

I also concentrate on good coding practice that prepares you to use future technologies of the Web, starting with Extensible HTML (XHTML). I believe that you might as well learn the proper coding technique now so that you don't have to unlearn your habits and form new ones later.

Finally, throughout the book I'll sprinkle hints and ideas for creating well-designed Web pages. Many times, your Web pages are the only thing your visitors and customers ever see. I want to make sure that the design and function of your Web site presents a professional-looking image.

I hope you'll enjoy following along with the tasks in this book. If you take the time to go through them all, you'll come away knowing HTML, and knowing it well. You'll be able to create Web pages and other HTML-based documents, and you'll also have an introductory knowledge of several of the most exciting and important emerging technologies on the Web.

Along the way, I hope you also have some fun. Thank you for reading!

Task

Part 1

Getting Started

Welcome to what might be the single most important part in this book! Throughout these pages, you will discover the possibilities that open up to you as you become proficient in properly coding HTML. However, the first step is to conquer any fears you might have as you approach this new—and perhaps somewhat intimidating—field. The importance of a solid understanding of the basics of the technology into which you are about to delve can't be overstated.

Just like any other mystery, the mystique surrounding Web development and HTML coding quickly evaporates as you examine the pieces. In this part, we'll look at the most basic of those pieces. You'll find that HTML is not so mysterious after all. You'll learn that the tools you use can be simple and relatively uncomplicated. You'll discover that the "code" that makes up HTML presents little challenge once you know how to structure it. And you'll see that even the most fancy HTML techniques are based on the same logical rules of construction that you'll learn in this part.

In the following tasks, I present the basic techniques you'll need as an author of HTML. In addition, as you learn more about HTML today, you'll be developing the solid coding techniques that will carry you into more sophisticated Web technologies tomorrow. You'll learn how to create a text document that you'll save as an HTML file. You'll learn how that HTML file becomes a Web page when you view it in a Web *browser* (a program that allows you to view Web pages on the Internet), and how that single page works with all the other pages you write to create a Web site.

No matter how good you turn out to be as a Web designer or how sophisticated the pages that you eventually code become, you must first get started. The tasks in this part are so important because they give you that start. Spend the time to thoroughly understand the information presented in these tasks. Don't let the basic nature of the information feed the urge to skim through without really learning it. Mastering these basics ensures that you will easily understand the techniques presented in the remainder of the book. Let's get started!

TASK 1 How to Organize Your Work

Before you start creating HTML, you need to do a little planning. How will the single HTML document (known as a Web *page*) you want to create be used? What will it accomplish? And how does it fit in with other pages in the Web site? You need to spend time exploring these issues. A Web site quickly grows from your first HTML page to many pages that can be linked together in countless ways. If you don't know where you're going, you probably won't be too happy with where you end up. Planning is the key to an organized, effective Web site. If you don't have a plan, you might wind up with a haphazard, disorganized, frustrating, and inefficient mess.

Plan for how your site will appear in the context of the Internet as a whole.

Plan the structure of the site.

No Time for Seat of Your Pants

No doubt you've been given this lecture before. In fact, we hear so much about planning and goal-setting that it almost becomes part of the background noise. But I guarantee that you'll be better off for the preparation and planning you do up front. Web sites can get very, very confusing. Especially when you start linking pages together. One of the things that makes the Web great is that links can exist from anywhere to anywhere else. That's also one of the features that breeds confusion during development. At the start, it's easy to think you've got it all in your head. But take my word for it...things can quickly become confusing and unmanageable. Take the necessary steps to be as prepared as you possibly can before you start coding, and you'll make your job much easier.

1 Assess the Needs

As the very first step to creating a Web page, you must figure out why the world needs it. Maybe the page contains critical information, or maybe you're creating it just for fun. Maybe it teaches, or maybe it entertains. Maybe it does both. These needs define the page—and the site as a whole. Think about the need, and write your ideas down. Then refer back to this list as you develop your pages.

Proposal for www.myvacations.com
List of Needs

1. People are busy. Busy people need vacations
2. Busy people don't have time to waste when researching vacation possibilities
3. Vacation destinations need publicity

2 State Your Goals

Now that you know the needs you want your Web page to satisfy, you must define specific goals. For example, if you find that people need more information about vacation destinations, make it a goal to describe an interesting new destination each month. Write down the goals. Make them specific, measurable, and most of all, achievable. Refer to this list often and don't be afraid to refine it along the way!

Proposal for www.myvacations.com
List of Goals

1. Profile one new vacation destination each month
2. Supply a minimum of six varied photos of each destination

3 List the Requirements

To achieve your goals, you'll have to fulfill a number of requirements. You'll have to gather the information. You might have to collect images. Your goals might also dictate specific technical requirements. Maybe you can get by with HTML, but you might also need other tools such as JavaScript or database-driven technologies. (Don't worry if you're not yet familiar with these terms, I'll explain them in later parts.) Underneath the goals you listed in Step 2, list the requirements for achieving those goals.

Proposal for www.myvacations.com
List of Requirements

1. Profile one new vacation destination each month
   a) A backlog of information on destinations
   b) Work at least one month in advance

4 Create a Map or Flowchart

Now that you know where you're going, create a map of how to get there. Decide what sections you want in your site and draw a square for each. You'll have to have a *home page* (sort of like the "front door" to your Web site). From there, you might *link* (that is, build pathways) to any of the major sections within the site. Draw boxes for those sections and draw arrows pointing to and from them to demonstrate desired link paths. Go as deep as you can because it makes your job from here on out much easier.

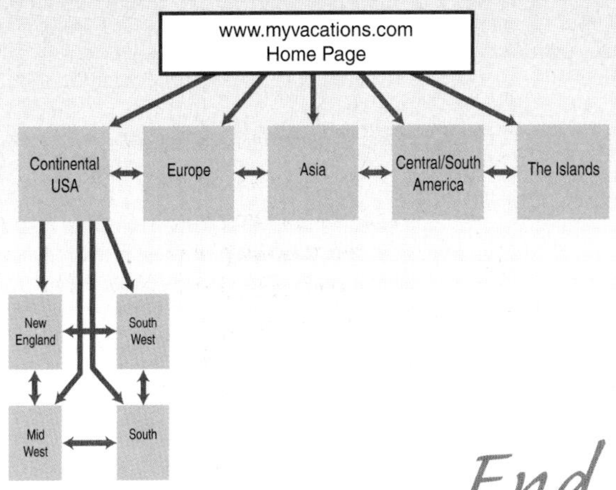

End

TASK 2 How to Gather the Tools You Need

Before you can get any work done, you have to gather the proper tools. Allow me to dispel the first major misconception of coding HTML—although there are many tools available, you don't need any particularly sophisticated tools to do the job. In fact, even that five-year-old computer can get you by. This task walks you through the collection of the simple tools you'll use throughout the remainder of the book.

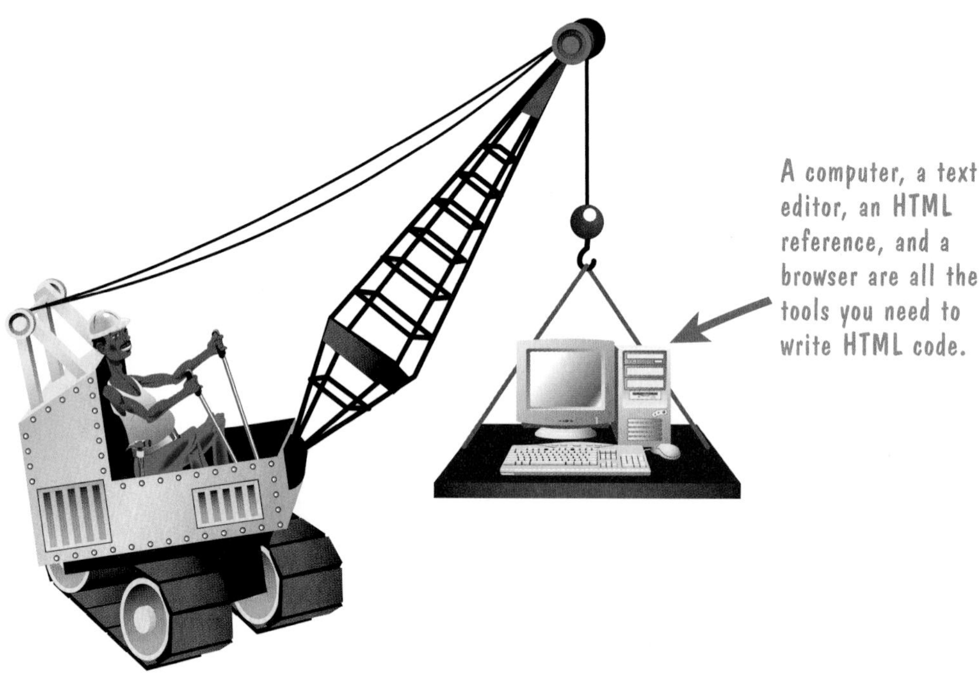

A computer, a text editor, an HTML reference, and a browser are all the tools you need to write HTML code.

What You See Is What You Get (WYSIWYG)

Many people use *WYSIWYG editors* to create Web pages. Programs such as Macromedia Dreamweaver and Adobe GoLive write the HTML for you. You work with a view that looks like your page will appear in a browser, and you format the page much like you would in a word processing or layout program. For instance, to make bold text, you select the text and click a button. The software codes the HTML in the background, and you see the results. Although they are improving, these editors tend to write code that contains unnecessary HTML. This makes the file size of the page larger than it needs to be; that means that your visitors have to wait longer to see your page. Some people use these programs for the initial setup and then clean up the HTML manually. With an editor program, you can get away with not knowing any HTML at all, but for serious Web development, I suggest that you continue learning the code!

1 Choose a Computer

The processing requirements for coding HTML are minimal. Choose a computer that's powerful enough to run a simple *text editor* and a *browser*. Although it's always better to have more computing power, that old Pentium I machine or your old Macintosh Ci is probably adequate. There's more good news: You can develop HTML pages on virtually any computer platform or format and deliver them to virtually any other format. So, pages created in Windows can be served by a UNIX box and viewed on a Macintosh.

2 Pick a Text Editor

Know what you need to write HTML? A text editor. It can have the latest bells and whistles, or it can be a basic, stripped-down model with last year's paint job. Some editors have features that color-code your work or automatically fill in code for you. Me? I use the plain-old, no-frills Notepad that comes on every Windows machine. On the Macintosh, you might use Simple Text. It doesn't really matter. Just choose something with which you can create an *ASCII text* document.

3 Find a Browser

You'll want to check your progress as you write your HTML, and the only way to see what you've created is to open your page in a Web browser. A Web *browser*—the most popular are Internet Explorer and Netscape Navigator—allows you to view the pages you create. Deciding which browser to use is an art in itself; I discuss the process in the following task.

4 Find an HTML Reference

You'll be happy to know that you've already taken this step! It's always a good idea to have a thorough HTML reference handy while you work. That way, you can quickly look up the tags you don't use all that often. This book can serve as that reference.

Figure 1.10 will be a shot of the cover art, which won't be available until later. Please make a note so the book doesn't ship with a blank spot.

TASK 3 How to Decide Which Browsers to Code For

Almost everyone who's heard of the Web knows of the "browser wars." It's a sad fact that the browser manufacturers have not made your job as an HTML author easy. Different browsers support different features. Browser manufacturers invent their own features that no one else supports. Standards seem nonexistent, and recommendations from the World Wide Web Consortium (W3C) are often ignored or incorrectly implemented. And none of this addresses the problem of the wide range of browser versions in use. It's enough to make you throw up your hands. In this task, you'll learn how to make logical decisions about the browsers you'll target for your Web page.

Building a Web site is like building a house: You need a plan, tools, and building skills.

Browsers are the windows into the structure of your Web site.

A Browser Here, a Browser There

You can quickly become overwhelmed with the options out there in browser land. Why can't they all just work the same? When you find the answer, will you please let the rest of us know? The sad truth is that browsers vary widely in their support for some features and in their interpretations of others. So, what should you use to test your code? Realistically, I think you can probably get by testing your code in two or three browsers. Any more than that, and you start to wonder whether the extra time you're sacrificing is worth the testing efforts. It's also handy to have a reference of which browsers support what features. This reference can help you make decisions about which browsers you need to test, given the features you want your Web site to support. You can find a great comparison chart at **http://hotwired.lycos.com/webmonkey/reference/browser_chart/**.

1 Know Your Target Audience

Before you can decide which browsers you should test with, you need to know something about your target audience. Simply put, what browsers do your target audience use? If your audience is cutting-edge Web designers, the latest browsers might cover the whole group. If your audience is relatively unsophisticated, you might assume that they use somewhat outdated browsers. Find out who they are and what they use. Then use the same browsers for your testing.

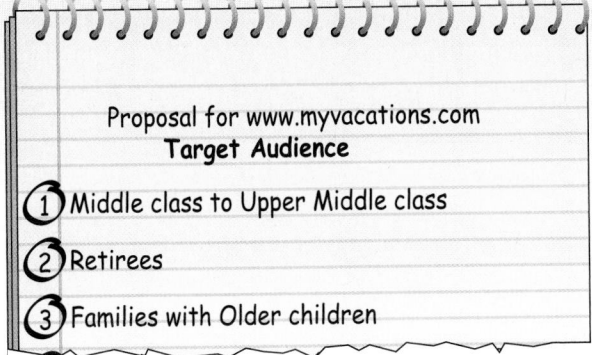

Proposal for www.myvacations.com
Target Audience

1. Middle class to Upper Middle class
2. Retirees
3. Families with Older children

2 Revisit Your Goals

Take another look at the lists of needs, goals, and requirements that you assembled during Task 1, "How to Organize Your Work." These lists might give you clues about which browsers to code for. For example, if your list of requirements dictates that you need to supply the visitor with a running time clock, you might have to include JavaScript in your page. In that case, older browsers are of no use because they lack JavaScript support.

Proposal for www.myvacations.com
List of Requirements

1. Profile one new vacation destination each month
   a) A backlog of information on destinations
   b) Work at least one month in advance

3 Decide on Feature Support

Are there any features that you absolutely must have on your Web page? Buttons that change when you point at them? Moving objects? Frames? These features might dictate that older browsers are out because they don't support many of the techniques required to provide such features. Decide what features you feel you must include. That will tell you a lot about the browsers your page requires.

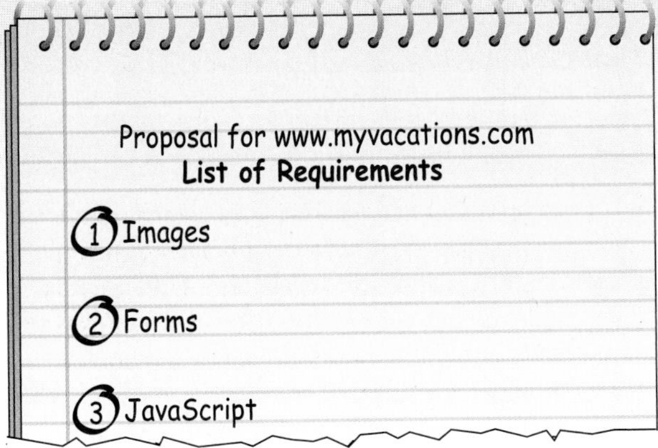

4 Identify Your Comfort Level

After making all these decisions, you ultimately have to decide what you're comfortable with. If you came up with a long list of "must have" features, can you live with the fact that many people won't be able to properly view your pages because they don't have an adequate browser? Or is accessibility more important than all the frills? Determine what you're comfortable with, and choose the browsers that support that comfort level.

End

TASK 4

How to Create HTML Tags and Add Attributes

The secret to making your pages look like you want them to look is knowing not only which HTML *tags* to use, but also how to properly construct them. HTML tags have a definite structure. Although there is some leeway when it comes to exactly how you arrange a few of the pieces, you won't find any forgiveness if pieces are missing. In this task, you'll build a sample HTML tag and add your first tag attributes. After you learn the basic structure, you'll use this knowledge countless times as you add new tags to your bag of HTML tricks.

Not the Forgiving Type

HTML is actually a somewhat forgiving language. For instance, it's not case sensitive. So, HTML considers **<garyshirt>** and **<GaryShirt>** and **<GARYSHIRT>** and **<GARYshirt>** to be the same thing. In fact, many HTML authors traditionally used all caps for tags to make them easier to locate on their pages. But the future is a technology called XHTML (you'll learn all about it in Part 10), which is not nearly so forgiving. For instance, you must always use lowercase letters for your XHTML codes because, although HTML might not care, XHTML does. In this book, I focus on teaching methods that not only work in HTML but also get you ready to move on to XHTML. Get into the habit now of doing it the XHTML way, and you'll be poised for the future.

1 Type Identifying Characters

When you're coding HTML, you need a way to alert the browser to the existence of an HTML tag. Something must separate the text from the tags. Therefore, each tag is bracketed by the less-than symbol on the left (<) and the greater-than symbol on the right (>). To identify a tag, type **< >**. You must have both symbols. If you forget either, the results are unpredictable, but more than likely unfavorable.

```
< >
```

2 Type the Tag Name

Now that you've alerted the browser of the existence of a tag, you must identify the tag. Type the tag name between the identifying symbols. For the hypothetical tag **garyshirt**, you would type **<garyshirt>**. Every tag is actually half of a tag pair. You have the opening tag (**<garyshirt>**) and its corresponding closing tag. Most closing tags are identified by the inclusion of a forward slash between the less-than symbol and the name. Type the closing tag as **</garyshirt>**.

```
<garyshirt>
</garyshirt>
```

3 Type the Attribute

Some tags contain *attributes*. Attributes describe the tag. For instance, one of the attributes of my shirt is "age," and the current attribute value is "old." The attribute name follows the tag name, separated from the tag by a single space. An equal sign (=) follows the attribute name, and the attribute value (enclosed in quotation marks) follows that. To specify the attribute of my shirt, type **<garyshirt age="old">**. Do not include attributes in the closing tag. Here the closing tag remains **</garyshirt>**.

```
<garyshirt age="old">
</garyshirt>
```

4 Type Additional Attributes

Some tags contain more than one attribute, and you can specify any or all of them. After the first attribute, type a space, and then the next attribute followed by the equal sign, and then the value in quotation marks. To further define my shirt, type **<garyshirt age="old" state="notfolded" condition="embarrassing">**. For most tags (but again, not all), specifying attributes is optional.

```
<garyshirt age="old" state="notfolded"
condition="embarrassing">
</garyshirt>
```

End

TASK 5 How to Structure Every HTML Page

Now that you know how to construct an HTML tag, let's talk about how to properly construct an entire page, and introduce the first four actual tags. After you've learned how to put a page together, you'll use that knowledge on every page you write. There are rules regarding tags that you must learn early.

Computers are literal. They read exactly what you write; the only way to ensure that they interpret your code correctly is to write it correctly. Follow the steps in this task to build an understanding of the skeletal structure of a properly coded HTML page.

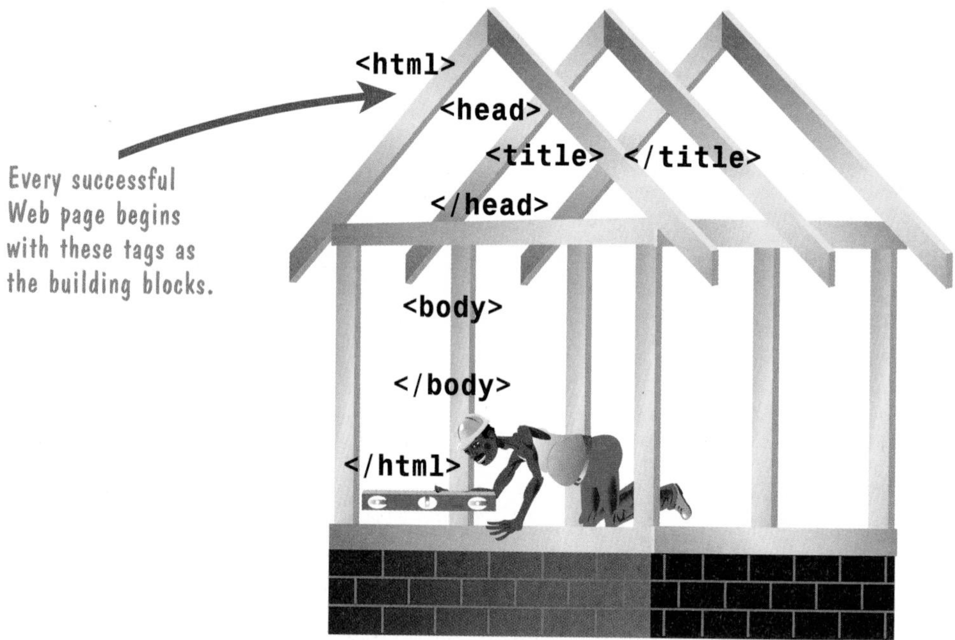

Every successful Web page begins with these tags as the building blocks.

An Open and Shut Case

Develop the habit now of closing every tag you open. Even though HTML doesn't always require this level of neatness, XHTML does. XHTML also insists on properly nested tag pairs. Think of it this way: First one in, last one out. You open the **<html>** tag before you open the **<head>** tag, so you must close them in the opposite order. You'll be glad you've developed good coding habits when you start working with XHTML later.

Organizing Your Text Document

Add tabs to your code to make it easier to read. For instance, the **<head>** tag pair is nested within the **<html>** tag pair, and the **<title>** pair is within the **<head>** pair. To make this easier to see in your text editor, type the **<html>** tags at the left edge of the document. Add one tab before the **<head>** pair, and two tabs before the **<title>** pair. Now each of the three pairs sits on its own level, and it's easy to see the relationships of the tags.

1 Add the <html> Tag Pair

Our first actual tag is the **<html>** tag. It appears as the first tag in every basic HTML page. This tag identifies the document as an HTML document and alerts the browser to expect more HTML to follow. Everything that you include in your page resides between the members of the HTML tag pair (this is referred to as *nesting*). To start a new HTML page, type **<html>** followed by a return (press **Enter**), and then type the closing **</html>** tag.

```
<html>

</html>
```

2 Add the <head> Tag Pair

The **<head>** tag follows the **<html>** tag. This tag pair encloses "invisible" heading information such as your page title, indexing information, expiration and creation dates, and author information. For pages that use scripting technologies such as JavaScript, the head area may contain scripting information. To add the **<head>** tag, type **<head>** under the **<html>** tag, followed by a return, and then type **</head>**. Do not include text you intend to be visible on your page within the **<head>** tag pair.

```
<html>
<head>
</head>
</html>
```

3 Add the <title> Tag Pair

The **<title>** tag pair is nested within the **<head>** tag pair. Whatever you type within the **<title>** tag pair appears in the title bar at the top of most browsers. This is the text that also appears on someone's bookmark or favorites list if they choose to add your page; many search engines use the title information you provide here to identify your page. So, type something descriptive and relatively short. Add the **<title>** tag directly below the **<head>** tag, followed immediately (don't add a return) by the **</title>** tag.

```
<html>
<head>
<title></title>
</head>
</html>
```

4 Add the <body> Tag Pair

The body of the page is where all the real action takes place! The information you type between the **<body>** tag pair appears on your Web page when it is viewed in a browser. You'll write most of your HTML within the **<body>** tag pair. Add the **<body>** tag directly under the **</head>** tag, followed by a return, and then the **</body>** tag directly above the **</html>** tag. Now you have it...the skeletal structure of virtually every HTML page you will ever code!

```
<html>
<head>
<title></title>
</head>
<body>
</body>
</html>
```

End

TASK 6 How to Give Your Page a Title

Everything you've learned so far lurks behind the scenes. Although anyone can view your code after you publish your work (Task 15, "How to Learn from Others' Source Code," explains how), most people never see the tags you write or the underlying structure of your pages. In this task, you create the first viewable results of your HTML work. The preceding task introduced the **`<title>`** tag; in this task, you'll use the **`<title>`** tag pair to give your page a title.

The text between the `<title>` tag pair is what appears in the vistor's browser's title bar.

What's in a Name?

Remember that you can't control who links to your page after the page is published to the Web. Therefore, you don't know where your visitors will come from—and you can't guarantee that they know anything about your page. The title you provide for your page should be something that helps people identify the topic of the page quickly. Don't make the title too long, or there might not be room for it all in the browser's title bar.

If you don't add a title at all, the browser might create one of its own. At best, this manufactured title might have something to do with the file path of the page. Whatever title the browser comes up with, you can bet it won't be all that helpful to your visitors. The moral of this hint is to provide a useful title for every Web page you create.

1 Identify a Main Topic

Many HTML authors overlook the importance of titles. As explained in Step 3 of the previous task, the title shows up in many places, so it's important to have a useful title. "Useful" means "descriptive, if relatively short." What key idea do you want to convey? Is there a "catch phrase" that will grab your visitors' attention? Identify the main topic and then write it down. After that, the title will almost write itself.

(1) This page is the home page for www.myvacations.com. The purpose of the page is to quickly convey the idea that vacations are fun, and this Web page is where your next vacation should start because it is full of great information on a wide variety of travel destinations.

2 Invent a Title

But because, in reality, the title won't really write itself, you need to come up with a title. It can be a challenge, but again, it's worth spending some time on. Look at the main topic you wrote down in Step 1. Maybe it's already suitable as a title, but more likely it needs to be somewhat reworded so that it is descriptive, yet not too long.

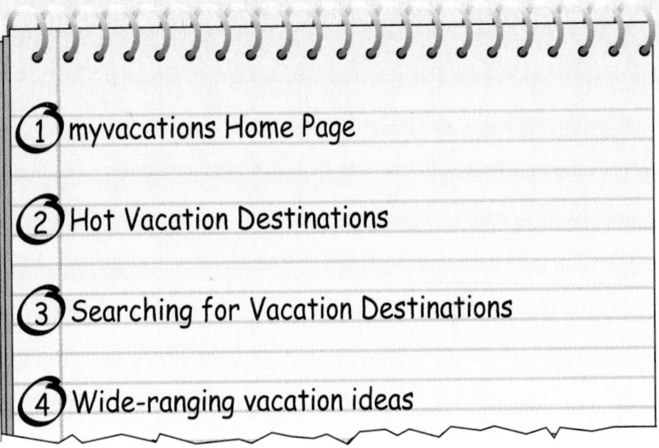

(1) myvacations Home Page
(2) Hot Vacation Destinations
(3) Searching for Vacation Destinations
(4) Wide-ranging vacation ideas

3 Add Text to the <title> Tag

When you have decided on a title, the hard work is done. Now you only have to add it to the right spot on your page. And you might have already guessed that the "right spot" sits squarely between the **<title>** and **</title>** tags. You have already added these to your page, so place the insertion point in your editor between those tags and type your title.

```
<html>
<head>
<title>Hot Vacation Destinations</title>
</head>
<body>
</body>
</html>
```

4 View Your Title

Now, save your HTML document and open it in your test browser (see the next two tasks). Look at the title bar; you'll see the title you typed in Step 3. If you don't see it, check your code to make sure that you've done everything correctly. Check the title for spelling and capitalization errors and the like, and return to the HTML document to correct anything that you see is wrong. Congratulations! You're now officially an HTML author!

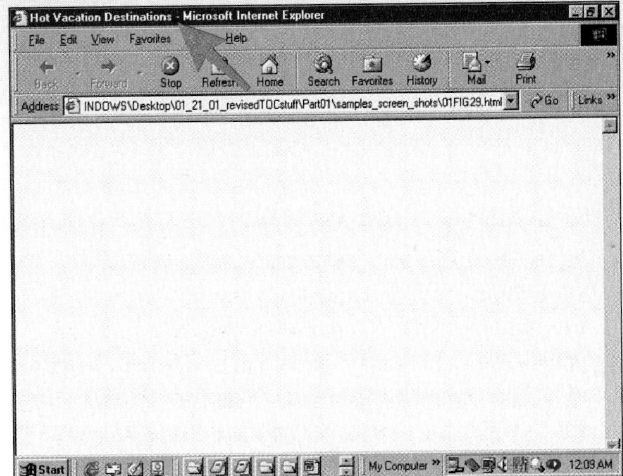

End

TASK 7 How to Save Your HTML Page

We haven't gotten all that far with the page, but it's never too early to save your work. Besides, it doesn't hurt to check on your progress as you move along. What does your page look like in a browser? To find out, you must first save the page as an HTML document. In the last task, you added the first piece of code that can be seen in a browser, so now's a good time to save the document. Then you can follow the steps in the next task to see what it really looks like in your target browser.

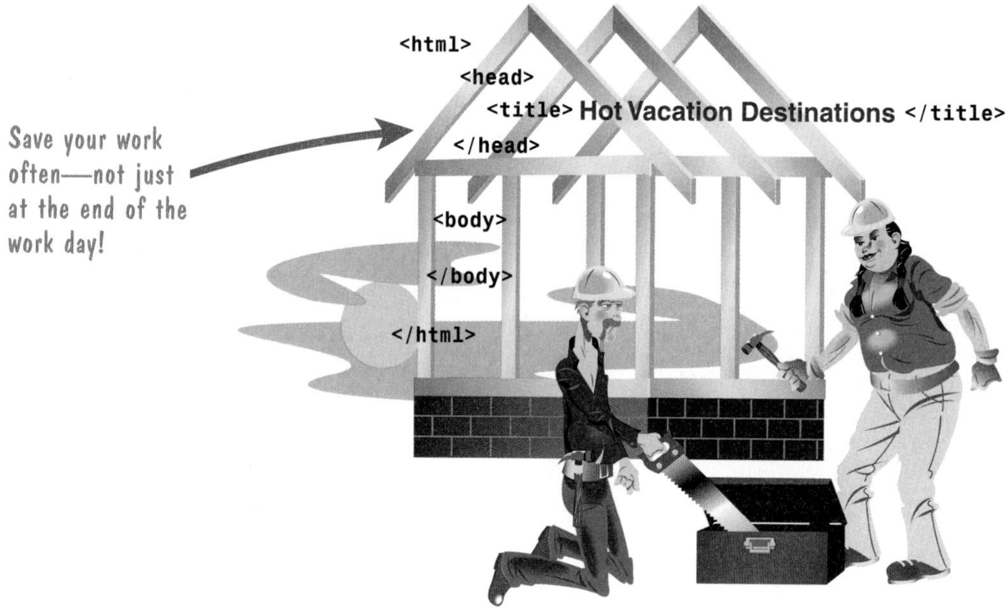
Save your work often—not just at the end of the work day!
<html>
<head>
<title> Hot Vacation Destinations </title>
</head>
<body>
</body>
</html>

Save Early, Save Often

I guarantee that you will never lament saving too many times, but you will suffer one of the greatest frustrations of the computer experience when you realize that you haven't saved your work for 10 minutes...just seconds after your computer crashes. Besides, there's no way to check your progress—or the accuracy of your code—if you don't save the page and view it in your browser.

Don't Neglect That Extension

Your browser will not recognize your page as an HTML document unless you remember to save it with either the **`.html`** or **`.htm`** file extension. You can have the most perfect code ever written in the history of the Web, but no one will ever see the results if you don't give the text file you are creating one of these file extensions. If your page does not show up in your test browser, the first thing to check is whether or not you remembered that all-important file extension.

1 Choose the Save Command

In your text editor, choose **File, Save**. Your text editor might also support the typical keyboard shortcuts for save (**Ctrl+S** on a Windows machine and **„+S** on the Macintosh). Alternatively, you might find a **Save** button on your text editor's toolbar. Because this is the first time you've saved the file, the **Save As** dialog box opens.

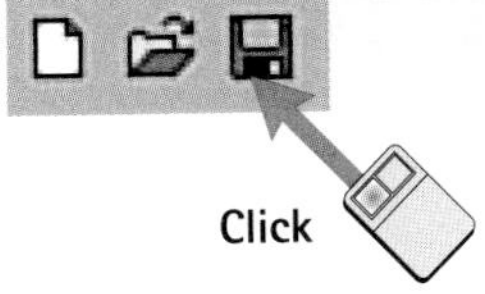

2 Define a Storage Location

Navigate to the location in which you want to save this page. Create a hierarchy of folders into which you'll store the files related to your project. For example, you might have a folder called `funvacationweb` under which you have subfolders to hold the related pieces of the Web site. This is another stage at which it pays to spend time organizing your work. That organization pays off as soon as you start building file paths to other pages and pieces.

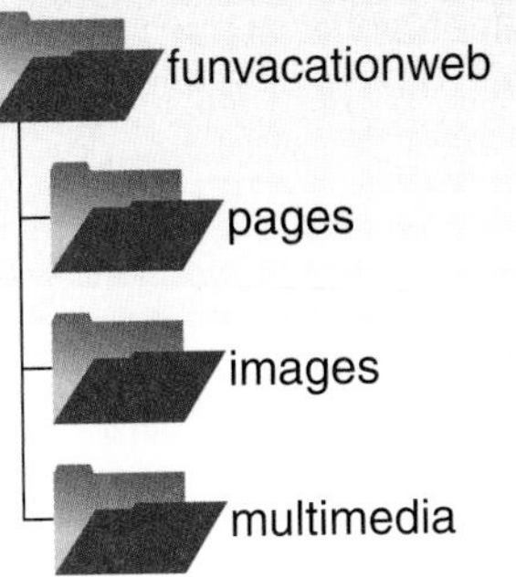

3 Name the File

In the **Save As** dialog box, type a name for the file that you can easily remember. Do not use spaces or special symbols in the filename. Use only letters (I suggest all lowercase letters) and numbers. You'll see why these guidelines are important as you move through this book. Try to use a name that suggests the content of the page without having to open it. Remember that the filename you're specifying here and the title you added in Task 6, "How to Give Your Page a Title," are two different things.

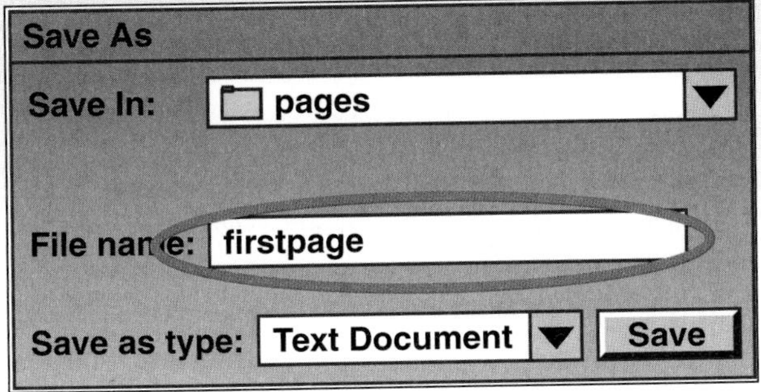

4 Add the File Extension

HTML pages require either an `.html` or an `.htm` file extension. I suggest that you use `.html` unless you work on a DOS or older Windows system that supports only three-character extensions. Whichever extension you use, stick with it for all your pages to avoid confusion. If your text editor does not give you an `.html` or `.htm` option in the **Save as type** drop-down list, choose **Text Document** and manually add the extension to the filename. Click **Save**.

Save As

Save In: pages

File name: firstpage.html

Save as type: Text Document   Save

End

TASK 8

How to Test Your Page in a Browser

Even though you've saved your page as an HTML document, you still don't know what it looks like to those who will view it when you're done. Here's where the browsers you chose to use during development (way back in Tasks 2, "How to Gather the Tools You Need," and 3, "How to Decide Which Browsers to Code For") come into play. This task walks you through the process of viewing your page locally (that is, on your development machine) so that you can test it during development, verify that your code works as intended, and make any additions or changes that might be necessary.

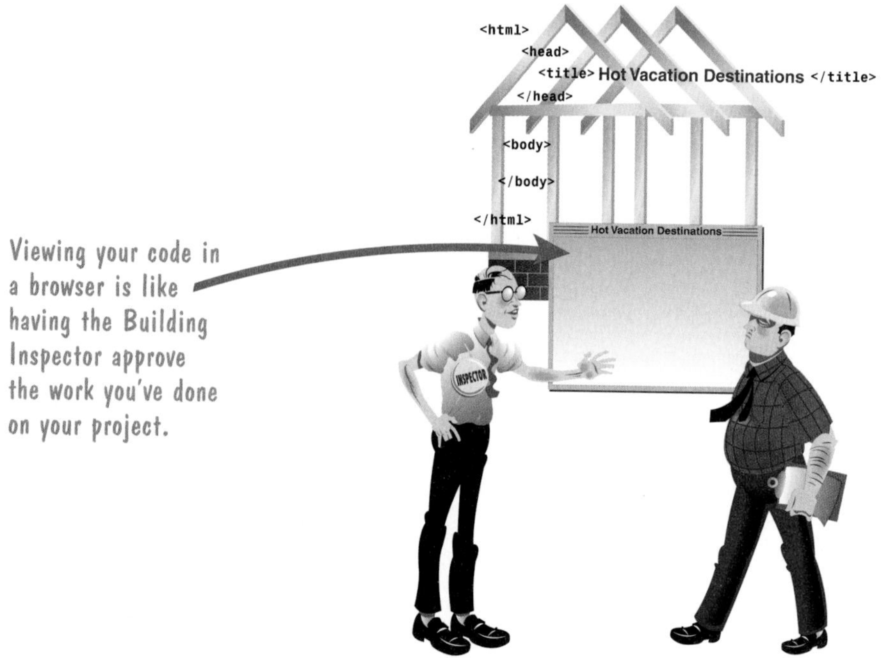
<html>
<head>
<title> Hot Vacation Destinations </title>
</head>
<body>
</body>
</html>
Hot Vacation Destinations
INSPECTOR

Viewing your code in a browser is like having the Building Inspector approve the work you've done on your project.

How's It Look?

Personally, I get a little kick every time I add another tag, check it out in my browser, and see that it looks just the way I'd hoped it would look. Checking your work in the browser is instant gratification. I always launch my browser and leave it open as I'm working in my text editor. That way, I can switch back and forth from the text editor to the browser to evaluate my code as often as I need to.

When you think about it, you don't really have a choice. The only way you can see what the page looks like in a browser is to view it in that browser. Even if you use a WYSIWYG editor, you can't rely on what it shows you. You still have to take the page to your browser and verify that things look the way they should in that particular piece of software.

1 Launch Your Browser

Using your computer's file-navigation program (Windows Explorer on a Windows machine), open the folder that contains your new HTML page. Your default browser assigns all HTML pages an icon. This figure shows the icon for Internet Explorer on a Windows machine. Double-click the file to launch the default browser and open the selected file in the browser. To view the file in an alternative browser, you must first launch the browser in the normal way.

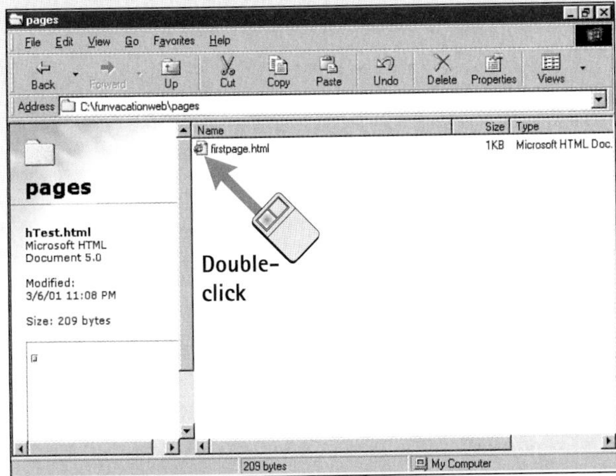

2 Choose File, Open

If you double-clicked the file in Step 1, you have automatically launched the browser and opened the page in it. If you manually launched an alternative browser, you must now choose **File, Open** to find the file you want to view. Because you can have only one default browser on your computer, you must use this alternative approach to launch any other browsers installed on your machine if you want to test your Web pages in more than just the default browser.

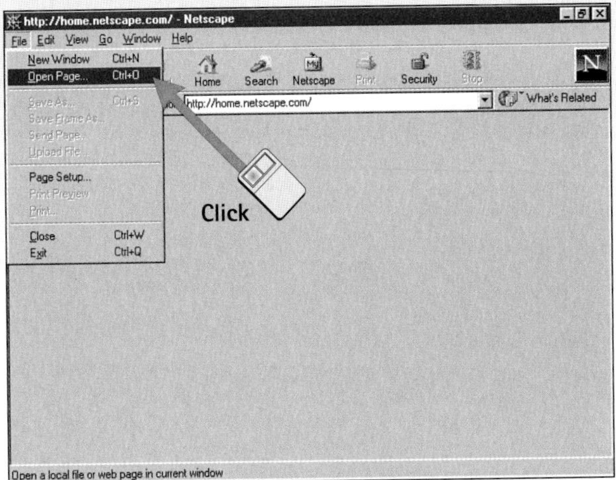

3 Navigate to the Desired Page

In the **Open** dialog box, browse to the page you created, or type the file path to the page, and click **Open**. The page now appears in the browser window. You can now review and proofread your work, as well as evaluate whether the browser displays the page in the way you intended it to appear. If a problem exists, go back to your text editor, make the necessary changes, and save the file again.

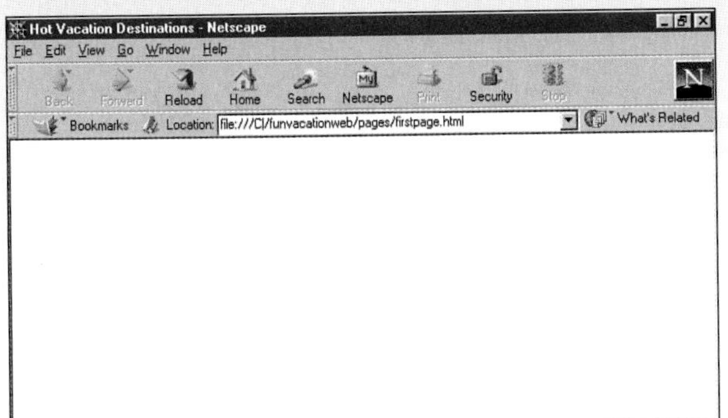

4 Refresh Your Browser

If you change code in the text editor while you have that same page open in a browser, you must tell the browser about those changes. Click the browser's **Reload** button. (Your browser might call this function something else, such as "**Refresh**.") This function instructs the browser to reload the updated page. You'll almost always have the page on which you're working open in both the text editor and the browser so that you can constantly evaluate the results of your work.

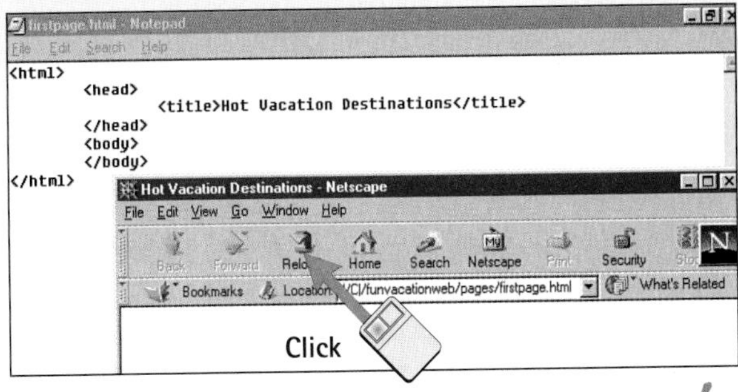

End

TASK 9 How to Add Visible Text

Now we're getting serious! Here's how you get your message across to the viewers of your Web page. Most of the HTML coding you complete from now until the end of your career will involve working with the text that you want people to see when they visit your completed pages. This task shows you where you have to put this text so that it is visible in a browser.

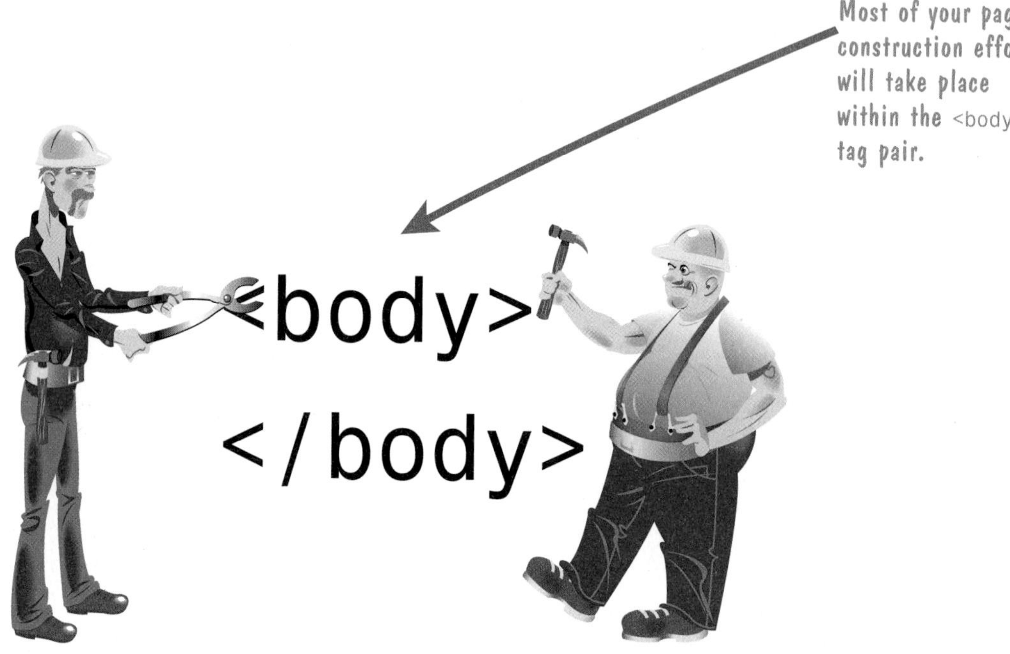

Most of your page-construction efforts will take place within the <body> tag pair.

What You See Is Not What You Get

Don't fall into the common trap of thinking that just because it looks good in your text editor, it will look fine in the browser. Browsers do not understand many things that a text editor does. The example given in this task involves the use of returns (which are inserted in the text file whenever you press **Enter**). A browser reads the page the same whether you put in returns at the end of paragraphs or just run everything on a single line in your editor with only a regular, single space between paragraphs. Still, feel free to put in paragraph returns in when you're coding. The same with tab characters. They won't cause any problems in your browser, and these things make your HTML text file much easier to read and edit. Just don't rely on these keyboard characters to do the task that the proper HTML tag is meant to do—and that is to communicate with your browser.

1 Place Your Cursor

In Task 5, "How to Structure Every HTML Page," you learned that most of the action takes place within the **<body>** tag pair. Well, we're finally there! To prepare to enter text that will be visible in the browser, place your cursor on the line directly under the **<body>** tag, in front of the **</body>** tag. You are now ready to enter your text.

```
<html>
<head>
<title>Hot Vacation Destinations</title>
</head>
<body>
|</body>
</html>
```

2 Enter Your Text

Now it's just a matter of typing your message. Well, almost. There are certain things that your browser won't recognize. For example, enter one line of text, followed by a return, and then another line. Although it looks fine in your editor, you'll see in the next two steps that the browser incorrectly interprets that return character as a space and not as an end-of-paragraph marker.

```
<html>
<head>
<title>Hot Vacation Destinations</title>
</head>
<body>
Here is one line of text. Now press Enter.
This line of text is on a new line.
</body>
</html>
```

3 Save the Page

I've already mentioned this step and the next, but they're worth repeating because I want to make sure that you understand the development process: Make changes to the text file, save your work, refresh the browser. You'll do it a million times, so you might as well learn it now!

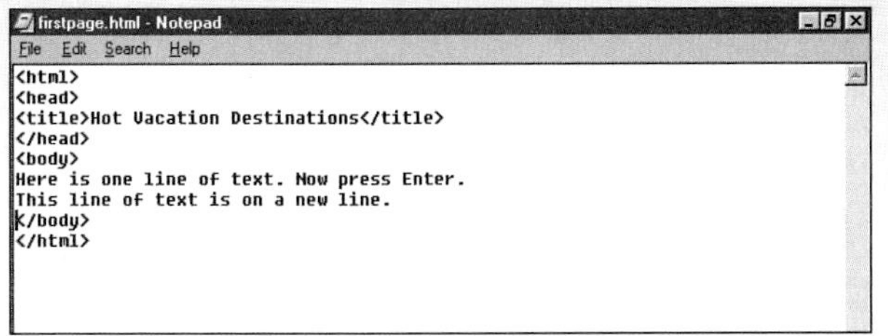

4 Refresh the Browser

Refresh your browser and evaluate your changes. Notice that (as promised) your browser does not recognize the return you entered. What gives? Well, remember that HTML's job is to tell the browser what to do. Your job is to write the HTML that accomplishes that goal. If you want the browser to recognize a return, you have to supply it with the HTML code that says, "Hey Browser, put a paragraph return here!" You'll learn how to do that in Part 2, "Working with Text," Task 6, "How to Control Line Breaks."

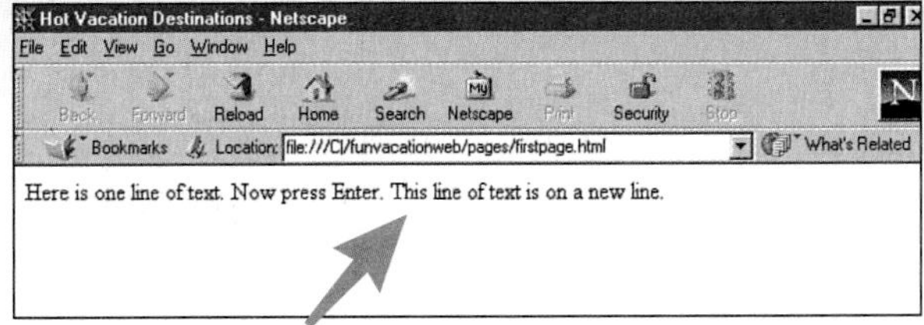

End

TASK 10 How to Specify Colors

There are several different places where you'll want to specify colors as you develop your HTML pages. Text, page background, borders, links, and other objects can be assigned virtually any color you desire. There are two ways to specify colors in HTML, although one is more dependable than the other. This task shows you how to specify colors in HTML.

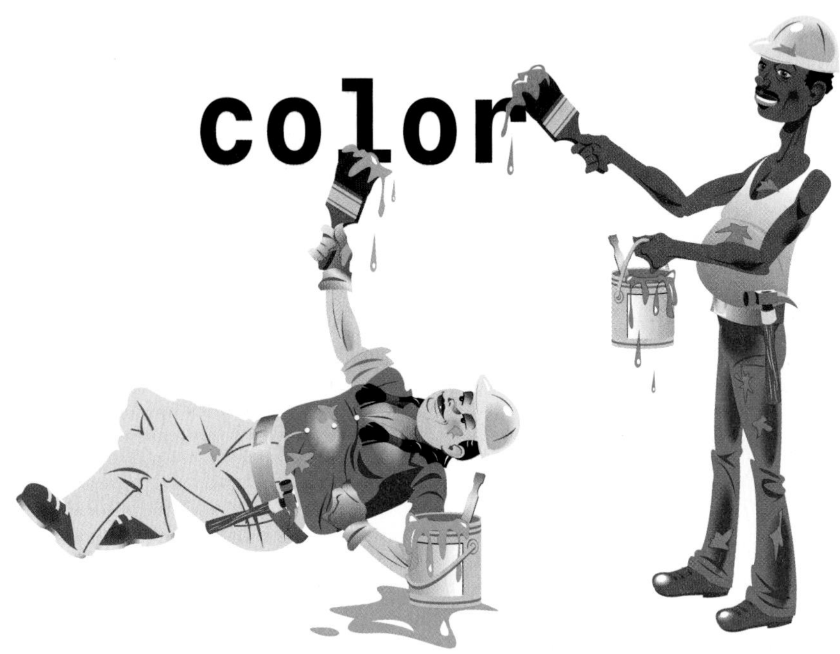

You Put a Hex on Me

The **color** attribute uses the *hexadecimal* model, which might seem confusing at first. Most image editors give you the color information in terms of Red, Green, and Blue values (the more familiar RGB color model) instead of hex. From there, you can find a lookup table that gives the hex equivalent of an RGB color. Visit **http://www.dreamartists.com/hexcode.html** to find a tool that lets you specify a color, and that gives you the hex value of that color.

Browser Safe

There are 216 Web-safe colors that will show up properly on an 8-bit (low resolution) monitor. Browsers replace non-safe colors with ones from the Web-safe palette. Usually this doesn't result in the best-looking graphics. If you don't want this to happen, create images and pages using browser-safe colors. In hex, browser-safe colors use combinations of these hex pairs: **00**, **33**, **66**, **99**, **cc**, and **ff**. In RGB, the numbers are multiples of **51**. Personally, I don't lose too much sleep over the issue.

1 Add the Color Attribute

To define the color of many objects in HTML, just add the **color** attribute to the appropriate tag. Let's go back to our hypothetical tag to demonstrate the **color** attribute. To define the color of my shirt, type **<garyshirt color="value">**. Steps 2 and 3 explain two ways to fill in the missing **"value"** in the code.

```
<garyshirt color="value">
```

2 Use Predefined Color Labels

You can use simple color names to assign a value to the **color** attribute. In the preceding example, you could type **<garyshirt color="black">**. The value **"black"** comes from a list of predefined color names. This is the easiest way to define the color value, but support for this method is not consistent from browser to browser, and there are a limited number of colors you can define this way. You'll probably be safe using this method for very basic colors with Internet Explorer or Navigator, but other browsers might not recognize color names at all.

```
<garyshirt color="black">
```

3 Specify a Hexadecimal Color

The most accurate and dependable method is the hexadecimal (hex) color model. The hex model uses three pairs of digits to define the amounts of red, green, and blue (in that order) in a color. Each of these digits falls within the range, 0–9, a–f. A value of **0** indicates the lowest level (none), whereas a value of **f** indicates the maximum level. To define my shirt color, type **<garyshirt color="#000000">** which specifies none of all colors—that is, black.

```
<garyshirt color="#000000">
```

4 Learn Common Hex Values

As mentioned in Step 3, the hex value for black is **#000000**. You should learn a few other common values such as white (**#ffffff**), red (**#ff0000**), green (**#00ff00**), blue (**#0000ff**), and gray (**#999999**). The appendix lists many hex codes and associated colors. Experiment with changes to the various digits in the hex value to become familiar with how each affects the resulting color. Notice that each hex value begins with a hash symbol (**#**). This symbol is required, so don't forget it!

Hex Value	Color
#000000	Black
#ffffff	White
#ff0000	Red
#00ff00	Green
#0000ff	Blue
#999999	Gray

End

TASK 11 How to Specify a File Path

Another common task involves specifying a file path in your HTML code. At some time, you'll have to direct the browser to the location of images, multimedia elements, and other Web pages. All these require the specification of an exact file path.

Remember that computers understand only what you tell them—and exactly what you tell them. Close is not good enough in this case. Here you learn how to build exact paths.

Specifying a path to an image or music file is a lot easier in HTML than it is for our constuction crew!

Don't Overcomplicate Things

Because you constantly build file paths to images, files, other HTML pages, and so on, it really pays to keep your file organization simple. For example, I usually keep all my images in one big folder that I call (appropriately enough) **images**. That way, I can become very familiar with that part of my file path; no matter where the page I'm working on resides, I need only build a path to the **images** folder to link to the proper file. Likewise, you'll really appreciate simplicity in file structure when you start building links from this page to that and back again. Naturally, you'll want to put related pages in separate, logical folders, but don't take it too far. If you create folder systems that are too many levels deep, you're only creating more work for yourself and introducing more opportunity to make coding errors.

1 Visualize the File Path

To re-create a file path in HTML, you must first know the path. Is the file you're looking for in the same folder as the one you're in? Or is it up three directory levels and buried in the fourth subdirectory along a different route? Whatever the case, it often helps to write out or draw complicated paths on a sheet of scratch paper so that you can easily visualize the path while trying to build it into your HTML.

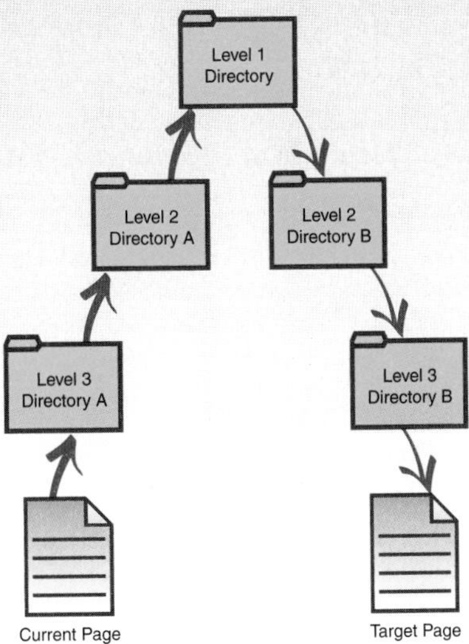

2 Back Up One Directory Level

You might find that the path you need to follow dictates that you must first back out of the folder or directory in which your page resides. Two periods followed by a forward slash accomplish this for you. Type `../` to back up one directory level. To back up three directory levels, type `../../../` and so forth.

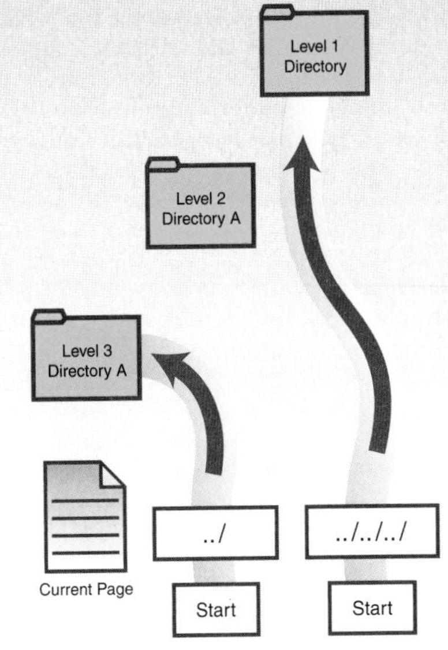

3 Enter the Next Directory

To enter a directory (or folder), type the directory name. Make sure that you type the name exactly as it appears on your computer system, including matching the case correctly. Although case doesn't always matter, it's better to be safe than sorry. If you want to back out of the directory in which your page resides and then enter a different directory called **newdirectory**, type **../newdirectory/** as your file path.

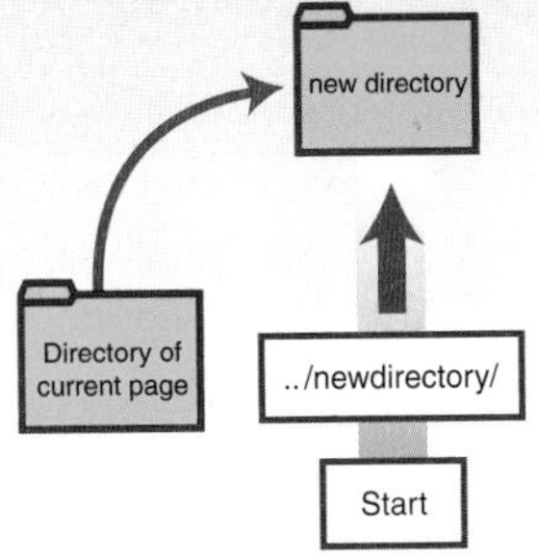

4 Specify the Desired File

After you have accessed the proper directory, specify the file that you are ultimately trying to find. Your complete path might look like this: **../newdirectory/ultimatefile.ext** where **.ext** is the file extension. If the ultimate file is an HTML page, for example, you might type **../newdirectory/ultimatefile.html** to specify the complete path.

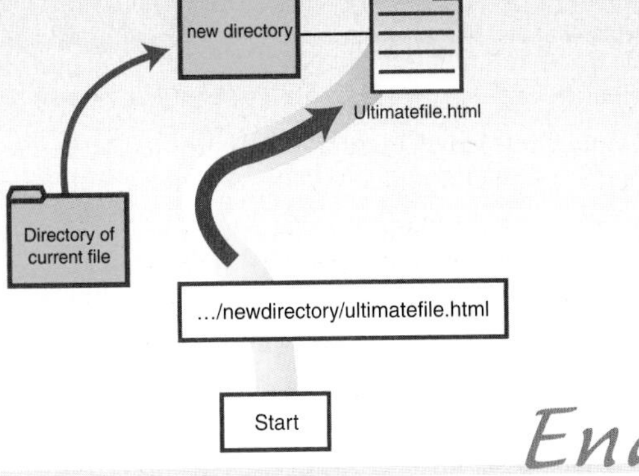

End

TASK 12 How to Change the Background of a Page

You've probably seen Web pages that have colored backgrounds, or even images in the background. Although this practice raises some serious graphic design issues, you should know how to change the background of your pages in case you ever need or want to. The techniques you learned in the last two tasks come in handy during this task, so you might want to review them. The steps in this task teach you how to add any background you want to your Web page.

Ever Write on Wrapping Paper?

A wise person once said, "There's a reason we don't use Christmas wrap for letterhead." And yet, HTML authors publish page after page of text printed over the top of busy, multicolored background images. If you want to make reading your Web page an annoying, unpleasant, sometimes next-to-impossible experience, go ahead and use that "cool" background image. Who cares if parts of it happen to be the same color as the text? Maybe the content of your page is so important that you could print it in invisible ink and people would still do whatever they had to in order to read it. Me? I'd rather make it as easy as possible to read the text on my pages. After all, if what I have on my page weren't important, I wouldn't publish it.

1 Add the bgcolor Attribute

In Task 10, "How to Specify Colors," you learned about the **color** attribute. The **<body>** tag contains a similar attribute called **bgcolor**. The **bgcolor** attribute works exactly the same as the **color** attribute, but it defines the background color of the entire page. For instance, to specify the background color of your page, type **<body bgcolor="value">** where **"value"** defines your color choice (see Task 10, Steps 3 and 4).

```
<body bgcolor="value">
</body>
```

2 Specify the Desired Color

Enter the appropriate hex value for the **bgcolor** attribute. For example, to make the background color of your page red, type **<body bgcolor="#ff0000">**. Remember to include the hash mark (**#**) so that browsers will properly recognize the value you enter.

```
<body bgcolor="#ff0000"
</body>
```

3 Add the background Attribute

You can also use an image as the background. To do so, add the **background** attribute to the **<body>** tag. When you add an image this way, everything else you add to your page prints right over the image. If you don't pick the right image, it could cause severe readability problems, so choose the image wisely. The HTML looks like this: **<body background="value">** where **"value"** is the file path leading to the image you want to use.

```
<body background="value">
</body>
```

4 Specify the Background Image

In Task 11, "How to Specify a File Path," you learned how to specify a file path. You can use that new skill to define the value for the **background** tag. You need only build the file path that leads to the image you want as your background. Here's an example: **<body background="../images/mountainbackground.gif">**. Notice that you should not specify both the **bgcolor** and **background** attributes. In most browsers, **background** overrides **bgcolor**, but that might not be the case in all browsers. Pick one attribute or the other.

```
<body background="../images/
mountainbackground.gif">
</body>
```

End

TASK 13

How to Change the Default Text Color

Another use for specifying a color as described in Task 10 is to change the default text color of your page. This can be critical if you have changed the background of a page (refer to Task 12, "How to Change the Background of a Page"). When you specify a default text color, all the text that you add to your page appears in the default color you specify. It's common to override the default text in several instances. The most common example is text links that appear in a different color. Learn how to set the default text color by following the steps in this task.

Not to Belabor a Point...

If you use a background image, make it simple and subtle. Then pick a font color that stands out well against the background image. But quite frankly, unless you're in a field that requires you to impress your visitors with fancy graphics (in which case, you are probably qualified to make sensible design decisions), I see little need for using a background image at all. It just gets in the way.

They Must Be Cool

I wish I had 10 bucks for every site I've seen that uses a black background and white text. Apparently somebody, somewhere started the rumor that if you wanted to show everyone how hip and cool you are, you absolutely have to make your Web pages with black backgrounds and white text. It seems that music-related sites are the strongest believers in this adage. The trouble is that this color scheme happens to be the exact opposite of what's easiest to read. Did you ever wonder why paper is traditionally white?

1 Add the text Attribute

The **<body>** tag contains another attribute that lets you specify the default text color of your page. Most times, when you include the **bgcolor** or **background** attributes, you'll need to change the default text color to ensure that text can be read against the background. You do this with the **text** attribute. Add the **text** attribute to the **<body>** tag like this: **<body bgcolor="#ff0000" text="value">** where **"value"** specifies the color you want.

```
<body bgcolor="#ff0000" text="value">
</body>
```

2 Specify the Desired Color

By now you're getting familiar with specifying color values for attributes. The **text** attribute receives the same kind of color value as the **color** and **bgcolor** attributes you've already worked with. To make the default text color white and the background color red, type **<body bgcolor="#ff0000" text="#ffffff">**.

```
<body bgcolor="#ff0000" text="#ffffff">
</body>
```

3 Save the Page

Save your HTML page so that you can open it in your test browsers.

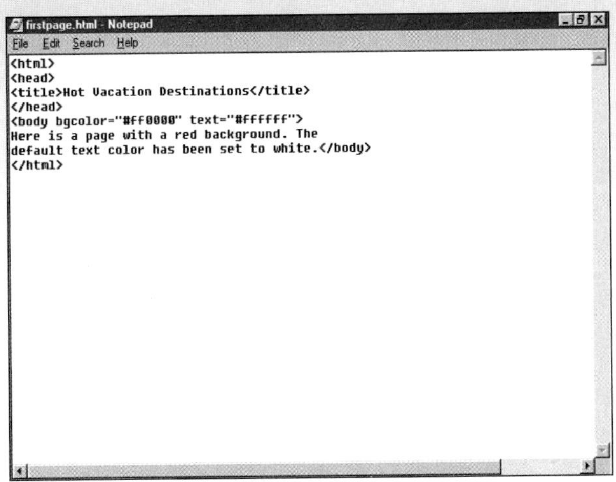

4 Evaluate the Results

Open the page in your browser. Make sure that your code achieves the intended results. If not, correct the problems in the HTML file. If the code is correct, you must next decide whether the page looks good. Don't use these color techniques just because you know them. Use them only if they make your page more effective. If you can't read the text because of a busy background, change the text color or get rid of the background image altogether. You're trying to impart information, not hide it!

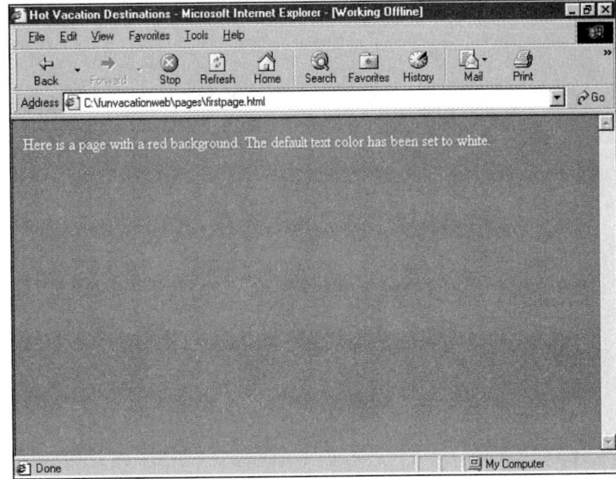

End

TASK 14 How to Add Invisible Comments

Not everything you type in your HTML document is for public consumption. It's always a good idea to make liberal use of *comments* in your code. Comments help organize the document and make it much easier to read what was written—and to remember why it was written—when you (or others) work with the HTML document in the future. After following the steps in this task, you'll know how to add comments to your HTML pages.

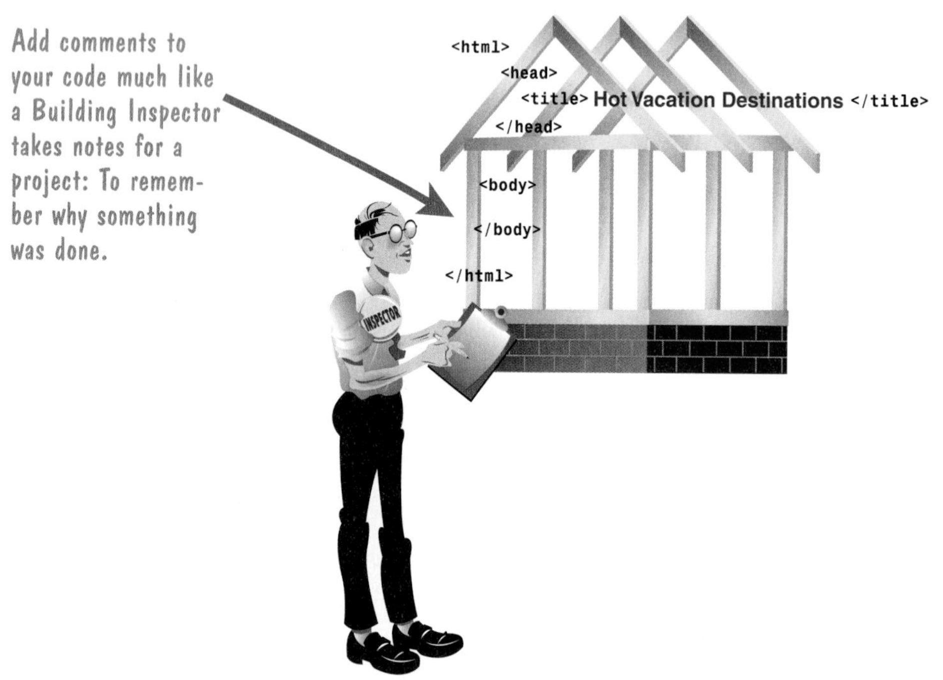
Add comments to your code much like a Building Inspector takes notes for a project: To remember why something was done.
<html>
<head>
<title> Hot Vacation Destinations </title>
</head>
<body>
</body>
</html>
INSPECTOR

They Really Are Useful

Adding comments to your code is one of those "things." You know, those "things" that don't really seem important at the time. Well, of course they don't...at the time. When you're working on the code, you know exactly why you're doing what you're doing. But trust me, if you have to go back to that code a year, a month, or even a day later, you'll often find that you can't remember why you did something the way you did to save your life. Take a few seconds to add comments to your code. You'll be glad you did...sooner or later, you'll be glad.

Watch What You Say

Don't get careless with your comments. As you'll see in Task 15, "How to Learn from Others' Source Code," anyone can view the source code of your page—and that includes the comments. Don't put anything into your comments that you wouldn't want your boss or your mother to read. At the same time, reading other people's comments can be a very enlightening (and sometimes amusing) experience, especially when you are trying to figure out just how they coded an effect similar to what you are trying to accomplish.

1 Add the Opening Elements

As I said earlier, when you know how to make one HTML tag, you know how to make them all. *Uhm,* except for comment tags. Comment tags have their own unique structure. To tell the browser to treat what follows as an invisible comment, type `<!--` where you want the comment to begin.

```
<!--
```

2 Type the Desired Comment

Next, type the comment that you want to add to your code. Your comment might be a reminder of the date on which certain content was added. Or it might be a description of what a complicated piece of code accomplishes. Your comment might be any number of things. Comments are very useful.

```
<!--Here is my very first comment.
```

3 Add the Closing Elements

To tell the browser that you've said all that you need to say and that what follows should be treated like regular HTML (that is, it should be made visible on the page), type `-->`. So, your entire comment looks like this: **`<!--Here is my very first comment.-->`**. Your comments can consist of multiple lines, and the **`<!--`** can be on a separate line than the comment, which can be on a separate line than the `-->`.

```
<html>
<head>
<title>Hot Vacation Destinations</title>
</head>
<body bgcolor="#000000" text="#ffffff">
<!--
Here is my very first comment.
-->
This text shows white in your browser.
</body>
</html>
```

4 Verify the Results

Don't forget to save your page and view it in your test browser. You want to make sure that the browser interprets what you intended to be an invisible comment as a comment. If it doesn't, it'll be immediately evident because you'll probably see your comment, and maybe even parts of the tag. Go back to your text editor, find the mistake, correct it, and verify the results again. When you construct your comments correctly, the average reader never knows they exist.

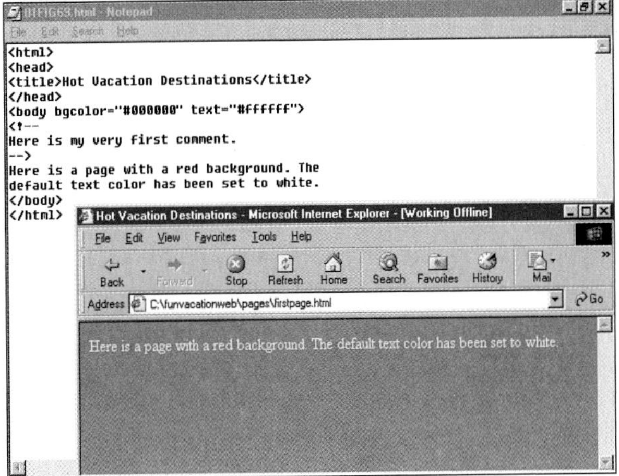

End

TASK 15

How to Learn from Others' Source Code

Now that you know how HTML works, you'll find it easy to recognize HTML tags—if you can find some existing code to study. Well, you're in luck because you can look at the code for any page you can browse to. This is an excellent way for you to learn more about HTML and to discover some of the techniques used by others. When you find yourself wondering, "How'd they do that?" go view the code and figure it out! Follow the steps in this task to learn how to view the HTML code of a Web page.

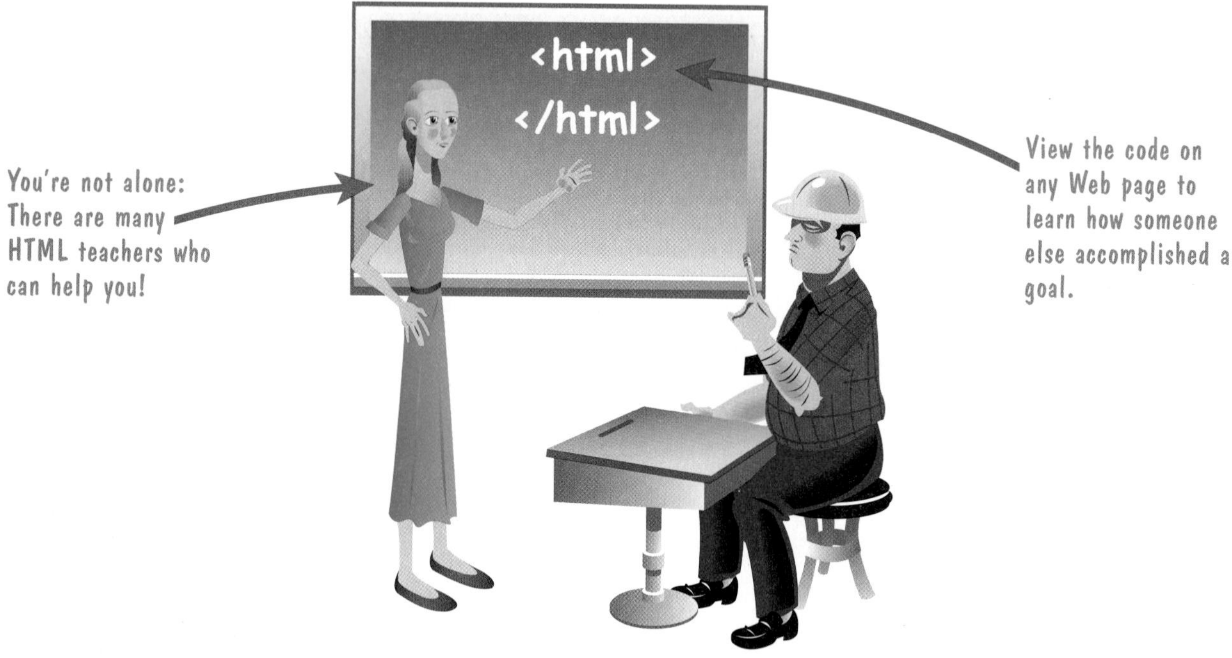
<html>
</html>
You're not alone: There are many HTML teachers who can help you!
View the code on any Web page to learn how someone else accomplished a goal.

Who's Messing with My Code?

It follows that because you can open the source code to any HTML document into your text editor, you can also edit that code. And anyone can edit yours. "You mean people can change my Web page to whatever they want? This is intolerable!"

Well, yes and no. Although anyone can edit your code, they can't publish it to your Web site, so they can't suddenly change your Web site. What they *can* do is copy your code and use it on their own pages. Or copy *pieces* of your code and incorporate them into their own code. Is that legal? Probably. Is there anything you can do about it? Not really. You'd probably never even know about it.

You know what I suggest? Learn from other people, but write your own code. And don't lose sleep over somebody else using your code. Now if you find someone who's stealing your *content*, that's a different issue. Never publish content you copied from somebody else's pages. That's clearly illegal.

1 Launch Your Browser

Virtually every browser allows you to view the source code of the page that it currently displays. Launch whichever of the test browsers you've been using, or launch your favorite browser for surfing the Internet.

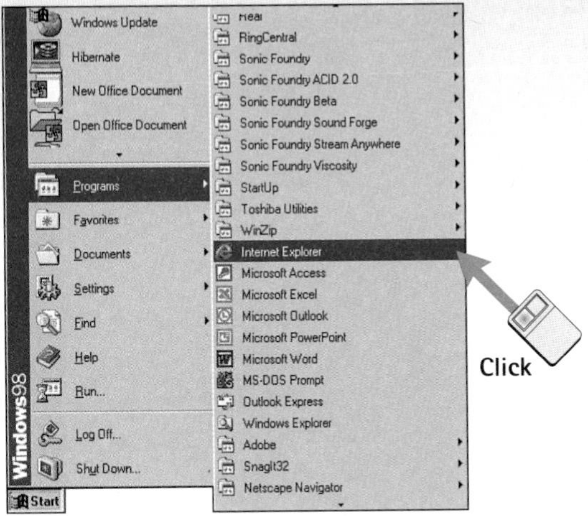

2 Browse to the Desired Page

Type a Web address or conduct a search on a topic that interests you. Go to your favorite Web site. It doesn't matter where you go...you'll be able to see the code behind any page.

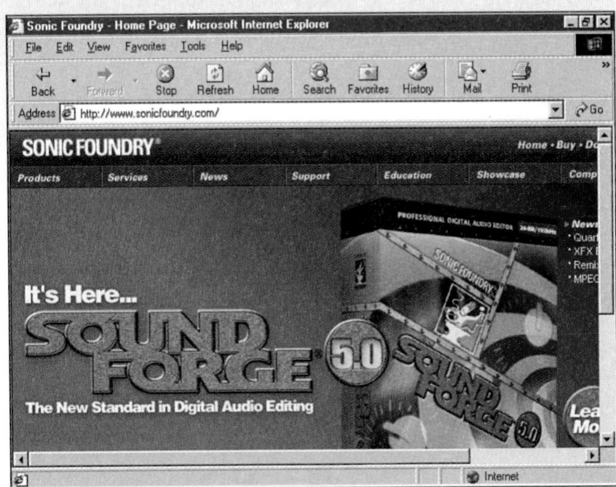

3 Use the Menu Bar

Somewhere in the menus of your browser you'll find an option that lets you view the source code of the page you're looking at. A good place to start looking is in the **View** menu. Look for something called **Source** or **Code**. You shouldn't have to look too hard. When you choose the option, your browser launches your text editor and, like magic, you find yourself reading the code that creates the Web page.

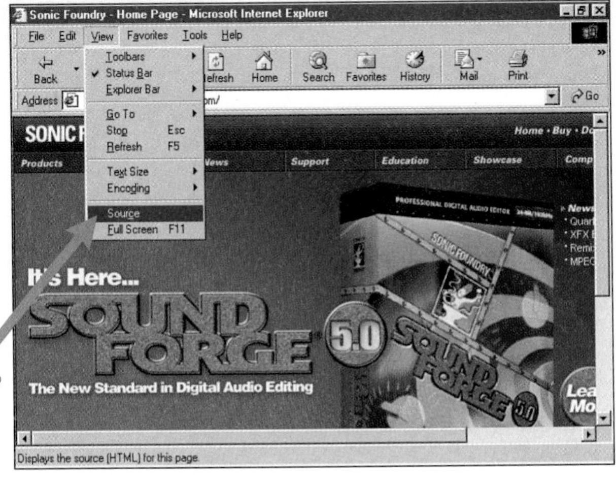

4 Use the Pop-up Menu

You might also be able to right-click („+click with the Macintosh) anywhere on the Web page; in the shortcut menu that pops up, look for the **View Source** or **Code** option. Choose that option to launch your text editor and view the code.

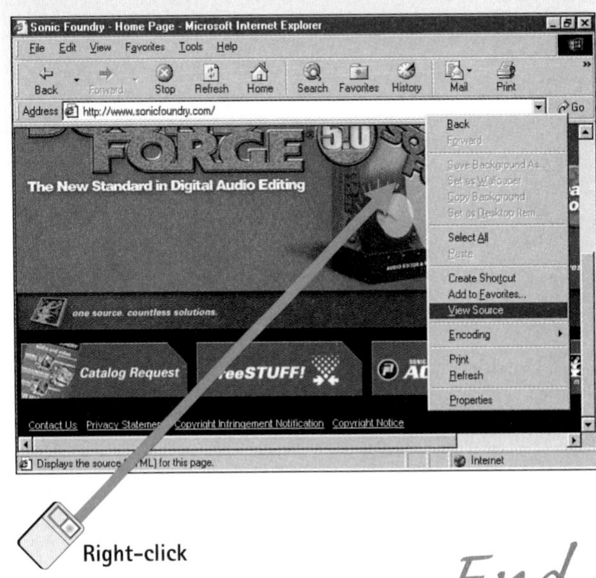

End

Task

PART 2

Working with Text

The real value of the World Wide Web is information. If the Web is nothing else, it's an amazing and diverse source of information. A true reflection of the people who feed the information into the vast machine, some of the available information is good, and some of it is bad. Some is profoundly important, and some is ridiculously useless. And of course, it all depends on the perspectives of the Web author and the Web surfer. What I find interesting might bore you to tears. What you find entertaining, I might find offensive.

You can find pictures on the Web to show you information. There are movies on the Web so that you can watch information move. And you can seek out audio on the Web so that you can hear information. But by far the most common form information takes is the written word. There are millions of words on the Web. They are constantly being added, continually being revised. These words are written in virtually every language spoken by the human tongue. And regardless of the language the words come from, the topic they talk about, or the ideological slant that shades them, all these words have one thing in common: Each was put there by humans (or at least by a machine built by humans).

And what all these humans know how to do is to format their HTML so that those words show up in your browser. As I mentioned in Part 1, "Getting Started," some people use WYSIWYG editors to format the words; others code the HTML themselves. The second is the group you'll fall into by the time you're done working through the tasks in this part.

This part shows you how to work with font size, color, and typeface. You'll learn how to make bold text and italic text. (I might even show you how to make italic text that's bold!) You'll learn how to make line breaks without creating a new paragraph. Don't worry; you'll learn how to work with paragraphs in Part 3, "Working with Paragraphs."

Finally, you'll learn about some special problems that HTML introduces when you're working with text. For instance, consider the less-than symbol. You've already learned that it's an important symbol in HTML because it tells the browser that it should expect an HTML tag. So what do you do when you want to write a mathematical equation like this: `7 < 10`? I'll show you in Task 7, "How to Use Special Text Characters." ●

TASK 1 How to Specify Text Size

There are a number of reasons you might want to change the size of the text on all or part of your Web page. You might want some text to stand out. Maybe your target audience is older, and you know that older people sometimes have trouble reading small text. Whatever your reason, you can use the techniques taught in this task to resize text on your HTML pages.

The Browser Still Rules

The browser has a great deal of control over the way it displays your page. As an example, Internet Explorer gives the viewer the power to override any text size, style, or color specifications you make in your HTML. To see this in Internet Explorer, choose **Tools, Internet Options**, and then click the **Accessibility** button. In the **Accessibility** dialog box, you can set the browser to ignore several different things. No matter how hard you work, the ultimate power still lies in the hands of the Web surfers because the tools they have to override your settings outweigh those you have to create them in the first place. In reality, very few people invoke these weapons. After all, most people are interested in nice-looking Web pages, and as long as you're making good-looking Web pages, you give them little incentive to override your decisions. Still, be aware that the possibility exists.

1 Add the <font> Tag Pair

Introducing the **<font>** tag and, of course, its sidekick, the **</font>** tag. You use this tag pair to control the look of your text. Be aware that some browsers don't recognize this tag pair, although the major ones do. To control the size, color, and typeface of your text, type **<font>…</font>**.

```
<html>
<head>
<title>Working with the Font Tag</title>
</head>
<body>
<font>
Here is text within the font tag pair.
</font>
</body>
</html>
```

2 Add the size Attribute

You add attributes to the **<font>** tag in exactly the same way as you've added attributes to tags in earlier tasks. Type **<font size="value">**. You'll specify the value of the font in the next step.

```
<html>
<head>
<title>Working with the Font Tag</title>
</head>
<body>
<font size="value">
Here is text within the font tag pair.
The size attribute has been
added, but the value has not
yet been specified.</font>
</body>
</html>
```

3 Absolute or Relative Size

You can specify an *absolute* or *relative size* for text. To specify an absolute size, type **<font size="X">**, where **X** is a number from 1 to 7. The default is 3, the size you'll get if you don't specify the **size** attribute. To specify a relative size, type **<font size="+ (or -) X">**. Relative sizes are always based on the default size of 3, regardless of any absolute size you might have set earlier, so if you want a size of 2, type either **<font size="2">** or **<font size="-1">**.

```
<html>
<head>
<title>Working with the Font Tag</title>
</head>
<body>
<font size="4">
Here the value for the size attribute has
been set to "4", one higher
than the default. I could also specify a
value of "+1" to achieve the same result.
</font>
</body>
</html>
```

4 Change the Base Font Size

As mentioned in Step 3, the default size for text is 3. You can change that default with the **<basefont>** attribute. To specify a new default size, type **<basefont size="X">** where **X** is between 1 and 7. Now any relative sizes you specify in the **<font>** tag will be based on the size you specified in the **<basefont>** tag.

```
<html>
<head>
<title>Working with the Font Tag </title>
</head>
<body>
<basefont size="4">
<font size="-2">Notice that here I use the
basefont tag pair to set the base font size
to "4". In the font tag, I use the size
attribute to set the font size to "-2". I
could achieve the same results with a font
size of "2".
</font>
</basefont>
</body>
</html>
```

End

TASK 2 How to Specify Text Color

Text color can be used to help make text stand out. This task shows you how to change the color of your words. It also discusses changing the color of a single word within an already-colored sentence. The possibilities are endless, and that's why you have to be careful. Too much colored text is more akin to a nightmare than it is to pleasant reading. Exercise caution when it comes to changing the colors in your Web site, and that includes the text.

Judicious use of colored text on your page will enhance your message; too many colors can distract and confuse the reader.

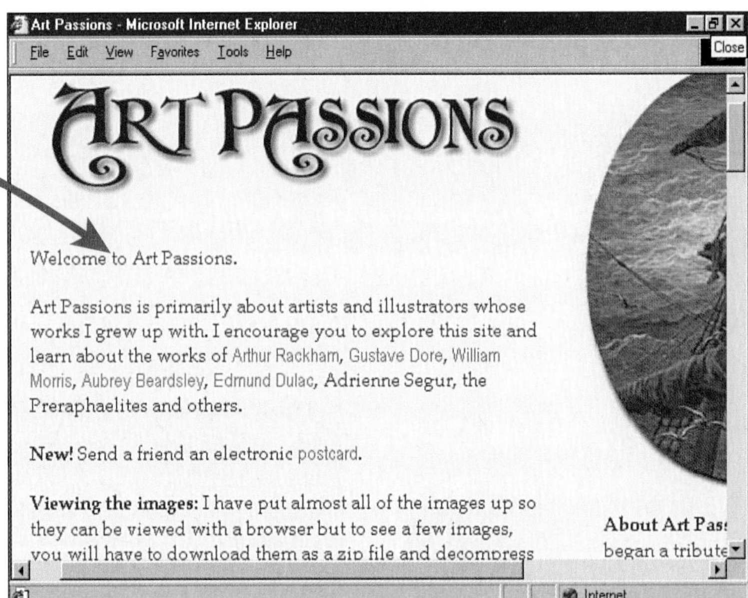

Help! Aliens Colored My Page!

I've seen Web sites where there is definitely something other-worldly going on. It's the only way to explain the horrendous designs evident on the Web today. Many people seem to subscribe to the "I can, therefore I must" school of HTML authoring. They believe that the more techniques they use, the more people will love their Web sites.

Wrong! You can quickly over-do your use of color. Two or three colors of text have more impact than a dozen. Many more, and the colors cease to mean anything. I'll teach you how to change the color of your text. But I urge you to use the technique sparingly and tactfully. It's up to you to resist the "I can, therefore I must" syndrome.

1 Add the <font> Tag Pair

Another use of the **<font>** tag is to change the color of your text. Type **<font>…</font>**.

```
<html>
<head>
<title>Working with the Font Tag</title>
</head>
<body>
<font>
Here is text within the font tag pair.
</font>
</body>
</html>
```

2 Add the color Attribute

Add the **color** attribute. Type **<font color="value">…</font>** where **value** is specified using either of the methods discussed in Part 1, Task 10, "How to Specify Colors."

```
<html>
<head>
<title>Working with the Font Tag</title>
</head>
<body>
<font color="#3300ff">
Here is text within the font tag pair.
The color attribute has been
added, and a hex value specified to
make the text blue with a touch of red.
</font>
</body>
</html>
```

3 Nest Colors

There might be times when you want to have a few words of one color appear within a paragraph of text in another color. To do this, simply nest one **<font>** tag within another. Type **<font color="#ff0000">…<font color="#00ff00">…</font>…</font>**.

```
<html>
<head>
<title>Working with the Font Tag</title>
</head>
<body>
<font color="#3300ff">
Here I am embedding a couple words of
<font color="red">red text</font>
within a line of blue font. Notice
that to do this I simply nest one
font tag pair within
the other.</font>
</body>
</html>
```

4 Test the Page

You've made a number of changes to your text over the past couple of steps. Hopefully, you've been saving your page and checking your results in a browser all along. If not, do so now. Try setting your browser to override these settings to get an idea of how your page could be changed by the viewer.

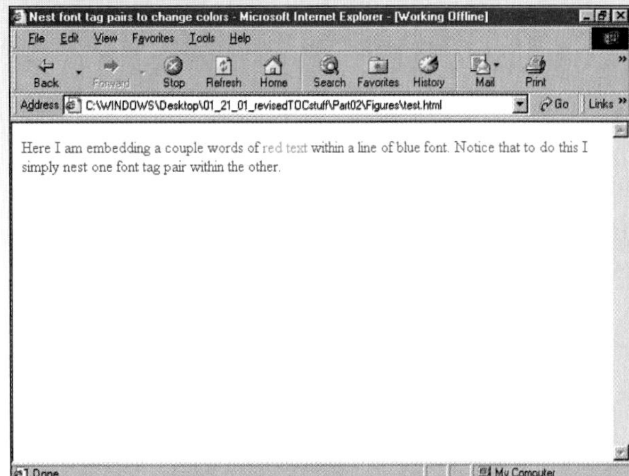

End

TASK 3

How to Specify Text Fonts

Wouldn't it be great if you could use any font in the world for your Web page? Guess what...you can. Sort of. This task shows you how to specify any font you want on your Web page. But you can't prevent the reader from overriding these wonderful font settings with a simple click or two in a browser dialog box.

By now, you get the picture: You can work hard to make your Web pages look "just so." But you can never guarantee how they will ultimately appear to the viewer. Browser differences—and browser options—see to that!

When All's Said and Done

Most browsers can be set to ignore the **<font>** tag and use a default font. Another consideration is font availability. Remember that HTML merely tells the browser which font to use. You're not including the actual font with the document. What does that mean? Well, a font might look great when you view it on your machine. But what happens when I surf to your page? My browser comes across the **face** attribute, which tells it, "Use this fancy font." My browser goes in search of the font. But if I don't have that font on my system, my browser can't find it, and it falls back to use the default font on my machine. The point? Unless you can be sure that your audience has the font you choose, stick to basic fonts. Standard Windows machines come with Times New Roman and Arial; Macintosh machines come with Times and Helvetica (which is essentially the same as Arial). You should stick with these fonts.

1 Add the face Attribute

Another important attribute of the **<font>** tag is the **face** attribute. Add it just as you add any other attribute. Type **<font face="value">** where **value** is the desired typeface.

```
<html>
<head>
<title>Working with the Font Tag</title>
</head>
<body>
<font size="4" face="value">
Here I have left the size
attribute in and added
the face attribute to the font tag.</font>
</body>
</html>
```

2 Specify a Font

You can specify any font you desire in the **face** attribute. For instance, to specify the typeface Comic Sans MS, type **<font face="comic sans ms">…</font>**.

```
<html>
<head>
<title>Working with the Font
Tag</title></head>
<body>
<font size="4" face="comic sans ms">
Here I have chosen Comic Sans MS for
the value in the
face attribute.</font>
</body>
</html>
```

3 Specify Font Alternatives

If you specify a different font, you should also specify alternatives for people who don't have that font on their computers. To do so, separate the alternatives by a comma. Type **<font face="comic sans ms, arial, helvetica">**. The browser first looks for Comic Sans MS; if it can't find that font, it looks for Arial, and so on. If it can't find any of the fonts in the list, it uses the system default.

```
<html>
<head>
<title>Working with the Font
Tag</title></head>
<body>
<font size="4" face="comic sans ms,
arial, helvetica">
Here I have chosen Comic Sans MS for the
value in the face attribute. I also list
two alternatives: Arial and Helvetica.
Because Comic Sans MS is loaded on my
system, the alternative fonts are not
called on by the browser.</font>
</body>
</html>
```

4 Test Your Page

Save your page and test it once again in a browser. Explore your browser's options. Set the browser to ignore the page's **<font>** tag settings so that you can see how your page looks to any viewer who makes this adjustment to his own browser.

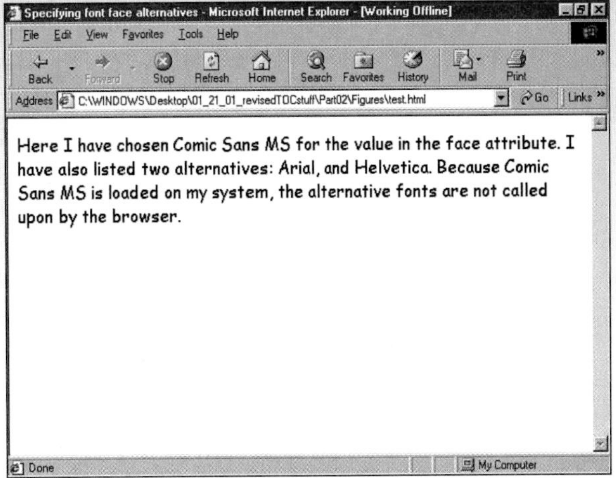

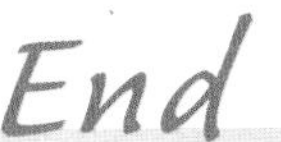

TASK 4

How to Format Text

I'll admit right here at the start of this task that I'm not going to show you a step-by-step process for adding every formatting option available in HTML. Instead, I'll discuss a few of the most common formatting options. After you've learned how to incorporate these, you'll know how to use the others as well. Specifically, this task shows you how to create bold and italic text and how to underline your text. Step 4 lists some additional formatting options that work essentially the same way as these three common ones.

Let's Get Physical...or Logical

The tags discussed in this task are either physical or logical. *Logical tags* tell the browser of your intended use for the text, but leave it to the browser to decide how to display it. For instance, the **<em>** tag tells the browser that you're using this text for emphasis. Most browsers translate this to italics, but you can't count on that treatment from all browsers. On the other hand, the **<i>** tag (a *physical tag*) tells the browser specifically, "make this text italic." My suggestion is, if you want italics, use **<i>**. It's the only way you can be sure that everyone sees italics.

Here are other logical tags: **<strong>**, **<code>**, **<samp>**, **<kbd>**, **<var>**, **<dfn>**, **<cite>**, **<abbr>**, and **<acronym>**. Other physical tags are **<b>**, **<tt>**, **<u>**, **<s>**, **<big>**, **<small>**, **<sub>**, and **<sup>**.

1 Create Bold Text

You can create bold text on your page by specifying a bold-faced font in the **face** attribute of the **<font>** tag. For example, instead of choosing Helvetica as your font, choose Helvetica Bold. Another way is to use either the strong (**<strong>**...**</strong>**) or bold (**<b>**...**</b>**) tag pairs. The strong tag is a logical tag; the bold tag is a physical tag.

```
<body>
<font size="2" face="arial, helvetica">
In this example, I use the now familiar font
tag pair. Within this pair, I use the
bold tag pair to make <b>bold text</b> and
the strong tag pair to make <strong>strong
text</strong>. In most browsers the two
tag pairs bring similar results.</font>
</body>
```

2 Create Italic Text

To create italic text, use either the emphasis tag pair (logical) or the italic tag pair (physical). Type either **<em>**...**</em>** or **<i>**...**</i>**. To create bold and italic text, you can type **<b><i>**...**</i></b>**. Notice the proper nesting of these tags: Because the italic tag is opened after the bold tag, it is closed before the bold tag. Remember that proper nesting, although important in HTML, is *critical* in XHTML.

```
<body>
<font size="2" face="arial, helvetica">
In this example, I use font tag pair. Within
this pair, I use the italic tag pair to
make <i>italic text</i>, and the
emphasis tag pair to make <em>emphazised
text</em>. In most browsers, the two tag
pairs bring similar results. I also nested
the italic tag pair within the bold tag
pair to make <b><i>bold-italic text</i></b>.
</font>
</body>
```

3 Create Underline and Strikethrough Text

To underline your text, use the underline tag. Type **<u>**...**</u>**. To strike through (or cross out) your text, use the strikethrough tag. Type **<s>**...**</s>**.

```
<body>
<font size="2" face="arial, helvetica">
Here I use the underline tag to
<u>underline a few words</u>, and the
strikethrough tag to <s>cross a few words
out</s>.</font>
</body>
```

4 Create Superscript and Subscript Text

Superscript text is smaller than regular text and is raised off the baseline. The 2 in 3^2 is written in superscript. To create superscript, use the superscript tag pair. Type **^{**...**}**. Subscript text is smaller than regular text and is lowered below the baseline. The n in X_n is subscript. To create subscript, use the subscript tag pair. Type **_{**...**}**.

```
<body>
<font size="2" face="arial, helvetica">
I want to indicate that there is a footnote
to this sentence. To do so, I use the
superscript tag pair to type my footnote
reference,like this<sup>4</sup>. To write 10
base 4, I use the subscript tag pair like
this: 10<sub>4</sub>. Then I continue on
as normal.</font>
</body>
```

TASK 5

How to Preformat Text

Remember earlier when I said that browsers ignore the returns, tabs, and extra spaces that you enter into your text editor? The **<pre>** (preformatted text) tag lets you get around this default behavior. By enclosing text within the preformatted text tag pair, you can force the browser to see all the extra spaces, returns, and tabs you type in your text editor. This task shows you how to use the **<pre>** tag.

You can "drop" preformatted text into your page without worrying about getting the formatting codes right.

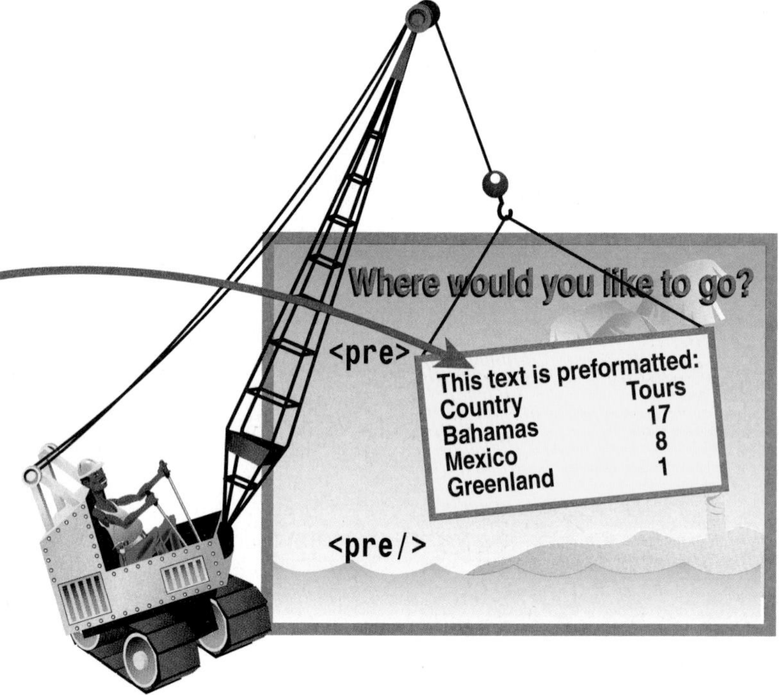

Where would you like to go?
<pre>
This text is preformatted:
Country Tours
Bahamas 17
Mexico 8
Greenland 1
<pre/>

Why Not Preformat Everything?

The **<pre>** tag has limitations. Preformatted text is usually presented in a monospaced font style, such as Courier. Monospaced fonts (like the one used by your old typewriter) are more difficult to read and don't look very nice. Another problem is that different browsers interpret tabs differently. This can cause tab stops that line up nicely in one browser to look sloppy in another.

Still, there are good uses for preformatted text. An example is when you have a word-processing document that you want to include on your Web page. It doesn't have to be a very long document before you start to lament the time it takes to add a paragraph tag for each new paragraph. You can quickly copy the page from your word processor and paste it within a preformatted tag pair in your text editor to preserve your paragraph breaks.

1 Begin Preformatting

To tell the browser where the preformatted text begins, type the preformatted text tag, **<pre>**.

```
<html>
<head>
<title>Working with the
Preformatted Text Tag Pair</title>
</head>
<body>
<font size="2" face="arial, helvetica">
To begin a preformatted text area,
I add the preformatted text tag.
<pre>
</font>
</body>
</html>
```

2 Type the Text

Type the text exactly as you want it to appear on the Web page. Make sure that you include returns, extra spaces, and any tabs you want to use. Be careful not to make your lines too long (generally less than 60 characters) because they might become too long to show up on the browser screen without making your visitor scroll.

```
<body>
<font size="2" face="arial, helvetica">
Next I type the information I want
preformatted, including extra spaces,
tabs, and returns.
<pre>
  Tropical      European   Domestic
  Hawaii        France     Southern California
  Puerto Rico   Germany    New England
  Bahamas       England    Midwest
</font>
</body>
```

3 End Formatting

After you've added all the text you want, close the preformatted text area. Type **</pre>**.

```
<body>
<font size="2" face="arial, helvetica">
Finally, after the text is entered,
I type the closing tag to close the
preformatted text area.
<pre>
  Tropical      European   Domestic
  Hawaii        France     Southern California
  Puerto Rico   Germany    New England
  Bahamas       England    Midwest
</pre>
</font>
</body>
```

4 Test the Page

Save your page and test it in your browser to see whether your preformatted text looks the way you hoped it would. One caution: Although some HTML tags work when embedded within a preformatted text area, not all do. And support for tags that work on your browser is probably not consistent in other browsers. In other words, don't include other HTML tags within the preformatted text tag pair.

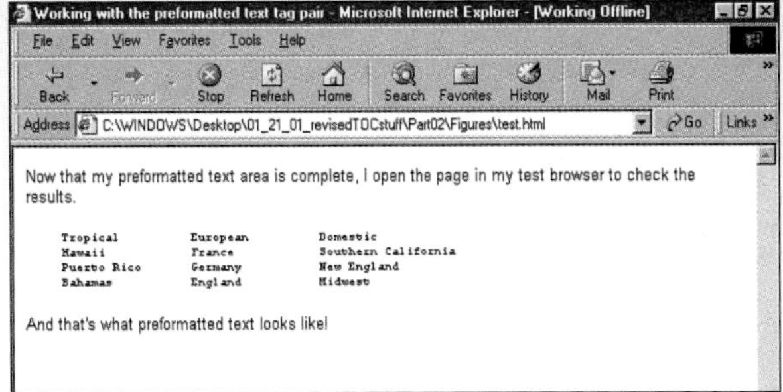

End

TASK 6 How to Control Line Breaks

Sometimes you want to start a new line of text, but you don't want to include a paragraph break. A good example of this is when you are typing out the lyrics of a song. You want each line of the verse to be on a separate line in your document, but you only want a paragraph break between the last line of the first verse and the first line of the second verse. This task shows you how to create this type of line break. Part 3, "Working with Paragraphs," explains the various ways of creating paragraph breaks.

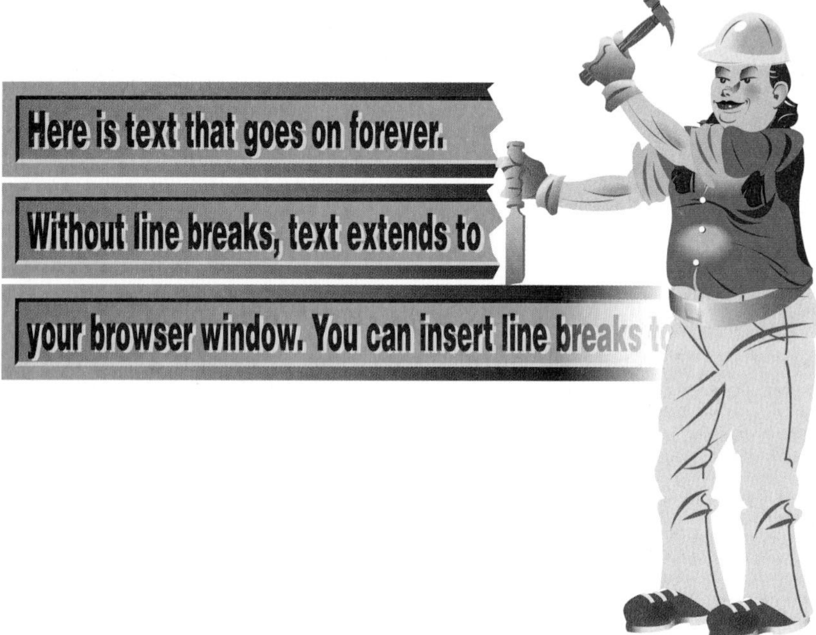

Achieving Closure

The line break tag is the first of several tags that have no closing tag in HTML. This is because unlike other tags, it doesn't affect a specific range of text. That is, nothing "goes between" the tag in the way that text goes between the `<font>` and `</font>` tags.

You could get away with never closing those line break tags, and you'd be writing perfectly acceptable HTML. But recall that one of my goals in this book is to prepare you for the future of Web technology, XHTML. No two ways about it, you must close every tag you use in XHTML.

Adding the closing part of the line break tag does not affect your HTML in any way. But it makes all the difference in the world to XHTML. In addition, it is easy to close the tag—even easier than the normal method. Therefore, there really is no reason not to get into the habit now. Remember, we all need closure!

1 Add a Few Lines of Text

To create a line break on your Web page, first type several sentences in your text editor. Don't worry about the length of your lines, just go ahead and type.

```
<html>
<head>
<title>Adding Line Breaks</title>
</head>
<body>
<font size="2" face="arial, helvetica">
Here I am going to demonstrate line breaks.
Notice that the  text I type does not break
until it reaches the edge of the browser
window. It does not matter how I type it
into my text editor, or where my text editor
breaks the lines. Only when I add HTML line
breaks can I control where the line breaks
occur.
</font>
</body>
</html>
```

2 Add the Line Break Tag

To create a line break, type **
** (**br**, a space, and a forward slash). The space and forward slash are the special closing portion of the line break tag. Now type a few more sentences.

```
<body>
<font size="2" face="arial, helvetica">
Here I am going to demonstrate line
breaks.<br /> Notice that the text I type
does not break until<br /> it reaches the
edge of the browser window.<br />
It does not matter how I type it into
my text<br /> editor, or where my text
editor breaks the lines.<br /> Only when I
add HTML line breaks can I control where the
line breaks occur.
</font>
</body>
```

3 Add the `clear` Attribute

In Part 5, "Implementing Web Graphics," Task 5, "How to Align Graphics to Text," you'll learn how to wrap text around images that you include in your HTML. You can use the **clear** attribute of the line break tag to override the specified text wrap. To use the **clear** attribute, type **<br clear />**. You'll see how this works in Part 5. Notice that the **clear** attribute is different from other attributes we've used in that it does not require a value.

```
<body>
<font size="2" face="arial, helvetica">
Only when I add HTML line breaks can I
control where the line breaks occur.<br />
I can also add the clear attribute to a
line break<br clear /> to override the wrap
around an image on my page.<br />
You'll learn more about that later.
</font>
</body>
```

4 Test the Page

Now that you've added line breaks, save your page and open it in your test browser. Notice that the line breaks cause the browser to move to the next line before showing the text that comes next. Also notice that the line break does not cause a paragraph break. It merely moves the text down to the next line without inserting additional space.

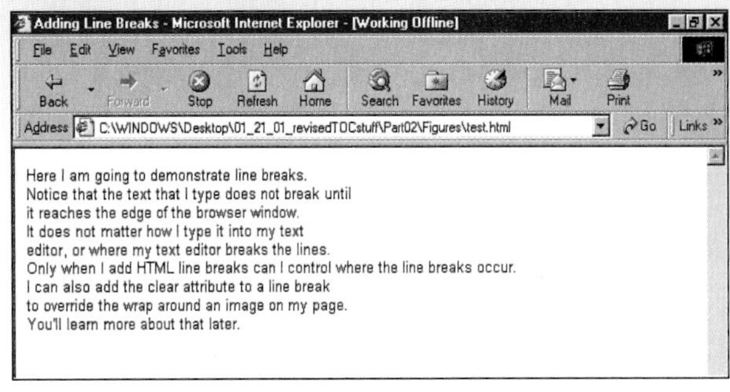

End

TASK 7 How to Use Special Text Characters

HTML is a lot like life. There's always some character or another causing you problems. Although you might not have thought about it, HTML uses some characters for very specific purposes. The obvious examples are the less-than and greater-than symbols. By now you know that these symbols signify the beginning and end of an HTML tag. When a browser sees these characters, it thinks it's being told to do something. This task shows you what you need to do to include these characters in your HTML as normal characters instead of as tag identifiers.

HTML interprets many "special" characters as the preamble to an HTML command. Escape codes let you include the characters as characters.

What's the Secret Escape Code?

Although the less-than and greater-than symbols are the obvious examples of characters that require special treatment in HTML, there are many others. How do you add an accent over that *e* or an umlaut over that *a*? How about that copyright symbol, or the registered trademark? In fact, if you can't type it on your keyboard without holding down something other than the key itself or the key in combination with the Shift key, you can't use it in your HTML. Browser support will be iffy at best. As a solution, HTML provides escape codes for these special characters. This task presents a few of the common codes, but there are too many to cover them all here. Escape codes come in two flavors: named entities and numbered entities. For a list of special characters and their escape codes, see the inside back cover of this book or visit **http://www.bbsinc.com/symbol.html**.

1 Include a Less-than Symbol

To include a less-than symbol that shows up on your Web page, type **<**. To include a greater-than symbol, type **>**. For example, to indicate that 6 is less than 9 but greater than 3, type **6 < 9 and 6 > 3**. What happens if you forget, and inadvertently use the less-than or greater-than symbol instead of the escape code? Your guess is as good as mine! Different browsers react differently, but the result won't be good.

```
<body>
<font size="2" face="arial, helvetica">
To write the mathematical equation, five is
less than 10, I use the escape character for
the less-than symbol, like this:<br />
5 &lt; 10 <br />
To write the equation 10 is greater than 5,
I write this code:<br />
10 &gt; 5<br />
Escape codes allow me to use symbols
that are reserved for HTML.
</font>
</body>
```

2 Add an Ampersand

Step 1 shows how to solve the less-than and greater-than problems, but you might have noticed that we introduced another problem. Notice that the special character codes both begin with the ampersand and end with a semicolon. In fact, this is the case with all special characters. So, what if you want to show the ampersand on your Web page? You need to type the escape code for it. Type **&**.

```
<body>
<font size="2" face="arial, helvetica">
The ampersand symbol is another special
character that is reserved for use in HTML.
Therefore, to use it on my Web page, I type
the escape code for it. I'll use it in
this phrase:<br />
Me &amp; you &amp; a dog named Boo.
</font>
</body>
```

3 Add a Nonbreaking Space

Remember that browsers ignore extra spaces in your HTML. You've learned how to use the preformatted text tag pair to get around this, but that can be cumbersome if you want just an extra space or two. In these cases, use the escape character for a nonbreaking space. To create an extra space in your HTML, type ** **.

```
<body>
<font size="2" face="arial, helvetica">
Because browsers ignore extra spaces, I must
use the escape code for a nonbreaking space
if I want to add more than one space in a
row. Here I'll add five spaces:<br />
Here come five spaces 
    in a row.
</font>
</body>
```

4 Add Other Characters

Here are a few other common escape codes: **"** for double quotation marks, **©** for the copyright symbol, **®** for the registered trademark symbol, **¢** for the cent sign, **°** for the degree sign, **¶** for the paragraph symbol, and **÷** for the division symbol.

```
<body>
<font size="2" face="arial, helvetica">
Here are some common escape codes<br />
&quot; for double quotation marks<br />
&copy; for the copyright symbol<br />
&reg; for registered trademark symbol<br />
&cent; for the cent sign<br />
&deg; for the degree sign<br />
&para; for the paragraph symbol<br />
&divide; for the division symbol.
</font>
</body>
```

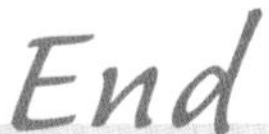

Task

PART 3

Working with Paragraphs

Now that you know how to add words to your HTML page and know something about how to control fonts, you next need to learn how to create paragraphs. Just as they do in any written document, paragraphs on your Web page help you organize your thoughts into related subtopics and make it much easier for the reader to follow along with what you've written.

The tags we talked about in Part 2, "Working with Text," fall into a category of tags called *inline elements*. As you've seen, these tags can be incorporated into a line of text without causing the text to break into a new paragraph. They simply tell the browser to make the text that falls between the opening and closing tags look a certain way.

HTML gives you many different ways to make a paragraph. There are a number of tags, referred to as *block elements* that create a paragraph break in addition to their main function. Task 1, "How to Create a New Paragraph," fully discusses the simplest of these, the paragraph tag pair (**<p>**...**</p>**). This is one of the most common tags you'll use when coding HTML. In fact, it might be the most common, so you'll get very used to it.

There are other block element tags that create a new paragraph. But unlike the paragraph tag, whose one and only function is to create a new paragraph, these tags have some other main function. Causing a paragraph break happens in addition to that function. List tags and headline tags fall into this second category.

The tasks in this part explore some of these tags and explain how you can use them to create structure for your Web page. You'll learn how to use them to take your page from a bunch of run-on words to an organized, easy-to-read document.

By the end of this part, you'll know enough HTML to put together a real page that you could actually use to share information across the World Wide Web. Therefore, in the last task, we'll walk through the creation of your very first Web page. That will serve as a great review of what you've learned so far—and will hopefully help you to see the practical potential of these techniques. •

TASK 1

How to Create a New Paragraph

Use the <p> tag to break long blocks of text into paragraghs.
You can add align attributes to center the paragraph or make it right-aligned.
<p>
Without block elements such as the paragraph tag, text will run on and on, filling the web page from left to

Another Open and Shut Case

In the first version of HTML, the **<p>** tag indicated the end of a paragraph instead of the beginning of the next paragraph, and it had no closing tag. Therefore, people became accustomed to ending each paragraph with this tag and moving on. That has changed, and now the **<p>** tag identifies the beginning of a paragraph. It also has a corresponding closing tag that goes at the end of each paragraph, although the closing tag is optional in HTML.

By now, you probably expect the situation to be slightly different in XHTML—and of course, you're right. As always, XHTML requires an opening and a closing tag. Because we're working toward developing good XHTML coding skills, we'll close all our **<p>** tags. Therefore you'll notice that all the paragraph examples in this book have a **<p>** tag at the beginning and a corresponding **</p>** tag at the end.

1 Add the Paragraph Tag Pair

By now, the form of tags should look very familiar. The paragraph tag pair is no different than other tags you have become familiar with. To start a new paragraph, type **<p>**.

```
<html>
<head>
<title>Creating a New Paragraph</title>
</head>
<body>
<font size="2" face="arial, helvetica">
<p>
</font>
</body>
</html>
```

2 Add the Paragraph Text

After the tag, you can type your paragraph as normal. Don't worry about line breaks—the browser will put them in when your text reaches the edge of the browser window. When you are done with the paragraph, type **</p>** to close it. Type another **<p>** to start the next paragraph.

```
<p>
Now that I've added the paragraph tag,
I can write my first paragraph. When I'm
done with this paragraph, I will close the
paragraph tag pair and open a new one. I'll
then be ready to write my next paragraph.</p>
<p>
Notice that the paragraph tag pair puts
space between the first paragraph
and the second. You see, making
paragraphs is really quite easy in HTML!</p>
```

3 Add the `align` Attribute

Sometimes you want your text to align to the left side of the browser, sometimes to the right, and sometimes you want each line to be centered. Add the **`align`** attribute to specify the alignment of the paragraph. For instance, to create a right-aligned paragraph, type **`<p align="right">`**. To create a center-aligned paragraph, type **`"center"`**. For a left-aligned paragraph, type **`"left"`**, or just leave out the **`align`** attribute completely because left is the default alignment.

```
<p>
This paragraph uses the default value for
the align tag, which is align="left".
Notice that the paragraph lines up on its
left edge.</p>
<p align="center">
This paragraph uses the value "center"
for the align attribute. Every line of this
paragraph is centered on the browser page;
both the left and right edges are ragged.
</p>
```

4 Test the Results

Save your page and view the results in your browser. Make sure that each of the paragraphs aligns the way you expect it to. If something doesn't align properly, correct any mistakes in your code, save the page, and refresh your browser to test the page again.

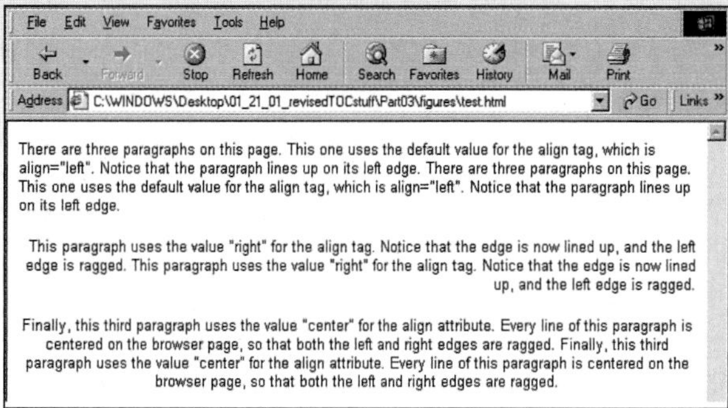

End

TASK 2

How to Add Headings

HTML provides six tags that create six different levels of headings. You can use these to create headlines, section headings, subheadings, and outlines. Each of these tags also creates a paragraph break. In other words, when you add a heading tag, you also add space between the heading and the paragraph that comes before it, as well as the paragraph that comes after it.

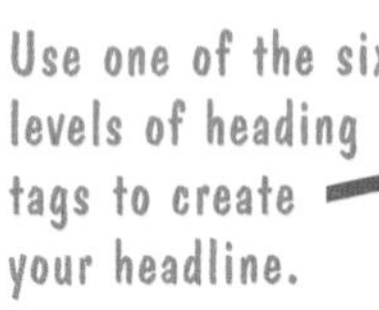

Use one of the six levels of heading tags to create your headline.

Heading tags are interpreted by the browser and may not have the formatting you expected.

That's the Logical Heading

Be aware that heading tags are much like the logical tags we discussed in Part 2, Task 4, "How to Format Text." When you use a heading tag, your HTML tells the browser, "Here comes a heading. Please treat it as such." But the browser decides how to display that heading. Most browsers use a combination of size and boldness to display headings. For instance, most browsers show **<h1>** headings as larger than **<h2>** headings, which are larger than **<h3>** headings, and so on.

But because it's up to the browser to decide how to show this hierarchy of significance, you can't always know exactly how your page will look on every browser. You need to keep this in mind when coding your HTML. If you depend on a larger, bolder text for your level-one headings, and you base your graphic design decisions on this assumption, your page could look disappointing when viewed on a browser that shows significance with underlining instead of bolding.

1 Add a Main Headline

Of all the six heading tags, browsers interpret the **<h1>** heading tag as the most significant. Thus it makes sense to use this tag for your main headings. The logical place to add the main heading is directly after the **<body>** tag. Type **<h1>**, followed by the heading itself, and close with **</h1>**.

```
<html>
<head>
<title>Adding Headings</title>
</head>
<body>
<font size="2" face="arial, helvetica">
<h1>
Here Is My Main Heading
</h1>
</font>
</body>
</html>
```

2 Add a Subhead

All the other heading tags work in exactly the same way as the <h1> tag. To add a second-level subhead, type **<h2>**...**</h2>**. For a third-level heading, type **<h3>**...**</h3>**, and so on.

```
<body>
<font size="2" face="arial, helvetica">
<h1>
Here Is My Main Heading
</h1>
<h2>
Here Is My Second-level Heading
</h2>
<h3>
Here Is My Third-level Heading
</h3>
</font>
</body>
```

3 Create an Outline

You can use the heading tags to easily delineate the different sections of an outline. Start with the **<h1>** tag pair for the main topic, move on to the **<h2>** tag pair for the next level, and so on.

```
<body>
<font size="2" face="arial, helvetica">
<h1>Main Topic</h1>
<h2>Second Level Heading</h2>
<h3>Third-level Heading</h3>
<h4>Forth-level Heading</h4>
<h5>Fifth-level Heading</h5>
<h6>Sixth-level Heading</h6>
</font>
</body>
```

4 Test the Results

Save your page and test the results in your browser. Make sure that you have properly closed all the tags. If you haven't, you might see strange results.

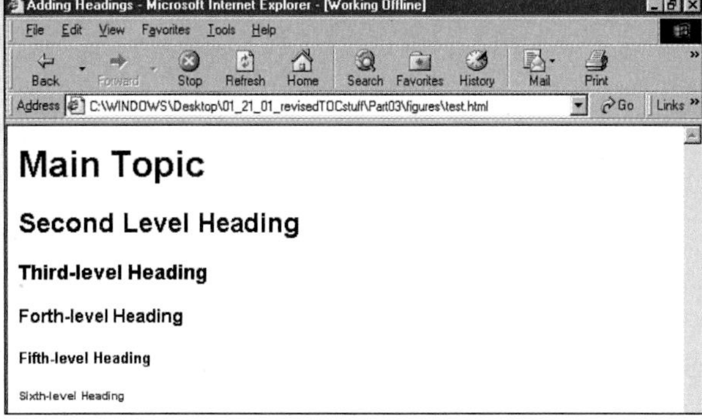

.End

TASK 3 How to Create a Horizontal Rule

Although the horizontal rule tag might not officially be considered a block tag, I include it here because it has essentially the same effect in that it creates a paragraph break as well as a horizontal rule. In other words, when you add a horizontal rule tag, the browser puts space between the previous line of text and the rule, as well as between the rule and the next line of text. You can use horizontal rules for any number of reasons. Any time you want to separate one section from another, consider doing so with a horizontal rule.

Horizontal rules can separate blocks of text to give your pages some structure.
<hr/>
<hr/>
You can set the thickness, length, and alignment of a rule.

Poor Man's Graphics

You can use horizontal rules for simple graphic design purposes. In Part 5, "Implementing Web Graphics," you'll explore creating graphics for your Web site using image-editing software. You'll also learn how to incorporate those graphics into your Web page. Part 9, "Working with the Layout of Your Web Pages," discusses decisions you'll have to make about the layout of your Web pages. But because you've not gotten that far yet, you can use horizontal rules to give your pages a little bit of graphic flare. Try using rules of different thickness and length for various effects. Even though its design possibilities are limited, the horizontal rule tag can nonetheless give you a way of defining sections of your page graphically. Hopefully, the techniques you learn later in this book will play a more important role in your graphic design scheme, but for now, see what you can accomplish with horizontal rules.

1 Add the Horizontal Rule Tag

To add a horizontal rule, type **<hr />**. This tag creates a horizontal rule that stretches across the full width of the browser window. When you resize the browser window, the horizontal rule adjusts along with it. Notice that this tag is similar to the line break tag you learned about in Part 2, Task 6, "How to Control Line Breaks," in that it has no closing tag. Therefore, you need to add the forward slash that closes the tag in XHTML.

```
<html>
<head>
<title>Working with Horizontal Rules</title>
</head>
<body>
<p>
To add a rule across the width of the
browser window, just add the
horizontal rule tag.</p>
<hr />
</body>
</html>
```

2 Define Size and Width

Use the **size** attribute to define the thickness of the line in pixels. The default thickness of two pixels is the smallest allowed. Use the **width** attribute to define the length of the line. You can specify the width either as an exact number of pixels or as a percentage of the width of the browser window. For example, type **<hr size="4" width="60%" />**. To specify an exact value for width, type **<hr size="4" width="350" />**.

```
<body>
<p>
To change the width and height of the
rule, use the width and size
attributes.</p>
<hr size="4" width="350" />
</body>
```

3 Align the Rule

By default, horizontal rules with a width less than the width of the browser window are centered in the browser window. Use the **align** attribute to change this behavior. To align the rule left, type **<hr align="left" />** and to align the rule to the right side of the screen, type **<hr align="right" />**.

```
<body>
<p>
Use the align attribute to change the
alignment of the rule from its default
("center") to either left
<hr size="4" width="350" align="left" />
or right
<hr size="4" width="350" align="right" />
</p>
</body>
```

4 Control the Rule Shading

By default (at least on most browsers), each horizontal rule has a shadow under it. If you don't want a shadow to appear under your rule, use the **noshade** attribute. To add a horizontal rule with no shadow, type **<hr size="4" width="350" noshade="noshade" />**.

```
<body>
<p>
Use the noshade attribute to remove the
shadow from the rule
<hr size="4" width="350" noshade="noshade" />
</p>
</body>
```

End

TASK 4

How to Create a Numbered List

HTML allows you to create several different types of lists. This task demonstrates how to create a numbered list, known in HTML as an *ordered list*. Use this type of list when you want to list items in order of importance. For instance, use it to display the steps of a recipe or your top five favorite vacation attractions. As you'll see, there are many variations of the basic ordered list that you can use to shape your list depending on your preference and specific needs.

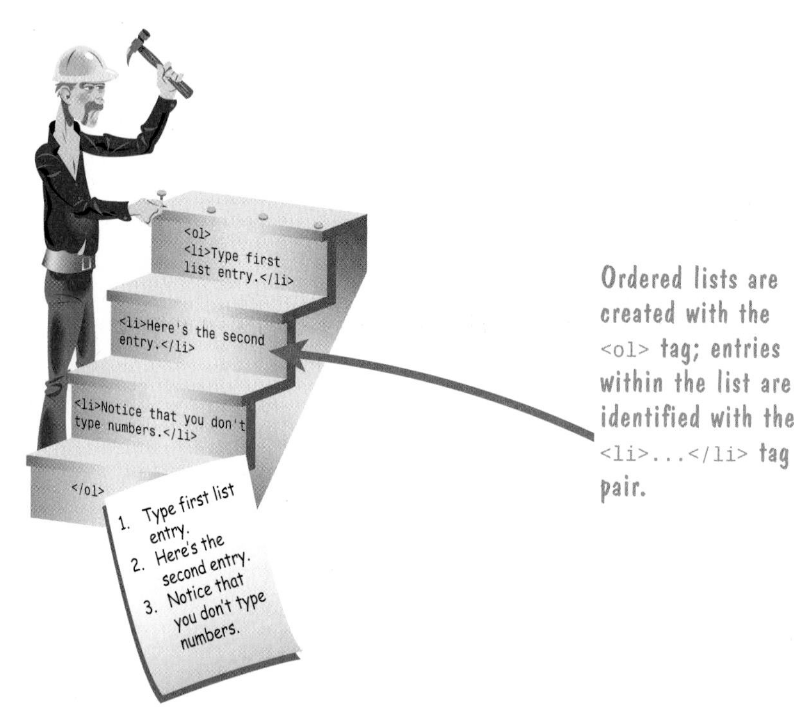

Ordered lists are created with the <ol> tag; entries within the list are identified with the <li>...</li> tag pair.

More Optional Closing Tags

Lists represent another area in which you can get away with omitting a few closing tags as long as you are writing HTML. Specifically, the closing tags **</dd>**, **</dt>**, and **</li>** are not really necessary for HTML. (In this task and the next, you'll see how to use the **<li>**...**</li>** tag pair; Task 6, "How to Create a Definition List," introduces the **<dd>**...**</dd>** and **<dt>**...**</dt>** tag pairs.)

As usual, however, you won't see any missing closing tags in my examples. Because the closing tags do not hamper HTML in any way, get used to using them now so that the habit is well entrenched when you begin writing XHTML. Remember, all tags must be closed in XHTML.

1 Identify an Ordered List

If you want to create a list of items in a specific order of importance, create an ordered list. To create this type of list, enclose its contents with the ordered list tag pair. Type **<ol>**...**</ol>**.

```
<html>
<head>
<title>Constructing an Ordered List</title>
</head>
<body>
<p>
Start an ordered list by adding the ordered
list tag pair:</p>
<ol>
</ol>
</font>
</body>
</html>
```

2 Identify List Items

You need to identify each item in the list with the list item tag. Don't worry about adding the number to the list item; the **<ol>** tag takes care of the numbering for you. To identify a list item, type **<li>**...**</li>**. The list item tag causes a line break, so each time you add a new list item, it starts on a new line. You can add as many list items as you want.

```
<p>
Start an ordered list by adding the ordered
list tag pair. Then, within the ordered list
tag pair, use the list item tag pair to
identify the individual list items.</p>
<ol>
<li></li>
<li></li>
<li></li>
</ol>
```

3 Add the List Items

Type the actual list item between the **<li>** and **</li>** tags. Each list item requires its own list item tag. You can use other HTML tags within the list. For instance, you can use the **<b>** tag to make a word in the list item bold.

```
<ol>
<li>Chocolate Cake</li>
<li>Cheesburgers</li>
<li>Pizza</li>
<li><i>More</i> <b>Chocolate Cake</b>!</li>
</ol>
```

4 Specify Number Style

By default, an ordered list gives each list item a number starting with the Arabic numeral 1. Use the **type** attribute to change the numbering to lowercase letters (**type="a"**), uppercase letters (**type="A"**), lowercase Roman numerals (**type="i"**), uppercase Roman numerals (**type="I"**), or back to Arabic numerals (**type="1"**). Use the **start** attribute to start the list at a specific number or letter. For instance, to create a list that orders its items by lowercase letters starting at *f*, type **<ol type="a" start="6">**. Notice that the **start** attribute always takes an Arabic numeral regardless of what you specify with the **type** attribute.

```
<body>
<ol type="i"  start="6">
<li>Chocolate Cake</li>
<li>Cheesburgers</li>
<li>Pizza</li>
<li><i>More</i> <b>Chocolate Cake</b></li>
</ol>
```

End

TASK 5

How to Create a Bulleted List

The second type of list (referred to as an *unordered*, or *bulleted list*) allows you to present a list of items that don't necessarily have a particular order. For instance, you might use an unordered list for the favorite foods you listed in the last task or for the list of the places you've visited on vacation in the past 10 years. When list order matters, use an ordered list. When order doesn't matter, use an unordered list. This task shows you how to make an unordered list.

<ul>
<li>Apples</li>
<li>Peaches</li>
<li>Pumpkin pie</li>
</ul>
Unordered lists use bullet points to set off the entries in the list.
·Apples
· Peaches
·Pumpkin Pie
Who's not hungry, holler "I"!
You can change the bullet character using the type attribute.

Automatic Paragraph Breaks

Remember that all the list types we're discussing are block elements. This means that when you add the appropriate tag to identify the list, you automatically create a line break and insert space between the previous paragraph and the list, as well as between the list element and the following paragraph. Therefore, you do not need to add a paragraph tag before your lists.

Tags Within Lists

You might (not unreasonably) assume that a list is what it is and that you can't change the look of it. This is not really so. In addition to the attributes that allow you to customize your lists, there is another way to change the appearance of your lists: You can include other tags within them. For example, if you want to make a word within your list italic, do so using the **<i>**...**</i>** tag pair you learned in Part 2, Task 4, "How to Format Text."

1 Identify an Unordered List

Sometimes you want your list to be a little less formal. When you want to make a list of items in which order doesn't necessarily matter, create an unordered list. To start an unordered list, type **<ul>**...**</ul>**. Unordered lists use bullet points instead of numbers or letters to separate list items.

```
<html>
<head>
<title>Constructing an Unordered List</title>
</head>
<body>
<p>
Unordered lists are structured just
the same as ordered lists.
First add the unordered list tag pair.</p>
<ul>
</ul>
</body>
</html>
```

2 Identify List Items

Identify the list items in an unordered list in exactly the same way you do for an ordered list. To add a list item, type **<li>**...**</li>**. Just as you don't have to include the numbers for your items in an ordered list, you don't have to provide the bullets in an unordered list; the unordered list provides those characters for you.

```
<p>
After the unordered list tag pair, identify
the list items with the list item tag pair.
</p>
<ul>
<li></li>
<li></li>
<li></li>
</ul>
```

3 Add the List Items

To add the contents of the list item, type the actual list item between the **<li>** tag and the **</li>** tag.

```
<ul>
<li>Sleep</li>
<li>Talk on the phone</li>
<li>Play with the kids</li>
<li>Eat chocolate cake</li>
</ul>
```

4 Customize the List

By default, filled, round bullet points mark the list items in an unordered list. Use the **type** attribute to change this default to a square (**type="square"**), a hollow circle (**type="circle"**), or back to a bullet point (**type="disc"**). For example, to create an unordered list whose items are marked by squares, type **<ul type="square">**...**</ul>**. The shapes mentioned here are the only shapes you can use for bullets.

```
<ul type="square">
<li>Sleep</li>
<li>Talk on the phone</li>
<li>Play with the kids</li>
<li>Eat chocolate cake</li>
</ul>
```

End

TASK 6 How to Create a Definition List

The *definition list* acts a bit differently than the other two lists you've learned about. Because the purpose of a definition list is also different, it follows that you construct this type of list a bit differently. Sometimes called *glossary lists*, definition lists give you a good way to present terms and their definitions. You might use a definition list to create a glossary of terms used on your Web site. You don't see these lists as often as the other two types, but they can be very handy in the appropriate situation.

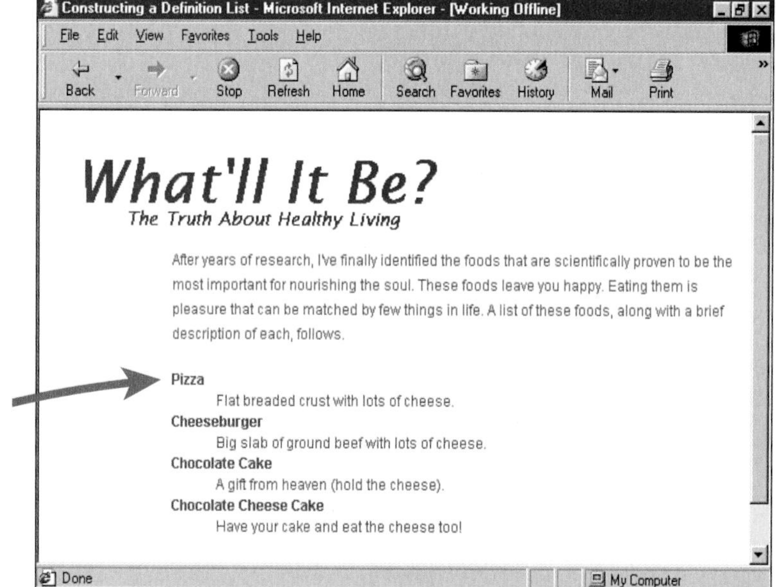

Definition lists place the term on a separate line and a definition or explanation of that term on the following line, slightly indented under the term.

That Nesting Instinct

What if you want one of the items in your list to be yet another list of items? Can HTML handle that? Sure. Simply add the new list where you want it. This is called nesting one list within another. As long as you properly construct them, you can nest lists within lists all day long.

Here's an example. Suppose that you make a list of classical composers. You include Bach, Schubert, Handel, Mendelssohn, and Mozart in an unordered list. You decide it would be helpful to include a few compositions by each that people might find particularly pleasing. Under the Mendelssohn list entry, you nest an ordered list that includes *A Midsummer Night's Dream*, *Symphony No. 4 in A Major*, and *Symphony No. 5 in D Minor*. You can create similar lists for the other composers.

1 Identify the Definition List

To identify a definition list, use the definition list tag pair. Type **<dl>...</dl>**.

```
<p>
Although definition lists are somewhat
different than the other two list
types, you start out the same. Type the
definition list tag pair.
</p>
<dl>
</dl>
```

2 Identify the Defined Term

You compose definition list entries in two steps. The first step is to type the term for which you want to provide the definition. To add this term, use the definition term tag pair. Type **<dt>...</dt>**.

```
<p>
Now type the definition term tag pair to
identify the terms to be defined.
</p>
<dl>
<dt>Pizza</dt>
<dt>Cheeseburger</dt>
<dt>Chocolate Cake</dt>
</dl>
```

3 Identify the Term Definition

The next step in creating a definition list entry is to define the term you specified in Step 2. Use the definition definition (yes, I meant to say definition definition) tag pair to specify this type of entry. Type **<dd>...</dd>**.

```
<p>
Finally, use the definition definition tag
pair to enter the definitions.
</p>
<dl>
<dt>Pizza</dt>
<dd>Flat bread with lots of cheese.</dd>
<dt>Cheeseburger</dt>
<dd>Slab of beef with lots of cheese.</dd>
<dt>Chocolate Cake</dt>
<dd>A gift from heaven (no cheese).</dd>
</dl>
```

4 Test Your Results

You've added three different list types over the past three tasks. Save your page and test it in your browser to see how each of these lists appears to the Web page viewer. Here you see the definition list in Internet Explorer.

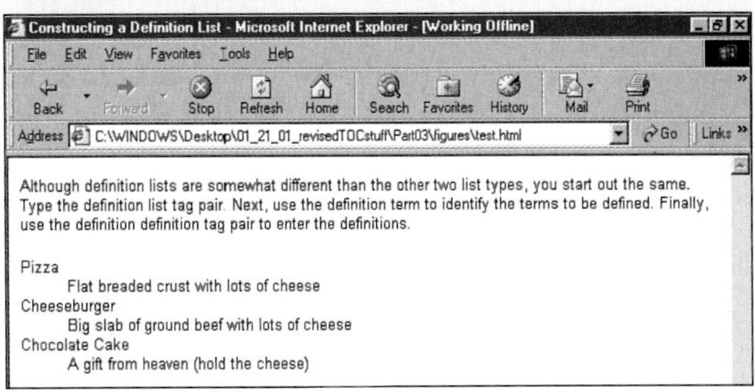

End

TASK 7

How to Format Quotations

There might be times when you want to include a quote on your Web page. For instance, you might want to include a famous line from your favorite book to illustrate a point. Or you might want to include an entire paragraph from the book. HTML provides two tag pairs specifically designed to allow you to do these things. This task shows you how to use these tags to present quotes in your HTML.

To show quotation marks, use the " escape character.
<blockquote>
</blockquote>
When you want to show a long quotation, use the <blockquote> tag.

And I Quote...

Using quotations from others can be a great way to make a point, emphasize your views, or substantiate your claims. For example, you can describe the perfect vacation in astounding eloquence, but just think of the extra punch your description will have if a poetic pondering from the pen of Longfellow backs up everything you're saying. If your Web page is trying to convince people that time travel is possible, wouldn't it be more convincing if you had a quote from Albert Einstein agreeing with your point of view?

Cite quotations on your Web pages just as you would in any document you prepare on your word processor. If it's not your original thought, give credit where credit is due. Plagiarism is just as serious an offense on Web sites as it is in written communications. And the penalties are the same, too.

1 Identify an Inline Quote

Sometimes you want to cite a short quote. For instance, you might want to write Mr. Lincoln's famous phrase, "Four score and seven years ago..." Use the **"** escape character to put the quote into quotation marks and use the **<cite>** tag to credit Abe with the quote. The **<cite>** tag is a logical tag, so you don't always know exactly how the text you include in it will be presented by every browser. (Most browsers present this type of tag in italics.) To use this tag, type **<cite>**...**</cite>**.

```
<p>
When you want to include a very short
quote within a line of text like this
one, use the cite tag pair. As an example,
I could write, &quot;Four score
and seven years ago...&quot;
<cite>Abraham Lincoln</cite>.
</p>
```

2 Test Your Results

Check your page in your browser to see how it presents the citation tag.

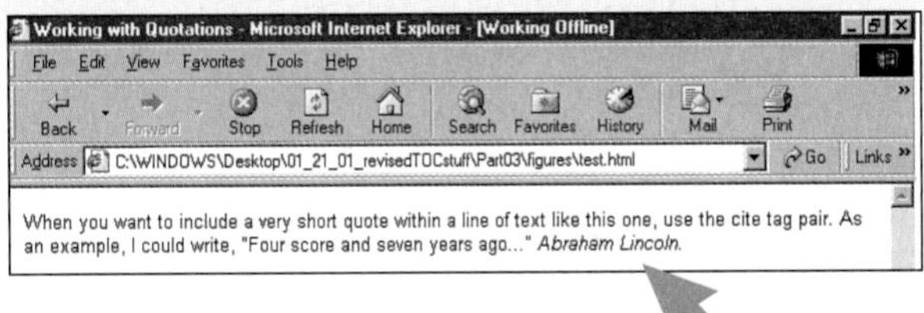

3 Identify a Block Quote

When the quotation you want to include gets long, you'll want to separate it from your regular text. Use the **<blockquote>** tag pair to do so. Most browsers set text within this pair off from the rest of the text using indentation, but some browsers might treat the text differently. For long quotations, type **<blockquote>**... **</blockquote>**.

```
<p>
When you have a long quotation, use the
blockquote tag pair to set it aside from
the rest of your text.</p>
<blockquote>
Well we all shine on<br />
Like the moon and the stars and
the sun<br />
Yeah we all shine on<br />
On and on, on and on<br />
--John Lennon
</blockquote>
```

4 Test Your Results

You can also include other HTML tags within a block quote (as well as the **<cite>** citation tag talked about in Step 1). For instance, you can make several words bold. Check your page in your browser to see how it presents block quotes.

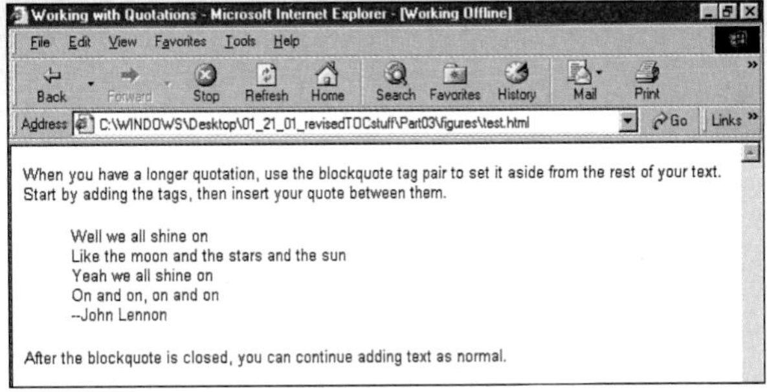

End

TASK 8 How to Create Your First HTML Page

You've come a long way already! You've learned a lot of HTML, and could probably use a little practical reinforcement. This task walks you through coding your first complete Web page. We'll use many of the tags and attributes discussed in the first three parts of the book. Hopefully, you can also solidify some of the concepts of graphic design and proper coding technique we've been talking about. Granted, there is still a lot to learn, but I think you'll be surprised by how much you already know, and what you can already create.

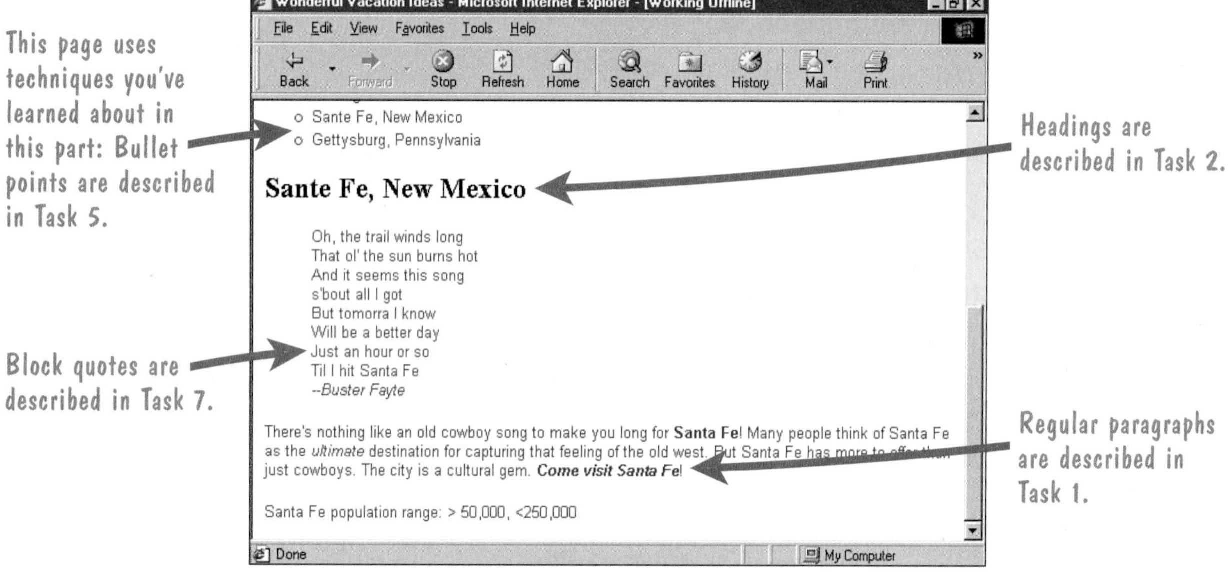

Coming Up Next...

Hopefully you're over any fears that HTML is too complicated. Although this task takes an important look back to where you've been, it is also an excellent time to contemplate what's to come. We've still got a lot to cover, including some of the key pieces to the puzzle. Some of it gets a bit more complicated, but you've got a solid base now for handling that. Besides, much of what you'll learn is no more complicated than what you already know.

In the next part, you'll learn how to transform your page from an isolated island of HTML code into a full-fledged member of the World Wide Web. You'll learn to create the links that make the Web so useful. In Part 5, you'll learn more about Web graphics. In Part 6, "Working with Tables," we'll explore one of the most useful (and confusing!) tools in HTML—tables. So settle in. The ride's just getting interesting!

1 Add the Structural Tags

Start this page just as you start every page: Add the basic structural tag pairs. Specifically, add the **<html>**, **<head>**, **<title>**, and **<body>** tag pairs. Don't forget to give your page a title! Refer back to Part 1, "Getting Started," Tasks 4, "How to Create HTML Tags and Add Attributes," and 5, "How to Structure Every HTML Page," if you need a refresher.

```
<html>
<head>
<title>Wonderful Vacation Ideas</title>
</head>
<body>
</body>
</html>
```

2 Add a Heading

Use the **<h1>** tag pair to add a main heading to your page. If you need help, refer to Task 2, "How to Add Headings," in this part. Don't forget to close the header tag!

```
<html>
<head>
<title>Wonderful Vacation Ideas</title>
</head>
<body>
<h1>Wonderful Vacation Destinations</h1>
</body>
</html>
```

3 Add a Horizontal Rule

Add a horizontal rule under the heading with the **<hr />** tag. (Don't forget the closing character for XHTML.) Add the **width** attribute to make the rule stretch a quarter of the way across the page. (*Hint:* Specify a percentage.) Use the **size** attribute to make the rule three pixels thick, and the **align** attribute to anchor the rule to the left edge of the window. See Task 3, "How to Create a Horizontal Rule," for help.

```
<html>
<head>
<title>Wonderful Vacation Ideas</title>
</head>
<body>
<h1>Wonderful Vacation Destinations</h1>
<hr align="left" size="3" width="25%" />
</body>
</html>
```

4 Specify Font Attributes

You are about to add your main text. First, add the **<font>** tag pair. Use the **face** attribute to specify the Arial typeface with an alternative of Helvetica; use the **size** attribute to set the font size to 2. Use the **color** attribute to specify a dark blue color for the text. See Part 2, Tasks 1, "How to Specify Text Size," 2, "How to Specify Text Color," and 3, "How to Specify Text Fonts," for help with the **<font>** tag; see Part 1, Task 10, "How to Specify Colors," for a refresher on specifying colors.

```
<html>
<head>
<title>Wonderful Vacation Ideas</title>
</head>
<body>
<h1>Wonderful Vacation Destinations</h1>
<hr align="left" size="3" width="25%" />
<font face="arial,helvetica" size="2"
color="#0000cf">
</font>
</body>
</html>
```

Continues

5 Add an Introductory Paragraph

Use the **<p>** tag pair to create a new paragraph, and type a two-paragraph introduction to your Web page. See Task 1 of this part for help with creating paragraphs.

```
<p>There are many wonderful places to spend
your next vacation. You can choose from a
lazy week on the beaches of Hawaii, or an
adventure hiking through the mountains and
canyons of New Mexico. Whatever your
preference, you can find a destination that
will make your next vacation the most
memorable one you've ever had.</p>
<p>This Web site is devoted to giving you
new ideas. We've researched the best
vacation destinations in the world and now
pass this valuable information on to you.
Take time to look at the options. No matter
where your travels take you, you'll be glad
your next vacation started here!</p>
```

6 Add a Bulleted List

Use the **<ul>** and **<li>** tag pairs to add an unordered list of the things covered in your Web page. Use the **type** attribute to show a hollow circle in front of each new list item. Task 5 of this part, "How to Create a Bulleted List," can help if you get stuck.

```
<p>
This month's featured trips are:</p>
<ul type="circle">
<li>The big island of Hawaii</li>
<li>Sante Fe, New Mexico</li>
<li>Gettysburg, Pennsylvania</li>
</ul>
</font>
</body>
</html>
```

7 Add a Subheading

After the list, add another heading. Use the **<h2>** tag pair to make this a level-two subhead. Task 2 of this part, "How to Add Headings," talks about creating headings.

```
<p>
This month's featured trips are:</p>
<ul type="circle">
<li>The big island of Hawaii</li>
<li>Sante Fe, New Mexico</li>
<li>Gettysburg, Pennsylvania</li>
</ul>
</font>
<h2>Sante Fe, New Mexico</h2>
</body>
</html>
```

8 Add a Comment

Use the special **<!--...-->** tags to write yourself a note that will not appear on the Web page, but that you can use for future reference. See Part 1, Task 14, "How to Add Invisible Comments," if you don't remember how to add comments.

```
<p>
This month's featured trips are:</p>
<ul type="circle">
<li>The big island of Hawaii</li>
<li>Sante Fe, New Mexico</li>
<li>Gettysburg, Pennsylvania</li>
</ul>
</font>
<h2>Sante Fe, New Mexico</h2>
<!--This section of the page focuses on the
areas surrounding Santa Fe.-->
</body>
</html>
```

9 Add a Block Quote

Add a verse from your favorite song. Enclose it within the **<blockquote>** tag pair to set it apart from your main text. At the end of each line of the verse, use the **
** tag to cause a line break before you type the next line. See Task 7 of this part, "How to Format Quotations," for step-by-step instructions on using the **<blockquote>** tag, and Part 2, Task 6, "How to Control Line Breaks," for help with the line break tag.

```
<font face="arial,helvetica"
size="2" color="#0000cf">
<blockquote>
Oh, the trail winds long<br />
That ol' sun burns hot<br />
And it seems this song<br />
s'bout all I got<br />
But tomorra I know<br />
Will be a better day<br />
Just an hour or so<br />
Til I hit Santa Fe<br />
<cite>Buster Fayte</cite>
</blockquote>
</font>
```

10 Create Bold and Italic Text

After the quote you added in Step 9, add another paragraph. Use the **<b>** tag pair to include at least one word of bold text, the **<i>** tag pair to include some italic text, and combine the two to create a few words of bold, italic text. See Part 2, Task 4, "How to Format Text," for help.

```
<p>
There's nothing like an old cowboy song to
make you long for <b>Santa Fe</b>!
Many people think of Santa Fe as the
<i>ultimate</i> destination for capturing
that feeling of the old west. But Santa Fe
has more to offer than just
cowboys. The city is a cultural gem.
<b><i>Come visit Santa Fe</i></b>!</p>
```

11 Add a Special Character

Next, add a mathematical equation to your page. Use the escape characters for the less-than (**<**) and greater-than (**>**) symbols. Add some additional escape characters if you can. Refer to Part 2, Task 7, "How to Use Special Text Characters," for a reference to find other escape characters.

```
<p>
There's nothing like an old cowboy song to
make you long for <b>Santa Fe</b>!
Many people think of Santa Fe as the
<i>ultimate</i> destination for capturing
that feeling of the old west. But Santa Fe
has more to offer than just
cowboys. The city is a cultural gem.
<b><i>Come visit Santa Fe</i></b>!</p>
<p>
Santa Fe population range:
&gt; 50,000, &lt;250,000</p>
```

12 Test Your Results

If you took my advice in Part 1, Task 8, "How to Test Your Page in a Browser," you've already completed this step several times during this task. Save your page and review the results in your test browser.

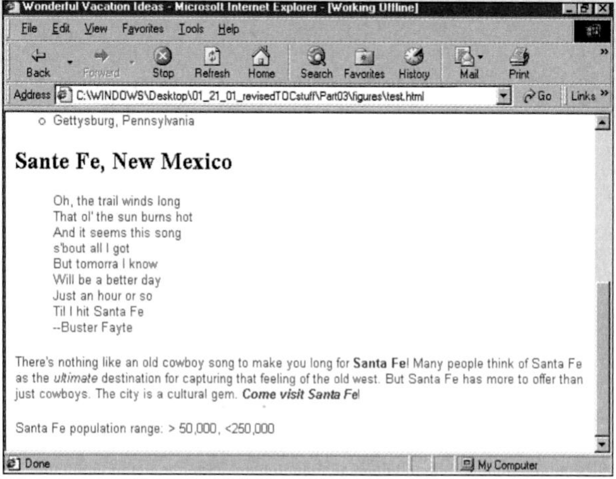

Task

PART 4

And Now, the Star of Our Show...Adding Hyperlinks to Text

It's time to transform your page into a dynamic member of the World Wide Web. How do you do that? With hyperlinks. Commonly referred to simply as *links*, these truly are the stars of the show. You've probably followed links already. These are the words you click to go from page A to page B. Without links, your page is just...well...a page. But with hyperlinks, you can tie your page to all the other pages in your site—and to a whole world of pages created by your fellow HTML authors around the globe. Your page becomes a launching pad for the wonderful journey into the World Wide Web.

Sound overly dramatic? Well, maybe it is...I get that way sometimes. But maybe it isn't. Think about it: With hyperlinks, you can link your page to any other page in the world. *Any page.* Whether that other page was created by you or the guy in the next office, or a woman across town, or a bunch of school kids upstate, or your grandmother on the opposite coast, or somebody you've never heard of on the other side of the planet, it doesn't matter. You can link your page to theirs, and they can link their pages to yours.

Something that important sounds a bit daunting, doesn't it? The good news is that for such an undeniably critical cog in the great wheel, a link is incredibly easy to make. In fact, you've already learned the majority of what you need to know. You know how to make a tag, add attributes, and specify file paths. And that's almost all there is to creating a link. Of course, there are always the details, and that's what the tasks in this part of the book cover.

One of those details is something that a surprisingly large number of HTML authors don't seem to take into account: You follow a link from one site to another, and then another, and another, and so on. And then you try to remember where you started, and how in the world you can ever get back. Now picture visitors to your site having the same experience. You can't just hope they'll find their way back; you have to make sure that they can. Task 3, "How to Link to a Page on a Different Web Site," shows you a simple technique that can help ensure that your visitors don't get lost.

TASK 1

How to Create a Link from One Page to Another

This task explores the anatomy of a link. Most of you have probably seen links on Web pages to which you've surfed. By default, links appear in the same font as the text around them; they are usually blue when you haven't visited them yet and a different color (depending on the browser) after you've visited them. You'll learn which tags you need to construct the link, which attributes to define to give the link directions to its destination, and where to put the text that shows up in the browser as the visible portion of the link.

Hey, "Link" Doesn't Start with "A"!

Most tags in HTML have some sort of logical relationship to the function they perform. For example, it makes sense that the bold tag is **<b>** and that the font tag is **<font>**. We can easily see why the paragraph tag is **<p>**. So, what gives with that crazy **<a>** tag? What this tag does is create a link. Therefore, you might logically expect the tag to be **<l>**, but it's not. Why? The tag is actually called the anchor tag, not the link tag. It is a bit confusing because links and anchors are two different things in HTML. Yet they both use the **<a>** tag. You use attributes to define whether the tag is an anchor or a link. In most of these tasks, you'll learn to use the tag to create links, but Task 4, "How to Link to a Specific Location on a Web Page," shows the tag's alternative use. After you work through these tasks, the difference will be clear.

1 Type the Anchor Tag Pair

The anchor tag pair defines a link. The structure of this tag pair surely looks very familiar to you by now. It is the same structure you've been using for most of the other tags you've learned so far. To add the anchor tag pair, type **<a>...</a>**. It almost seems anticlimactic that the tag for creating links is so simple, but that's the way it is!

```
<h1>Creating text hyperlinks</h1>
<p>
The anchor tag allows you to build links
so that your visitors can
surf from page to page.
To learn all about <a></a>, your visitors
can click the link in this sentence.
The link is not complete. We still need to
supply directions to the page we want and
supply the text that acts as the link. </p>
```

2 Specify the Destination Page

In Step 1, you built the basic structure of the link. Now you need to provide the location to which the link points. You use the hyper-reference attribute for this purpose. Type **href="value"** where **value** is the file path to the desired page. For instance, to link to the page called **vacations.html**, type **<a href="vacations.html">...</a>**. This is the simplest link because it points to a page in the same folder as the one that holds the link.

```
<p>To learn all about
<a href="vacations.html"></a>, visitors
can click the link in this sentence.
Notice that even though we've supplied the
directions to the page we want, the link
does not yet appear in the browser because
we have not defined the text that acts
as the link.</p>
```

3 Add the Link Text

Now you need a label for the link. The label is the word or phrase that shows up in your visitor's browser when he or she views your page. The label is what the visitor sees as the link. Anything you add between the opening anchor tag and the ending tag becomes a clickable link. For example, type **<a href="vacations.html">Dream Vacations</a>**. The phrase *Dream Vacations* shows up in the browser as the visible link.

```
<p>This paragraph contains the anchor tag.
The anchor tag allows you to build links
into your page so that visitors can surf
from page to page. To learn all about
<a href="vacations.html">
Dream Vacations</a>,
visitors can click the link in
this sentence.
If you test this page in your browser now,
you'll see that the link is complete.</p>
```

4 Test the Hyperlink

To test your link, create a new HTML page called **vacations.html** (save it in the same folder as the page you're working on). Make sure that you save the page containing the link, and then open that page in your test browser. If you did everything correctly, you'll see the link on your page. Click the link. If the current page closes, and **vacations.html** opens in its place, you've successfully created your first link!

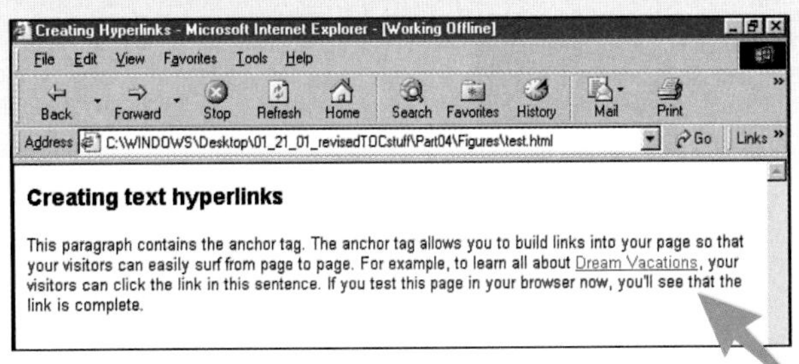

TASK 2 How to Link to a Page on Your Own Web Site

In the last task, you linked from your page to another page stored in the same folder. But usually, you'll have pages grouped in various logical folders or directories. For instance, you might have a directory called **pages** in which you have a directory called **past** and another called **current**. To link from a page in **current** to a page in **past** requires a little more work than what you learned to do in the last task. This task shows two ways to link to pages in your own directory structure. By the way, now would be a great time to review Task 11, "How to Specify a File Path," in Part 1, "Getting Started."

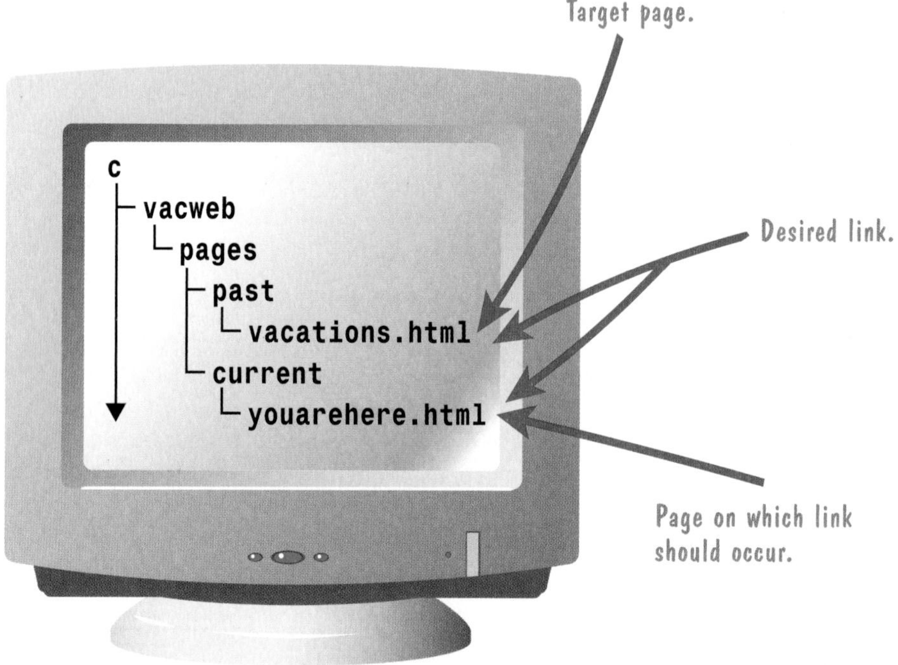

Local Links

The links you create in this task, as well as the one you made in the last task, are known as *local links* because they link to pages on your own Web site. In other words, they link to pages that reside locally (on the same Web server as the page containing the link). A typical Web site has more local links than the other type of link, *remote links*, which you'll learn about in Task 3. Local links provide a great way for you to build cross-references into your Web site. For instance, the visitor starts on your home page where several different paths can be taken to other pages on the site. But just because he or she chooses a particular path doesn't mean there's no going back. In a well-planned, well-designed site, there's always a way to get from one place to another: Just follow the appropriate local links! This is one reason I stressed planning so heavily back in Part 1.

1 Find the Destination File Path

Make a note of the exact file path leading to the page to which you want to link. You should have a good idea of where to look for the page because you spent time in Part 1 organizing your thoughts and planning your Web site. For the rest of this discussion, assume that the page you're linking to (**`vacations.html`**) resides at **`c:/vacweb/pages/past`**, and the page you're linking from resides at **`c:/vacweb/pages/current`**.

2 Use an Absolute Pathname

Absolute pathnames give you the advantage of not having to know the location of the page you're linking to in relation to the page you're linking from. However, they're somewhat risky because they'll instantly break if you change the name of any folder along the path. To create an absolute link to **`vacations.html`**, start the pathname at the top level of your computer filing system. Type **`<a href="/c:/vacweb/pages/past/vacations.html">Dream Vacations</a>`**. In the anchor tag, absolute pathnames always start with a forward slash.

```
<p>This paragraph contains a link built
with an absolute pathname. Notice that
the pathname to <a href=
"/c:/vacweb/pages/past/vacations.html">
  Dream Vacations</a>
starts at the root level of the C drive and
follows an exact (or absolute) path to the
desired page.</p>
```

3 Use a Relative Pathname

A *relative pathname* starts in the directory that holds the page containing the link and finds the new page from there (rather than from the top of the computer filing system as does an absolute pathname). In our example, both pages reside in folders that in turn reside in the **`pages`** folder. Type **`<a href="../past/vacations.html">Dream Vacations</a>`** to create the same link you did in Step 2. Relative pathnames are preferred over absolute pathnames because they are harder to break. You can change the name of the **`pages`** and **`vacweb`** folders without breaking this link. They also make your pages easier to move to your Web server.

```
<p>This paragraph contains a link built with
a relative pathname.
Notice that the pathname
to <a href="../past/vacations.html">
  Dream Vacations</a>
starts by backing out of the current
folder (../) and then builds the path to
the desired page from there.</p>
```

4 Test Your Links

Test the page in your browser. The two links you created should look exactly the same if you built them correctly. And they both achieve the same result—they take you to **`vacation.html`**. Remember that you're better off using relative links than absolute links. You might be surprised at the number of times you'll change folder names as you develop your Web site. Name changes are the death knell for absolute links, whereas relative links can ride them out more effectively.

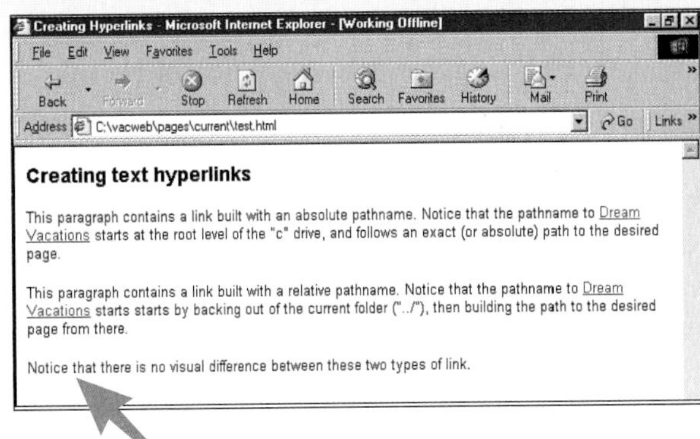

End

TASK 3

How to Link to a Page on a Different Web Site

The links you created in the last two tasks were local links, meaning that they linked from one page on your Web site to another page on the same site. Of course, what really makes the Web useful is the ability to link to different sites all over the world. You do so using *remote links*. This type of link is just as easy to construct as are local links, and they don't look or act any differently to the user. A great way to increase the usefulness of your Web site is to include a page full of related remote links.

Remote Issues to Ponder

Because you are linking to pages over which you have no control, sooner or later one of those pages will be removed from the remote Web site (or the whole Web site will go away or change addresses). Your page is left with what's called a dead, or broken, link. Visit your remote links regularly to make sure that they are still live. A helpful Web site is **http://siteowner.bcentral.com/sitecheck.cfm**.

Mail Call!

Another important type of link is the mailto link. This link allows you to specify an e-mail address to which your visitors can send messages about a subject relating to your page. To add this link, type **mailto:myemail@myisp.com**. When your visitors click this link, their e-mail software opens with the specified address in the address (or **To:**) field.

1 Find the Destination File Path

To find the file path that leads to the desired page, surf to the page to which you want to link. Most browsers have a **Location** or **Address** field that shows the pathname of the page you're currently viewing. Just copy the contents of that field into your computer's Clipboard. For instance, in Internet Explorer, highlight the contents of the **Address** field and choose **Edit, Copy**.

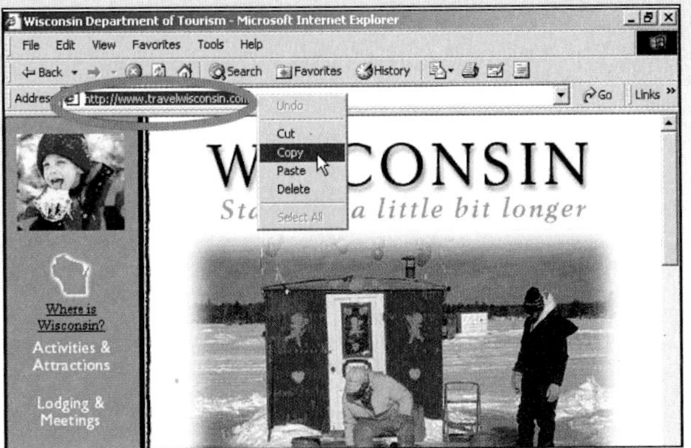

2 Create the Link

Use the anchor tag to create the link. For example, if you're creating a link to the Wisconsin Vacations page, type **<a href="http://www.travelwisconsin.com/"> Wisconsin Vacations</a>**. If you followed along with Step 1, the pathname that defines the **href** attribute is on your computer's Clipboard. Paste that text into place in the anchor tag. **http://www.** is at the start of every remote link. This is the part of the link that lets the browser know to look at the World Wide Web to find the link, and you must always include it.

```
<p>The link in this sentence is a remote
link meaning that it links to a page,
<a href= "http://www.travelwisconsin.com/">
Wisconsin Vacations</a>, that is on a
different Web site. Notice that the link
starts by using the "Hypertext Transfer
Protocol"--http:--and then specifies
the path to the desired page.</p>
```

3 Define a Target Behavior

It's a good idea to open remote pages in a new browser window while leaving the current window open. That way, the surfer can always get back to your page after following one of your links to a different site. Assign a value of **"_blank"** to the **target** attribute to accomplish this. Type **<a href="http://www.travelwisconsin.com/"target="_blank"> Wisconsin Vacations</a>**. You'll learn more about the **target** attribute when you learn about frames in Part 8, "Understanding Frames."

```
<p>Here's the growing link <a href=
  "http://www.travelwisconsin.com"
   target="_blank">
Wisconsin Vacations</a>, that is on a
different Web site. </p>
<p>The target attribute has been added
to the remote link so that the remote page
opens in a new browser window while our
page stays open in the original window.
This ensures that our visitors will always
find their way back to our page.</p>
```

4 Test the Link

Connect to the Internet and open your page in the test browser. Click the link. The remote page opens in a new browser window, while your page remains open in the old window. Follow the links you find on the remote site. Try to find a link to another site; from there, link to another site, and so on. When you're done, you can easily find your way back to your page because it remains open in the original browser window.

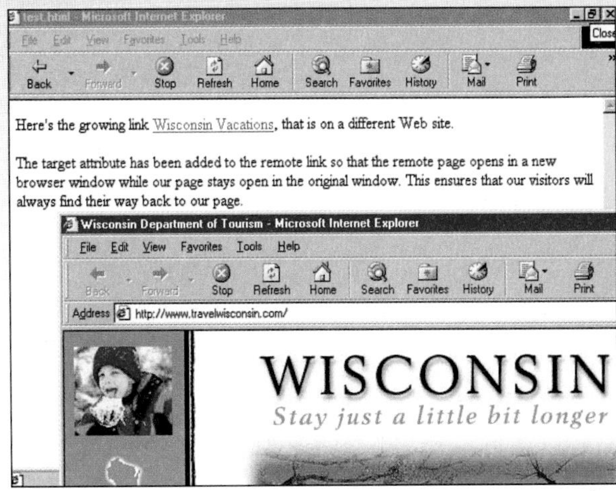

End

TASK 4

How to Link to a Specific Location on a Web Page

The anchor tag has another use in addition to creating links. You can also use it to create an anchor in your text. You can then create a link that not only navigates to the page containing the anchor, but also locates the anchor and scrolls the browser screen so that the text associated with the anchor is the first visible line. Anchors are especially useful in long text documents. You can build a list of topics at the top of the page and create anchors that link to the appropriate sections further down in the document. You build anchors in much the same way as you've learned to build links. This task shows you just how to do it.

An anchor marks the point on a page to which you want the visitor to go when he or she clicks the link.

Anchors Away!

Anchors have two critical components. You know most of what you need to know to make the first component—the link that leads to the anchor. But you also need the anchor itself. If you're linking to an anchor on your own page, you can easily drop the anchor yourself. But if you're trying to link to a specific point on a page written by someone else, you're pretty much out of luck because you have no way to drop an anchor on that page. Your only chance (and it's a small chance at that) is to convince the author of the other page to drop the anchors for you. Even if you can find the author of the page, most people are not going to be overly anxious to do so. Aside from the fact that they're busy maintaining and building their own pages, people don't generally want you to link to such a deep level in their sites.

1 Create the Anchor

To create an anchor, use the anchor tag pair you have been using to create links. But instead of defining a destination with the **href** attribute, use the **name** attribute to identify the anchor. To create an anchor, type **<a name="value">associated text</a>** where **"value"** is the name you'll use to refer to the anchor and **associated text** is the text to which you are attaching the anchor.

```
<p>In the text below, an anchor has been
added. However, since nothing appears
within the anchor tag pair, the anchor
is non-functional.</p>
<h4><a name="santafe"></a>
  Santa Fe, New Mexico</h4>
<p>Sante Fe has it all.</p>
```

2 Define the Anchor Name

The value you give to the **name** attribute can be anything you want. I keep my anchor names short so that they're easier to work with, yet long enough to be somewhat descriptive. I use the same standards for the associated text. To create an anchor named **"devilslake"** associated with the words "Devil's Lake" in a text document, type **<a name="devilslake"> Devil's Lake</a>**.

```
<h4><a name="devilslake">Devil's</a>
Lake, Wisconsin</h4>
<h4><a name="santafe">Santa</a>
  Fe, New Mexico</h4>
```

3 Create a Link to the Anchor

Now, create the link that points to the anchor. The link looks like any other link, except that you need to tack on a reference to the desired anchor. To do so, create the pathname to the page you want, and then tack **#anchorname** to the end of the tag (the pound sign **#** is required). A link to the description for Devil's Lake State Park would look like this: **<a href="../past/vacations.html#devilslake">Devil's Lake State Park</a>**. If the anchor is on the same page as the link that points to it, the **href** attribute value need only be the pound sign followed by the anchor name (as shown in the code example).

```
<ul>
   <li><a href="#santafe">
Santa Fe, New Mexico</a></li>
   <li><a href="#devilslake">
Devil's Lake, Wisconsin</a></li>
</ul>
<p>In the list above, we have added links
that point to the anchors in the text
below.</p>
<h4><a name="santafe">Santa</a> Fe, New
Mexico</h4>
```

4 Test the Anchor

Open the page in your test browser and test for two things: First, if the link points to a different page, make sure that it takes you to the correct page. Second, make sure that the browser found the anchor. You'll know that it did if the browser has scrolled the target page so that the text with which the anchor is associated is the first visible line (or as close to the top line as possible if the anchor is near the bottom of the page). Notice that, unlike a link, there is no visual indication that the text has an anchor.

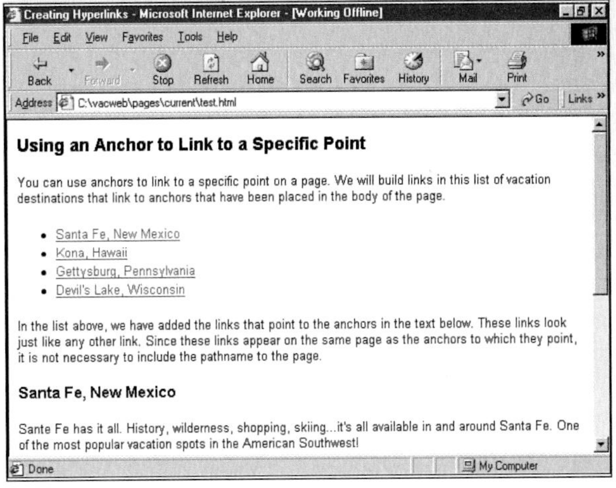

End

TASK 5

How to Specify Link Colors

Most of the text links you see on Web pages appear on the page as blue, underlined text. When you click the link, the text changes to a different color, such as purple, so that you can identify that particular link as one you've already followed. These link colors are the defaults, but you can change them (as you might need to do if you've changed your page's background color). This task shows you how to specify a new color for the unvisited link, the color of the link as the visitor hovers over it, and the color of the visited link.

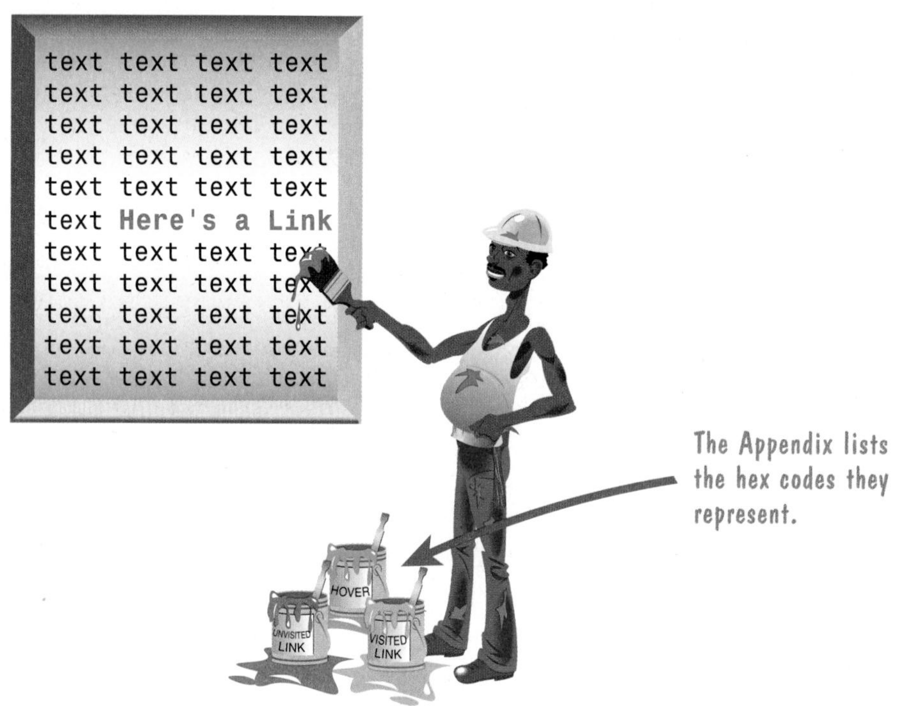

The Appendix lists the hex codes they represent.

Just Because You Can...

Think twice before changing your link colors. I understand that the default blue might not match your graphic color scheme, and that it would look better to have your links show up in an off-beige with a hint of mauve. But keep in mind that most people are expecting to see blue links. If you present them with something else, they might not recognize your links as links. Worse yet, unsophisticated surfers might think that they've encountered something other than an innocent link. They might even think that it's the dreaded "Gotcha!" button. (You know, the "you clicked here, and now we know your bank account password" link they suspect is lurking on your Web site somewhere.) Although it sounds a little silly, these thoughts occur to people when they see something on a Web page that looks out of the ordinary. My advice is to stick with the default link colors for all but rare special cases.

1 Specify the Unvisited Link Color

An *unvisited link* is one on which the visitor has not yet clicked. If you've done much Web surfing at all, you've probably seen (and clicked) lots of these. By default, unvisited links are usually blue and underlined. To change the color of unvisited links, use the **link** attribute of the **<body>** tag. For instance, type **<body link="#ff0000">...</body>** to make all the links on your page red.

```
<body link="#ff0000">
<h3>Specifying Link Colors</h3>
<p>On this page, the unvisited link color
has been set to red. Notice the addition of
the <b>link</b> attribute to the <b>body</b>
tag. The first link below shows the new
unvisited link color.</p>
<p><a href="vacations.html">
Vacation.com</a></p></font>
</body>
```

2 Specify the Hover Color

Some browsers change the color of the link when you hover over (that is, point at) it. You can specify the color to use for this hover state with the alink attribute of the <body> tag. For example, type **<body link="#ff0000" alink="#00ff00">...</body>** to set the hover color to green.

```
<p>In the second link that follows, the
<body link="#ff0000" alink="#00ff00">
<b>alink</b> attribute in the <b>body</b>
tag defines the hover color of links as
green.</p>
<p><a href="vacations.html">
Vacation.com</a></p>
<p><a href="trips.html">
FunTrips.com</a></p></font>
</body>
```

3 Specify the Visited Link Color

Most browsers keep track of the links you have visited (for a short time, anyway). They show that a link has been visited by changing its color. Different browsers use different colors to mark a link as visited. To make sure that visited links on your page are always a certain color, use the **vlink** attribute of the **<body>** tag. Type **<body link="#ff0000" alink="#00ff00" vlink="#999999">...</body>** to set the color of a visited link to gray.

```
<body link="#ff0000" alink="#00ff00"
vlink="#999999">
<p>Now the <b>vlink</b> attribute has been
added to the <b>body</b> tag to cause
visited links to show up as gray.</p>
<p><a href="vacations.html">
Vacation.com</a></p>
<p><a href="trips.html">FunTrips.com</a></p>
<p><a href="getaways.html">
Getaways.com</a></p></font>
</body>
```

4 Test Your Page

Open the page in your browser and look at an unvisited link to make sure that your settings work properly. Point to a link, and see whether the hover color works. Don't be surprised if it doesn't; some browsers don't support the hover color, and other browsers disable it by default (good reasons, in my opinion, not to bother with a hover color). Finally, click the link, return to the page, and check to see that your visited link color is correct.

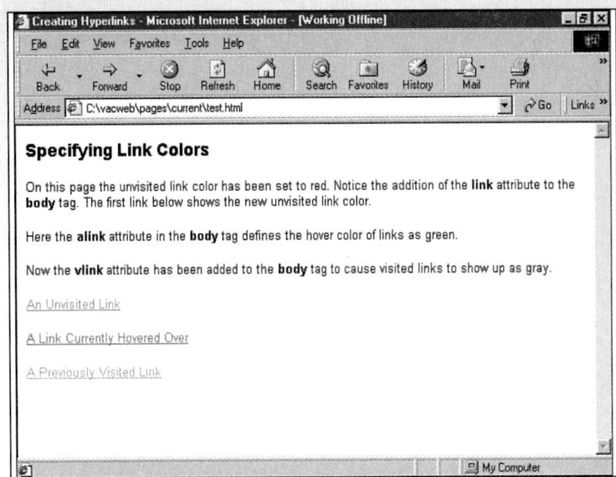

End

Task

PART 5

Implementing Web Graphics

So far, you've learned a lot of useful techniques for constructing your HTML pages. But I'm sure that you're anxious to get to the information in this part of the book.

Sometimes words just aren't enough. You want to show your readers what you're writing about. So, you want to include graphics and images on your pages. But there are many issues related to doing so.

Images are a great addition to almost any HTML page. But they can also cause no end of grief and frustration for visitors to your Web site. Few things lengthen the download time of a Web page more than a big, fat graphic file that you're trying to squeeze through a tiny little 56K modem connection. And few things about the Web irritate surfers more than long download times.

So, your job is not only to learn how to add graphic files to your Web pages, but also how to make the file size of those graphics as small as possible, while at the same time maintaining an acceptable level of image quality. It's not always easy to strike the balance between size and quality. In fact, for Web designers, it is one of the great never-ending struggles.

There are many tricks you can use to help suck file size out of your images without completely destroying quality. You'll need to know them. Still there are times when you just can't get around it...that image you want to include is just not going to get any smaller without the quality suffering. In that case, there are techniques you can use to make things less painful for your visitors as they sit through the download.

Preparing your images for the Web is somewhat beyond the scope of learning HTML—in fact, you can find complete books and countless Web resources on the subject. So, rather than concentrating on how to prepare your graphics, we'll spend most of the next several tasks learning how to handle the graphics you already have: You'll learn how to add them into your page. We'll talk about how to incorporate them with the text that surrounds them. You'll find out how to make your images act as links to other pages. All these techniques, and more, are explored by the tasks in this part.

By the time you've made it through this part of the book, you'll be prepared to create HTML pages that have the essentials: text, links, and graphics. Of course, I don't stop there, and I hope that you don't either. I hope you find it encouraging to know just how far you've come already. If you never learned another thing about HTML after this part, you could still put together complete, informative HTML pages.

TASK 1

How to Prepare Graphics for the Web

You can find many resources devoted to the topic of preparing graphics files for the Web. A couple of good places to start are **http://deezin.com/** and, for a comprehensive list of resources, **http://www.windweaver.com/searchpage7.htm**. Yahoo.com also has a number of resource links.

In this task, I'll give you some basic pointers about preparing graphics files. Remember, the trick to getting your graphics ready for the Web is to strike that delicate balance between file size and image quality. It's a constant trade-off: You can't have the highest quality and the smallest file size at the same time.

Are You Digitized?

To get an image on your Web page, you first have to get it onto your computer in digital form—a process known as *digitization*. If you're lucky enough to own a digital camera, you're almost all the way there already. A common method of digitizing graphics is to create the graphics yourself in a computer graphics program. A common use for this type of graphics is custom navigation buttons and icons for your page. For those times when you want to include a photograph on your page, but you don't have a digital camera, use a scanner to digitize the picture. There are three file formats you can use for images on the Web. One of these (PNG) is not yet widely supported, so we'll talk only about the two that are commonly found on Web pages: GIF and JPEG.

You can use your favorite paint program to prepare graphics for the Web. The most popular is Photoshop from Adobe, which is what I use in most of my examples. You might also find a shareware or freeware program you like. Try navigating to **www.webware.com** or **www.download.com** to see what is available.

1 Make the Image Small

The easiest way to lower the file size of your image is to make the image physically smaller. Resize the image in your image editor. You might also be able to *crop* your images. That means you cut out unnecessary portions of the image that often exist around the edges of pictures. Remember, smaller images mean smaller file sizes.

2 Compress the Image as a GIF

The GIF file format works best for images that have large areas of solid color, such as computer-generated art for logos and buttons. It uses *lossless* compression to make the file size smaller. This means that the quality of the image does not suffer as a result of the compression operation. You can also designate a color in a GIF image as transparent, which allows you to achieve many interesting effects.

3 Reduce the Number of Colors

You can further cut the file size of a GIF image by reducing the number of colors the image uses. Most image editors allow you to change the color depth (number of colors) in your image. Start with the lowest setting, and evaluate the results. If image quality suffers too much at this lower color setting, try the next lowest setting. Continue like this until you find the lowest color setting that gives you acceptable image quality.

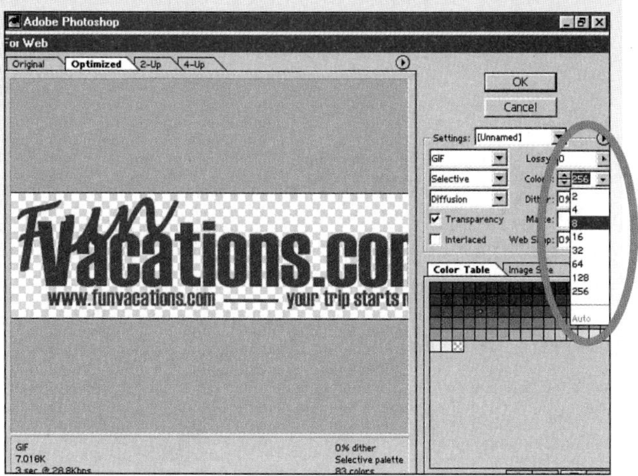

4 Compress the Image as a JPEG

For images with many colors (such as photographs), use JPEG (pronounced "jay-peg") compression. This is a *lossy* format, which means that you actually lose some of the information in the file. The more you compress, the more information you lose, and the more image quality suffers. Start with low quality, and check the results. If they're unacceptable, keep trying higher quality levels until you're satisfied.

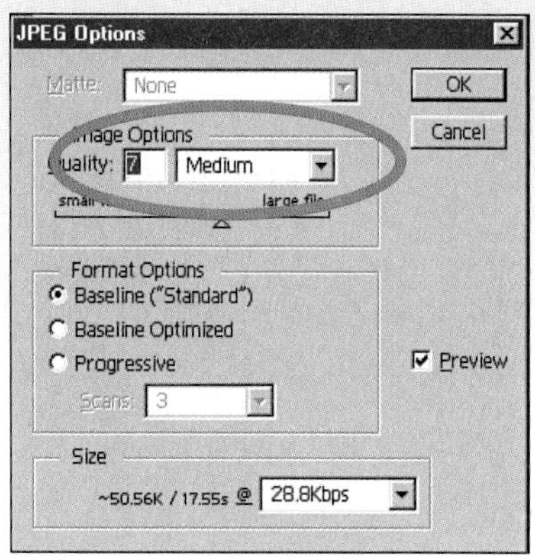

End

TASK 2 How to Insert a Graphic into a Web Page

Now that you have that graphic digitized and have struck the important balance between file size and image quality, it's time to get the graphic onto your page. You won't be too surprised to find out that there is no great mystery to accomplishing this task.

You've probably already figured out that all you have to know is the tag and any attributes that make it all happen. This task walks you through adding a graphic to your HTML page. The remaining tasks show you what you can do with the graphic after it's on the page.

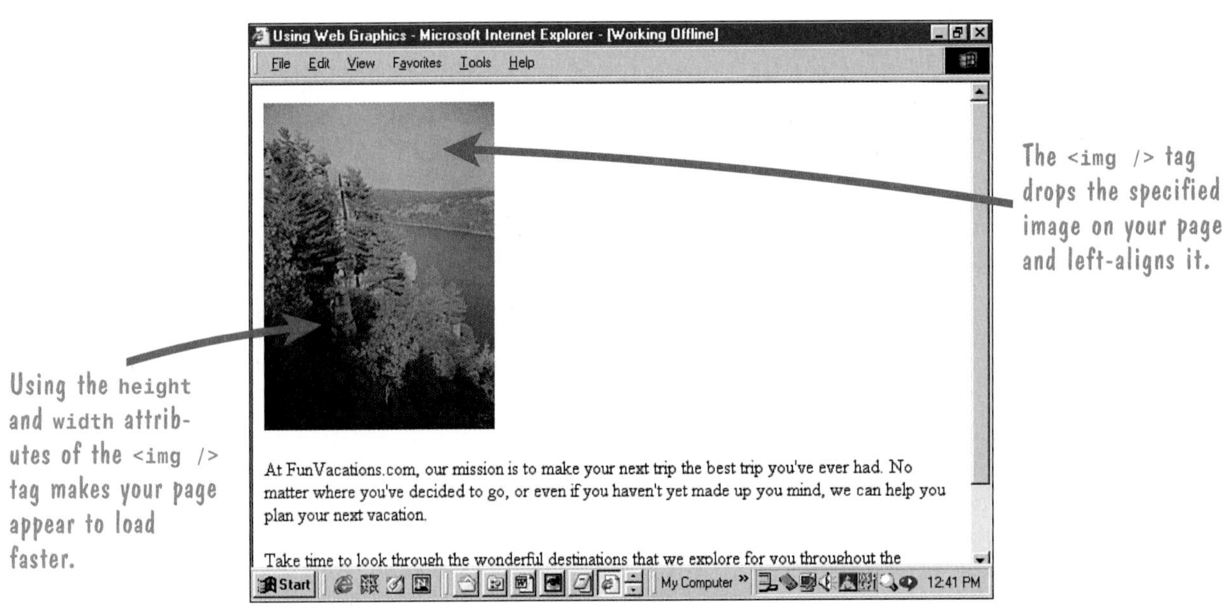

The <img /> tag drops the specified image on your page and left-aligns it.

Using the height and width attributes of the <img /> tag makes your page appear to load faster.

Images with Issues

There are a few things to keep in mind when adding images to your pages. First, don't waste your visitors' time with images that don't add anything to the message. No one likes downloading superfluous images.

Second, always include the **width** and **height** attributes in the **<img />** tag. They give the reader the illusion that your page is loading faster than it is. If you leave it to the browser to figure out an image's dimensions, the browser has to download the entire image before it can know the measurements. Therefore, anything that comes later in the download process has to wait for the entire image to download. When you supply the height and width information, most browsers continue downloading the text that comes after the image. Therefore, the visitor can read the text while the image downloads. Thus, the "appearance" of a faster download. The graphic doesn't really download faster, but your visitors have something to do while they're waiting for the image to appear.

1 Add the Image Tag

As with everything else you've already learned to do in HTML, a special tag exists for adding images to your page. To add the image tag, type **<img />**. Notice that the image tag is similar to the line break **
** tag in that it does not have a closing tag. You close the tag by adding the forward slash just before the less-than symbol so that the tag works for XHTML authoring as well.

```
<body>
<font face="arial" size="2">
<h3>Adding the Image Tag</h3>

<p>You can add the image
tag right into a line
of text. Here the <img /> tag is empty,
so it would show as a missing image in
your browser.</p>
</font>
</body>
```

2 Specify the Image

Add the **src** source attribute to the image tag and specify the file path that leads to your image. For instance, if the image called **bluffs.jpg** is in a folder called **images**, and the page you're coding resides in a folder called **current** in a folder called **pages**, type **<img src="../../images/bluffs.jpg" />** Notice that **.jpg** is the file extension for a JPEG file. If the image were a GIF file, its name would be **bluffs.gif**.

```
<p>
You can add the image tag right into
a line of text. Now the
<img src="../../images/bluffs.jpg" /> tag
contains the <b>src</b> attribute so the
image shows in the browser.</p>
```

3 Determine the Image Size

From your image editor, you can learn the exact physical size of the image you're including, as measured in pixels. Make sure that you note the size of every image you use on your HTML pages. You'll use that information in the next step.

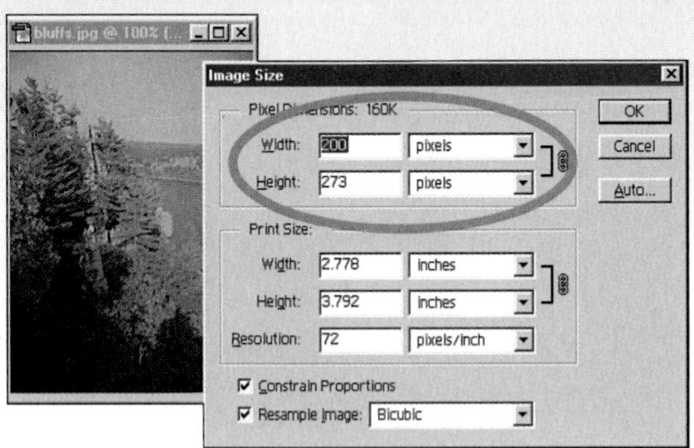

4 Specify the Image Size

Use the **width** and **height** attributes to specify the image size you noted in the last step. These attributes help your page appear to load faster. Resist the urge to resize your images using these attributes. A larger image sized down with these attributes still has the same file size, and actually loads more slowly than an image properly sized in the image editor to start with. A small image sized up with these attributes quickly loses image quality.

```
<p>The <b>width</b> and <b>height</b>
attributes have been added to the <img src=
"../bluffs.jpg" height="273" width="200" />
tag. It is important to include these
measurements with every image you show on
your page.</p>
```

End

TASK 3

How to Add a Text Message to Your Graphic

HTML offers a way to attach text to your graphics. One of the things you can do with this feature is to supply a ToolTip for anyone who hovers the mouse pointer over the graphic. The text you attach to the graphic pops up in a small window when the reader points to your graphic. It used to be that attaching text to your graphic was optional, but in HTML 4 and especially in XHTML, it is required. The hint below explains why you would want to do it even if it weren't required. This task shows how to attach a simple text message to your graphics.

The ToolTip-like text appears when you hover the mouse pointer over the image, if the user has disabled graphics, and in some browsers before the image is done downloading.

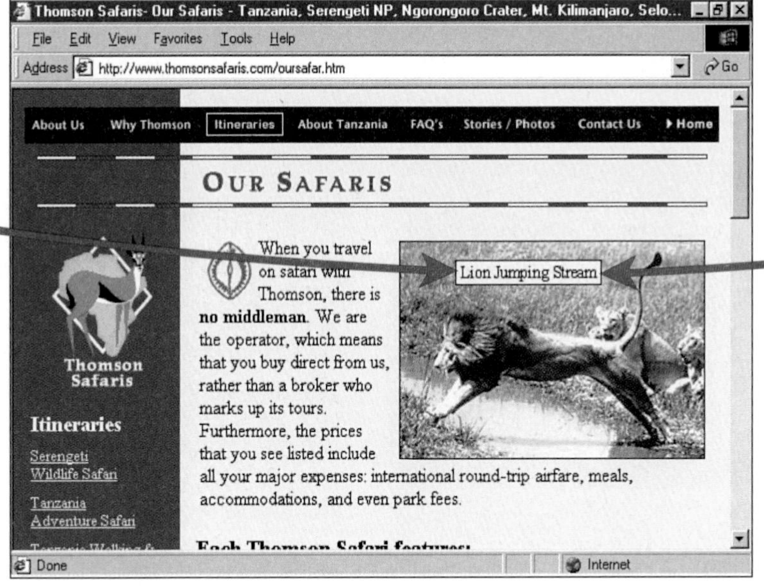

XHTML requires you to include alternative text when you put an image on the page.

Why Bother? There's a Picture

Sometimes, despite gallant effort, your images simply cannot be seen. There are a number of reasons this might be true. Maybe your reader is sight-impaired and is using a special browser. Maybe your reader is opening your page in a text-only browser that doesn't support images. Maybe your reader simply doesn't want to be bothered by the delays involved with downloading graphics and has disabled the graphics display in his or her browser. (Yes, browsers offer that option, and yes, I guarantee that some people really do surf the Web that way! I know...I'm often one of them.) Whatever the reason, the simple truth is that it pays to add a text message to every graphic you include on your page. If the picture can't be seen, the text you type appears in its place, so at least the visitor knows what picture *would* be there if it were visible. In the case of browsers for the sight impaired, a speech synthesizer speaks the text you put in the `alt` attribute.

1 Add the Alt Attribute

To include a text message with your image, add the alternate attribute to the image tag. Type **`<img src="../../images/bluffs.jpg" height="273" width="200" alt="value" />`** where **"value"** is the message you want to include.

```
<h3>Add the Alternative Text Attribute</h3>

<p>The alt attribute is important for
people who browse with images turned off,
or use text-only browsers or browsers
designed for the visually impaired.
<img src="../bluffs.jpg" height="273"
  width="200" alt=""/> Always include the
alt attribute. In this example, it has not
yet been given a value, so it would not
show up in your browser.</p>
```

2 Type the Alt Message

Now simply replace the word **"value"** in the last step with the message you want to include. Type **`<img src="../../images/bluffs.jpg" height="273" width="200" alt="The beautiful Baraboo bluffs surround Devil's Lake" />`**, for example. Don't go overboard with the length of the message. Something that quickly summarizes the image works best. You should include the **alt** attribute with every image to make sure that those who can't see your image can still get the information the image provides.

```
<p>In this example, we provide the alt
attribute for the image tag.
<img src="../bluffs.jpg"
height="273" width="200"
alt="The beautiful Baraboo bluffs surround
Devil's Lake" /> Always include the alt
attribute. The value of this attribute shows
up when the image does not.</p>
```

3 Test with Images On

You've added a lot to the image tag. Test it in your browser to see whether everything is working the way it should. Hover the mouse pointer over the image and wait to make sure that the text you typed into the **alt** attribute shows up in a ToolTip" window.

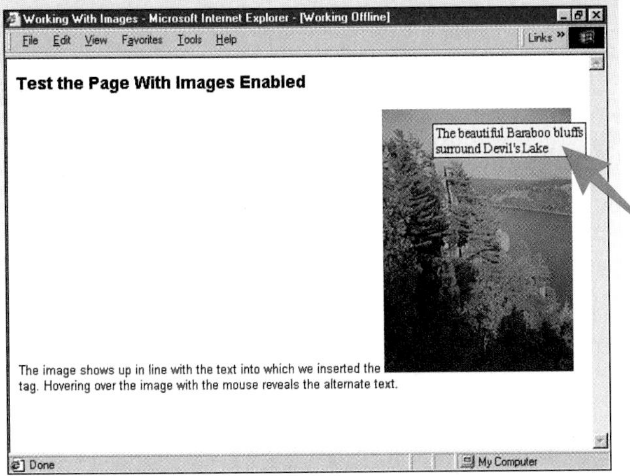

4 Test with Images Disabled

Now test your alternative text in the test browser with images turned off so that you can get an idea of what someone will see if images are disabled. To disable images in Internet Explorer, choose **Tools, Internet Options** and click the **Advanced** tab. Scroll to the **Multimedia** section and deselect the **Show Pictures** check box.

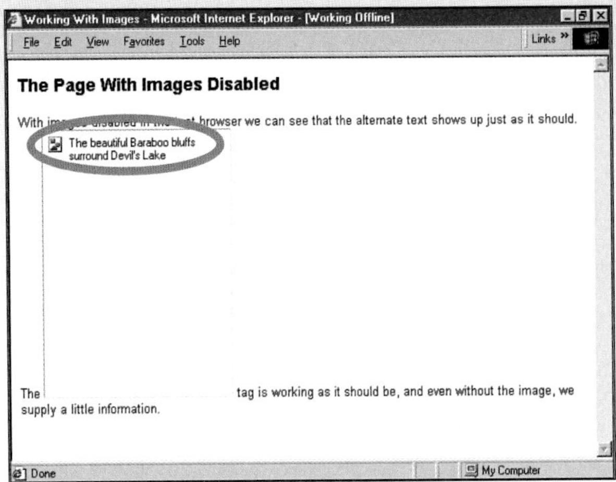

End

TASK 4 How to Add Borders and Space to Images

This task discusses two useful image-related features in HTML that help you as you work with the graphic design of your page. The first feature allows you to add a border around your image. In printing terms, this thin border is often called a *keyline* and can be a classy touch to your graphics when used properly.

The second feature discussed in this task allows you to add space around your images. This comes in very handy when you're trying to make sure that your text does not get too close to an image.

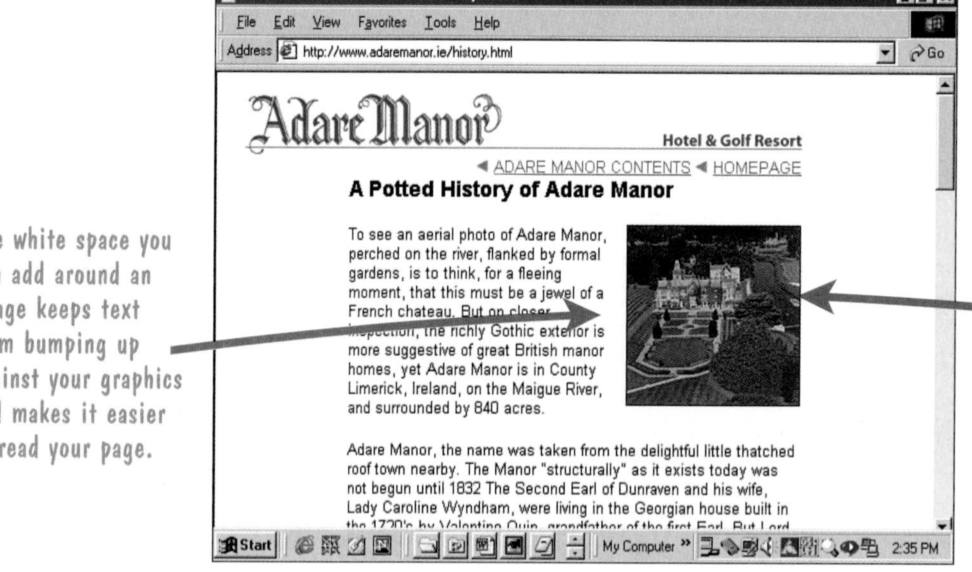

The One-Pixel GIF Trick

There's a trick Web designers use to "push things" around on their pages. In Task 1 of this part, "How to Prepare Graphics for the Web," I mentioned that you can specify a color to be transparent in a GIF image. Create an image that's one pixel wide and one pixel tall. Make it a one-color image and specify that color as transparent when you save the file as a GIF. Now add that invisible image to your page, and use the **hspace** and **vspace** attributes discussed in Steps 3 and 4 to create extra space around the image, thus adding space on your page. Why would you want to do this? Remember that in HTML you can't type a tab at the beginning of a paragraph to indent the first line. Instead, you could insert your one-pixel transparent GIF file and add a few pixels of **hspace** to indent the paragraph. That's just one simple example. The more sophisticated your layouts get, the more opportunities you'll find to use the One-Pixel GIF Trick.

1 Add a Border

Use the **border** attribute to tell the browser to show a border of the specified width around the graphic. Type **<img src="../../images/bluffs.jpg" height="273" width="200" alt="The beautiful Baraboo bluffs surround Devil's Lake" border="value" />** to show a border around your image. Here the word **"value"** should be replaced by the number of pixels wide you want the border to be.

```
<p>We've added the border attribute to the
<img src="../bluffs.jpg" height="273"
width="200" border="value" alt="The
beautiful Baraboo bluffs surround Devil's
Lake" /> tag. We have not yet added a value,
so the border would not show up in the
browser yet.</p>
```

2 Specify a Border Width

Now enter a whole number equal to or greater than 0. A value of 0 gives the same results as not including the **border** attribute. If you're looking for a guideline, I personally prefer no border, but if I add one, I rarely go wider than one pixel. Type **<img src="../../images/bluffs.jpg" height="273" width="200" alt="The beautiful Baraboo bluffs surround Devil's Lake" border="1" />** to specify a one-pixel border.

```
<p>We've added the border attribute to the
<img src="../bluffs.jpg" height="273"
width="200" border="1" alt="The beautiful
Baraboo bluffs surround Devil's Lake" /> tag.
We have added a value of 1 to specify a
one-pixel border.</p>
```

3 Specify a Horizontal Space

It's usually desirable to put some space between the image and the text that appears next to it. Use the **hspace** attribute to add a whole number of pixels' worth of space to both the left and right sides of the image, between the picture and adjacent text. For example, type **<img src="../../images/bluffs.jpg" height="273" width="200" alt="The beautiful Baraboo bluffs surround Devil's Lake" border="1" hspace="6" />** to add a six-pixel space.

```
<p>Here we've added horizontal space around
the image: <img src="../bluffs.jpg"
height="273" width="200" border="1"
alt="The beautiful Baraboo bluffs surround
Devil's Lake" hspace="6" /> in order to push
the text away from the image.</p>
```

4 Specify a Vertical Space

In the same way you added horizontal space before and after the image in Step 3, you can add vertical space above and below the image. To add three pixels of space above and below the image, use the **vspace** attribute: **<img src="../../images/bluffs.jpg" height="273" width="200" alt="The beautiful Baraboo bluffs surround Devil's Lake" border="1" hspace="6" vspace="3" />**.

```
<p>Here we've added vertical space around
the image: <img src="../bluffs.jpg"
height="273" width="200" border="1"
alt="The beautiful Baraboo bluffs surround
Devil's Lake" hspace="6" vspace="3" />.
This space pushes other objects (text) away
from the image.</p>
```

End

TASK 5 How to Align Graphics to Text

There are a number of ways to present a graphic in relation to the text around it. Being able to align the images and text in different ways gives you some flexibility in the layout of your pages. The three possibilities discussed in this task are generally used for associating headlines or captions with pictures.

The two additional options discussed in the next task are used more often for handling body text. All these techniques use the **`align`** attribute to dictate just where the graphic falls in relation to the text around it.

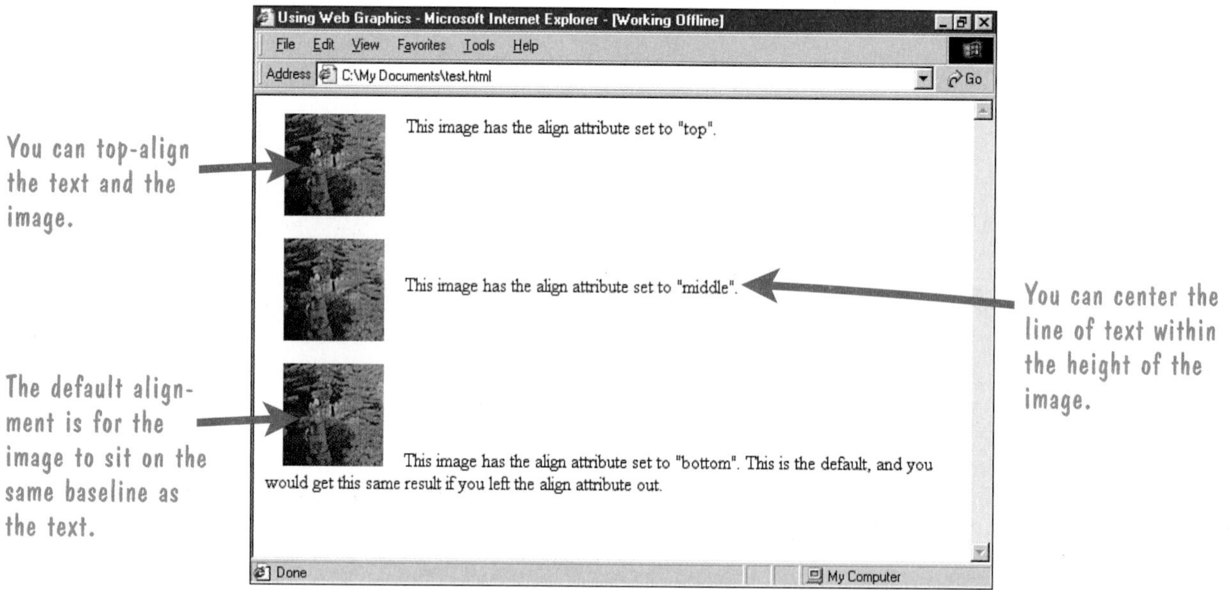

The Perfect Layout?

Many people who take up an interest in creating Web pages come from a graphic design background. Whether or not you fall into that category, you must get over the fact early that the "perfect" layout in HTML has a different definition than the "perfect" layout on the printed page. HTML is not a page-layout language. You can't expect to make the kind of fine adjustments to your layout in HTML as you can in a page-layout program such as QuarkXPress or Adobe PageMaker. However, there are some things you can do in HTML to fine-tune alignment. The techniques in this task represent a couple of the tools that are available to help control the layout of your HTML pages. Becoming familiar with these tools helps you develop solid page-layout skills because you come to know when to use what technique. If you ignore these issues and simply use the default settings, your pages will quickly be identified as amateurish.

1 Add the Align Attribute

When you add the bold **<b>** tag, it affects the text it modifies, but the tag does not force a line break. In other words, the command is inserted into the line; it is an inline command. The image tag is the same. By default, the bottom of the image sites on the baseline of the text. To change the alignment of the image, you add the **align="value"** attribute to the image tag.

```
<h3>Aligning the Text Around the Image</h3>
<p>We've add the align attribute here, but
have not yet assigned it a value.
<img src="../bluffs.jpg" height="273"
 width="200" border="1" alt="The beautiful
Baraboo bluffs surround Devil's Lake"
hspace="6" vspace="3" align="value" />
It will have no effect until the value is
specified.</p>
```

2 Align to the Top

To line the top of the image up with the top of the text line in which the image sits, specify **align="top"**. The browser will add as much text as can fit on the remainder of the line and then start a new line under the image. To align text to the top of the image, type **<img src="../../images/bluffs.jpg" height="273" width="200" alt="The beautiful Baraboo bluffs surround Devil's Lake" border="1" hspace="6" vspace="3" align="top" />**.

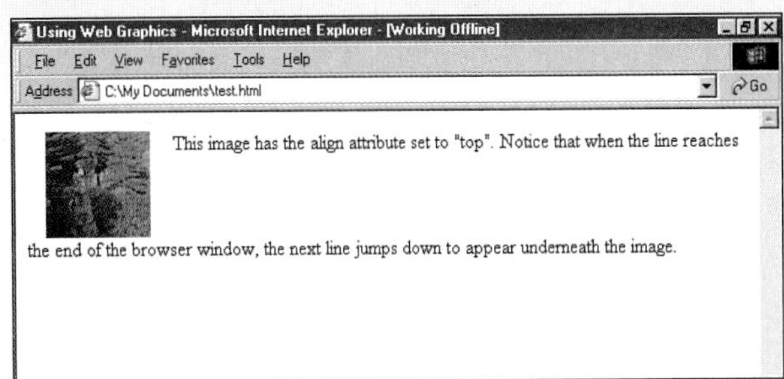

3 Align to the Center

You can also align the line of text in which the image sits to the center of the image. To do so, type **<img src="../../images/bluffs.jpg" height="273" width="200" alt="The beautiful Baraboo bluffs surround Devil's Lake" border="1" hspace="6" vspace="3" align="middle" />**.

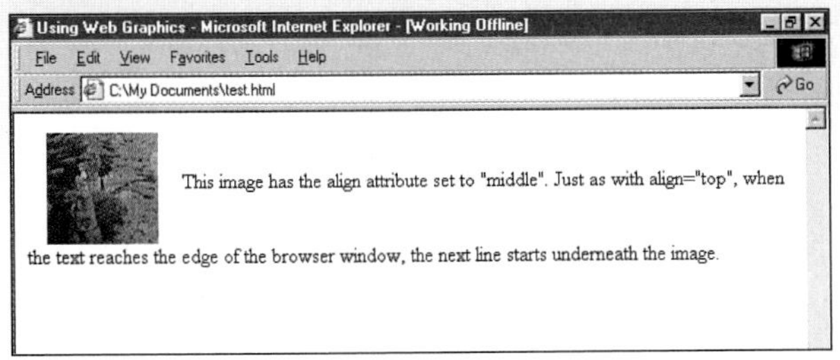

4 Align to the Bottom

To align text to the bottom of the image, type **<img src="../../images/bluffs.jpg" height="273" width="200" alt="The beautiful Baraboo bluffs surround Devil's Lake" border="1" hspace="6" vspace="3" align="bottom" />**. Because bottom alignment is the default state, you could leave the **align** attribute out and get the same result. If you're testing different settings, you can insert the **align** attribute and change to **"bottom"** alignment without deleting the attribute completely.

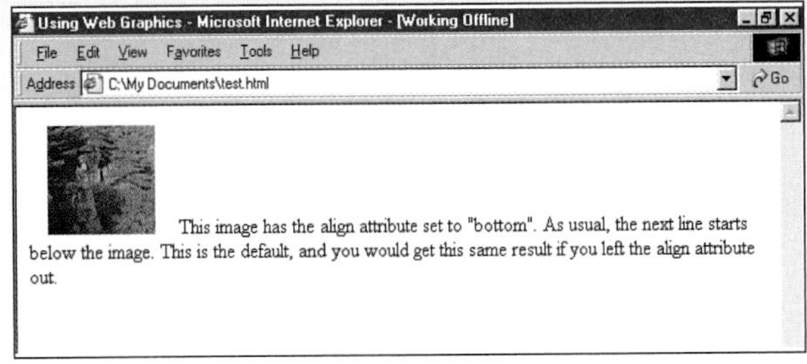

End

TASK 6

How to Wrap Text Around a Graphic

By default, an image is just like any other inline character in HTML. You can add it at any point in your code. As you saw in Task 5, "How to Align Graphics to Text," you can align the image in various ways to the text. However, all the methods presented in the preceding task can cause the space between the line on which the image sits and the line preceding or following the image to be unnaturally large—which usually doesn't look nice. You can tell the browser that you want the text to "wrap," or flow around the image, instead. This task shows you how.

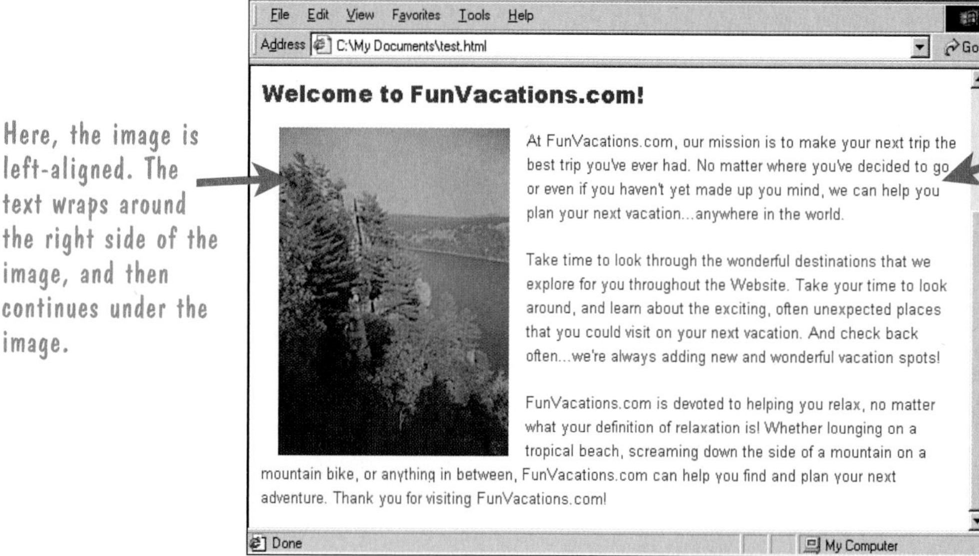

Here, the image is left-aligned. The text wraps around the right side of the image, and then continues under the image.

When you specify a text-wrap alignment option for an image, text flows around the side of the image.

Wrap It Up

Wrapping your text around images is another nice graphic design touch. It's one of those little things that, if done well, no one really notices. On the other hand, if you neglect to do it, your page is immediately pegged as amateurish. Here's a chance for you to bend that consistency rule a little bit. Try to build a little visual interest by staggering your pictures. For instance, if you have three pictures, see how you like the page when you wrap text around the right side of the first and third ones, and around the left side of the second one. Maybe you like your page better with the text wrapping around the right side of all three images. Try it a few different ways to see which you like best. The important point is that you wrap the text around the pictures in almost all cases. Your page looks more efficient and professional when you do.

1 Align the Image to the Left

When you align the image to the left, you wrap the text that follows it around the right side of the image. This is a good time to use a little extra **hspace** around the image, as you learned to do in Task 4, "How to Add Borders and Space to Images." To align the image to the left with text wrapping around its right side, type **<img src="../../images/bluffs.jpg" height="273" width="200" alt="The beautiful Baraboo bluffs surround Devil's Lake" border="1" hspace="6" vspace="3" align="left"/>**.

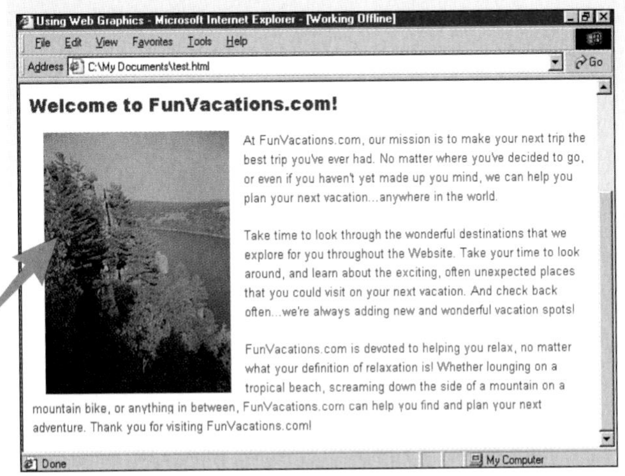

2 Align the Image to the Right

Similar to the effect achieved in the last step, you can align an image to the right, thus wrapping text around the left side. To do this, type **<img src="../../images/bluffs.jpg" height="273" width="200" alt="The beautiful Baraboo bluffs surround Devil's Lake" border="1" hspace="6" vspace="3" align="right"/>**. Notice that an image aligned to the right sits on the right side of the browser window, just as one aligned to the left sits on the left side.

3 Clear the Specified Alignment

When you reach a certain point in the text, you might want to stop the text from wrapping. To do this, add a **
** tag where you want the line to break, and add the **clear** attribute to the tag. Type **<br clear="all" />** to clear all the image-alignment options. You can also type **clear="right"** or **clear="left"** to override a specific type of alignment.

```
<p><img src="../bluffs.jpg" height="273"
width="200" border="1"  alt="The beautiful
Baraboo bluffs surround Devil's Lake"
hspace="6" vspace="3" align="left" />
Here the value is specified as left. The
text wraps around the image as usual until
the browser encounters the clear attribute
of the <br> tag: <br clear="all" />. The
rest of the text starts on a new line below
the image and fills in from there </p>
```

4 Test Your Page

I'm sure that you've been doing this as you've been learning all these techniques, but I'll remind you to save your page and view it in your test browser to make sure that you're getting the results you're after.

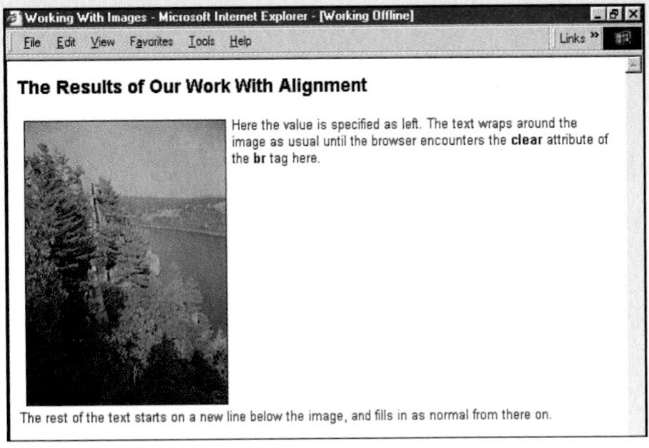

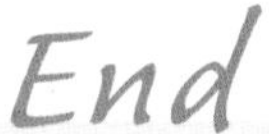

TASK 7

How to Provide a Quick-Loading Graphic

No one enjoys waiting for an image to load on the Web page they're looking at. And everyone enjoys it even less if waiting for that image means that they can't read anything until after the image finally appears. You can provide some relief from the download doldrums by creating a quicker-loading version of your image. HTML provides the tools to do it, and this task shows you how to use them.

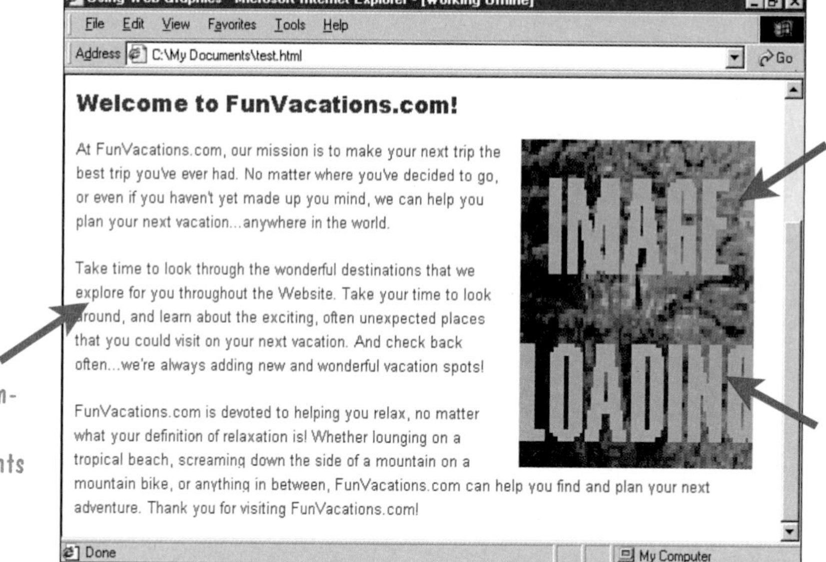

As the more-complex, larger image file is downloading, text and other page elements can be seen and read.

The quick-loading image file you provide can include text that explains what's happening.

You can use stylized, simple graphics as placeholders until larger image files are downloaded.

It's an Opportunity

At first, it seems that anything you do to make the image load more quickly will look bad. But that doesn't have to be the case. Here's a chance to do something unusual. One trick is to transform your color pictures into black-and-white images. Not grayscale (where the picture shows various shades of gray), but actually two colors: black and white. The effect can be interesting on the right type of image. If strict black-and-white doesn't work, try adding a few shades of gray or maybe a few other colors. Take a little time to experiment. Just keep in mind, the fewer colors your image uses, the smaller the image file is, and the quicker it downloads. Another idea is to create one image that acts as a placeholder for all the other images until they can finish loading. For example, you might create a simple image that includes the words, "Image now loading." People seem a little more willing to wait if you tell them what's going on up front.

1 Create the Stand-in Image

First create the image that you want to appear temporarily while the main image loads. As mentioned, you can create a vastly simplified version of the main image, or you can use a stylized version that loads quickly. You might also consider using a single placeholder image for all the images on the page. Whatever you decide, your first step is to create that "temporary" image. For this example, we'll call the image **bluffstemp.jpg**.

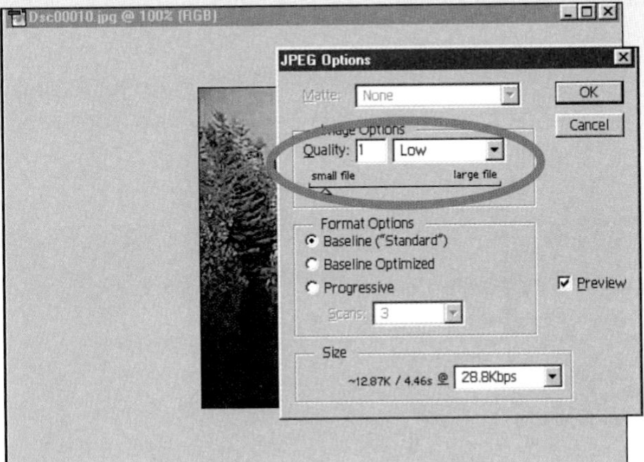

2 Specify the Main Image Path Name

To keep this example simple, I'll remove all the image attributes we've talked about so far except for the **src** attribute, which points to the main image. Type **<img src="../../images/bluffs.jpg">**. Even though I've left them out for this example, don't forget to add the **width**, **height**, and **alt** attributes (at the very least) to your **<img>** tag.

```
<h3>Using a Stand-in Image</h3>

<p><img src="../bluffs.jpg" height="273"
width="200" /> A much lower-quality version
of the main image serves as a stand in
until the main image with a larger file
size can completely download.</p>
```

3 Specify the Stand-in Image Path Name

Now add the **lowsrc** attribute to specify the temporary image. Assuming that you've stored the temporary image in the same place as the regular image, the path name will be very similar. Although the path names can be totally different (if that is necessary for some reason), it'll probably be easier to keep things straight if you put both images in the same location. Type **<img src="../../images/bluffs.jpg" lowsrc="../../images/bluffstemp.jpg" />**.

```
<p><img src="../bluffs.jpg" height="273"
width="200" lowsrc="../bluffstemp.jpg" />
A much lower-quality version of the main
image serves as a stand in until the main
image with a larger file size can completely
download.</p>
```

4 Test the Page

The reason you're including this temporary image is so that, when the page is downloading over a slow modem connection, the smaller file-size image can appear before the main image is completely downloaded. On your test machine, the main image will likely load virtually instantaneously. This is one case in which you might actually have to publish the page to the Internet and test it over your own modem before you can tell whether the image-swapping technique is working properly.

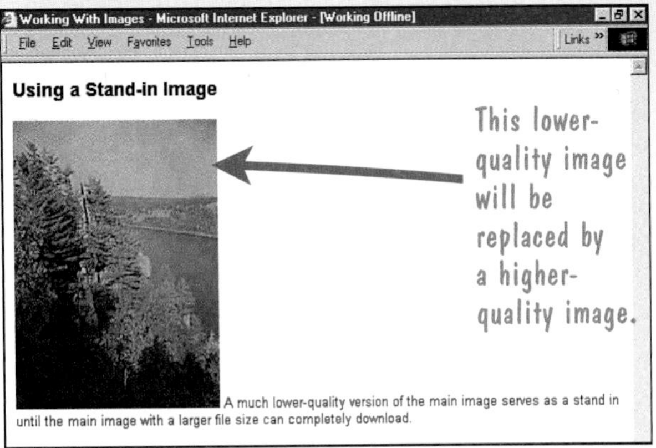

End

TASK 8 How to Link to External Graphics

You can greatly shorten the download time of graphics by making them physically smaller. But what if you need them large to show finer detail? In such cases, you can make the image that appears on the page a small version of the larger, detailed image (this smaller image is often called a *thumbnail*), and then create a link to the larger external graphic. (You'll learn how to make the thumbnail itself act as a link in Task 9, "How to Use a Graphic as a Hyperlink.") With this arrangement, visitors can view the thumbnail and decide for themselves whether they want to download the larger version. If so, they click on the link (typically the thumbnail itself) to view the larger image file.

The thumbnail is a smaller version of the larger graphic that the visitor can click to link to the larger image.

Use the same image in multiple places to get more bang from your download times.

The thumbnail can be either a low-quality, small version or a full-sized, cropped portion of the larger image.

Reduce and Reuse

In this part, we've explored a number of ways to reduce the file size of images to make them download faster. Here's another thing to consider: When a browser downloads an image, it stores it in a temporary folder on the visitor's computer. If the picture is used elsewhere on the page, the image loads much more quickly because it can be pulled from the temporary file instead of being downloaded again from the Web server. You can think of reused images as "download freebies" after the first time they appear. Try to come up with multiple uses for the same image. For instance, instead of making new navigation buttons for every page, use the same images. Not only will this help shorten your download times, it is also a good idea from the design-consistency standpoint we talked about earlier. You'll be surprised at how many opportunities you can devise to use the same image more than once. Just give it a little thought!

1 Create the Thumbnail Version

Use your image editor to create a thumbnail version of the large graphic. Consider simply resizing the entire graphic so that it is a smaller version of exactly what your reader will see when viewing the larger graphic. Alternatively, crop the larger image to show a small portion in the thumbnail, but at full size. Either way, make sure that the thumbnail provides enough information to allow the reader to judge the importance of the large image.

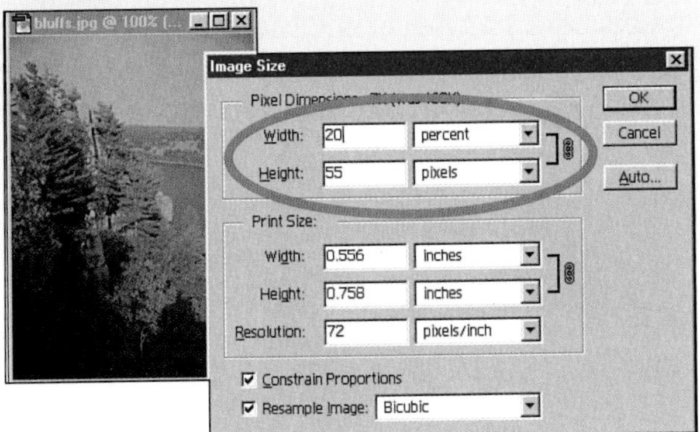

2 Add the Thumbnail to the Page

Add the thumbnail version of the larger image to your page just as you've learned to add any image: Type **`<img src="../../images/bluffsthumb.jpg">`**. Again, for simplicity, I've left out the **`height`**, **`width`**, and **`alt`** attributes, but make sure that you include these in your final code. You might also want to include a line or two of comments here to remind yourself of what you're doing and why.

```
<h3>Providing a Thumbnail Preview of a
Large Image</h3>
<!-- The following image gives the visitor a
preview of the large image -->
<p><img src="../bluffsthumb.jpg" height="55"
 width="40" alt="Bluffs Thumbnail" />
The thumbnail gives the reader an idea of
what the larger image looks like.</p>
```

3 Create a Link to the Large Image

Use the techniques you learned in Part 4, "And Now, the Star of Our Show...Adding Hyperlinks to Text," to create a link to the larger external image: Type **`<a href="../../images/bluffs.jpg">View the full image</a>`**. There is no need to include the **`width`**, **`height`**, or **`alt`** attributes here; in fact, they don't make sense in the **`<a>`** tag.

```
<p><img src="../bluffsthumb.jpg" height="55"
width="40" alt="Bluffs Thumbnail" />
The thumbnail gives the reader an idea of
what the larger image looks like. The reader
can click on the
<a href="../../images/bluffs.jpg">View the
full image</a> link to see the full version
of the image.</p>
```

4 Test the Link

Open the page in your test browser and click the link (the thumbnail) you've just created. The large image opens by itself in the browser window. When you're done viewing the large image, click your browser's **Back** button to return to the original page and the thumbnail image.

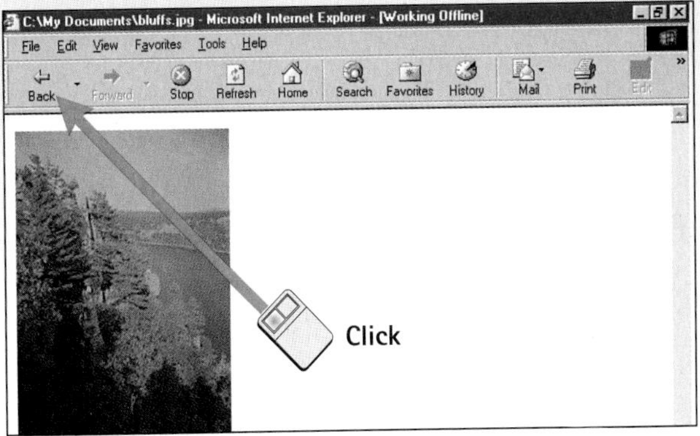

End

TASK 9 How to Use a Graphic as a Hyperlink

In Part 4, you learned how to create hyperlinks so that you can supply clickable text buttons that your readers can click. As you'll learn in this task, it is just as easy to use images as hyperlinks. Using images as links allows you to create interesting navigation buttons as well as links from inline graphics to larger external images (as discussed in Task 8, "How to Link to External Graphics"). It's very easy to make an image act as a hyperlink, and it is a very common technique on the Web today. By the way, it's also very easy to make poorly designed navigation buttons that are difficult use, so be careful.

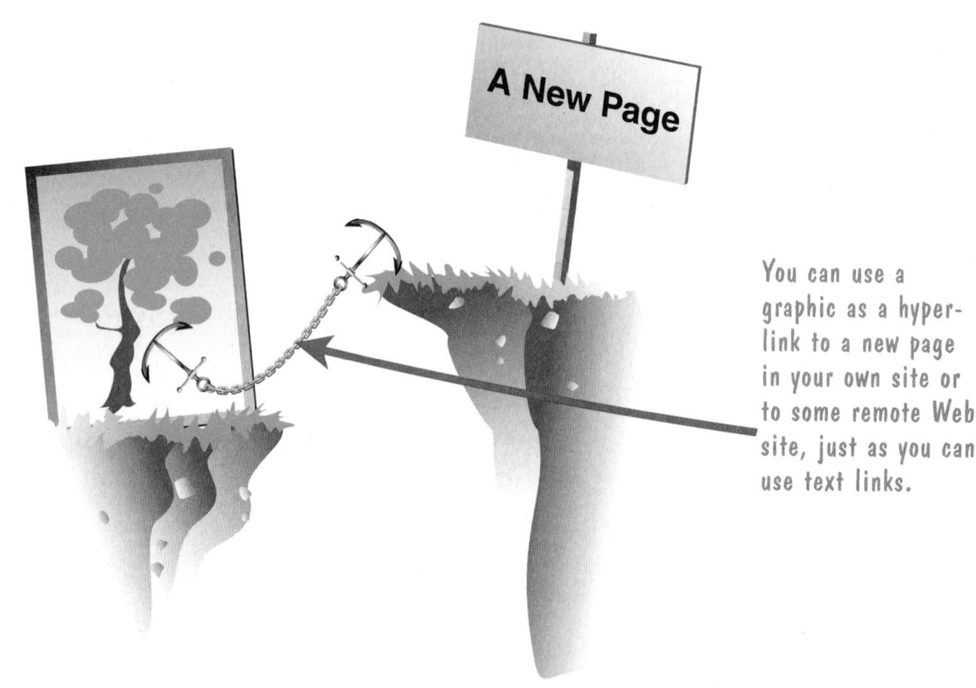

You can use a graphic as a hyperlink to a new page in your own site or to some remote Web site, just as you can use text links.

Good News, Bad News

So, this guy walks into the Webmaster's office with a one-eyed parrot on his shoulder. The parrot says, "I've got good news and bad news..." Okay, so the parrot doesn't really have anything to do with this, but there *is* good and bad news about using graphics as navigation buttons. The good news is that you can make nice-looking navigational tools using graphics. The bad news is that those fancy buttons come at a price. Remember, every image you include on your page has to be downloaded from your Web server across modem lines (most often at relatively slow connection speeds) to your readers' computers. That can cause nasty download delays. But as pointed out in the hint for Task 8, if you use the same buttons on each page, you only force the download the first time. You'll have to weigh the good news against the bad, and decide for yourself whether to use graphics as links.

1 Choose Text or Graphic Links

You must decide which is more appropriate for your page: a text link or a graphic link. Text links are generally more obvious because of their familiar blue, underlined appearance. However, well-designed graphic links can be obvious, too. In the case of the thumbnails we talked about in Task 8, people usually understand that the thumbnail is the link. Many authors cover all the bases...they make text links that point to the same locations as their graphic links.

2 Create the Image

Use your image editor to prepare the image you want to use as your link. You don't have to do anything different to the image at this stage. Everything you need to do to make the image act as a link is done in HTML. Prepare the image exactly the same as you'd prepare any other image; for example, if you want the image to be a thumbnail, make the image smaller and less detailed.

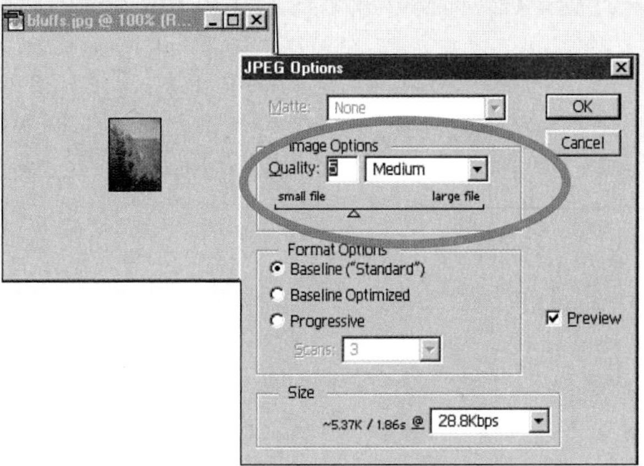

3 Specify the Image as the Link

Create a regular link, but instead of including text within the anchor tag pair, include a reference to the image. Type **<a href="devilslake.html"><img src="../../images/bluffsthumb.jpg" /></a>**. Notice that the image tag is placed between the opening and closing anchor tags. This is the same location into which you would type text when creating a text link. Again, I've left out a few important attributes of the image tag, but on a real page, you'll need them!

```
<p><a href="devilslake.html">
<img src="../../images/bluffsthumb.jpg" />
</a>The Thumbnail on this page acts as a
link to the larger graphic. It's rarely a
bad idea to include both a graphic and
<a href="devilslake.html">text link</a>.</p>
```

4 Remove the Image Border

This step is optional, but I never skip it. Most browsers put a blue border around image links. The blue matches the blue used for text links. Usually, this border looks ugly; if you've done a good job making your image links look obviously like links, you don't need the border to identify them. Add the **border** attribute as you learned in Task 4, and give it a value of **"0"**: Type **<img src="../../images/bluffs.jpg" border="0" />**.

```
<p><a href="devilslake.html">
<img src="../bluffsthumb.jpg" / border="0">
Bluff View</a><br />The Thumbnail on
this page acts as a
link to the larger graphic. The border
attribute is used to remove the link border
from the image. Notice that a text link has
also been added within the same anchor tag.
It's rarely a bad idea to
include both a graphic and a
  text link.</p>
```

End

TASK 10

How to Create Imagemaps

Sometimes you'll want to use an image as a navigational tool, but unlike the image we used in the previous task, you might want this single image to link to different places depending on where the user clicks. This useful tool is relatively easy to accomplish, although it can get a bit complicated. This task shows you how to use an image editor's measurement tools in conjunction with HTML to create *imagemaps*. Imagemaps, in turn, allow you to define individual regions of a single graphic that link to various locations.

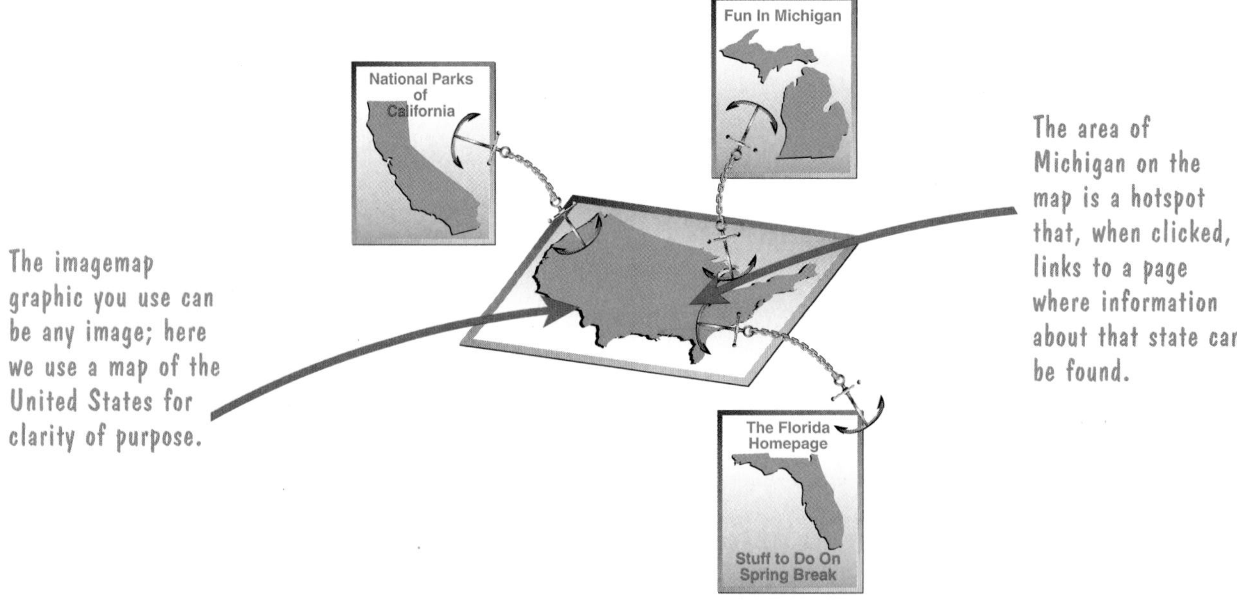

The imagemap graphic you use can be any image; here we use a map of the United States for clarity of purpose.

The area of Michigan on the map is a hotspot that, when clicked, links to a page where information about that state can be found.

Not Always Exact Science

Although creating imagemaps is in reality fairly simple, creating an imagemap with link areas, or *hotspots*, that follow complicated shapes can be somewhat challenging. Imagine making an imagemap over a graphic of the United States, and that each state is a separate link area. You can see that building the imagemap to conform exactly to the contours of the various states would be a big job. And no matter how you try, you could never really be exact. The more points you add to your map line, the more precisely you can follow the state borders, but you'll go cross-eyed trying to get exact. At some point, you'll just have to accept that "close enough is good enough" and live with the results.

1 Create Your Artwork

Use your image-editing software to prepare the graphic that you want to use. The graphic can be anything: a photo or computer-generated artwork. You can apply an imagemap to either a GIF or a JPEG image. The example used here is obviously simplistic, but it illustrates the technique well. Let's assume that this artwork is named **imagemapart.gif** so that we can use it in our code in later steps.

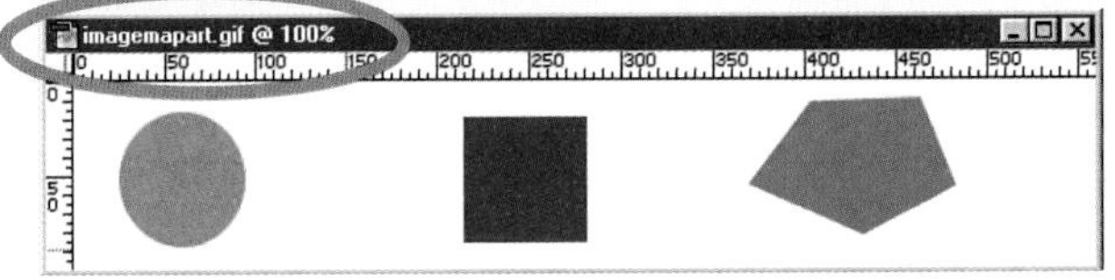

2 Determine the Coordinates of the Circle

To make a hotspot over the circle graphic in this example, first determine the coordinates of the circle. In your image-editing software, use the rulers and guides to find the coordinates of the center point of the circle (expressed in relation to the upper-left corner of the image), and the radius of the circle. In this example, the x coordinate of the circle is 59 pixels, the y coordinate is 40 pixels, and the circle's radius is 37 pixels. All these measurements are rounded to the nearest pixel.

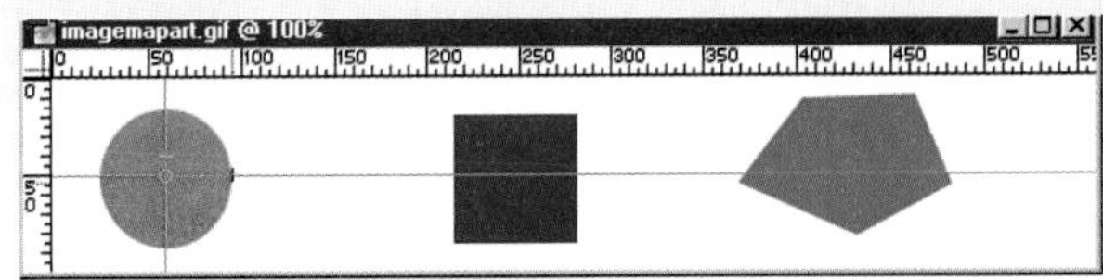

3 Create a Circular Hotspot

Now back to the HTML. Use the **<map>** tag and the **name** attribute to define the imagemap and give it a name. Use the **area** tag with the **shape**, **coords**, **href**, and **alt** attributes to define the hotspot. Type **<map name="navmap"><area href="circlepage.html" alt="To the circle" shape="circle" coords="59,40,37" /></map>** where 59 is the x measurement and 40 is the y measurement of the center point, and 37 is the circle's radius. Notice the **href** attribute that specifies the page to which you're linking.

```
<h3>Creating a Circular Hot Spot</h3>
<p>First we define the map and give it a
name. Then we specify a circular hotspot:
<map name="navmap">
<area href="circlepage.html"
alt="To the circle" shape="circle"
coords="59,40,37" /></map></p>
```

4 Determine the Coordinates of the Rectangle

In your image-editing software, use the rulers and guides to find the coordinates of the upper-left corner and the bottom-right corner of the rectangle (expressed in relation to the upper-left corner of the entire image). Given these two points, the browser can calculate the coordinates for the other two corners. In this example, these coordinates are 215, 17 and 281, 84. All these measurements are rounded to the nearest pixel.

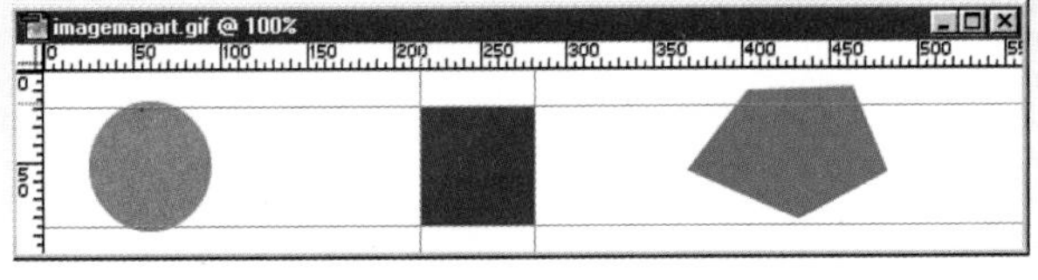

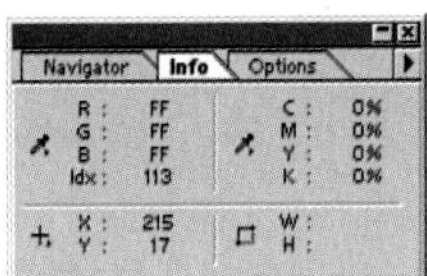

Continues

5 Create a Rectangular Hotspot

Still within the map tag pair, create a rectangular hotspot. To define the rectangular hotspot, type **<map name="navmap"><area href="rectangle.html" alt="To the rectangle" shape="rect" coords="215,17,281,84" /></map>**. Here, 215 is the x coordinate of the upper-left point, and 17 is the y coordinate of that point; 281 is the x coordinate of the lower-right corner, and 84 is the y coordinate.

```
<p>First we define the map and give it a
name. Then we specify a circular hotspot.
Next we add a rectangular hot spot:
<map name="navmap">
<area href="circlepage.html"
alt="To the circle" shape="circle"
coords="59,40,37" />
<area href="rectangle.html"
alt="To the rectangle" shape="rect"
coords="215,17,281,84" /></map></p>
```

6 Determine the Coordinates of the Polygon

The difficulty in finding the coordinates of a polygon grows in complexity with the number of sides in the polygon. In your image-editing software, use the rulers to find the coordinates of every corner point (expressed in relation to the upper-left corner of the entire image). Start with any point and work your way around the polygon clockwise until you have the coordinates for every corner.

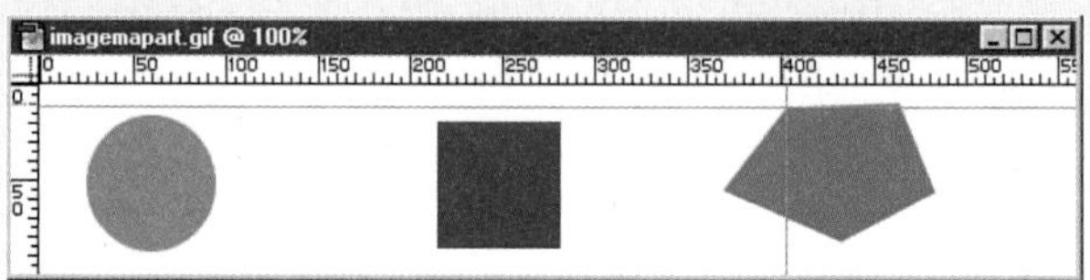

7 Create a Polygonal Hotspot

To define a polygonal hotspot, you must list the coordinates of each point on the polygon, one after another. For example, to specify the pentagon shape in my example, type **<map name="navmap"><area href="pentagon.html" alt="To the pentagon" shape="poly" coords="401,10,461,8,482,55,431,81,370,53" /></map>**.

```
<p>First we define the map and give it a
name. Then we specify a polygonal hot spot:
<map name="navmap"><area href="pentagon.html"
alt="To the pentagon" shape="poly"
coords="401,10,461,8,482,55,431,81,370,53" />
</map></p>
```

8 Add the Image to Your Page

Now use the techniques you learned earlier in this part to add the **imagemapart.gif** to your HTML document. Type **<img src="../../images/imagemapart.gif" />** Again, for the sake of making it easy to see the imagemap technique, I've left out a number of the important attributes discussed in earlier tasks—but don't you leave them out when you're coding actual pages! Notice that if you hover over or click on any of the shapes, nothing happens. In the next few steps, we'll apply the imagemap to this image.

```
<body>
<p>Here is our image. In contains the
three shapes for which we've created
an image map.</p>
<img src="../../images/imagemapart.gif" />
</body>
```

9 Call the Imagemap

Now add the **usemap** attribute to call the imagemap you created in the previous steps. Type **<img src="../../images/imagemapart.gif " usemap="#navmap" />**. Notice that the value for the **usemap** attribute is the name of the imagemap we defined in Step 3. Make sure that you precede the imagemap name with the crosshatch (**#**). In this code example, I've included the map definition we created in earlier steps so that you can see all the code together.

```
<map name="navmap">
<area href="circlepage.html"
alt="To the circle" shape="circle"
coords="59,40,37" /> <area href="rectangle.html"
alt="To the rectangle" shape="rect"
coords="215,17,281,84" /><area href="pentagon.html"
alt="To the pentagon"
shape="poly" coords=
"401,10,461,8,482,55,431,81,370,53" />
</map></p>
<p>Here is our image. In contains the
three shapes for which we've created
an imagemap.</p>
<img src="../../images/imagemapart.gif"
usemap="#navmap" />
```

10 Test the Page

Open the page in your test browser. When you hover over the shapes (and thus the invisible hotspots), the mouse pointer changes to a pointing finger indicating that the shape is a link. Notice that each shape also has its own alternative text because you added the **alt** attribute to the hotspot declaration. Click each shape to see whether the links work (you'll have to create the pages to which each spot links).

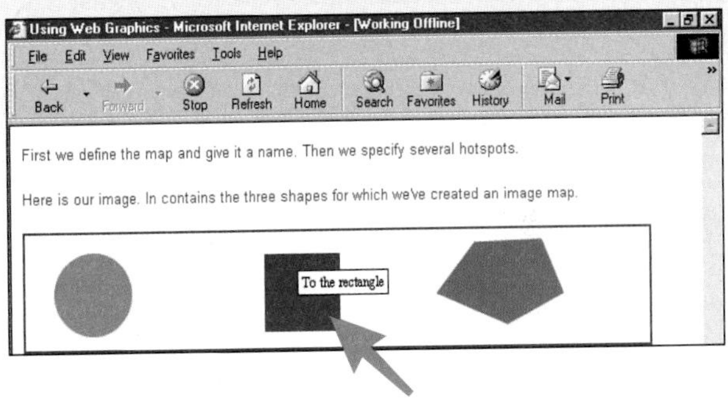

11 Remove the Border

After you've determined that your imagemap works properly, use the **border** attribute to remove the border from the image. Although you don't have to do this, it's usually a good idea because the border doesn't look all that nice. Type **<img src="../../images/imagemapart.gif" border="0" />** to remove the border. Now's also your chance to track down and correct any mistakes you might have made in your code.

```
<p>Here is our image. In contains the
three shapes for which we've created
an image map.</p>
<img src="../../images/imagemapart.gif"
usemap="#navmap" border="0" />
```

12 Retest the Page

Open the page in your test browser once again. The blue border is now gone, and the imagemap works just as it should. Each shape links to the page specified for it in the imagemap. Although I've used a simple example here, you can use imagemaps on any image. For instance, you might have graphics of compact discs, each of which uses a circular hotspot to link to more information about the disc. The possibilities are endless.

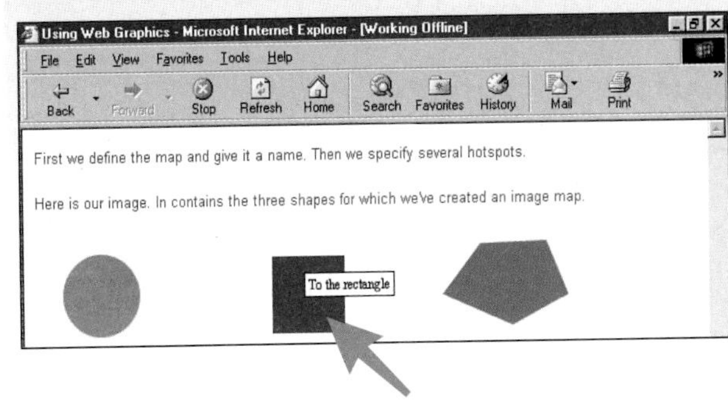

End

TASK 11 How to Create Animated GIF Files

One of the things that many people feel make the **.gif** format so useful is its ability to show movement. Creating movement in your GIF files—that is, creating an animated GIF file—is pretty much the same as creating any regular GIF file. The main difference is that, instead of creating one image, you create a series of slightly different images. When played in quick succession, these images give the illusion of movement. You'll need some type of GIF animation tool for putting all the individual frames of your animation together. This task gives you the basic outline of how to create GIF animations and also shows how to add the animation to your Web page.

ANIMATED GIF
The number of frames used by the animated GIF should be 10 or fewer.
The graphic you animate should be simple.
Animated GIF files do not require special players.

Against My Better Judgment

It sort of pains me to tell you about animated GIF files. I think these animations are among the most overused, badly implemented, and misguided techniques on the Web. Because they move, they draw the reader's eye from anything that's not moving—such as words. And more often than not, they're not important enough to sacrifice the readability of your page. For instance, is it really necessary for the door on that silly little mailbox to flap open and shut incessantly? If it's so important that your readers learn what's new, why draw their eyes away from the words that describe that new item to a flashing "New!" icon? This task tells you about these little pests because I can't deny that some people have found clever and creative uses for animated GIF files. But I urge you to ask yourself what they really bring to your page. The reviewers might pan me for this, but I say most of the time these animations equal bad graphic design. Avoid using them.

1 Create the Individual Images

Use your image editor to create a series of progressively different images. All the techniques you've learned for making small graphics are just as important when creating animated GIF files. Animated GIFs are best for simple animations with a limited number of frames.

2 Assemble the Animation Sequence

Many tools can help you assemble the individual frames into a single animation file. Use one to assemble the individual graphics you made in Step 1 into an animation sequence. A good place to start looking is **`www.download.com`**. Here I use Sonic Foundry Viscosity. A shareware option is the GIF Construction Set, which you can find at **`www.mindworkshop.com/alchemy/gifcon.html`**.

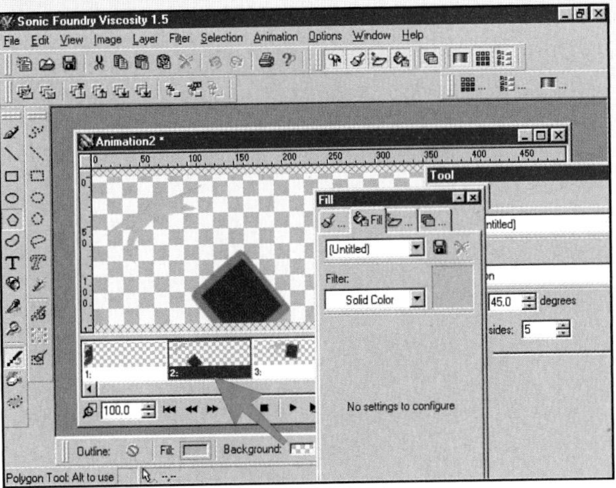

3 Adjust the Animation Timing

Adjust the delay between each frame to fine-tune the animation. A bit of trial and error is in order here. Just keep working with the timing until you are happy that people can process the information in one frame before it transitions to the next frame. If there are words involved with the animation, the frame rate might have to be slower than if the animation is strictly visual.

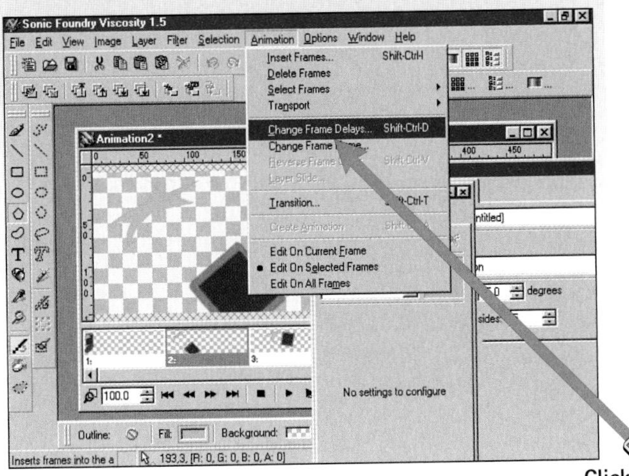

4 Add the Animation to Your Page

After you save the animated GIF file, it looks exactly the same as any other GIF image until you view it in a browser. By looking at the icon, you can't tell the difference between the two. And you add it to your page in exactly the same way as you add a normal GIF file: Type **`<img src="myanimation.gif" alt="My first GIF animation" height="50" width="500" />`**.

```
<h3>Adding a GIF Animation</h3><p>The GIF
animation is added to the page
just as a regular GIF is added:
<img src="myanimation.gif"
alt="My first GIF animation" height="50"
width="500" /></p>
```

End

Task

Part 6

Working with Tables

Welcome to possibly the most confusing subject of the book: tables. Tables can be confusing not so much because the techniques used to make them are more difficult to master than any of the others that you've learned so far. Rather, tables can be confusing because of the complexity they can spawn.

Used for their original purpose—presenting information in logical, tabular form—tables are quite straightforward. They are also easy to understand in this basic form. But tables are called on to play a much more prominent role in the way HTML is used in the everyday, real world of the Web. Tables are not just rows and columns of numbers any more! As a matter of fact, tables haven't been used much for that purpose since Web page designers realized that they could be used effectively to control page layout. It's safe to say that page-layout applications are undoubtedly the main use of tables these days.

The tasks in this part of the book take a detailed look at how to construct tables. They show you the parts and pieces you can combine to make tables that work effectively and that turn out the way you want them to.

I should mention one more thing before we get started. Many people think that it is foolish to code tables by hand. They suggest that you would be well served to use a WYSIWYG editor to create the tables for you. I disagree, but then I can be a bit of a purist sometimes. I think you are always better off to maintain complete control of your code. As soon as you start relying on software to write the code for you, you run the risk of writing sloppy code in which you might never catch the errors and which can lengthen the download times for your pages. True, tables can be complicated. But if you learn the techniques and follow the steps I outline in the following tasks, you'll become adept at building them.

Perhaps a compromise is in order. Consider building your tables in your favorite WYSIWYG editor and then spend time combing through the code to make sure that it is well constructed. You can do that only if you thoroughly understand how the code works. Still, if you're going to spend time verifying the code anyway, why not just roll up your sleeves, dig in, and build the table properly in the first place? I promise, after you become familiar with building tables, you will be able to put even the toughest tables together surprisingly quickly. And guess what; I think it's actually kind of fun to make tables by hand. But then, I'm pretty easily amused....

TASK 1 How to Use Tables

If you're like most people, when you hear all this talk about tables, you immediately think of rows and columns of numbers all neatly tucked underneath descriptive headings. And you can find plenty of tables on the Web today that accomplish that very task. But table usage has grown well beyond that initial concept. Tables have become the workhorses of HTML. This task gives you an idea of some of the things for which tables are commonly used.

This part of the table used for page layout contains navigation tools used throughout the Web site, and contains a different background color than the rest of the page.

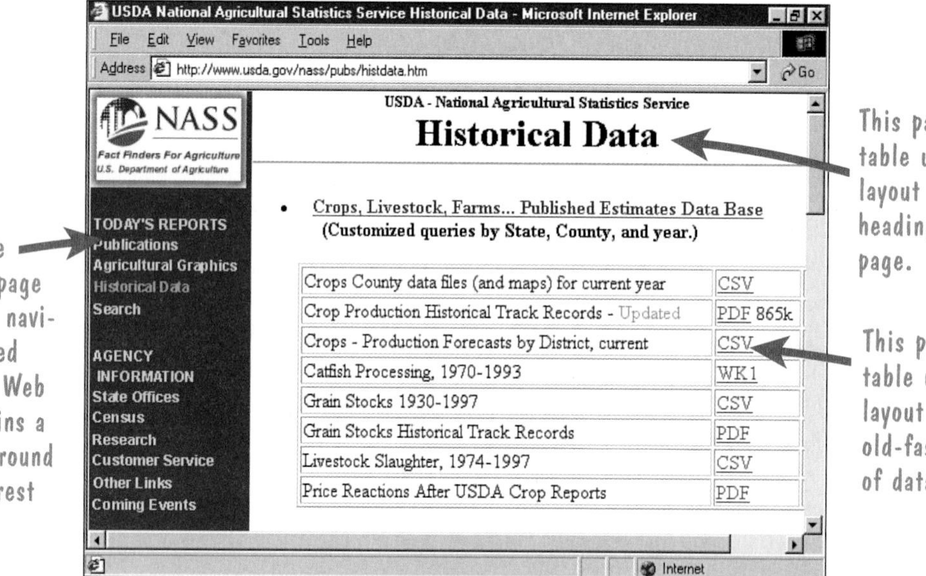

This part of the table used for page layout contains the heading for this page.

This part of the table used for page layout contains an old-fashioned table of data.

Not the Definitive List

The ideas in this task represent just a few possible uses for tables. After you get to know them, tables will become invaluable to you, and you will more than likely devise your own uses for them. Those uses might be modifications of the ones discussed here, or you might think of something totally different. The point is, don't limit your thinking. Tables can solve all kinds of problems for you. And most of these problems (let alone the table-related solutions) were never even dreamed of by the wise people who decided that HTML needed a way to make tables. Go through the steps in this task with your mind open to whatever idea pops into it. Ask yourself, "Could I use a table to accomplish this or that?" You'll probably have to get to some level of proficiency before you can really answer those questions, but it helps to start thinking about it early.

1 Organize Your Data

Probably the most obvious use for tables is as a way of presenting data. Tables are a simple way to list related pieces of information in a manner that makes them easy to read and understand. You can quickly show relationships, make comparisons, point out differences, highlight similarities, and more by putting together a logical table. Tables are perfect for temperature charts, schedules, performance histories, reference lists, priority lists, evaluation results, and so much more.

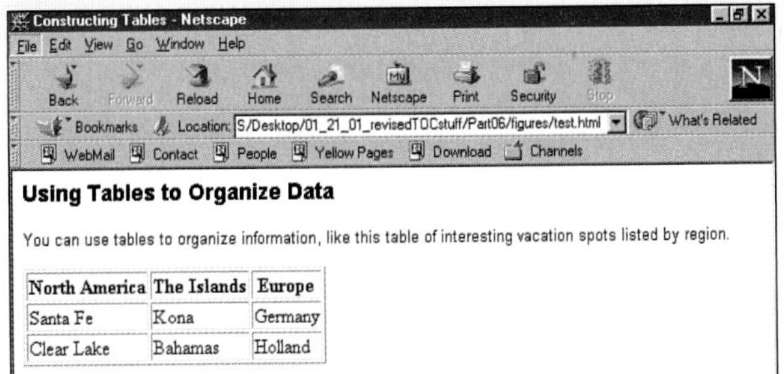

2 Control the Layout of Your Page

By far the most common use for tables in HTML today is as a powerful way of controlling the layout of pages. Tables have literally revolutionized the way HTML pages are structured. Tables allow the HTML author to achieve layouts that were impossible before their advent. Eventually, tables will be displaced as the king of page layout by other Web technologies such as Cascading Style Sheets (which you'll learn about in Part 10, "XHTML and Cascading Style Sheets"), but for now, they rule.

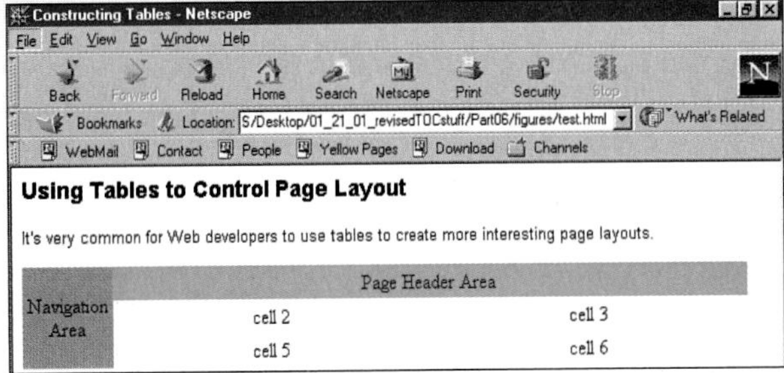

3 Make Multicolored Backgrounds

In Part 1, "Getting Started," you learned to change the color of your page's background. In Tasks 5, 6, and 7 of this part, you'll learn break the page into multiple color areas using tables. For example, you can create a gray bar down the left side of the page and leave the rest of the page white. There is no limit to how you can break up the page with various colors—except good taste and solid graphic design sense!

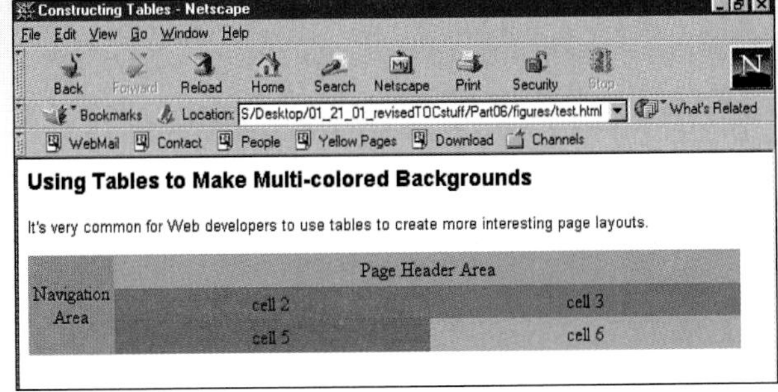

4 Reassemble Sliced Images

Task 14, "How to Slice Images with Tables," shows how to use tables to reassemble images that you have sliced apart in your image editing software. You can use this technique to help improve the download time of your pages in certain instances. As you can see in the figure, if you do it correctly, the results are seamless.

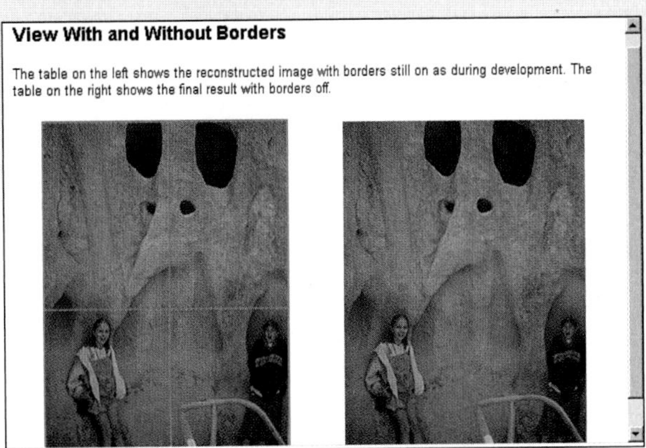

End

TASK 2 How to Plan a Table

You can avoid headaches by carefully planning out what you want your table to accomplish. If you're using it to present a chart of average temperatures by date and location, a very basic table might be all you need, and planning won't be so important. But if you're using tables nested within tables to control the layout of your page, planning pays. Don't let yourself be fooled into thinking that it's best just to dive in and see what happens. Tables can get too complicated for that. Make a plan and follow it. Making tables will be much less of a chore if you do.

Use paper and pencil to plan your table. If you rely on your memory to hold all the details, something will be left out!

Paperless, Indeed

Are you old enough to remember how computers were going to put an end to our use of paper? Not that I am, but I've heard stories.... Well, it has not come to pass, and again I find myself advocating the use of that old pencil and paper. Building tables in HTML can become abstract. Place a **<tr>** here and a **<td>** there, and make sure not to forget the **colspan** and **</table>**. You might think you've got it all squared away in your head only to find that it doesn't work on your page. Do yourself another big favor: Draw your table by hand first. This helps tremendously to keep things straight and is an effective way to visualize what you must do to build the table you have in mind. You can do your planning on paper and still save a tree if you use the back of that junk-mail letter you just received!

1 Assess the Need for the Table

Admittedly, most of the time this step takes place right inside your head. You'll become adept at recognizing instances in which a table will solve your particular problem or fill a specific need. It's easy to recognize that you need a table when you want to illustrate a relationship between pieces of data or control the layout of your page. Still, this is the first step in building a table, so it deserves mention.

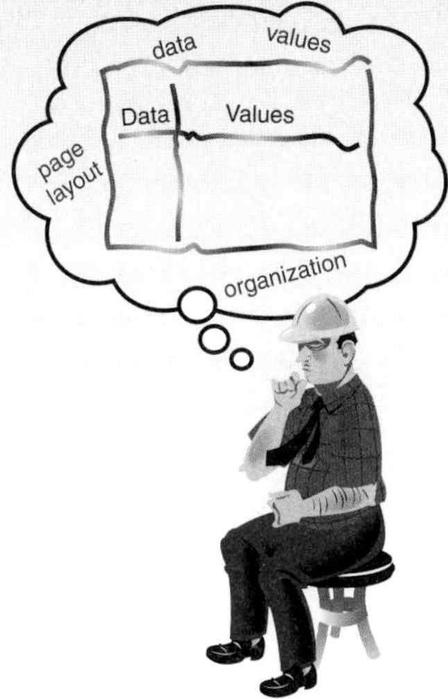

2 Organize the Table Contents

Organize—isn't that what the *table* does? Right. But you have to organize your thinking before you can build the table that organizes the information. What are you trying to show? What relationships do you need to emphasize? Which pieces of information are important, and which can be left out? You'll need to answer these types of questions before you can construct a logical table.

3 Sketch Your Table on Paper

This is really the most important step from a construction point of view. As your tables become more and more complex (and they most likely will!), you'll need a reliable blueprint you can use while putting them together in code. After the table has been sketched out on paper, you can—and will—refer to it over and again to figure out what tag has to go where to achieve the results you're after.

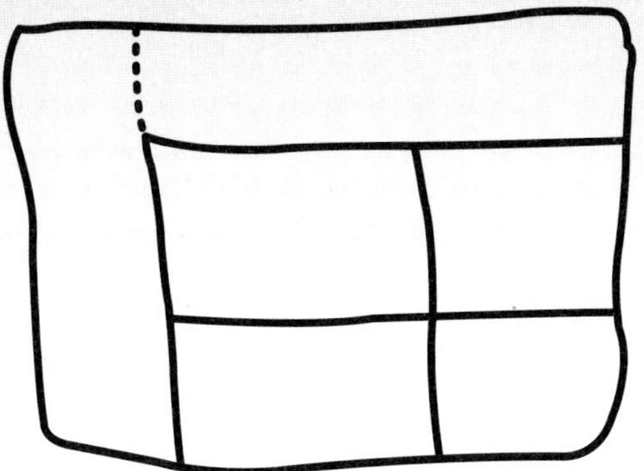

4 Make Notes on Your Sketch

After you've sketched out the look of your table, mark your sketch with notes that help you translate the idea from paper to HTML. Identify areas that require particular tags or attributes. For instance, if a row is to serve as a header, mark it as such. If a column needs to span several rows, note the attribute that will make it so. A quick sketch and a few meaningful notes can cut development time.

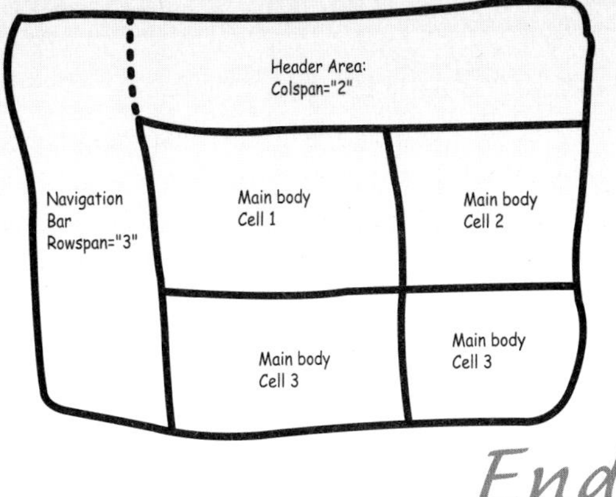

End

TASK 3 How to Structure a Table

Just as every HTML page has a basic structure, every table has a definite and particular structure. Every table you ever create will have the same underlying framework. It's what you tack onto that framework that makes one table different from the next. In this task, we'll explore the skeletal structure of all tables and define a few of the important concepts that will appear over and over again as you work with tables. Everything you do after this builds on the frame, so solid skills in this area are crucial. This task gives you those skills.

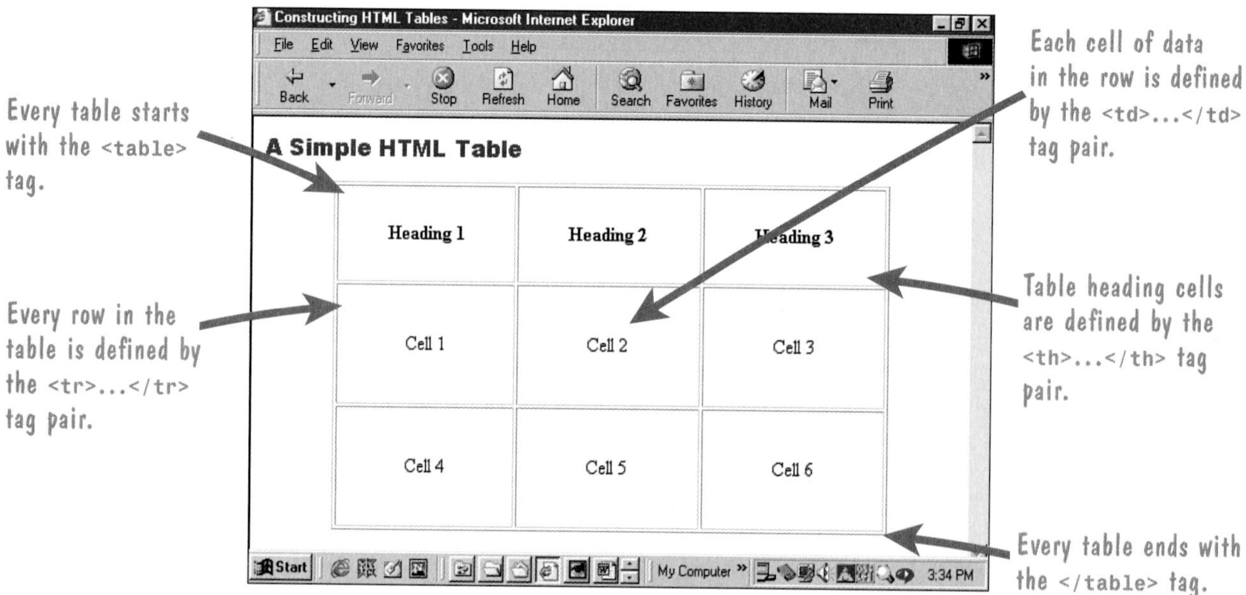

Constructing HTML Tables - Microsoft Internet Explorer
A Simple HTML Table
Heading 1
Heading 2
Heading 3
Cell 1
Cell 2
Cell 3
Cell 4
Cell 5
Cell 6
Every table starts with the <table> tag.
Every row in the table is defined by the <tr>...</tr> tag pair.
Each cell of data in the row is defined by the <td>...</td> tag pair.
Table heading cells are defined by the <th>...</th> tag pair.
Every table ends with the </table> tag.

Organize Your Code

I mentioned earlier in the book that it sometimes helps to indent various levels of code. The indentations make your HTML code easier to read. Nowhere in HTML is this as true as when you're working with tables. As you'll see in this task, the structure of tables is quite hierarchical. The **<table>** tag sits on one level, the **<tr>** tag sits on the next, and the **<td>** tag sits on yet another level. If you have another table nested within the first, things can get very complicated. Anything you can do to organize your table work is well worth the effort. Arranging your code so that it reveals the hierarchy of the table at a glance is one of the biggest aids you can give yourself. And don't forget about your old friend the HTML comment either. A comment at the beginning of a table can be a lifesaver when you must later try and figure out not only what the table does, but also how it does it.

1 Identify the Table

Use the table tag pair to alert the browser of the existence of the table. Every table you ever create must begin with the opening table tag and end with the closing table tag. Type **<table>**...**</table>** to begin the table structure. It is also a good idea (although not an official requirement) to get into the habit of including a comment that summarizes the purpose of the table and that includes other important information worth remembering.

```
<p>Use the table tag pair to identify your
table. If you view this
page in your browser,
you won't see the table. We have not yet
added any content, we have simply identified
it as a table.</p>
<table>
</table>
```

2 Identify the Table Rows

We'll go into much more detail about this step and the next two steps in later tasks, but I'll introduce the concepts here. Create new table rows using the table row tag pair. Type **<tr>**...**</tr>** within the table tag pair.

```
<p>Here a table row tag has been added to
identify a new row. Again, you won't see
this in the browser. We still haven't
added content, just identified the row.</p>
<table>
  <tr>
  </tr>
</table>
```

3 Identify Table Cells

Each row contains one or more table cells. As you'll see, the cells in one row line up with the cells in the next row to create the columns of the table. To create most cells, you use the table data tag, so called because cells hold the actual data in your tables. For each cell in a row, type one set of **<td>**...**</td>** tags within the table row tag pair.

```
<p>Within the table row tags, we've added a
table data tag pair. No content yet, but
we're getting closer! You still won't see
this table in your browser.</p>
<table>
  <tr>
    <td></td>
  </tr>
</table>
```

4 Identify Table Headings

Table headings are a special type of cell. Browsers display the data you include in these cells differently than the way they display regular cells to set that information apart. Other than that, table heading cells behave exactly like other cells; you add them to the table in essentially the same way. The difference is that you use the table heading tag pair. Type **<th>**...**</th>** within the table row tag pair.

```
<p>Here we add a table heading tag pair.
This is where we can type the contents of
a heading cell. Notice that a new row was
added to hold the table heading cell.</p>
<table>
  <tr>
    <th></th>
  </tr>
  <tr>
    <td></td>
  </tr>
</table>
```

End

TASK 4

How to Use Borders and Colors in Tables

HTML allows you to place borders around your tables. You can also change the background color of tables and the individual table cells. As the hint for this task explains, I use borders on every table...and I don't use borders on any table. In this task, I'll show you how to add borders and colors to your tables. I'll also show you how I use these tools not for the final product (as they were originally intended), but as an indispensable aid during the construction of tables.

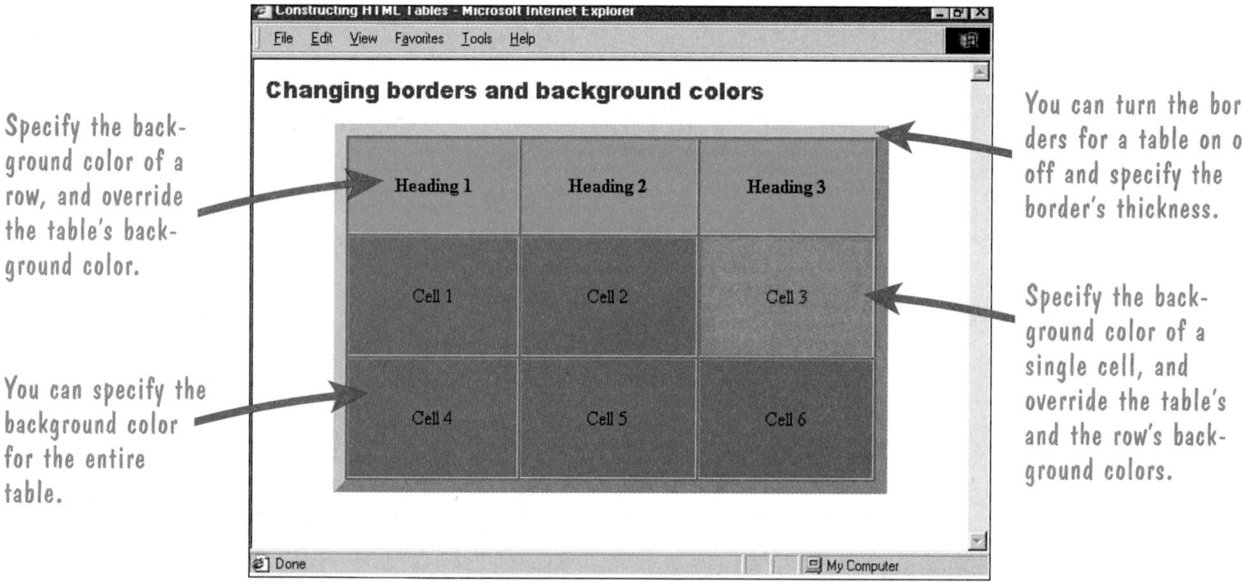

Constructing HTML Tables - Microsoft Internet Explorer
File Edit View Favorites Tools Help
Changing borders and background colors
Heading 1
Heading 2
Heading 3
Cell 1
Cell 2
Cell 3
Cell 4
Cell 5
Cell 6
Done
My Computer
Specify the background color of a row, and override the table's background color.
You can specify the background color for the entire table.
You can turn the borders for a table on or off and specify the border's thickness.
Specify the background color of a single cell, and override the table's and the row's background colors.

All That Work for Nothin'?

I add borders to nearly every table I create, yet no one ever sees them but me. *Huh?* Well, I try to avoid borders because I don't like the way they look. I don't think I've ever come across a situation in which I felt that the table border added anything to the finished page. From a graphic design standpoint, borders and lines separating rows and columns are ugly, and they don't add anything to the functionality of the table. In fact, some might argue that these lines hurt readability. So, what do I mean when I say that I add them to every table? Borders play an invaluable role in table construction because they help you keep track of the results of your code. This is especially true when you nest tables within tables. If you have four tables on a page, give each table a different-colored border so that you can keep them straight during development. When you're done, remove all the borders. No one will be the wiser, except for you!

1 Add a Border to the Table

Use the **border** attribute of the **<table>** tag to add a border to the table. Type **<table border="1">** to make a one-pixel-thick border. To specify the color of the border (useful for development purposes), use the **bordercolor** attribute. For a red border, type **<table border="1" bordercolor="#ff0000">** (refer to the Appendix, "Colors and Hex Equivalents," for a list of the hex colors). Switch the border on and off during development by changing its thickness back and forth between **"0"** and **"1"**. A value of **"0"** is the same as omitting the border attribute.

```
<table border="1" bordercolor="#ff0000">
   <tr>
      <th></th>
   </tr>
   <tr>
      <td></td>
   </tr>
</table>
```

2 Change the Table's Background Color

You can change the background of the entire table to any color you choose with the **bgcolor** attribute. Type **<table bgcolor="#00ffff">** for a light-blue table background. (Although I don't know why you would ever subject your readers to a table of that color!) Some people prefer to use table color instead of borders to keep their various tables straight during development.

```
<table border="1"
bordercolor="#ff0000" bgcolor="#00ffff">
   <tr>
      <th></th>
   </tr>
   <tr>
      <td></td>
   </tr>
</table>
```

3 Change the Background Color of a Row

You can also add the **bgcolor** attribute to the **<tr>** tag to change the color of just that row. To make a green row in your table, type **<tr bgcolor="#00ff00">**. The row color overrides any background color of the table that you specified in the table tag.

```
<table border="1"
bordercolor="#ff0000" bgcolor="#00ffff">
   <tr bgcolor="#00ff00">
      <th>yep</th>
   </tr>
   <tr>
      <td>nope</td>
   </tr>
</table>
```

4 Change the Background Color of a Cell

You might have already guessed that you can even change the color of an individual cell with the **bgcolor** attribute. Just add the attribute to the **<td>** or **<th>** tag. To create a red cell, type **<td bgcolor="#ff0000">**.

```
<table border="1" bordercolor="#ff0000"
bgcolor="#00ffff">
   <tr bgcolor="#00ff00">
      <th></th>
   </tr>
   <tr>
      <td bgcolor="#ff0000"></td>
   </tr>
</table>
```

End

TASK 5 How to Define Table Rows

Now that you have defined the table with the table tag pair and have turned on the border with the **border** attribute, it's time to specify the number of rows you want in the table. Because you've already sketched out your table on a sheet of paper, you can easily count the number of rows you've drawn.

The sketch you made in Task 2 of this part is already coming in handy! This task shows you how to define the rows you'll need in your new table. After you define the rows, you can move on to adding content to the table.

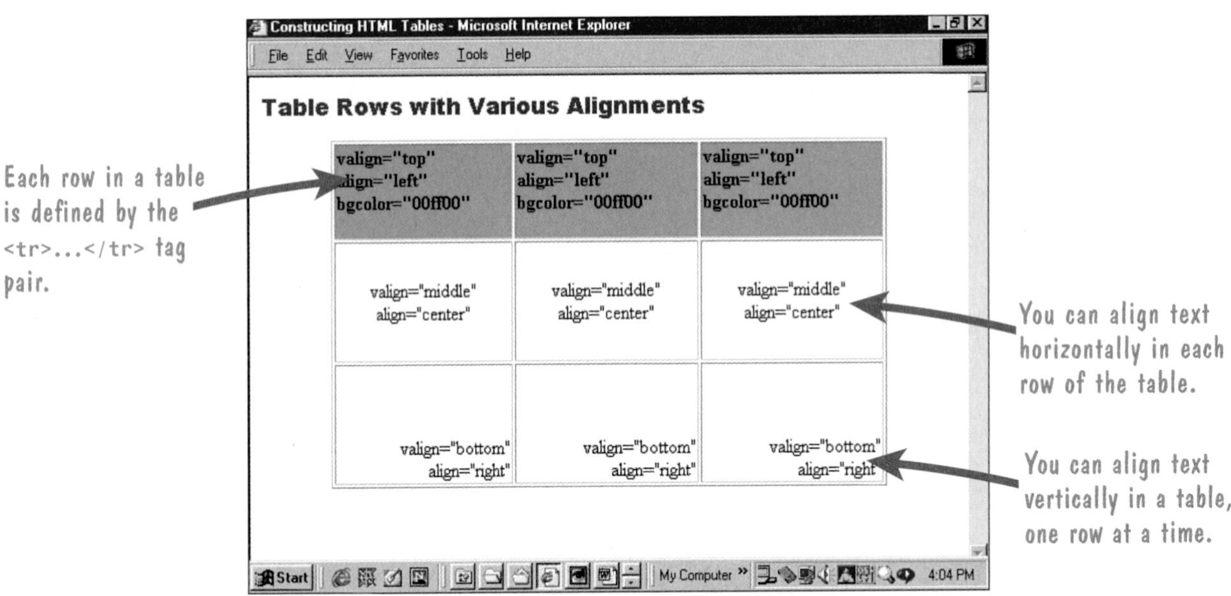

Row Upon Row Upon Row...

You might wonder about the limit on the number of rows you can have in your tables. As far as HTML is concerned, there is no limit. You can add as many rows as you need. But there are some practical considerations you should take into account. Large tables can be quite difficult to read, especially if the entire table can't fit in the browser window, and the reader is forced to scroll the browser to read the whole table. If your table is growing bigger and bigger, try to come up with a way of breaking the information into multiple, smaller tables; doing so might make the tables more manageable for you to create and will make the data easier for your readers to digest. Because this isn't always possible, you sometimes just have to bite the bullet and build a huge table with lots and lots of rows. But if you can break the table down, it can help to do so.

1 Add the Desired Rows

If you have a sketch of your table on the desk next to your computer, you can quickly see how many rows your table needs. For each row, add another table row tag pair. You'll probably find it helpful to type the opening tag on the first line and the closing tag on the next line. I also suggest that you add a tab before each of these tags so that the row information is indented one level from the table tag pair.

```
<table border="1" bordercolor="#ff0000"
bgcolor="#00ffff">
   <tr>
   </tr>
   <tr>
   </tr>
   <tr>
   </tr>
</table>
```

2 Specify the Horizontal Alignment

For each table row, use the **align** attribute to define the positioning of the text that will appear in the cells on that row. Adding the **align** tag to a row affects every cell in that row. You can choose **"left"**, **"center"**, or **"right"** for the value of the **align** attribute. The default is **"left"**, and you'll get that alignment if you don't specify the attribute. To center everything in the cells of a row, type **<tr align="center">**.

```
<table border="1" bordercolor="#ff0000">
   <tr align="center">
   </tr>
   <tr>
   </tr>
   <tr>
   </tr>
</table>
```

3 Specify the Vertical Alignment

The **valign** attribute allows you to position the contents of every cell on a row vertically. Your choices are **"top"**, **"middle"**, and **"bottom"**. To place the contents of every cell in a row at the top of the cell, type **<tr valign="top">**. If you want the default value of **"middle"**, you can leave the **valign** attribute out.

```
<table border="1" bordercolor="#ff0000">
   <tr align="center" valign="top">
   </tr>
   <tr>
   </tr>
   <tr>
   </tr>
</table>
```

4 Specify the Background Color

Change the color of an entire row with the **bgcolor** attribute of the **<tr>** tag. To change the color of a row to gray, type **<tr bgcolor="#999999">**. In this way, you can specify the color of each row in your table independently of any other row.

```
<table border="1" bordercolor="#ff0000">
   <tr bgcolor="#999999" align="center"
   valign="top">
   </tr>
   <tr>
   </tr>
   <tr>
   </tr>
</table>
```

End

TASK 6

How to Define Table Columns

After you have specified the rows in your table, you can add columns to the table. This task shows you how to create table columns. Again, refer to the sketch you made of your table back in Task 2.

If you've taken the time to thoroughly plan the table, it will be easy to see what you need to do now to add the correct number of columns.

You can specify the width and height of a single cell either in pixels or as a percentage of the table size.

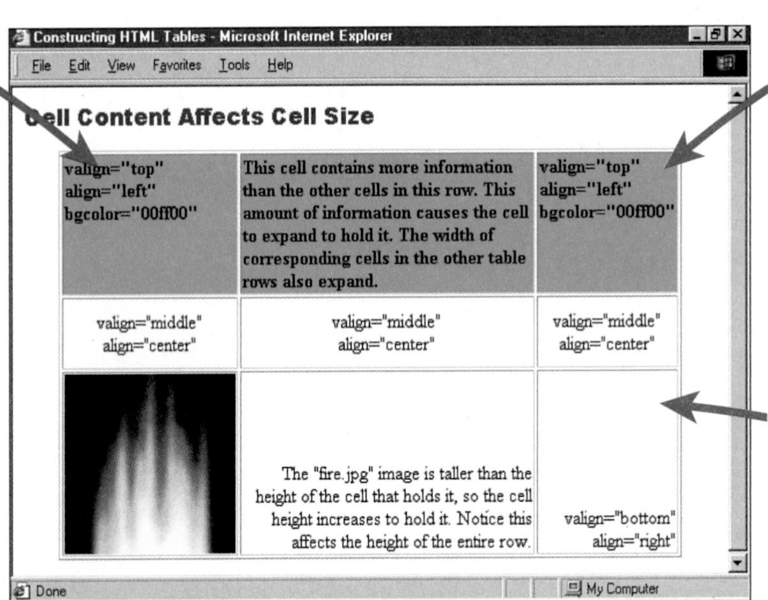

You specify the columns in a table simply by consistently defining the same number of cells for each row.

The height of the row and the width of the column adjust to fit the tallest and widest cells, overriding the width and height attributes you set if necessary.

Consistency Is Crucial

HTML creates columns differently than it creates rows. Each row spans the entire width of the table. But when you create columns, you create them within individual rows. In other words, if you create two columns in row one, you'll need to create two corresponding columns in rows two, three, four, and so on. If you're not consistent about this, you'll introduce errors into your table and achieve unpredictable results. It might be helpful to think of it another way: Instead of creating columns, you're actually creating table cells within each row. Think of a one-row table and imagine that you've added five cells to that row. You now have a one-row table with five cells. For the table to work properly as you add rows, you must make sure that you include the same number of cells in each row. When you do this, the cells of the various rows line up to imply columns.

1 Add the Desired Table Cells

Refer to your sketch to see how many cells you need in each row. For each cell in a row, insert one table data tag pair between the appropriate table row tag pairs. Make sure that you have an equal number of cells in each row so that the cells line up to form columns. Add two tabs in front of the table data tags so that those tags are indented from the table row tags. To add a cell, type **<td>...</td>**.

```
<table border="1" bordercolor="#ff0000">
<tr bgcolor="#999999"
align="center" valign="top">
    <td></td>
    <td></td>
    <td></td>
</tr>
<tr>
    <td></td>
    <td></td>
    <td></td>
</tr>
</table>
```

2 Specify Alignment

Use the **align** attribute in the **<td>** tag to control the horizontal alignment (**"left"**, **"right"**, or **"center"**) of the cell's contents; use **valign** to control the vertical alignment (**"top"**, **"middle"**, or **"bottom"**). To align the contents of a cell to the top and right, type **<td align="right" valign="top">…</td>**. Remember that when you add these attributes to the **<td>** tag, you affect only that cell.

```
<tr bgcolor="#999999"
align="center" valign="top">
    <td align="right" valign="top"></td>
    <td></td>
    <td></td>
</tr>
<tr>
    <td></td>
    <td></td>
    <td></td>
</tr>
```

3 Specify Background Color

To change the background color of an individual cell, add the **bgcolor** attribute to the **<td>** tag. With this method, you can specify different background colors for each cell in your table (but just because you can doesn't mean you should). To change the color of a cell to yellow, type **<td bgcolor="#ffff00">**.

```
<tr bgcolor="#999999"
align="center" valign="top">
    <td align="right" valign="top"></td>
    <td bgcolor="#ffff00"></td>
    <td></td>
</tr>
<tr>
    <td></td>
    <td></td>
    <td></td>
</tr>
```

4 Specify Cell Size

Specify the width and height of the cell in pixels or as a percentage of the table width and height with the **width** and **height** attributes of the **<td>** tag. Type **<td width="100" height="30">**. If you specify measurements that are too small to hold the object you put into the cell, the cell expands to fit the contents. A column is as wide as its widest cell, and a row is as tall as its tallest cell.

```
<tr bgcolor="#999999"
align="center" valign="top">
    <td align="right" valign="top"></td>
    <td bgcolor="#ffff00"></td>
    <td width="100" height="30"></td>
</tr>
<tr>
    <td></td>
    <td></td>
    <td></td>
</tr>
```

End

TASK 7 How to Add Table Headings

You might want to include headings for your table columns. As you'll learn in this task, you can use the table heading tag pair to accomplish this goal. Just as is true for the regular HTML heading tags you learned about in Part 3, Task 2, "How to Add Headings," it is up to the browser to decide exactly how it will show the table headings. All you can be assured of is that when you designate something as a header, it will appear different in some way than the regular text on the page. Most often, browsers show table headings as bolder than normal text.

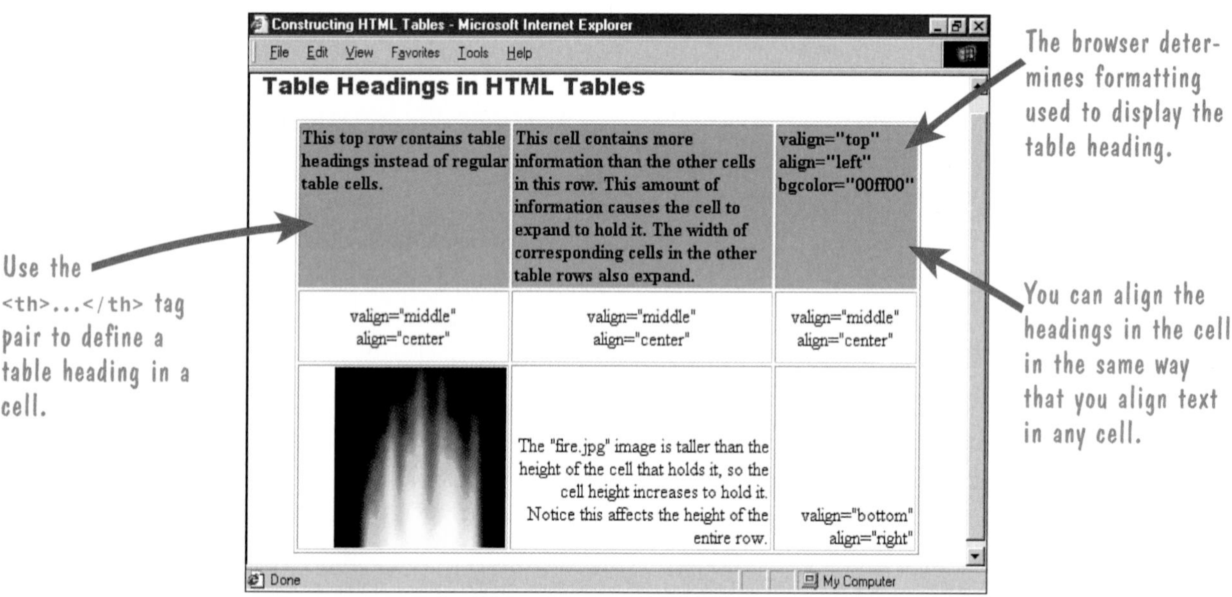

I Want Control

I usually find the fact that the browser is going to dictate the appearance of my table headings to be unacceptable. Therefore, if I'm including headings at all (table headings are optional, and more often than not, I leave them out), I prefer to define what they'll look like myself. To do this, I leave out the table heading tags all together. Instead, I use regular table cells and use HTML font tags to define the look of the text. For instance, in a regular table cell, I add the text I want to act as a header, but I enclose that text within HTML tags that make it look different than the rest of the table. I'll use the font tag pair to change font size or color, or the bold tag pair to make my heading bold. Using this method, I get to decide how my table headings appear, and not the browsers.

1 Add the Desired Table Cells

Refer to your sketch to quickly learn how many cells you need to designate as headings. To create a heading cell, use the table heading tag pair. Type **<th>...</th>**. Normally, you'll want a table heading for each column in your table.

```
<tr bgcolor="#999999"
align="center" valign="top">
<th></th>
<th></th>
<th></th>
</tr>
```

2 Specify Alignment

Use the **align** attribute of the **<th>** tag to specify the horizontal alignment as **"left"**, **"center"**, or **"right"**. Use the **valign** attribute to specify the vertical alignment as **"top"**, **"middle"**, or **"bottom"**. To align the contents of a heading cell to the bottom left, type **<th align="left" valign="bottom">**.

```
<tr bgcolor="#999999"
align="center" valign="top">
<th align="left" valign="bottom"></th>
<th></th>
<th></th>
</tr>
```

3 Create Your Own Headings

As mentioned earlier, I like to create my own custom headings using the **<font>** tag within the **<td>** tag. To do so, add the font tag pair to define the contents of the table data tag pair. You also can use the bold tag to make the heading bold. Type **<td><font face="arial" size="+2"><b>Custom Heading</b></font></td>**.

```
<tr bgcolor="#999999"
align="center" valign="top">
<td><font face="arial" size="+2">
<b>Custom Heading 1</b></font></td>
<td><font face="arial" size="+2">
<b>Custom Heading 2</b></font></td>
<td><font face="arial" size="+2">
<b>Custom Heading 3</b></font></td>
</tr>
```

4 Specify Cell Size

Use the **width** and **height** attributes to define the size of the table heading cells. To define a cell that measures 60 pixels wide by 40 pixels high, type **<th width="60" height="40">**. You can specify the size of the cell in exact pixels or as a percentage of the table dimensions. Regardless of your size specifications, the cell will expand as much as it needs to in order to hold the entire contents.

```
<tr bgcolor="#999999"
align="center" valign="top">
    <th align="left"
    valign="bottom"></th>
    <th bgcolor="#ff9933"></th>
    <th width="60" height="40"></th>
</tr>
```

End

TASK 8 How to Add the Contents of a Table

Well, this is it! You've finally finished the framework of the table, and now it's time for the content. This task shows you just where to place the information (sometimes called the *table data*) you want to include in your table.

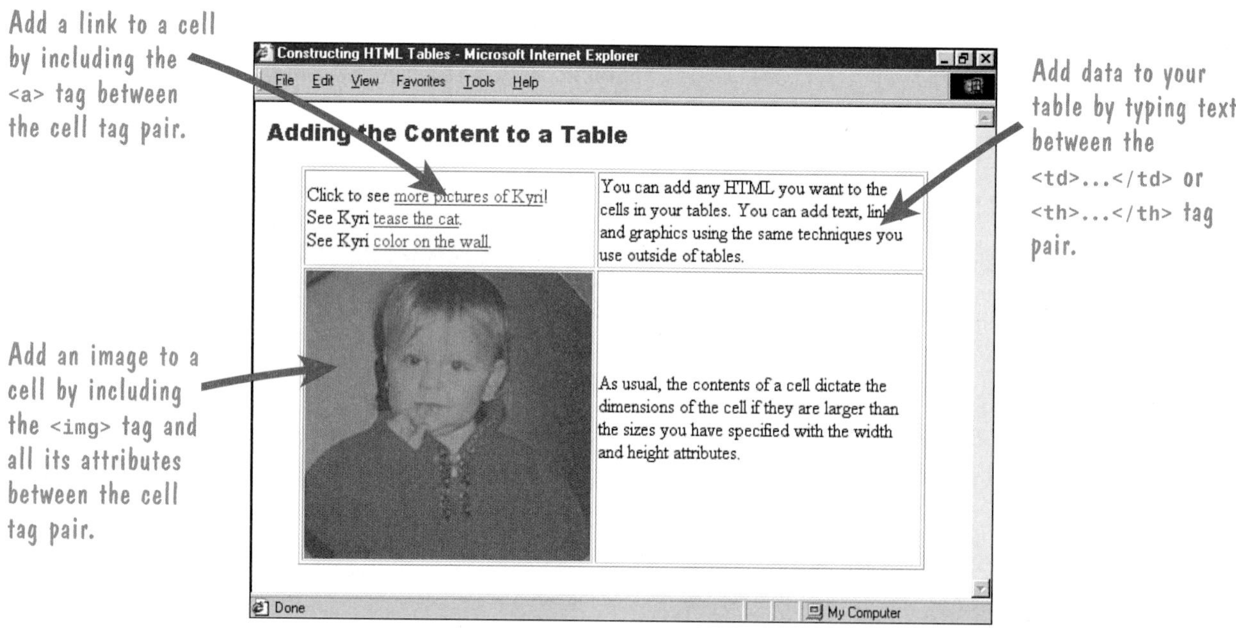

What Can a Table Hold?

The thing that really makes tables so powerful is that they can hold anything you can create using HTML. Any of the tags you've learned to use for manipulating text, adding images, and creating links can also be used within a table. The ability to add anything at all to your tables is what makes tables so useful as aids to controlling the layout of your pages. You can use a table to define the sections of your page; within that table, you can code your page as normal. You can even include tables within a table (a process called *nesting*). Use discretion when nesting tables because if you get too carried away (for instance, a table nested within a table that's nested within a table...), you might lengthen the download time of your page. Generally one or two levels of nesting won't cause problems, but be careful going beyond that.

1 Add Text to a Cell

To add text to your table, type the information between the <td> or <th> tag and the </td> or </th> tag of the cell in which you want the text to appear. If the text line is longer than the table cell is wide, the text will break and continue on the next line. For example, type `<td>Here are the contents of my first table cell!</td>`.

```
<tr>
    <td>Cell 1</td>
    <td>Cell 2</td>
    <td>Cell 3</td>
</tr>
```

2 Add an Image to a Cell

Add an image to a cell using the techniques you use to add images (refer to Part 5, Task 2, "How to Insert a Graphic into a Web Page"). Just include the <img> tag within the table data tag pair. For instance, type `<td><img src="../../images/kyri.jpg"></td>` (don't forget the **width**, **height**, and **alt** attributes). If the image is larger than the size of the cell you put it in, the cell will expand to fit the image.

```
<tr>
  <td><img src="../kyri.jpg"
  width="248" height="240"
  alt="A picture of Kyri"></td>
  <td>Cell 5</td>
  <td>Cell 6</td>
</tr>
```

3 Create a Link in a Cell

As you know, it is easy to include text in a table cell; you might have concluded that it's just as easy to add a link within a table cell. You're right. Just add the anchor tag as usual, but within the cell tag pair. For example, type, `<td><a href="http://www.travelwisconsin.com/" target="_blank">Wisconsin Vacations</a></td>`.

```
<tr>
 <td>
  <a href="../../pages/past/vacations.html">
  Kyri's first vacation</a></td>
 <td>Cell 8</td>
 <td>Cell 9</td>
</tr>
```

4 Test the Page

You've done a lot of work on your table. Hopefully, you've been testing it in your browser all along so that you can see the results of every new line of code you write. But it never hurts to be reminded! Test your page now to make sure that your table looks like you think it will.

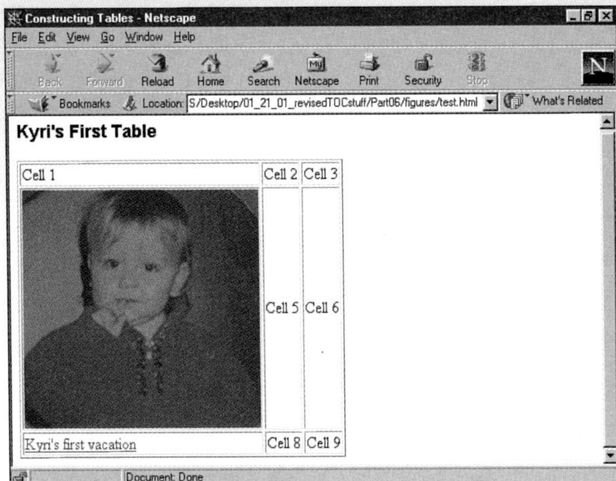

End

TASK 9 How to Control Table Dimensions

By default, a table lives in a state of constant flux. The width adjusts with the width of its contents, and maybe with the width of the browser window. Different cells have different widths depending on the content they hold. This variation can result in sloppy-looking tables. But you can override the default settings and exercise control over the dimensions of your tables and cells. This task shows you how to define the width of your tables and their cells so that you can display nice-looking tables, or tables that define specific areas for layout purposes.

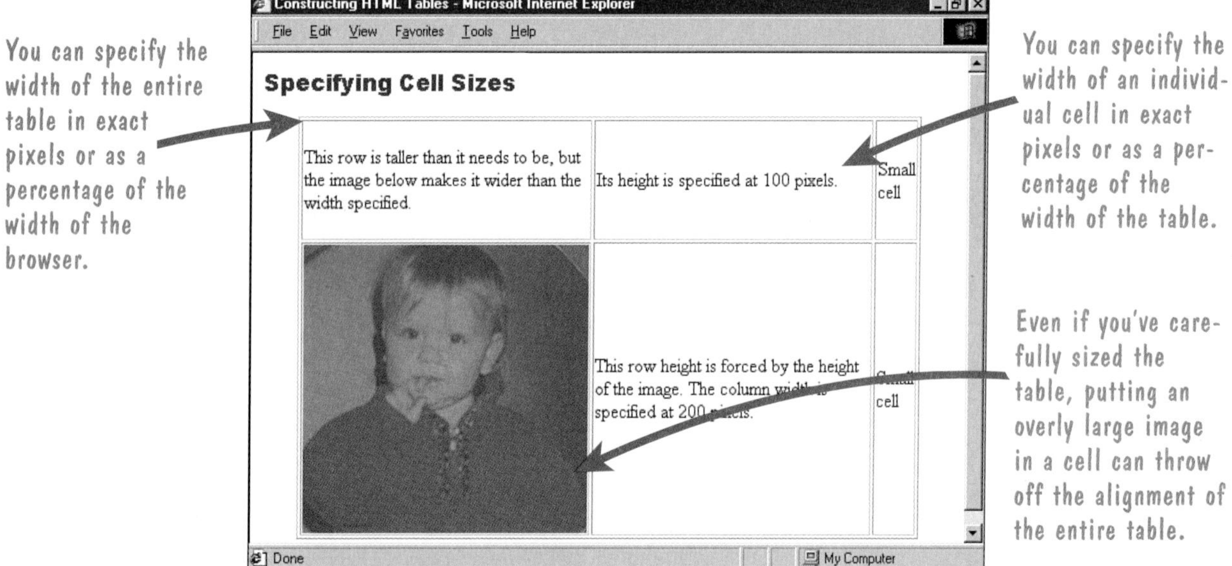

What the Big Dog Says, Goes

One thing you must consider when placing content—and especially images—into your table cells is that the "biggest" content defines not only the width of the cell that holds it, but also the width of any corresponding cells in other rows. Suppose that cell 1 in row 1 holds an image that is 150 pixels wide. The cell must be 150 pixels wide to hold the image. Now imagine that cell 1 of row 2 holds an image that is only 20 pixels wide. Even though this cell technically needs to be only 20 pixels wide, it is resized to correspond to the biggest cell in its column (in this case, 150 pixels wide to match cell 1 in row 1). You can picture how odd that will look. Cell 1 in row 2 will look sort of silly because it has so much empty space. If possible, make the images the same size. If you can't, try another layout so that they are not in the same column.

1 Specify Width as a Percentage

By default, a table and individual cells are only as wide as they need be to fit the contents. You can end up with unbalanced-looking tables this way. Specify a width as a percentage of the browser window width (for the table) or as a percentage of the table width (for cells) to make sure that things look balanced. For example, if you want the table to always be 70 percent as wide as the window, type **<table width="70%">**.

```
<table width="70%" border="1"
bordercolor="#ff0000">
    .
    .
    .
</table>
```

2 Specify Exact Width in Pixels

Another way to specify the width of a table or cell is to use an exact pixel value. This is especially useful when you're using a table to control page layout. To specify an exact pixel value, type **<table width="500">**.

```
<table width="500" border="1"
bordercolor="#ff0000">
    .
    .
    .
</table>
```

3 Specify Cell Width

You can also specify the width of individual cells in either a percentage of the table width or in terms of exact pixels. These techniques are useful for page layout purposes. To specify a percentage width for your cell, type **<td width="10%">**.

```
<tr>
  <td>Cell 1</td>
  <td width="10%">Cell 2</td>
  <td>Cell 3</td>
</tr>
```

4 Watch the Overall Size

Even with all the hard work you do defining specific table and cell sizes, you must be careful not to add content (usually an image is the culprit) that is bigger than the cell into which you are putting it. If you do, the cell will expand beyond the specified width to hold the content. The entire table will expand beyond the specified width if it has to hold content that is too wide.

```
<tr>
  <td width="100"><img src="../kyri.jpg"
    width="248" height="240"
    alt="A picture of Kyri"></td>
  <td>Cell 5</td>
  <td>Cell 6</td>
</tr>
```

End

TASK 10

How to Control Spacing

There are a couple of different ways you can control the spacing of cells within your tables. You can control the amount of space between the contents of a cell and the edge of the cell (called *cell padding*), and you can control the space between two adjacent cells (called *cell spacing*). Because they achieve similar results, these techniques can sometimes cause confusion for the HTML author. This task sorts it all out. You'll learn the difference between cell spacing and cell padding and how to define either or both for your tables.

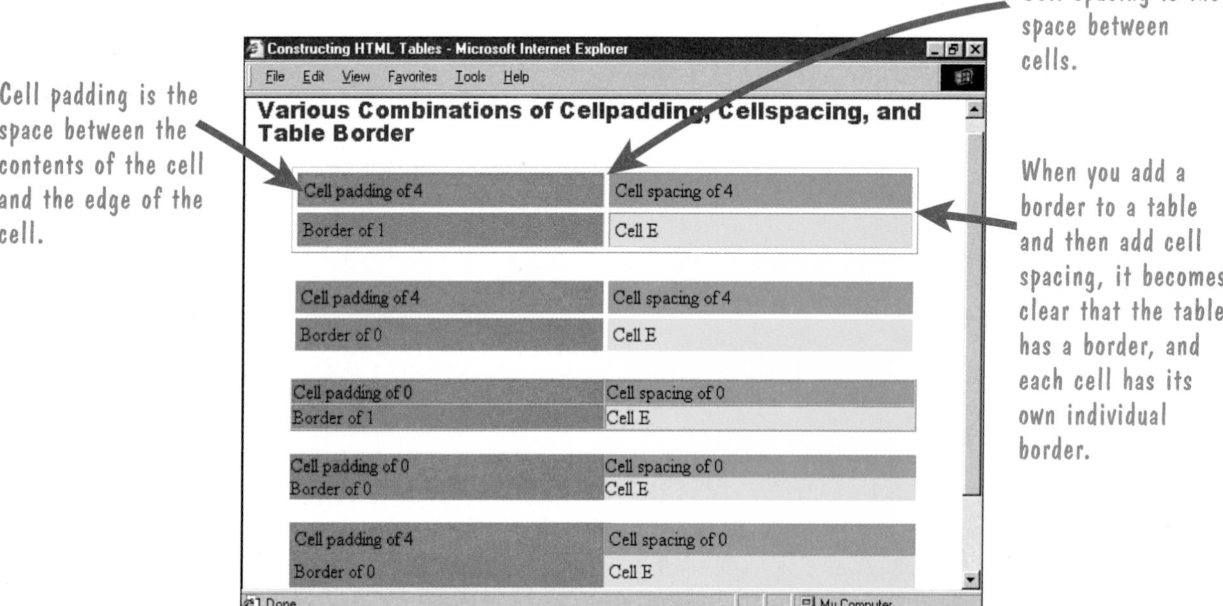

Which Should I Use?

If you're like me and dislike borders around your tables and cells, it makes virtually no difference whether you use cell spacing or cell padding to add space between the contents of your cells. With borders turned off, and all table cells having the same color, there is no visible difference between the two spacing options. On the other hand, when you do include borders on your table, you'll have to decide which technique to use. Maybe you'll even use a combination of the two. It's another instance where the decision boils down to what you like. With borders on, you'll instantly see the results of adding space with one or the other of these techniques. It's then up to you to look at those results and decide whether or not you like them.

Note that these attributes apply to the entire table, not to individual cells. Therefore, you cannot specify a cell padding value for cell 1, and a different value for cell 2. What you set for the table applies to all cells.

1 Use the Default Spacing

By default, all table cells have a two-pixel space between the contents of the cell and the edge of the cell (or the cell border, if it's visible). There is also a default of a two-pixel space between the edge of one cell and the edge of its neighboring cell. These spaces help maintain the readability of a very full table. If you want to use these defaults, you do not need to add attributes to specify these spacings.

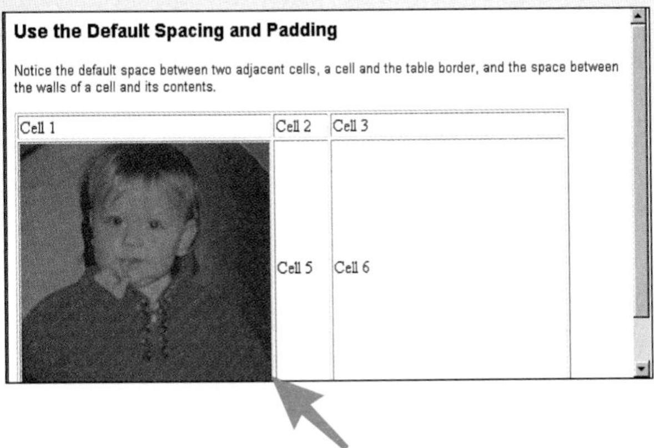

2 Specify Cell Spacing

The **cellspacing** attribute of the **<table>** tag defines the space between adjacent cells and between a cell and the edge of the table. To specify a space of 10 pixels between cells, type **<table border="1" cellspacing="10">**. The result of this large space is evident when you test the table with its border turned on.

```
<table width="550" border="1"
bordercolor="#ff0000"
cellspacing="10">
    <tr>
    .
    .
    .
    </tr>
</table>
```

3 Specify Cell Padding

The **cellpadding** attribute lets you specify the amount of space between the edge of a cell and its contents. Create a **cellpadding** of 10 and set the **cellspacing** to 0 by typing **<table border="1" cellspacing="0" cellpadding="10">**. Compare the difference between the results you achieved in the last step and the results for this step.

```
<table width="550" border="1"
bordercolor="#ff0000"
cellspacing="0" cellpadding="10">
    <tr>
    .
    .
    .
    </tr>
</table>
```

4 Test With and Without Borders

Try different combinations of **cellpadding** and **cellspacing** values. Test these combinations with and without borders turned on to see how borders affect the look of the table. Notice that when you add **cellspacing** and you have a border on the table, you also add individual borders around each table cell. Notice also that with borders turned off, the results of these two attributes are indistinguishable.

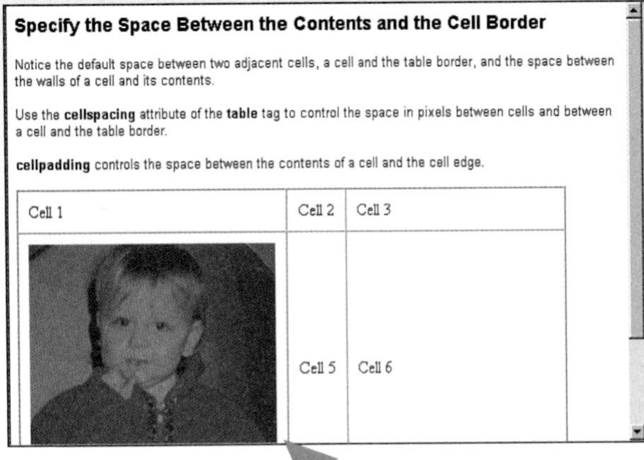

End

TASK 11

How to Span Columns

Earlier in this part, you learned that if row 1 has three columns, you must make sure that rows 2, 3, and 4 have three columns as well. In this task, you'll see that there is a bit of an exception to that rule. You can use the **colspan** attribute to create a row that spans multiple columns. For instance, row 1 has three equal columns. Although row 2 would typically have three equal columns, you can build the row so that it has only two columns, one of which occupies the space of two columns. Confusing? This task sorts it out for you.

Use the colspan attribute of the <td> or <th> tag to make a single cell stretch across multiple columns in the table.

The top row of this table contains the navigation imagemap and spans four columns.

When you use the colspan attribute, you'll have to delete the cell tags for the cells you "bumped over" and off the table.

Extra! Extra! Read All About It!

Here's an example that I hope will help you visualize what's going on with the **colspan** attribute. Take a look at your local morning paper. Look at the main headline. It stretches over a good portion of the page. Now look at the article that goes with the headline. It's broken into several columns. In my local weekly, *The Mount Horeb Mail*, the article is broken into five columns. Now think of this article and its headline as an HTML table. The table has two rows: Row 1 holds the headline, and row 2 holds the article. As mentioned, row 2 has five columns. On the other hand, row 1 has just one column, and that column occupies the same horizontal space as the five columns in row 2. In other words, the single column in row 1 *spans* the five columns in row 2. Speaking in HTML terms, the **colspan** attribute of the cell in row 1 has been set to **"5"**.

1 Construct a Table

To see how **colspan** works, first create a simple table with three columns and three rows. For the contents of the table, just type **Cell 1**, **Cell 2**, and so on between the **<td>**...**</td>** tag pairs. You'll have a total of nine cells when you're done.

```
<table width="90%" border="1"
bordercolor="#ff0000">
   <tr align="center">
      <td>Cell 1</td>
      <td>Cell 2</td>
      <td>Cell 3</td>
   </tr>
   <tr align="center">
      <td>Cell 4</td>
      <td>Cell 5</td>
      <td>Cell 6</td>
   </tr>
   <tr align="center">
      <td>Cell 7</td>
      <td>Cell 8</td>
      <td>Cell 9</td>
   </tr>
</table>
```

2 Create the Column Span

To cause a cell to span more than one column, add the **colspan** attribute to the **<td>** tag. Then specify the number of columns that cell should span. For instance, to cause cell 1 in row 1 to span all three columns of our sample table, type **<td colspan="3">Cell 1</td>**. Notice that when you test the results, cells 2 and 3 hang out over the edge of the table.

```
<table width="90%" border="1"
bordercolor="#ff0000">
   <tr align="center">
     <td colspan="3">Cell 1 now spans three
       columns</td>
     <td>Cell 2</td>
     <td>Cell 3</td>
   </tr>
   .
   .
   .
</table>
```

3 Remove Displaced Table Cells

Because the single cell you created in Step 2 now spans all three columns, you no longer have room for the other two cells in that row. Delete the second and third table data tag pairs from the first row. Think of it this way: Because this is a three-column table, you have only three cell slots available. The first cell now takes up all three slots, so you must remove the two extra cells.

```
<table width="90%" border="1"
bordercolor="#ff0000">
   <tr align="center">
      <td colspan="3">Cell 1 now spans three
        columns,<br />
        so Cells 2 and 3 have been removed.</td>
   </tr>
   .
   .
   .
</table>
```

4 Test the Results

Take a look at the table in your test browser. Does the first cell of the first row span all three columns? If the answer is yes, you've coded the **colspan** correctly. Are there any extra table cells hanging off the right edge of the table in row 1? If so, go back to Step 3 and remove the extra cells.

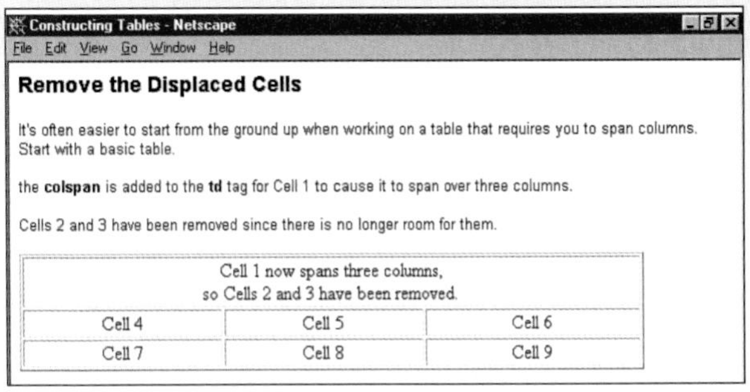

Constructing Tables - Netscape

File Edit View Go Window Help

Remove the Displaced Cells

It's often easier to start from the ground up when working on a table that requires you to span columns. Start with a basic table.

the **colspan** is added to the **td** tag for Cell 1 to cause it to span over three columns.

Cells 2 and 3 have been removed since there is no longer room for them.

Cell 1 now spans three columns, so Cells 2 and 3 have been removed.		
Cell 4	Cell 5	Cell 6
Cell 7	Cell 8	Cell 9

End

TASK 12 How to Span Rows

In the last task, you learned how to make a single cell span a number of columns by adding the **colspan** attribute to the cell in that row. You can also make one column span a number of rows in a similar fashion. In this case, you use the **rowspan** attribute to specify the number of rows to be spanned by the column, or more accurately, the cell. The technique for doing this is very similar to what you learned in the last task. This task walks you through the process.

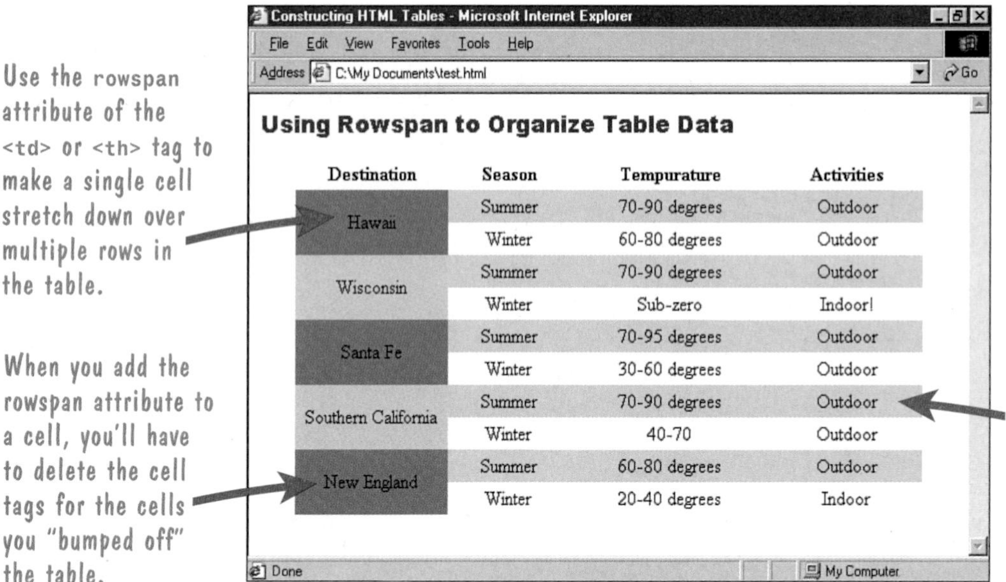

Here, color is used to help organize the table and make it easier to read.

Creating a Split Chart of Data

Here's an illustration of a situation in which a table that uses the **rowspan** attribute comes in handy. Suppose that you are constructing a table of information on possible vacation spots for your vacation Web site. You have four destinations in mind, but you want to list information for each of these sites in both the summer and winter seasons. In the first column, you list the four destinations—you have four rows. In the second column, you have two separate rows (summer and winter) for each destination. Subsequent columns list various facts related to the destination broken into summer facts and winter facts. So, columns 2 and up have eight rows, whereas column 1 has only four rows. In this case, each cell in column 1 spans two rows in columns 2 and up. The **rowspan** attribute for the cells in column 1 has been set to **"2"**.

1 Use the Table from the Last Task

Use the table that you started in the last task. This table now has seven cells, the first of which spans three columns (which accounts for the space of three full cells). In the next few steps, we'll modify this table even more by adding the **rowspan** attribute to the first cell in the second row (cell 4).

```
<table width="90%" border="1"
  bordercolor="#ff0000">
 <tr align="center">
   <td colspan="3">Cell 1 now spans three
    columns</td>
 </tr>
 <tr align="center">
   <td>Cell 4</td>
   .
   .
   .
  </tr>
</table>
```

2 Create the Row Span

To cause cell 4 to span rows 2 and 3, add the **rowspan** attribute to the **<td>** tag for the cell. Type **<td rowspan="2">**. When you view the results, notice that cell 4 now spans rows 2 and 3. Notice also that cell 9 hangs down over the bottom edge of the table in row 3. Because you're now spanning two rows with cell 4, there's no room for cell 9.

```
<tr align="center">
  <td rowspan="2">Cell 4 now spans<br />
   Rows 2 and 3.</td>
  <td>Cell 5</td>
  <td>Cell 6</td>
</tr>
 <tr align="center">
 <td>Cell 7</td>
 <td>Cell 8</td>
 <td>Cell 9</td>
</tr>
```

3 Remove Extra Table Cell

Because cell 4 now spans two rows, cell 9 must be eliminated so that the table balances. Delete the **<td>** tag pair for cell 9. You now have a table in which Cell 1 spans three columns, and cell 4 spans two rows. Cells 2, 3, and 9 have been removed to make room for the span commands we've used.

```
<tr align="center">
 <td rowspan="2">Cell 4 now spans<br />
  Rows 2 and 3.<br />
  Cell 9 has been removed<br />
  because there is no room for it.</td>
 <td>Cell 5</td>
 <td>Cell 6</td>
</tr>
<tr align="center">
 <td>Cell 7</td>
 <td>Cell 8</td>
</tr>
```

4 Test the Results

Verify that the table you have built looks like the sketch you used to guide you through the table-creation process. If it does, give yourself a pat on the back. For easy cases like the one in these examples, the sketch might not really have been that necessary. But as your tables and spans get more complicated, you'll be glad that you have that roadmap down on paper so that you can refer to it whenever necessary.

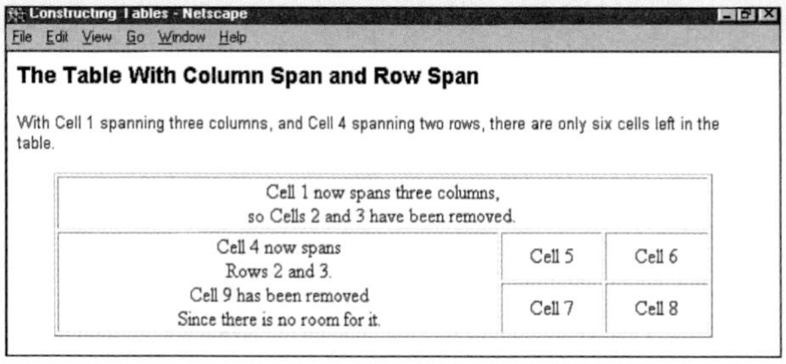

Constructing Tables - Netscape

File Edit View Go Window Help

The Table With Column Span and Row Span

With Cell 1 spanning three columns, and Cell 4 spanning two rows, there are only six cells left in the table.

Cell 1 now spans three columns, so Cells 2 and 3 have been removed.		
Cell 4 now spans Rows 2 and 3. Cell 9 has been removed Since there is no room for it.	Cell 5	Cell 6
	Cell 7	Cell 8

End

TASK 13 How to Nest Tables

I've already mentioned that you can include anything in a table that you can specify using HTML. That includes other tables. In this task, you'll build a table within another table. You should start to get an idea of how tables can get complicated, and how some of the development techniques we've discussed in this part will help you keep track of what you're doing. We'll use borders to help identify which table is which, comments to remind ourselves why we're building the tables, and indentation to help us quickly identify different parts of the tables.

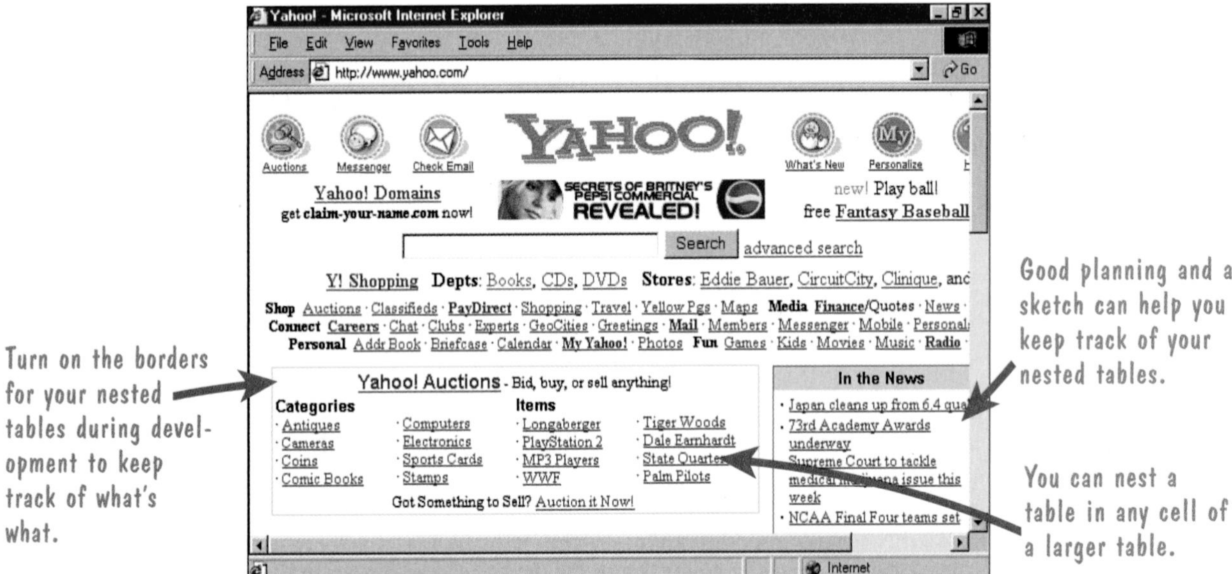

Turn on the borders for your nested tables during development to keep track of what's what.
Good planning and a sketch can help you keep track of your nested tables.
You can nest a table in any cell of a larger table.

A Case for Nesting

As soon as you decide that you are going to do anything beyond the basic layout functions on your HTML page, you're into tableland. Typically, when you use tables to control page layout, you'll open one big table at the beginning of your page that defines the various sections of the page layout. As you're writing the page, you might come to a point at which you want a table to present information. When you start this second table, you are nesting it within the large table that controls your page layout. It is the ability to nest tables within tables, and to include any other HTML within your tables, that allows you to use tables as layout tools. I don't think it's an exaggeration to say that tables have done more than virtually any other technique available in HTML to foster interesting graphic design on the Web. Many a graphic-designer-become-Web-designer has been thankful for the ability to nest tables when laying out pages!

1 Plan It on Paper

Time to grab that pencil again. By now, you know that a table requires a lot of tags. There's a **<table>** tag and a bunch of **<tr>** and **<td>** tags. And these tags might have a bunch of attributes. It gets confusing enough to make one complicated table. So, what happens when you nest another table into all that? It's very easy to get confused. Drawing it out on paper helps tremendously.

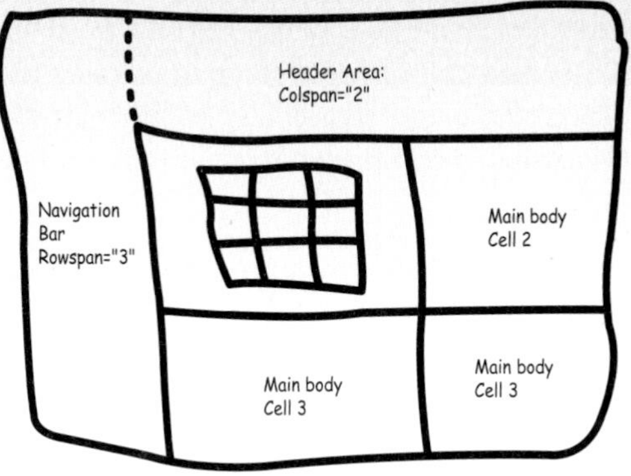

2 Create the First Table

Using all the techniques we've been exploring in this part, create the first table. You can use the table you made during the last two tasks, or you can create a simple four-cell table. You can nest another table in a simple table just as you can nest it in a complicated table. Make sure that you turn on the border of the first table at least during development.

```
<tr align="center">
    <td colspan="3">Cell 1</td>
</tr>
<tr align="center">
    <td rowspan="2">Cell 4</td>
    <td>Cell 5</td>
    <td>Cell 6</td>
</tr>
<tr align="center">
    <td>Cell 7</td>
    <td>Cell 8</td>
</tr>
```

3 Create the Nested Table

Choose a cell into which you'll nest the new table. Include a comment to remind yourself why you're nesting the table. Within the table data tag pair for the cell, build the second table. Define a different-colored border for the second table so you can distinguish the two in your browser.

```
<td>
    <table border="1"
    bordercolor="#00ff00">
    <tr>
        <td>Cell A</td>
        <td>Cell B</td>
        <td>Cell C</td>
    </tr>
    <tr>
        <td>Cell D</td>
        <td>Cell E</td>
        <td>Cell F</td>
    </tr>
   </table>
</td>
```

4 Test the Results

Use indentation to keep your tags straight. Indenting is especially helpful in keeping the **<tr>** and **<td>** tags from the first table separate from those in the second. Don't forget the closing tags. And don't feel bad if you get confused—it's easy to do so. When you're done, test your page. If you're happy with the results, remove the borders if you don't want them to show on your final page.

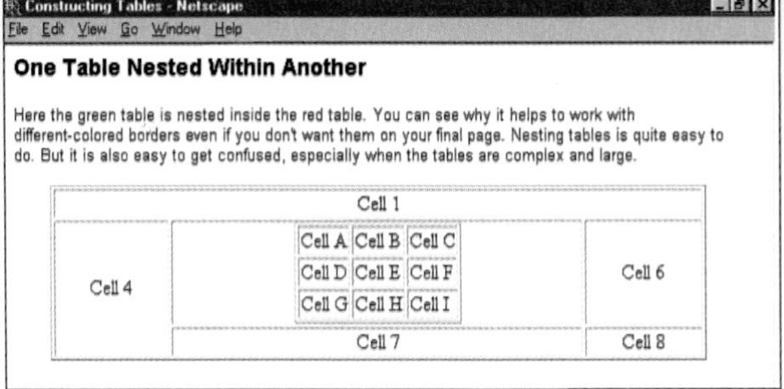

End

TASK 14 How to Slice Images with Tables

Sometimes it is a good idea to break a large image into smaller pieces before you add it to your Web page. This technique is often referred to as *image slicing*. After you have sliced the image into pieces, you need a way to reconstruct it in HTML. The only way you can accomplish this—and end up with an unbroken image on your page—is to make use of a table. This task shows you how to use a table to reconstruct an image that you've sliced apart in your image-editing software.

Slice an image in your image editing software and save the pieces as separate files.

Use a table to assemble the pieces of the image in a logical manner.

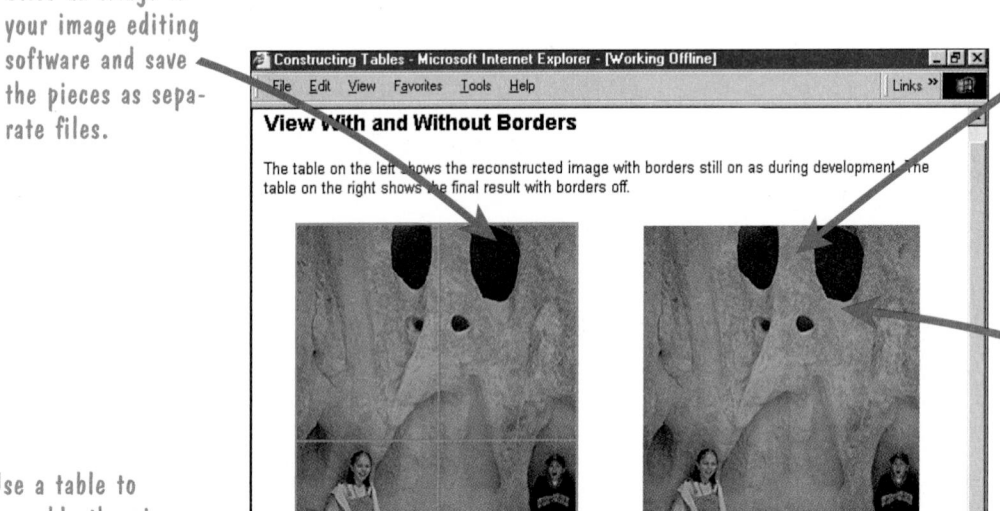

Don't bother specifying a width and height for the table; the image pieces will dictate the size of each cell.

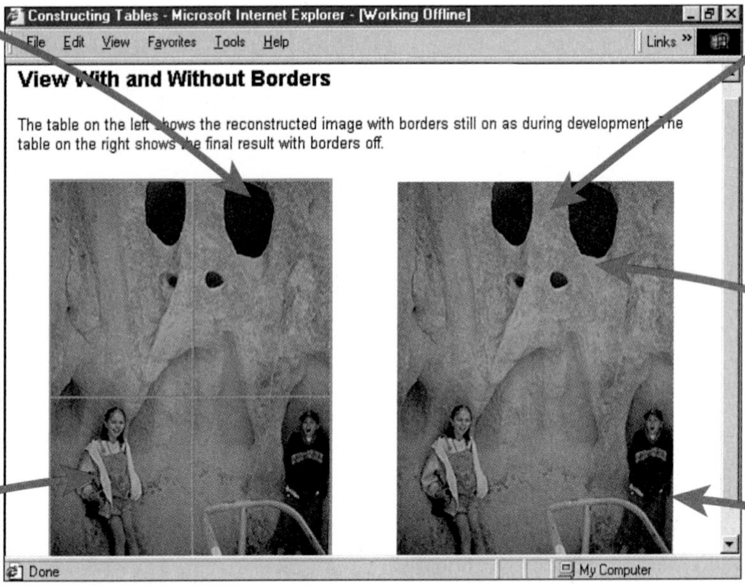

Don't forget to include the `alt`, `width`, and `height` attributes for each piece of the image for all the reasons discussed in Part 5.

Turn off the borders of the table after the image is successfully stitched together.

Why Bother?

What's the point of slicing an image up only to reconstruct it in a table? Image slicing is a way to create the illusion that the page is loading faster than it is. Instead of waiting to show the entire large image until it is totally downloaded, smaller pieces of the image show up one by one. Image slicing is also valuable when you have an image that is the same on several pages except for one portion; you can slice the image to isolate the changing portion. After the non-changing portion is downloaded, it can be called quickly from the temporary file on the visitor's hard drive the next time it's used (as you should remember from Part 5, "Implementing Web Graphics"). On the next page, only the new portion has to download. You might also be able to isolate a portion of your picture that you can compress more effectively as a GIF file while another portion works better as a JPEG file.

1 Slice the Image

Use your image editor to slice the image into pieces. Use the selection tools to copy pieces and paste them into separate files. Alternatively, use the software's crop tool to isolate the portion of the image you want and use the **Save As** command to save that portion as a separate file. However you accomplish it, you need multiple files, each containing just a piece of the overall image. Make sure that there is no overlap between pieces.

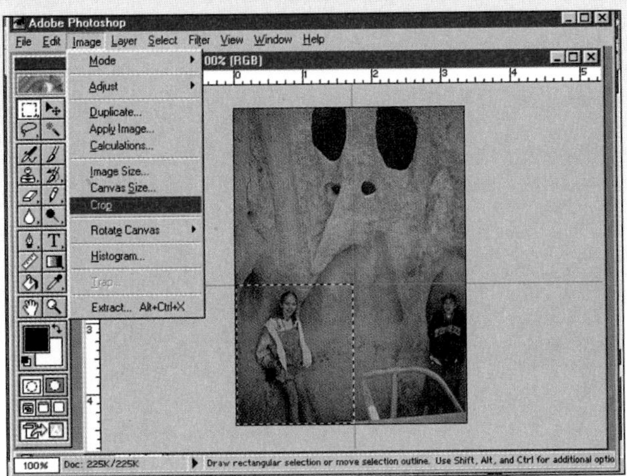

2 Build the Table

Now the image is broken into separate pieces, sort of like a jigsaw puzzle, but all the pieces are nice, neat rectangles. Now you must build a table with which you'll put the puzzle back together. You'll need as many cells in your table as you have pieces of the puzzle. Depending on how you sliced the image, you might need to use the **colspan** and **rowspan** techniques.

```
<table align="center" border="1"
bordercolor="#ff0000">
    <tr>
        <td>Cell 1</td>
        <td>Cell 2</td>
    </tr>
    <tr>
        <td>Cell 3</td>
        <td>Cell 4</td>
    </tr>
</table>
```

3 Eliminate Table Spacing

I'm sure that I don't have to mention once again that it might help to make a sketch, so I won't. As usual, while you're constructing the table, it can help to work with the border turned on. Remember that, by default, your table has **cellspacing** of **"2"** and **cellpadding** of **"2"**. Add these attributes to your **<table>** tag and set them both to **"0"** so that you can stitch the image pieces back together seamlessly.

```
<table align="center" border="1"
bordercolor="#ff0000" cellspacing="0"
cellpadding="0">
    <tr>
        <td>Cell 1</td>
        <td>Cell 2</td>
    </tr>
    <tr>
        <td>Cell 3</td>
        <td>Cell 4</td>
    </tr>
</table>
```

4 Reassemble the Image

Now you have a table with one cell for each piece of the puzzle. Use the **<img>** tag to add each piece to the proper cell in your table. Although I've left them out of my example to save space, don't forget to include the **width**, **height**, and **alt** attributes for each **<img>** tag. When you're done, test the page in your browser.

```
<table align="center" border="0"
cellspacing="0" cellpadding="0">
  <tr>
      <td><img src="jakeleah1.jpg" /></td>
      <td><img src="jakeleah2.jpg" /></td>
  </tr>
  <tr>
      <td><img src="jakeleah3.jpg" /></td>
      <td><img src="jakeleah4.jpg" /></td>
  </tr>
</table>
```

End

Task

PART 7

Building Forms

So far, everything you've learned has been focused on enabling you to present information to visitors to your Web site. You've made words people can read, pictures they can look at, and links they can follow. But how do they feel about everything they've read, seen, and experienced? Do they like it? Hate it? Understand it? Have questions about it? Or comments that might help you make your Web site even more useful? Are they convinced? Would they like to buy something now? How many do they want? What size? What color? Cash, check, or charge? Wouldn't it be nice to know the answers to all these questions?

It's time to talk a little bit about how your readers can communicate back to you. The simplest way to gather information from your visitors is to include a **`mailto:`** link on your page. Type **`<a href="mailto:myemail@myisp.com"`** to supply such a link. Although this method is simple, it's not very sophisticated. *Forms* make it possible to gather feedback from your visitors and then work with the data to provide better service. The concept of an HTML form is exactly the same as any form you've ever filled out with a pen and paper. It's a way for you to lead your readers into making their choices and preferences known. A way for you to gather important information so that you can better serve your audience. Forms provide a vehicle for all-important feedback and two-way communication.

When a visitor fills out the form you provide on your Web page and clicks the Submit button, what happens to the information? Where does it go? How does it get used? This part of the book gives basic answers to those questions and teaches you everything you need to know to build the form in HTML.

Coupled with the technologies that allow you to write something called "server-side scripts," a form is one of the most powerful tools in your HTML toolbox. We'll touch a bit on server-side scripts in this part, but the technologies involved in creating them can easily fill an entire book (make that an entire series of books), so we'll merely scratch the surface to gain a little understanding of the potential that forms allow you to achieve.

Still, for all this big talk about the importance of the HTML form, you'll be happy to know that with the base of HTML knowledge you already have, forms are a breeze to create. And they're kind of fun, too. They're not unlike a treasure hunt. You're after feedback, and it's up to you to figure out how to gather it. Using the tools that you are about to learn, you'll be able to tap into a wealth of information! •

TASK 1

How to Begin a Form

You're gaining enough HTML knowledge that you might have already guessed that to include a form on your page, you must first let the browser know that a form is coming. Just as with tables in Part 6, "Working with Tables," there is a special tag pair for forms. When the browser encounters the opening tag, it knows that it must treat what follows as a form. This task shows you how to begin your HTML forms.

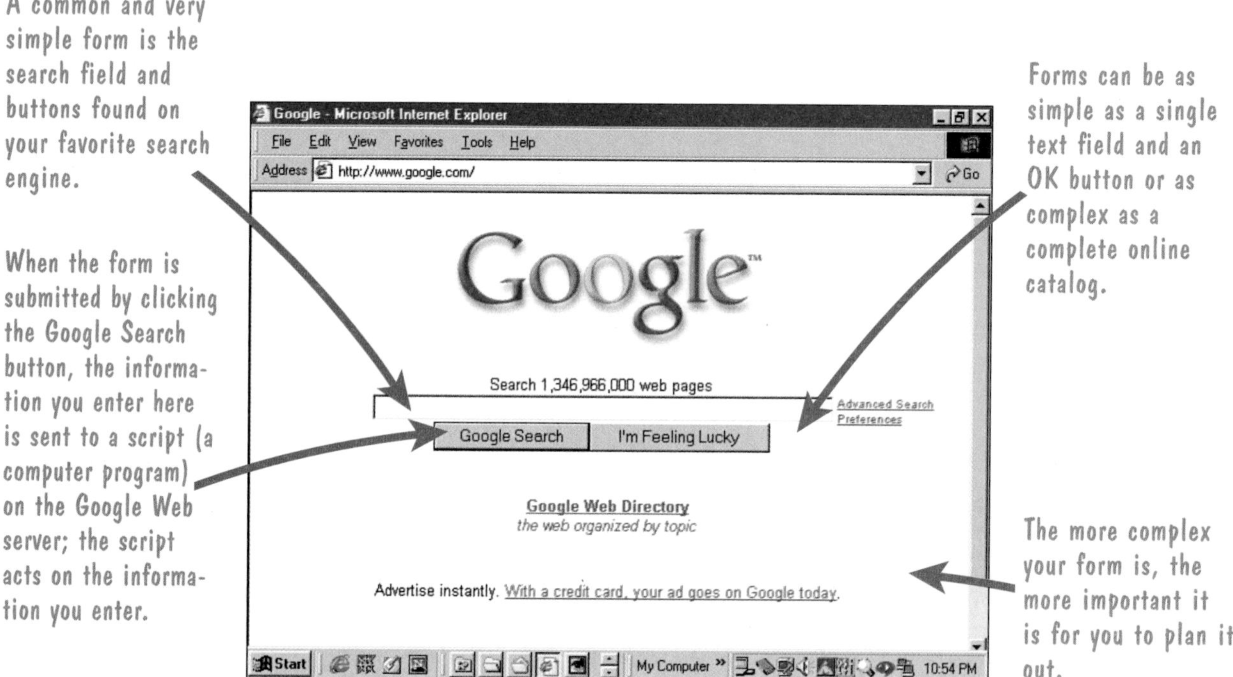

A common and very simple form is the search field and buttons found on your favorite search engine.
When the form is submitted by clicking the Google Search button, the information you enter here is sent to a script (a computer program) on the Google Web server; the script acts on the information you enter.
Forms can be as simple as a single text field and an OK button or as complex as a complete online catalog.
The more complex your form is, the more important it is for you to plan it out.
Google - Microsoft Internet Explorer
File Edit View Favorites Tools Help
Address http://www.google.com/
Go
Google
Search 1,346,966,000 web pages
Advanced Search
Preferences
Google Search
I'm Feeling Lucky
Google Web Directory
the web organized by topic
Advertise instantly. With a credit card, your ad goes on Google today.
Start
My Computer
10:54 PM

Not an Exclusive Club

Everything that comes between the opening and closing tags of a form belongs to the form. But just as tables can hold non-table-specific content, forms aren't made up of strictly form-specific content. Of course, forms certainly do contain special form-related tags that create form elements (sometimes called form "controls"), but you can use any element of HTML in a form. You can insert regular text, specify font attributes, add an image, build a link, construct a list, or include a table, all within the form structure. Forms can be very simple, such as a form that gives the reader a chance to enter a name and password. Forms can be very complex, such as a complete and detailed online store. But regardless of what the form does, it's always pretty easy to make because whether it's short or long, big or small, the complexity lies on the other end—that is, what you do with the information after the form gathers it.

1 Organize Your Thoughts

You might be getting a little tired of me telling you every time you turn around that you have to plan this or plan that. But planning really does pay off in terms of the development time you'll save. Planning your forms is no different. The first step to building an effective form is to decide what the form must accomplish. Maybe it'll help you to put it on paper. Regardless, get your thoughts together to avoid a sloppy form.

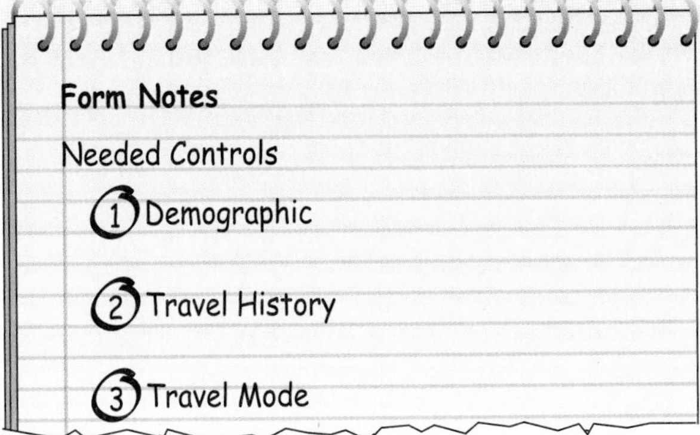

Form Notes
Needed Controls
1 Demographic
2 Travel History
3 Travel Mode

2 Formulate Specific Questions

I also find it very helpful to figure out what questions I want to ask before I start coding the form. Identify exactly which questions, options, and buttons you'll have to include in order to gather the information you really need. Pay close attention to how questions are worded—the wording has much to do with the perception people have when they read. This perception assuredly affects the answers users provide.

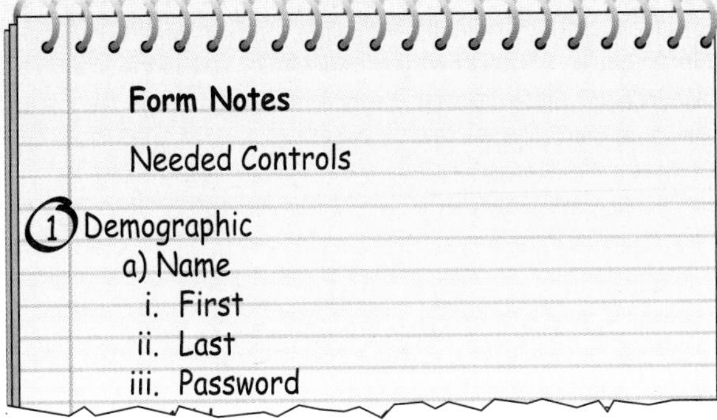

3 Decide on the Form Tools

After you have figured out the questions, it's simply a matter of choosing the right form control for the question. Form *controls* are the tools you use to construct your form. The following tasks teach you all you need to know about the various form elements, and when you might want to use one over another.

Form Notes

Needed Controls

1 Demographic
- a) Name
  - i. First (text field)
  - ii. Last (text field)
  - iii. Password (password field)
- b) Address
  - i. Street (text field)
  - ii. City (text field)
  - iii. State (text field)
  - iv. Phone (text field)
  - v. E-mail (text field)

4 Identify the Form

Now that you have jotted down some important notes and guidelines, add the form tag pair to your HTML page. The **<form>** tag alerts the browser to the fact that what follows is a form, and of course the **</form>** tag indicates the end of the form. Everything you type between these two tags is recognized as part of the form. The values of all the form elements are passed on to the *script* when the user submits the form.

```
<h3>Defining the Form</h3>
<!-- This form gathers information about
the site's visitors and their travel
preferences.-->
<form>
</form>
```

End

TASK 2

How to Specify a Form's Actions

A form's *actions* is where all the real...*uhmmm*...action is. Actions dictate what happens to the information after it's collected and submitted. An action usually references a script on your Web server. Scripts are miniature software programs that perform an action, or series of actions, based on the input provided through the form. Suppose that you build a form to sell computer software. Scripts log the order, calculate the sales tax, register the buyer, and remove the purchased item from the inventory list. Unfortunately, I still haven't found a script that'll clean my kitchen floor!

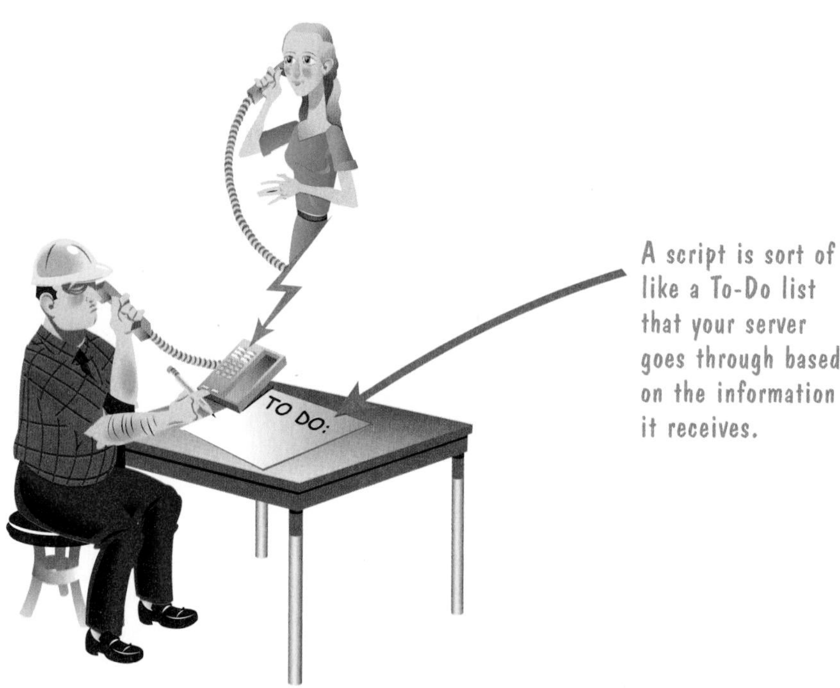

TO DO:
A script is sort of like a To-Do list that your server goes through based on the information it receives.

But I Can't Write Scripts!

A technology called Common Gateway Interface (CGI) drives most of the scripts behind Web forms. In basic terms, CGI is a standard for communications between the Web server and the script. The script is written in a programming language, most often a language called Perl. Another common scripting technology is Microsoft's Active Server Pages (ASP), most often written in a language called VBScript. Now that your heart has sunk because you don't know these or any other programming languages, fear not. Many people out in Webland love to write Perl scripts. And some of them will give their work away free! A great place to start is Matt's Script Archive at **`http://worldwidemart.com/scripts/`**.

1 Acquire the Script

There are several ways to get the scripts you'll need to process your forms. You can use Matt's Script Archive, mentioned in the hint in this task, to find scripts you can use. You also might be able to find an ISP that provides scripts for its customers (maybe free, but maybe not—don't forget to ask). Finally, you or a friend can develop custom scripts if you (or the friend) know something about programming.

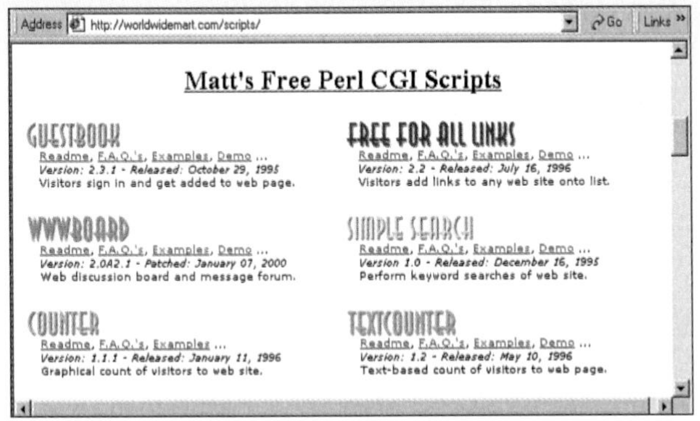

2 Add the Action Attribute

In the last step of the previous task, you used the **<form>** tag to identify the form to the browser. Now you need to specify the action of the form. Use the **action** attribute, and specify it with the pathname to the desired script. Type **<form action="value">** where **"value"** is the pathname to the script that resides on your Web server.

```
<form action="value">
</form>
```

3 Specify the Action

Specifying the action is much like creating a remote hyperlink. Because the script resides on a machine other than the machine on which the visitor is browsing, you must give the browser exact instructions on where to find the script. For instance, if the script is called **myscript.cgi** and the URL for the server on which that script will reside (after you publish the form) is **myserver.com**, type **<form action="http://www.myserver.com/myscript.cgi">**.

```
<p>The pathname that points to the location
of the CGI or ASP script on your Web server
is added as the value to the action
attribute.</p>
<form action=
  "http://www.myserver.com/myscript.cgi">
</form>
```

4 Specify the Form Method

The two **method** types you can use to process the form are **post** and **get**. In simplistic terms, the **post** method sends the form data to the server as a block of information that the script analyzes and uses. The **get** method tacks the form data onto the end of the URL specified in the **action** attribute. You'll almost always use the **post** method. To specify the form method, type **<form action="http://www.myserver.com/myscript.cgi" method="post">**.

```
<form action=
  "http://www.myserver.com/myscript.cgi"
   method="post">
</form>
```

End

TASK 3 How to Lay Out a Form

As mentioned at the beginning of this part, you can enter virtually any HTML element within a form. This flexibility allows you to give your forms an effective user interface. For example, a blank text entry field means nothing to your visitor. But everyone knows what to do with a text entry field with the label *First Name* next to it. This task discusses some of the issues related to designing a clear, concise form. Such a form is more likely to be filled out properly than a sloppy, unidentified hodge-podge of form elements laid out in a haphazard manner.

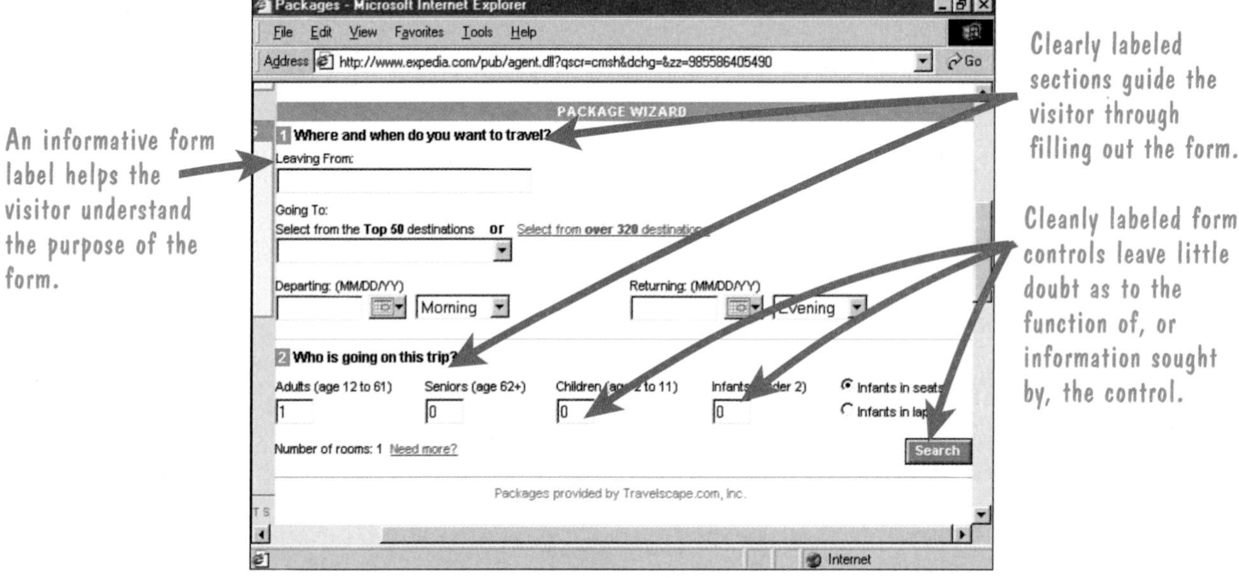

Don't Slight the User Interface

It's easy to get caught up in the decisions of whether to use a radio button here or a text field there and to forget about how usable the form is for visitors who've never seen it before. Solid graphic design decisions are just as important in a form as they are anywhere else. If you make the form uninviting, confusing, and intimidating, people are not going to take the time to fill it out unless they are extremely interested in the subject matter. And even then, the chances for improperly completed forms introduced by sloppy design are high. True, you're not building a $500 software program here. You're not creating the most complicated interface ever, and you probably don't have three months to devote to interface design. But give the interface a reasonable amount of thought. Your visitors will be glad you did, and ultimately that means you'll be glad you did.

1 Develop Related Sections

As always in graphic design, it makes sense to put related elements together in an easily distinguishable section so that those elements can be easily identified. If you planned your form as discussed in Task 1, "How to Begin a Form," it'll be easy to know what elements to put together in a section. The challenging part is to find a way to distinguish graphically between one section and the next.

```
<hr width="25%" align="left" />
<form action="http://www.myserver.com/
  myscript.cgi" method="post">
<h3>Customer Information Form</h3>
<p>To help us better understand and serve
your vacation desires, please take a few
minutes to fill out this form. There are
five sections, and each has only a few short
questions.</p>
</form>
```

2 Clearly Identify Each Section

After the form controls are grouped into logical sections, you can make it even easier on the reader by clearly identifying each section. Because you can include any HTML within your form, you can label each section with text or create some sort of graphic that you can incorporate with the **<src>** tag. Don't be afraid to use a table to help organize your sections!

```
<form action="http://www.myserver.com/
  myscript.cgi" method="post">
<h3>Customer Information Form</h3>
<p>To help us better understand and serve
your vacation desires, please take a few
minutes to fill out this form.</p>
<h5>Demographics</h5>
<h5>Travel History</h5>
<h5>Travel Mode</h5>
<h5>Comments</h5>
<h5>Navigation</h5>
</form>
```

3 Clearly Label Each Control

It sounds obvious, but make sure that the reader knows what information you're trying to acquire. Few of the form controls we'll discuss in the following tasks supply a way to identify themselves, so you need another tactic. Use regular text to label the controls in your form. Avoid becoming too "wordy" because too much information can sometimes be as useless as too little. Strive for short, descriptive labels.

```
<form action="http://www.myserver.com/
  myscript.cgi" method="post">
<h3>Customer Information Form</h3>
<h5>Demographics</h5>
<p><font size="1">First name: </font></p>
</form>
```

4 Provide Help

Include brief paragraphs, sentences, or even phrases designed to help the reader fill out the form. Again, don't get too wordy, or you'll almost surely lose the reader's interest. Remember that if your readers have to work too hard, you'll lose them. Web surfers don't have to bother trying to decipher your information because there's always another Web site to visit. In your own interest, make it easy on them!

```
<form action="http://www.myserver.com/
  myscript.cgi" method="post">
<h3>Customer Information Form</h3>
<h5>Demographics</h5>
<p>Please supply important
contact information.</p>
<p><font size="1">First name: </font></p>
</form>
```

End

TASK 4

How to Gather Short Information

One of the first things you'll probably want to do with your form is to gather demographic information from your Web site's visitors. Data such as name, address, phone number, customer number, registration numbers, and so on requires your visitors to type information into a field that your CGI scripts will read. This task shows you how to supply a text field on your form into which your visitors can type this important information.

You can make a field read-only so that the user cannot change the value contained in that field.

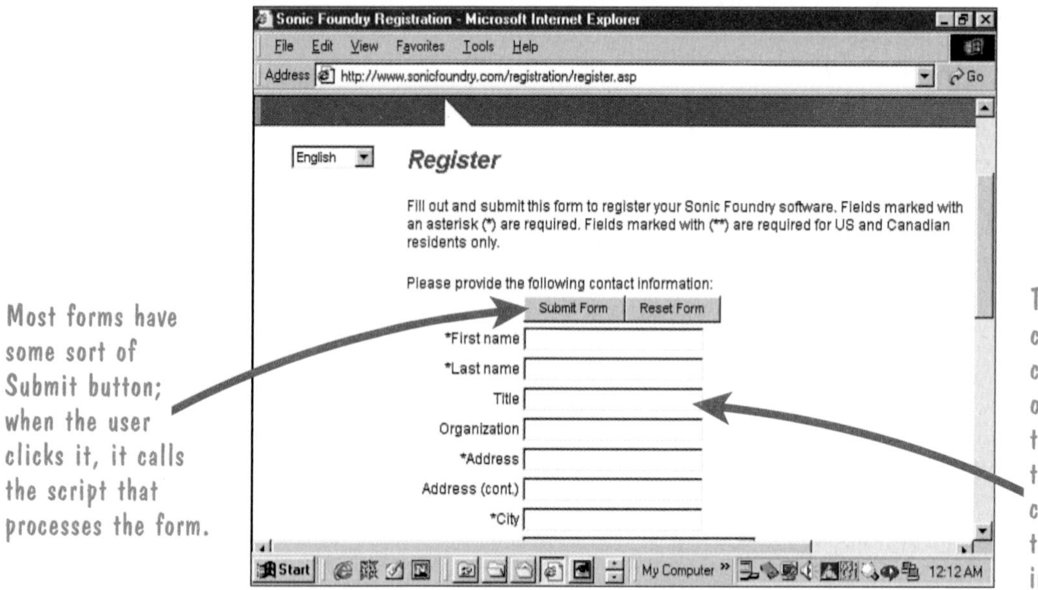

Most forms have some sort of Submit button; when the user clicks it, it calls the script that processes the form.

The text field control is used to collect little pieces of textual information; if you want the reader's lengthy comments, use the text area control instead.

A Little Cooperation, Please

In most cases, you'll have to check with your Internet Service Provider (ISP) to see whether it allows its customers to run CGI or ASP scripts on the servers. Not all ISPs do. Some don't want to deal with the hassles; others are concerned about security issues. Still, you can find many ISPs that are not only willing to let you run scripts on their servers, but also have scripts that they make available for you to use.

Creating Pages "On the Fly"

One of the great things about forms and scripts is that your script can analyze the information supplied in a form, create a custom HTML page based on that information, and then serve it back to the visitor. This is one way that the time can appear in a text field, as mentioned in Step 4 of this task.

1 Identify the Form Control

As you do with most form controls, you use the **<input>** tag to identify the text control. Add the **type="text"** attribute to create a text field. For example, type **<input type="text" />**. Notice that the **<input>** tag does not have a corresponding closing tag, so you must close it the same way you close the line break tag: with a trailing slash within the angle brackets of the tag.

```
<form action="http://www.myserver.com/
  myscript.cgi" method="post">
<h3>Customer Information Form</h3>
<h5>Demographics</h5>
<p>Please supply important contact
information.</p>
<p><font size="1">First name:
<input type="text" /></font></p>
</form>
```

2 Specify a Name and Default Value

When a form containing a text field is submitted (which happens when the visitor clicks a button that sends the information to the server), the script refers to the field's name and reads the value. Name the text control with the **name** attribute and specify a default value (which shows up in the field until the user changes it) with the **value** attribute. If you don't include a default value, the field is blank when the user first views it. Type **<input type="text" name="firstname" value="First Name" />**.

```
<p><font size="1">First name: <input
  type="text" name="firstname"
  value="First Name" /></font></p>
</form>
```

3 Specify a Size and Maximum Length

To specify the length of the text field in characters, use the **size** attribute. Use the **maxlength** attribute to define the maximum entry length in characters that the field will accept from the user. If you don't specify a maximum length, the user will be able to enter more information than actually fits in the visible field. Type **<input type="text" name="firstname" value="First Name" size="15" maxlength="15" />**.

```
<p><font size="1">First name: <input
  type="text" name="firstname"
  value="First Name" size="15"
  maxlength="15" /></font></p>
</form>
```

4 Make the Field Read-Only

Perhaps, depending on the user's answers to previous questions, certain information may be filled in by the script and appear in an unchangeable field. To make a text field unchangeable by the reader, use the **readonly** attribute. Type **<input type="text" name="visittime" value="9:46 AM" readonly />**. In this example, the script has determined the time and filled in the **value** attribute. The reader can't change that value. Notice that the **readonly** attribute does not require you to specify a value.

```
<form action="http://www.myserver.com/
  myscript.cgi" method="post">
<h3>Customer Information Form</h3>
<font size="1">Time of Visit: <input
  type="text" name="visittime"
  value="9:46 AM" readonly /></font></p>
</form>
```

End

TASK 5 How to Gather a User's Password

Creating a field designed for gathering a user's password is very similar to creating a text field, as you learned in the last task. A password field is used to gather a short piece of information. The difference between the password control and the text field control is that when the user types something into the password field, the browser shows asterisks (****) instead of the actual letters or numbers typed. This standard technique prevents anyone from seeing what the user is typing so that they cannot "steal" the password.

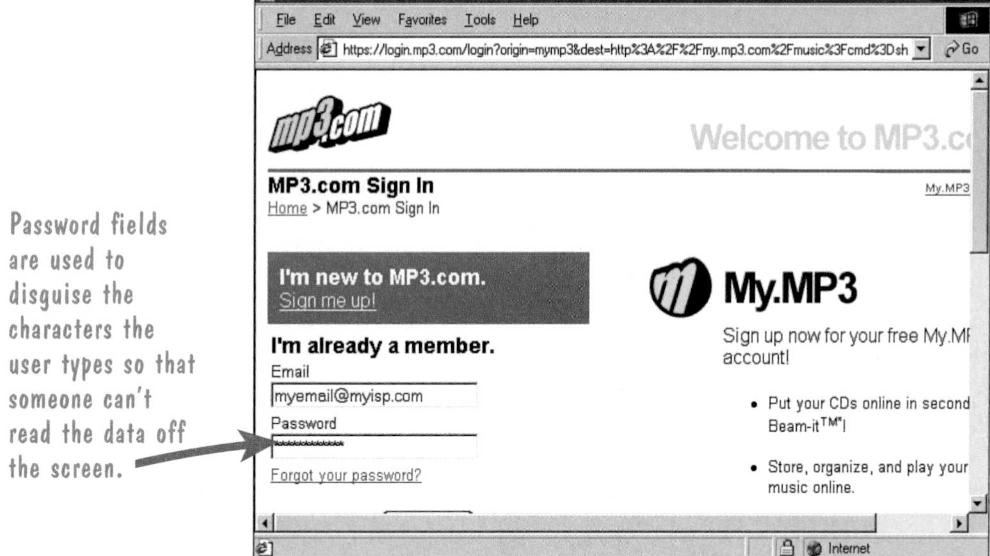

Password fields are used to disguise the characters the user types so that someone can't read the data off the screen.

A False Sense of Security

The password field makes it impossible for someone to read over your shoulder and see what your password is. It provides no real security against someone who might be snooping around electronically trying to read what's coming to and from your Web site. The information typed into a password field is in no way encrypted, coded, or otherwise protected by the field. You cannot rely solely on the password field to transmit sensitive information. There are ways you can try to protect this type of information, but the password field is not one of them. If you need a truly secure technology, check with your ISP to see what safeguards it can offer.

Note that you can use the password field control to collect any kind of information, not just a password. You can use the control to collect a serial number, Social Security number, or virtually anything else.

1 Create a Label for the Field

Use regular HTML text to create a label for the password field. Remember to make the label descriptive, yet succinct.

```
<form action="http://www.myserver.com/
  myscript.cgi" method="post">
<h3>Customer Information Form</h3>
<p><font size="1">Please enter your
  password: </font></p>
</form>
```

2 Define the Password Control

Use the **<input>** tag and the **type** attribute to identify the field as a password field. You don't have to specify a default value for this control (although you can). Type **<input type="password" />**.

```
<form action="http://www.myserver.com/
  myscript.cgi" method="post">
<h3>Customer Information Form</h3>
<p><font size="1">Please enter your
  password: <input type="password" />
</font></p>
</form>
```

3 Specify the Size of the Field

Use the **size** attribute to specify the length in characters of the password field. Type **<input type="password" size="10" />** to make a field that displays 10 characters. Even though the field has been set up to show only 10 characters, the user can type more than 10 characters unless you specify the **maxlength** attribute in the next step.

```
<form action="http://www.myserver.com/
myscript.cgi" method="post">
<h3>Customer Information Form</h3>
<p><font size="1">Please enter your
  password:
  <input type="password" size="10" />
</font></p>
</form>
```

4 Specify a Maximum Length

To make sure that the user doesn't enter too many characters into the password field, include the **maxlength** attribute. Type **<input type="password" size="10" maxlength="10"** to make the display size of the field and the maximum number of characters that can be entered into the field the same. Even though these examples for the password and text fields show that the **maxlength** and **size** attributes match, there is no requirement that this must be so. The attributes are independent of one another.

```
<form action="http://www.myserver.com/
  myscript.cgi" method="post">
<h3>Customer Information Form</h3>
<p><font size="1">Please enter your
password: <input type="password"
size="10" maxlength="10" /></font></p>
</form>
```

End

TASK 6 How to Provide a Large Text Entry Area

Sometimes you want to gather information that calls for a much larger text area than what the text field control provides. For instance, you might want to invite your reader to give you feedback about the usefulness and user-friendliness of your site. (Not a bad idea!) You're looking for more than a word or two, so you need to provide a large area into which users can type as much as they please. This task shows you how to create a text area.

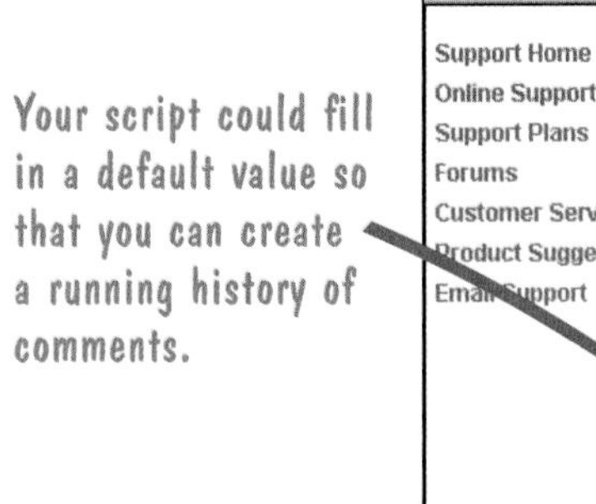

Your script could fill in a default value so that you can create a running history of comments.

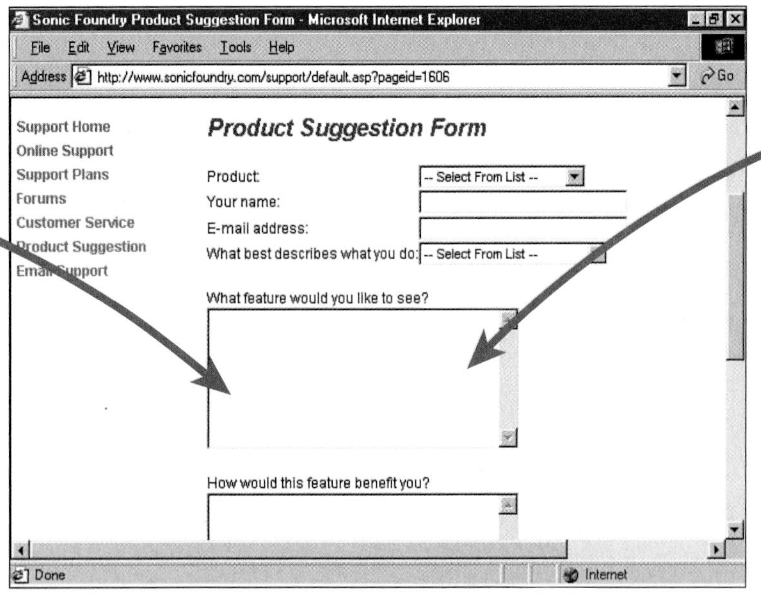

Use the text area control to provide a large area on your form into which the user can type lengthy textual responses.

Let's Talk

You can use a large text area for a number of different things. One thing you might do with it is to host a simple chat area on your site. You might use it for a section in which users can enter reviews about books, records, movies, vacations, and so on. With the proper CGI or ASP script behind the scenes, you could save each review to a database and then write the reviews back out to the page so that anyone considering buying the item could check out a string of reviews or a few user comments in a chat. You can see how valuable forms are, and how it's worth the effort to learn not only how to create HTML forms, but how to incorporate the feedback into a script that can then manipulate the data, act on it, and feed it back to your Web pages.

1 Identify the Text Area

The text area control does not use the **<input>** tag. Instead, it uses the **<textarea>** tag pair to define the area. Type **<textarea>...</textarea>** to create the control. You might want to include some sort of heading or introduction to the text area to help guide your readers as they fill in the form.

```
<form action="http://www.myserver.com/
  myscript.cgi" method="post">
<h3>Customer Information Form</h3>
<p><font size="1">
We value your comments!
Please let us know what you
are thinking:<br />
</font>
<textarea>
</textarea></p>
</form>
```

2 Give the Text Area a Name

As usual, the script that will process your form uses a name to refer to the text area. The script can then access the data that the user has entered into the text area. To give the text area a name, use the familiar **name** attribute: Type **<textarea name="feedback">...</textarea>**.

```
<form action="http://www.myserver.com/
myscript.cgi" method="post">
<h3>Customer Information Form</h3>
<p><font size="1">
We value your comments! Please
let us know what you are thinking:<br />
</font>
<textarea name="feedback">
</textarea></p>
</form>
```

3 Specify the Size of the Area

Use the **rows** and **columns** attributes to define the size of the area. The **rows** attribute defines the height of the area; it does not limit the amount of text the user can enter in it. If all the text that is entered does not fit in the area, scrollbars appear to allow the user to scroll through the entire text. To define the size of the area, type **<textarea name="feedback" rows="15" cols="55">...</textarea>**.

```
<form action="http://www.myserver.com/
  myscript.cgi" method="post">
<h3>Customer Information Form</h3>
<p><font size="1">
We value your comments! Please
let us know what you are thinking:<br />
</font>
<textarea name="feedback" rows="15"
cols="55">
</textarea></p>
</form>
```

4 Providing a Default Entry

You can provide a default entry for the text area. In fact, you can write a script that provides the default entry. Using this technique, you could include a running history of notes that various users have entered into the text areas (such as you've seen in a user group section of various sites). Assuming that you don't have a script that can do it for you, add the default entry yourself within the text area tag pair. Type **<textarea name="feedback" rows="15" cols="55">We're interested in your feedback! Add your comments here.</textarea>**.

```
<form action="http://www.myserver.com/
myscript.cgi" method="post">
<h3>Customer Information Form</h3>
<p><font size="1">
We value your comments! Please
let us know what you are thinking:</font>
<br /><textarea name="feedback" rows="15"
cols="55">We're interested in your feedback!
Add your comments here.
</textarea></p>
</form>
```

End

TASK 7 How to Create Checklists

When you want to allow your visitor to choose multiple items from a list, create a checklist. A *checklist* is a list of items, each of which is followed by (or preceded by) a check box. Users can read through the list and click the appropriate check boxes to indicate their choice of an item, or multiple items, in that list. This task shows you how to construct a list of related items and provide the reader the opportunity to choose one or more items from that list.

Checklists present options from which the user can select simply by clicking multiple check boxes.

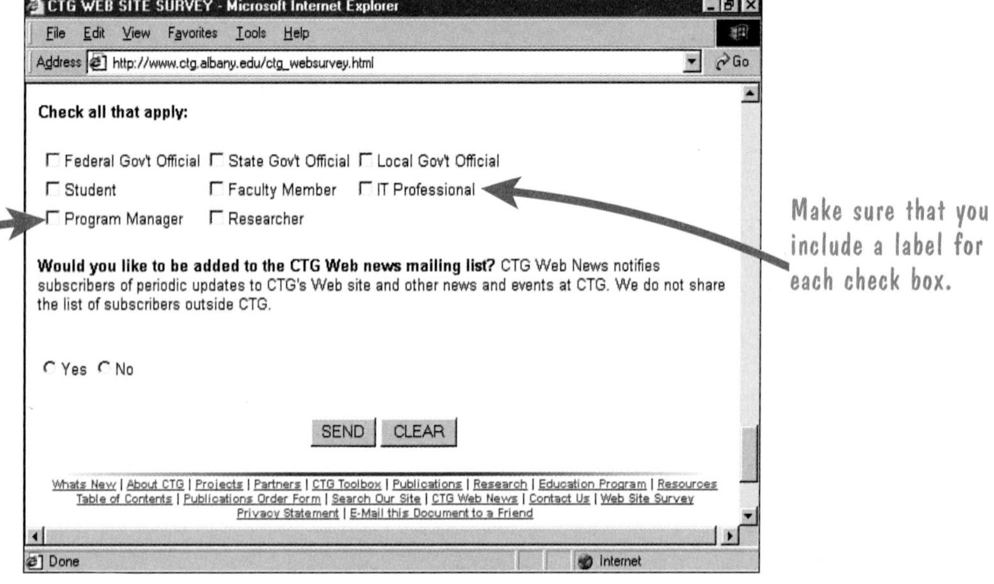

Make sure that you include a label for each check box.

The More, the Merrier

Check boxes are not exclusive, meaning that they allow your visitors to choose more than one item in the list. For example, you might create a checklist that asks the user to check all the vacation destinations for which they'd like to receive a brochure. There are many, many uses for check boxes. But don't rely too heavily on them. In fact, that's good advice for each of the form controls we're talking about in these tasks.

Check boxes are great, but they're not the right control for every situation. You need to become familiar with all the various form controls so that you can make more logical decisions regarding which one is right to use in this or that situation.

1 Plan Your List

It helps to get your thoughts together before you start coding. What is the nature of the list, and which type of list is more appropriate: a checklist or an exclusive list (discussed in the next task)? When you know what you want to include in the list, use HTML to create labels that will identify the check boxes.

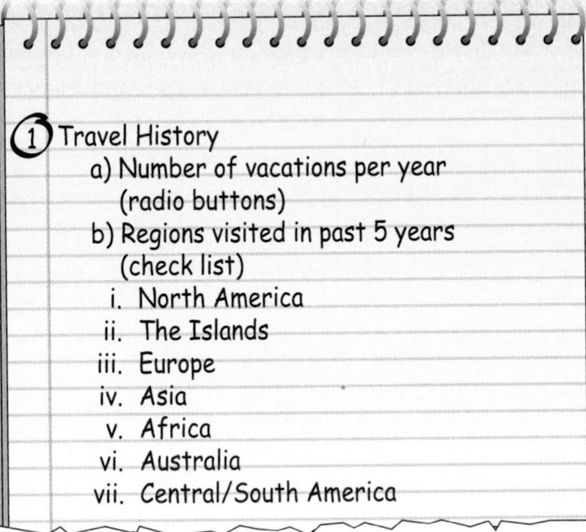

1 Travel History
a) Number of vacations per year
(radio buttons)
b) Regions visited in past 5 years
(check list)
i. North America
ii. The Islands
iii. Europe
iv. Asia
v. Africa
vi. Australia
vii. Central/South America

2 Define the Checklist

Add the **<input>** tag to your HTML code and use the **type** attribute to define each list item as a check box. Use the **checked** attribute to set the default state of the box to checked (the reader will see that box as pre-checked). For example, type **<input type="checkbox" checked />**. Notice that the **checked** attribute does not require a value.

```
<form action="http://www.myserver.com/
  myscript.cgi" method="post">
<h3>Customer Information Form</h3>
<p>Please check the names of all the regions
you've visited in the past 5 years:<br />
<font size="1"><input type="checkbox"
checked />North America</font></p>
</form>
```

3 Give the Check Box a Name

Use the **name** attribute to give the check box control a name. Type **<input type="checkbox" name= "interested" checked />**. If you want to group the check boxes, you can give all the check boxes in a list the same name; the script will then use each of the values of the check box controls to complete its operations. Check box values are discussed in the next step.

```
<form action="http://www.myserver.com/
  myscript.cgi" method="post">
<h3>Customer Information Form</h3>
<p>Please check the names of all the regions
you've visited in the past 5 years:<br />
<font size="1"><input type="checkbox"
name="interested" checked />
North America</font></p>
</form>
```

4 Give the Check Box a Value

Use the **value** attribute to assign a distinct value to a check box. Type **<input type="checkbox" name= "interested" value="northamerica" checked />**. The value is what the script will use when it processes your form; the user never sees this value.

```
<form action="http://www.myserver.com/
myscript.cgi" method="post">
<h3>Customer Information Form</h3>
<p>Please check the names of all the regions
you've visited in the past 5 years:<br />
<font size="1"><input type="checkbox"
name="interested" value="northamerica"
checked />North America</font></p>
</form>
```

End

TASK 8 How to Force an Exclusive Choice

Another type of list you will undoubtedly make use of on your HTML forms is a list made up of radio buttons. Use radio buttons when you are creating a list that requires an exclusive choice. For instance, to ask the readers to specify their gender, use radio buttons so that they can choose only one answer. This task shows you how to make a list using radio buttons.

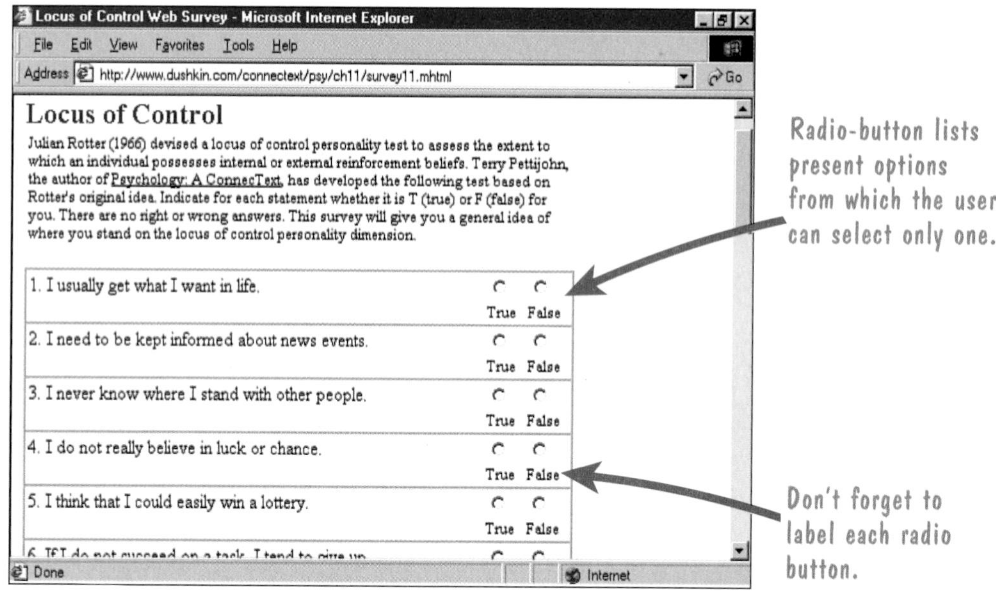

Make Up Your Mind

Lists created with radio buttons are more rigid than those created with check boxes. Radio-button lists force you to choose just one option. Let's say that you choose option number one and then decide that you want to choose option number five. Nothing stops you from clicking the radio button for option five, but when you do, not only do you select that option, you also deselect the option you chose first. Radio-button lists are great when you want to zero in on specific information about your readers. However, they can also be harder for your reader to select from because they require a little more thought and decision-making. For obvious and simple options, radio buttons pose no problem. But as the decision gets more complicated, it can be very difficult for your readers to make a choice. Be careful not to scare them away with too many tough choices!

1 Organize Your List

Decide whether a list with radio buttons is appropriate for the content you are trying to collect. Carefully craft the questions you ask so that an exclusive choice makes sense. After you determine the choices you want to present in the list, add your text labels to identify them.

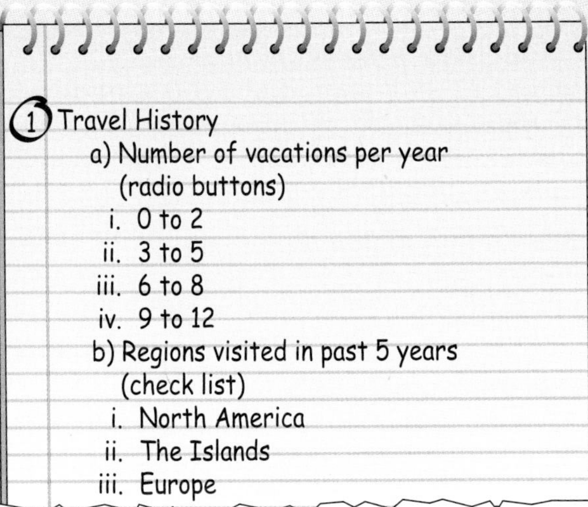

1 Travel History
a) Number of vacations per year (radio buttons)
i. 0 to 2
ii. 3 to 5
iii. 6 to 8
iv. 9 to 12
b) Regions visited in past 5 years (check list)
i. North America
ii. The Islands
iii. Europe

2 Create the Radio Button

Use the **<input>** tag and the **type** attribute to define the button as a radio button. Use the **checked** attribute to make one of the options the default. Type **<input type="radio" checked />**.

```
<form action="http://www.myserver.com/
myscript.cgi" method="post">
<h3>Customer Information Form</h3>
<p>Please click the button that represents
your preferred payment method:<br />
<font size="1">
<input type="radio" checked />
Check</font></p>
</form>
```

3 Name the Button

All buttons in an exclusive group must have the same name. This is how the browser knows that only one in the group can be chosen at a time. Use the **name** attribute to name the button. Type **<input type="radio" name="paymentmethod" checked/>**.

```
<form action="http://www.myserver.com/
myscript.cgi" method="post">
<h3>Customer Information Form</h3>
<p>Please click the button that represents
 your preferred payment method:<br />
<font size="1"><input type="radio"
 name="paymentmethod" checked />Check</font>
</p>
</form>
```

4 Give the Button a Value

Each button has a unique value that is passed along to the script as the value of the **"name"** variable in the script. Use the **value** attribute to give each button a value. Type **<input type="radio" name="paymentmethod" value="check" checked />**.

```
<form action="http://www.myserver.com/
myscript.cgi" method="post">
<h3>Customer Information Form</h3>
<p>Please click the button that represents
your preferred payment method:<br />
<font size="1"><input type="radio"
name="paymentmethod"
value="check" checked />
Check</font></p>
</form>
```

End

TASK 9

How to Create a Drop-down List

Another way to allow your users to make a choice from a list of items is to build a *drop-down list*. If you've spent any time at all with computers, you've seen this type of list (also sometimes called a *pull-down menu*). You can create a list from which the user can choose only one option—or multiple options. You can create a version of this type of list that shows multiple items in a window. You also can create a scrollable list if you want. This task shows you how to make each type of drop-down list.

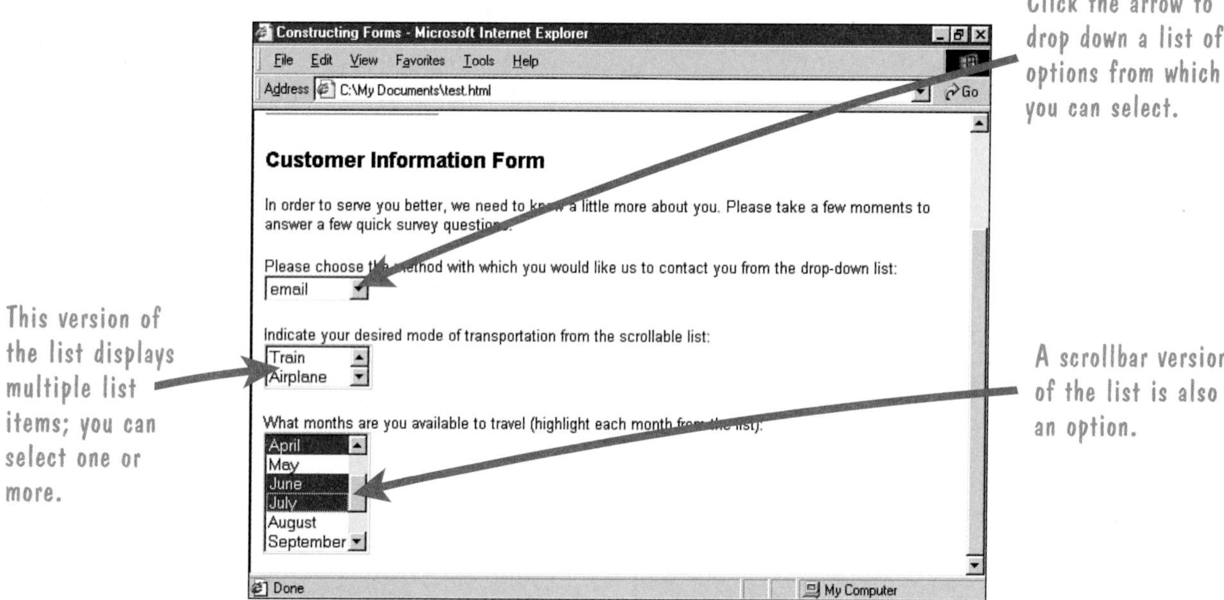

In Your Face, or Save Some Space?

The last two tasks discussed creating lists from which users could make choices of related items. This task shows you a third method. Why all these different techniques for accomplishing basically the same function? We've already talked about the differences between radio buttons (good for exclusive choices) and check boxes (good for multiple choices). Both of these types of lists take up a good deal of space. You have to devote space not only to the question, but also to every possible option. A drop-down list, on the other hand, is very compact. You must devote space to just the question itself because the options "pop up" only when you expand the list. Radio buttons and checklists, however, have the advantage of all options being visible at once. Drop-down lists require a little extra work before you can see the entire contents of the list. Yes, it's another of those infamous tradeoffs in life. You'll decide which list is best for which situation.

1 Define the List

The drop-down list is another form control that does not use the **<input>** tag. Instead, you use the **<select>** tag pair to define the list. Make sure that you give the list a name using the **name** attribute. After you use text to introduce or label the drop-down list, type **<select name="travelchoice">...</select>**.

```
<form action="http://www.myserver.com/
myscript.cgi" method="post">
<h3>Customer Information Form</h3>
<p><font size="1">Please choose the method
by which you would like us to contact you
from the drop-down list:
<select name="contactchoice">
</select></font></p>
</form>
```

2 Define the Options

Use the **<option>** tag pair to define the various list options. Between the opening and closing tags of the **<option>** tag pair, type the item that you want to appear in the drop-down list. Add the **value** attribute to the **<option>** tag to define what is sent to the script for this list when the form is submitted. If you don't specify the **value** attribute, the list item itself is passed to the script. Type **<select name="travelchoice"> <option>email</option></select>**.

```
<form action="http://www.myserver.com/
myscript.cgi" method="post">
<h3>Customer Information Form</h3>
<p><font size="1">Please choose the method
by which you would like us to contact you
from the drop-down list:
<select name="contactchoice">
<option>email</option>
<option>Telephone</option>
<option>Snail Mail</option>
</select></font></p>
</form>
```

3 Create a Scrollable List

Use the **size** attribute of the **<select>** tag to define the size of the window. The number you specify for the **size** attribute determines how many list items will be visible. If there are more items than the number that are visible, the list will have a scrollbar instead of a drop-down arrow. To create a list with a scrollbar, type **<select name="travelchoice" size="2"><option>email</option></select>**.

```
<form action="http://www.myserver.com/
myscript.cgi" method="post">
<h3>Customer Information Form</h3>
<p><font size="1">Please choose the method
by which you would like us to contact you
from the scroll list:
<select name="contactchoice" size="2">
<option>email</option>
<option>Telephone</option>
<option>Snail Mail</option>
</select></font></p></form>
```

4 Allow Multiple Choices

Use the **multiple** attribute of the **<select>** tag to allow the user to select multiple list items by holding down the **Shift** or **Ctrl** key in Windows (the ⌘ key on the Mac) while clicking items in the list. To allow multiple choices, type **<select name="contactchoice" multiple>...</select>**.

```
<form action="http://www.myserver.com/
myscript.cgi" method="post">
<select name="contactchoice"
size="2" multiple>
<option>email</option>
<option>Telephone</option>
<option>Mail</option>
</select>
</form>
```

End

TASK 10 How to Create Submit and Reset Buttons

After your visitors have filled out all the information on your HTML form, you must give them some way of sending that information to you (more accurately, to the scripts on your server). There are two default button types for use in forms. The first of these is the **Submit** button. This button transmits the contents of the form to the server script. The second button is the **Reset** button; it allows your visitor to set the entire form back to its default state, deleting all the answers and choices he or she has already made. This task shows how to add these buttons to your form.

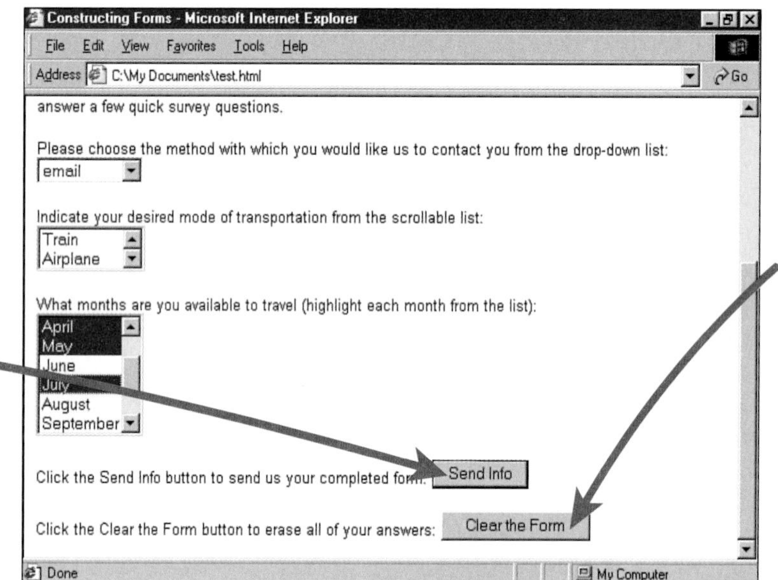

Click the Submit button (here named "Send Info") to send the information in the form to the server script, which will process the form data.

Click the Reset button (here called "Clear the Form") to clear the form and return all the options to their default values.

Help, I'm Trapped!

Web surfers are a suspicious bunch. We tend to get so wrapped up in our development technologies that we forget how young the World Wide Web really is. Many people have had only a year or two to get used to it. Some people coming to your site might be surfing for the very first time. It's a lot to ask these people to supply personal information and then click a button that magically sends that information to who knows where. The Reset button can help allay their fears a little. When they see a Reset button, they know that they can "get out" of the form any time they get cold feet. You'll never gain total trust—some people fear that the second they type their name into a form field, they've handed over the deed to the ranch whether they submit the form or not. It'll take a lot more than a Reset button to gain the trust of this group! But a Reset button helps. Never leave one out of your Web forms.

1 Add the Submit Button

Use the `<input>` tag with the **type** attribute set to **"submit"** to create a Submit button. The button contains the label **Submit Query**. This special button has one function: to send the information that the form has collected to the script specified in the form's **action** attribute. To add a Submit button, type `<input type="submit" />`.

```
<form action="http://www.myserver.com/
myscript.cgi" method="post">
<h3>Customer Information Form</h3>
<p><font size="1">Click the Submit Query
button to send us your completed form:
<input type="submit" /></font></p>
</form>
```

2 Specify the Submit Value

Use the **value** attribute to replace the label **"Submit Query"** with the value you enter. You can add more than one Submit button on your form; use the **value** attribute to give each a different name. To give your Submit button a different label, type `<input type="submit" value="Send Info" />`.

```
<form action="http://www.myserver.com/
myscript.cgi" method="post">
<h3>Customer Information Form</h3>
<p><font size="1">Click the Send Info
button to send us your completed form:
<input type="submit" value="Send Info" />
</font></p>
</form>
```

3 Add the Reset Button

Another special button is the Reset button. The sole function of this button is to reset the form back to its default state. Use the `<input>` tag with the **type** attribute set to **"reset"**. To add the Reset button, type `<input type="reset" />`.

```
<form action="http://www.myserver.com/
myscript.cgi" method="post">
<h3>Customer Information Form</h3>
<p><font size="1">Click the Send Info
button to send us your completed form:
<input type="submit" value="Send Info" />
</font></p>
<p>Click the Reset button to erase all your
answers:
<input type="reset" /></p>
</form>
```

4 Specify the Reset Value

Just as you can change the default label of the Submit button, you can change the label of the Reset button from **"Reset"** to whatever you choose. Use the **value** attribute to specify a different label. To add a Reset button, type `<input type="reset" value="Clear the Form" />`.

```
<form action="http://www.myserver.com/
myscript.cgi" method="post">
<h3>Customer Information Form</h3>
<p><font size="1">Click the Send Info
button to send us your completed form:
<input type="submit" value="Send Info" />
</font></p>
<p>Click the Clear the Form button to erase
all your answers:
<input type="reset"
value="Clear the Form" />
</p>
</form>
```

End

TASK 11

How to Create Custom Buttons

Often, you'll want buttons on your form that do things other than submit and reset the form. For instance, you might have a button that references a script that performs a tax calculation. There are countless uses for buttons. This task shows you how to make two types of custom button. First, you learn to create a Submit button for which you provide custom artwork. Then you learn to create a button that looks just like the Submit or Reset button you added in the last task, but that is somewhat limited. This kind of button is sometimes called a *push button.*

You can create a special button that, when clicked, calls a script that is embedded within your HTML document and performs a particular action.

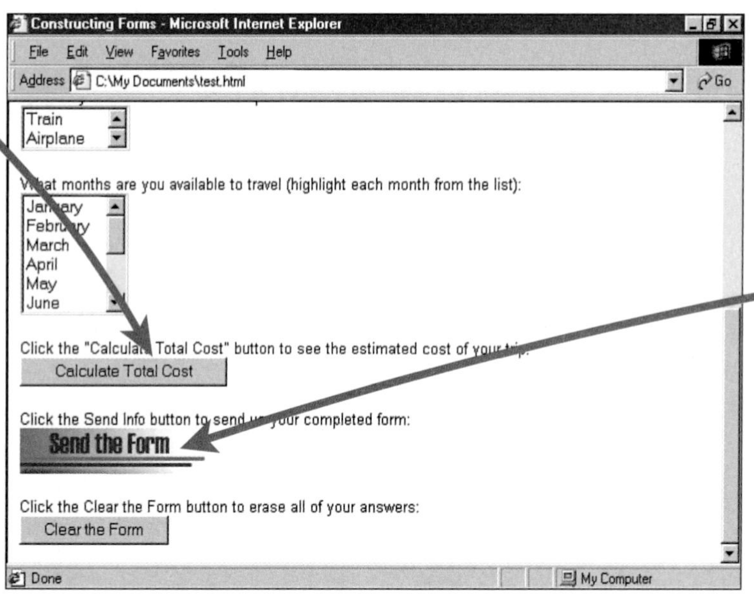

You can jazz up the looks of your Submit button by providing a custom graphic for the button face.

Server-side, Client-side

All the form elements you've learned about so far send information to the CGI or ASP scripts you specify on your Web server (these scripts are called *server-side scripts*). Push buttons activate scripts that you build right into your Web pages (called *client-side scripts*). These terms get us into an area of Web development that is well beyond the scope of this book—Dynamic HTML and client-side scripting technologies such as JavaScript. Because server-side scripts run on your Web server, you can interface those scripts with a database that helps you use the information you gather. You'll often hear the term *database-driven Web site* to define this type of setup. Because client-side scripts don't communicate with your server, you can't gather information for your database using them. But they do allow you to accomplish many other things, and they are a powerful component of the Web. Advanced sites often use both server- and client-side scripting technologies.

1 Create a Button Image

Use image-editing software to design your buttons. Remember all the tips you've accumulated for keeping the file size of your images low (refer back to Part 5, "Implementing Web Graphics"). It's best not to get too fancy with your button designs. You want them to look good, but more than that, you want them to be recognized as buttons.

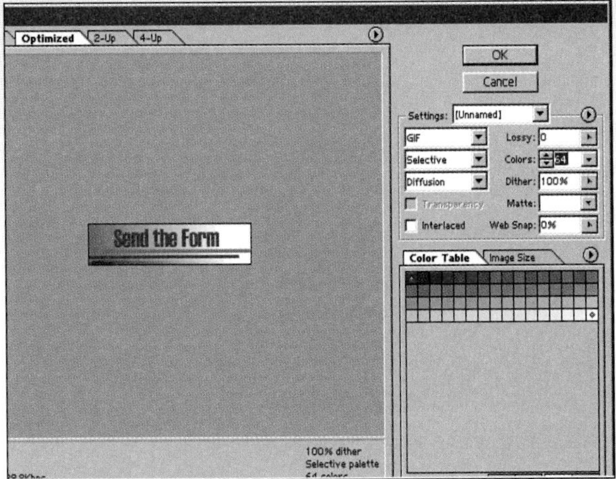

2 Add the Graphical Button

Use the **<input>** tag with the **type** attribute set to **"image"** to add a Submit button using your custom graphic. Then specify the pathname of the image using the **src** attribute. When the user clicks the button, not only is the form submitted, but the x and y coordinates of the click point are also passed to the script. If you name the button with the **name** attribute, the name is passed with the coordinates tacked onto it. Type **<input type="image" src="../../images/sendtheform.gif />**.

```
<form action="http://www.myserver.com/
myscript.cgi" method="post">
<h3>Customer Information Form</h3>
<p><font size="1">Click the Send Info
button to send us your completed form:
<input type="image" src="../../images/
  sendtheform.gif" /></p>
</form>
```

3 Create a Push Button

Use the **<input>** tag and set the **type** attribute to **"button"**. Give the button a name and a value. Whatever you type in to the **value** attribute shows up as the label for the button. To add a push button to your form, type **<input type="button" name="calculate" value="Total" />**.

```
<p>Click the Total button
to calculate a total:
<input type="button" name="calculate"
value="Total" /></p>
<p><font size="1">Click the Send Info button
to send us your completed form:
<input type="image"
  src="../../images/sendtheform.gif" /></p>
<p>Click the Clear the Form button to erase
all your answers:
<input type="reset" value="Clear the Form" />
</font></p>
</form>
```

4 Write a Client-side Script

The basics of client-side scripting are fairly easy. Visit a Web development site such as **www.webmonkey.com** and search for **"javascript"** for resources that will get you started. When you're done with the script, specify it by name with the **onclick** attribute of the push button you're creating. To associate the script with the button, type **<input type="button" name="calculate" value="Total" onclick="calculatetotal()" />**.

```
<p>Click the Total button to calculate:
<input type="button" name="calculate"
value="Total" onclick="calculatetotal()" />
</p>
<p><font size="1">Click the Send Info button
to send the completed form:
<input type="image"
src="../../images/sendtheform.gif" /></p>
</font></form>
```

End

TASK 12

How to Use Form Data

Now that you know how to build a form, let's talk a little more about how you can use the data you gather. I've mentioned repeatedly throughout the tasks in this part that you will typically have a CGI or ASP script running on the Web server that will accept and work with the information gathered by your form. This task reviews these ideas and introduces an alternative to server-side scripts for dealing with HTML form data.

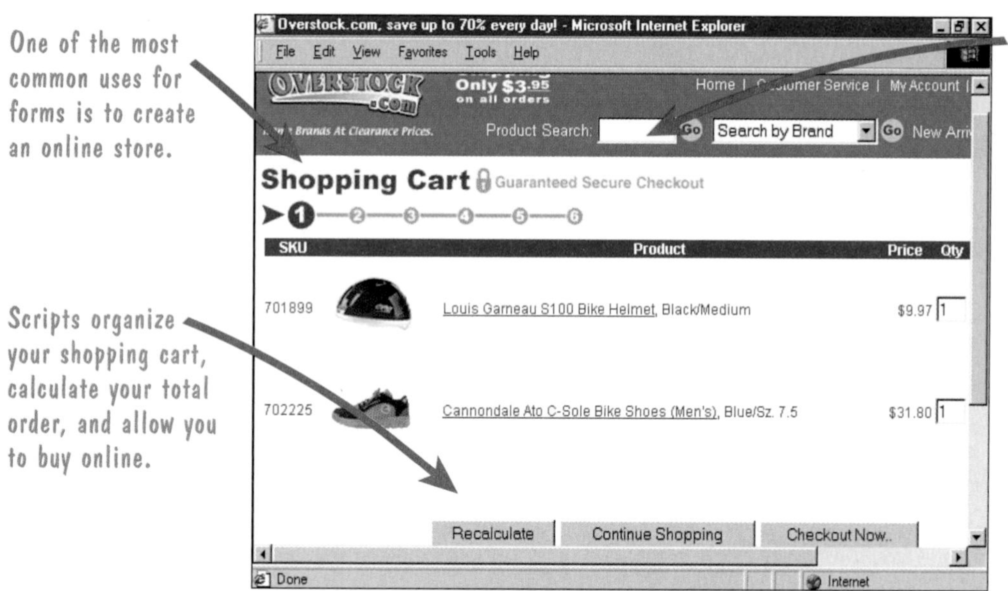

Another of the most common uses for forms is to make your site searchable.

You Need Information

You'll need a lot of information about the server-side scripts you're going to use to process the information you gather with your forms. You have many details to work out. For one thing, you need to know the exact pathname to the script on the server so that you can properly add that pathname to the **action** attribute of the **<form>** tag. In the preceding tasks, you've given each form control a name. Unfortunately, you can't just choose those names arbitrarily. They are used as variables in the script, so it is critical for them to match the script exactly. Depending on who's writing your scripts, the task of gathering the proper information can range from a snap to a nightmare, but you don't have a choice. If you are going to use scripts, you are going to have to get the details you need to implement them properly. Fortunately, most good sources for scripts will give you all the information you need.

1 Use a Server-side Script

Server-side scripts can perform tasks ranging from simple to complex. Scripts can make calculations and return the results to the user. They can write HTML pages that allow you to customize the Web experience depending on the information your user supplies. Matt's Script Archive supplies extensive information (including frequently asked questions) about each script and its uses as well as thorough instructions on how to implement the script into your Web site.

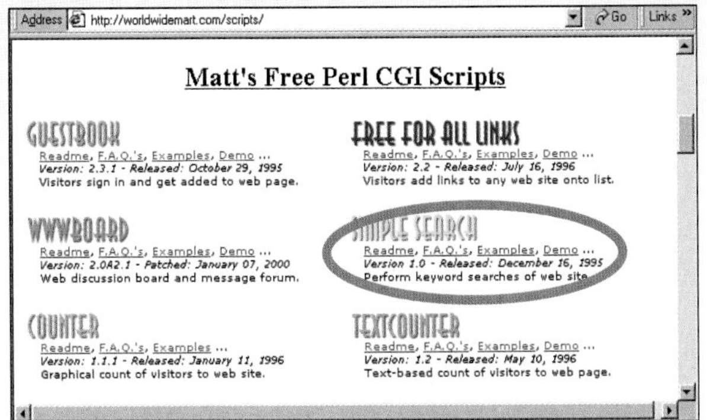

2 Use a Database

Database-driven Web sites are very powerful because they allow you to change and update your Web pages automatically. For example, when a user submits a form, your script can compare the information supplied in the form with information stored in your database; the script can then serve back to the user customized pages. Integrating a database to your pages through HTML forms and CGI or ASP scripts allows you to set up a complete online store, customized customer support, instantly updated news items, and much more.

3 Provide Responses

After the script processes the form information, it can generate an HTML page that gives the reader instant feedback. This feedback is a valuable public relations tool for someone who's taken the time to fill out and submit your form. It shows the person that you've received the information and provides assurance that the appropriate action is being taken.

4 Use a `mailto:` Action

If you can't use a CGI or ASP script, the least you can do is mail the results of the form to a specific e-mail address. To e-mail the results of the form, type **`<form method="post" action="mailto:myaddress@myisp.com">...</form>`**. This approach is a much less powerful way to use the information you collect, but it is better than not collecting the information at all. Unfortunately, some browsers (particularly older ones) don't support this technique.

```
<form action="mailto:myaddress@myisp.com"
 method="post">
      .
      .
      .
</form>
```

End

Task

PART 8

Understanding Frames

Frames. You either love 'em, or you hate 'em. Me? Well, I'll show you how they work anyway. But regardless of whether or not I've ever found a good reason to use frames, there might be times when frames work better than a regular HTML page. And lots of people love frames, so there must be something to them. To show my fair-minded side, the tasks in this part show you how to make frames for your HTML pages. *Frames* are multiple HTML pages that are grouped together to act as a single page (called a *frameset*). You can change each frame independently of the others on the page.

Why would you want to put multiple pages on a single page? Well, they can make it easier for your visitors to navigate your site. For example, you can designate one of the frames to act as your navigation section. You can then code the navigation frame so that it causes the HTML document in one of the other frames to change. This way, you can keep presenting new content in one frame without getting your visitor lost because the other frames are always there to orient the visitor.

However, frames have their limitations. First, there are still many browsers in use that don't support frames. If you use frames and want to make sure that these people can see your site, you'll have to develop a no-frames alternative to your site as well. Frames also take up valuable screen real estate because you will typically have at least one frame that never goes away unless you leave the site. In fairness, some new browsers enable visitors to maximize a single frame so that they can have better control over framed pages, but older browsers don't offer these options.

Framed pages also limit the effectiveness of adding a page to your favorites or bookmarks list: No matter where you navigate to on a framed site, the URL the browser sees always remains that of the frameset document (that is, the "main page" of the framed page). If you add such a page to your favorites list, you're really saving the frameset as a favorite; returning to the page in the future using the bookmark might not take you just where you thought it would.

Finally, frames are generally not very friendly to sight-impaired visitors. Debate rages over whether or not it's possible to create framed pages in compliance with the Americans with Disabilities Act (ADA).

By now, the defenders of frames are up in arms. The question of whether frames are useful has spawned a heated argument, to say the least. In the tasks in this part, I will show you how to make frames and will try to help you decide for yourself whether frames are right for you.

TASK 1

How to Decide Whether to Use Frames

Give some thought to why you might want to use frames on your Web site. Pretty much all the arguments you see for why you should use frames relate to the sophisticated navigational tools you can build using frames. You must decide whether those techniques and the navigational aids they provide are worth the downside of frames. I don't think they are, but I hope that I can help you work toward a decision of your own. This task will help.

Keep an Open Mind

My biggest gripe against frames is that they don't play nicely with my **Favorites/Bookmark** lists or search engines. Not only that, but I just can't stand the thought of someone forcing me to look at something and not giving me a way to make it go away. Still, there really *are* a lot of people who feel that frames are great, and they have good arguments to support their opinions. I urge you to keep an open mind. You might have an application that justifies using frames in some way that I've never run across. You can find many Web sites that present the arguments for and against frames. Start by going to **`http://altavista.com`** and running a search on **`+html +frames`**. You can find all kinds of opinions there!

1 Design Pages Without Frames

It might sound silly, but the first step in determining whether you should use frames is to see how the page works without frames. If you use frames (and you do it right), you'll have to create a no-frames option anyway for people who can't view frames, so the work you do in this step won't be wasted. Build a navigation system that works without frames.

```
<tr>
<td rowspan="2" width="175">
<a href="frame4.html">News</a><br />
<a href="frame5.html">Products</a><br />
<a href="frame6.html">Archives</a><br />
<a href="frame7.html">About Us</a><br />
<a href="frame8.html">Contact Us</a><br />
<a href="frame9.html">Employment</a></td>
<td>Here is the Header</td>
</tr>
```

2 Evaluate the No-Frames Version

After you've completed the no-frames version of the page, evaluate its effectiveness. You might find that there is no reason to go ahead with the framed version. If navigation is not a problem, chances are good that you can stop right here. On the other hand, if your page has some sort of special navigational needs that can't be served by a standard HTML page, the page might be a good candidate for frames.

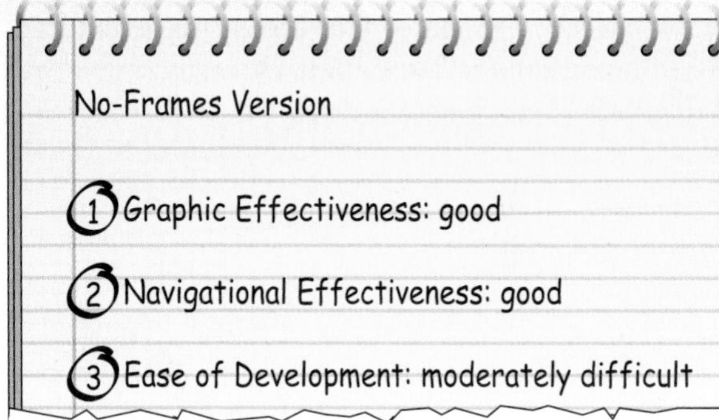

No-Frames Version
1 Graphic Effectiveness: good
2 Navigational Effectiveness: good
3 Ease of Development: moderately difficult

3 Weigh the Pros

Frames allow you to create navigational structures beyond what straight HTML can provide. They also make it possible to show two HTML documents simultaneously, which might come in handy. Frames ensure that certain content (such as a banner ad) stays visible as long as your site is open because you can put that content in a frame that never goes away.

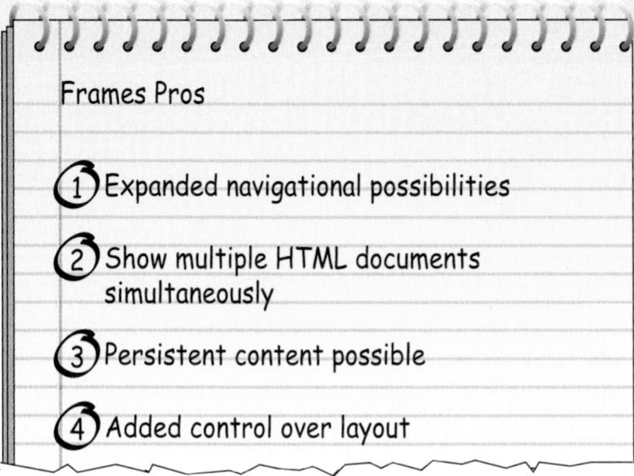

Frames Pros
1 Expanded navigational possibilities
2 Show multiple HTML documents simultaneously
3 Persistent content possible
4 Added control over layout

4 Weigh the Cons

Building a framed site requires at least twice the work of building a regular site because you should include a no-frames alternative to every page. Frames do not work well with bookmarks (favorites) or search engines because the URL is always the URL of the frameset, not of the important content in a specific frame.

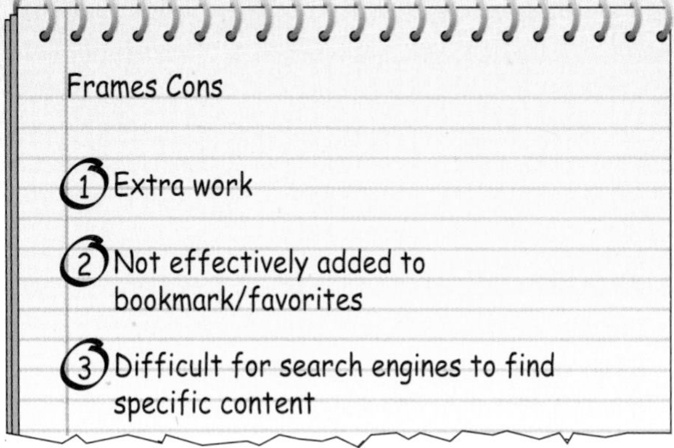

Frames Cons
1 Extra work
2 Not effectively added to bookmark/favorites
3 Difficult for search engines to find specific content

End

TASK 2

How to Structure a Frameset

After you've decided to create a framed Web site, the first step is to create the frameset that will hold it all together. Remember that one of the advantages of a framed page is that it allows you to present several HTML documents as a single page. The frameset is the structure that holds all the individual documents together. You'll want to give some real thought to your frameset because it dictates the layout of your page. This task walks you through the framing of your framed pages.

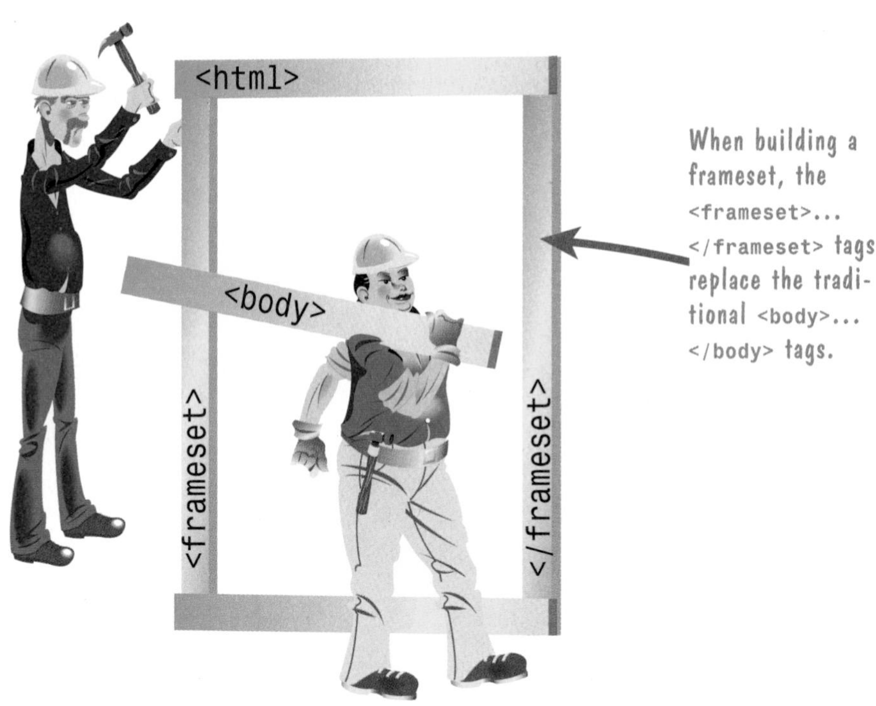

When building a frameset, the <frameset>... </frameset> tags replace the traditional <body>... </body> tags.

I Wouldn't Call It a Lie, Exactly...

Way back in Part 1, Task 5, "How to Structure Every HTML Page," I presented some basics. You've been building your pages based on your faith in my declaration that every page must have an **<html>** tag pair, a head tag pair, a title tag pair, and a body tag pair. Well, I didn't tell you the entire story back then. There is an exception to the rules I presented there, and that exception is the frameset you build in this task.

When you build a frameset, you'll see that here is an instance of building an **<html>** tag that does not contain the body tag pair. In a frameset, the frameset tag pair takes the place of the body tag pair. In addition, you should not type anything in the frameset page other than the tags you'll use to define the frameset, which you'll learn more about over the next couple of tasks.

1 Plan Your Layout

You use frames to define the structural layout of your pages. In much the same way as it was important to plan your tables back in Part 6, it can be a very big help to plan your frameset layout and draw it out on paper. The drawing becomes especially important when your framed layout gets more complicated. Make a note of the height of your rows and the width of your columns either in percentages or pixels.

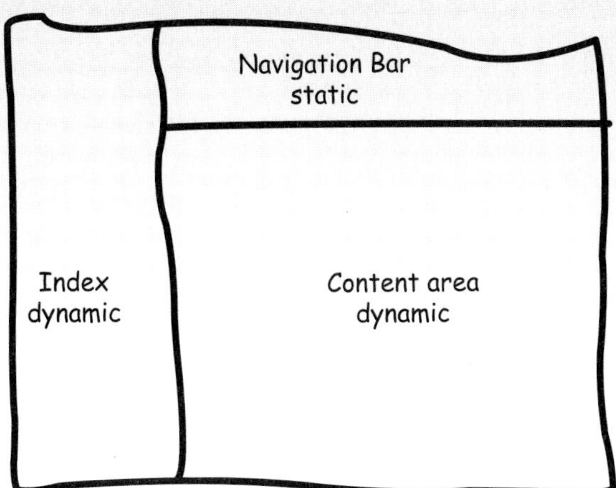

2 Start with the Basic HTML Structure

The basic structure of the frameset page is very similar to that of the regular HTML page structure. If you've developed a page template that you use when starting new pages, call up that template now. Such a template would have the normal HTML, head, title, and body structure you've used on all the pages you've created so far.

```
<html>
<head>
<title>My First Frameset</title>
</head>
<body>
</body>
</html>
```

3 Add the Frameset Tag Pair

The frameset tag pair replaces the body tag pair you're used to seeing in the page structure. On your template, make that switch now. Now add the noframes tag pair. Within these tags, you'll code the HTML that will show in browsers that don't support frames. (For space reasons, I'll omit the noframes tag pair after this example. That doesn't mean you can forget about it!)

```
<html>
<head>
<title> My First Frameset </title>
</head>
<frameset>
<noframes>
</noframes>
</frameset>
</html>
```

4 Specify Rows and Columns

Refer back to the drawing you made in Step 1. Use the **row** and **cols** attributes in the **<frameset>** tag to specify these values along with the depth of the rows and the width of the columns in percentage of the frameset or pixels. For the last measurement, you can use an asterisk (*****), which tells the browser to use the remaining available space for that row or column.

```
<html>
<head>
<title> My First Frameset </title>
</head>
<frameset rows="250, *"
cols="175, 35%, *">
</frameset>
</html>
```

End

TASK 3 How to Add Individual Frames

Now that you've defined the frameset, you can add the individual frames that make up the page. These frames are nothing more than standard HTML documents. In the code example in Step 4 of the preceding task, we specified a frameset that contains two rows and three columns. Therefore, we'll need a total of six HTML pages to fill the slots we've created in the frameset. This task shows you how to assemble your framed pages using your frameset as a guide.

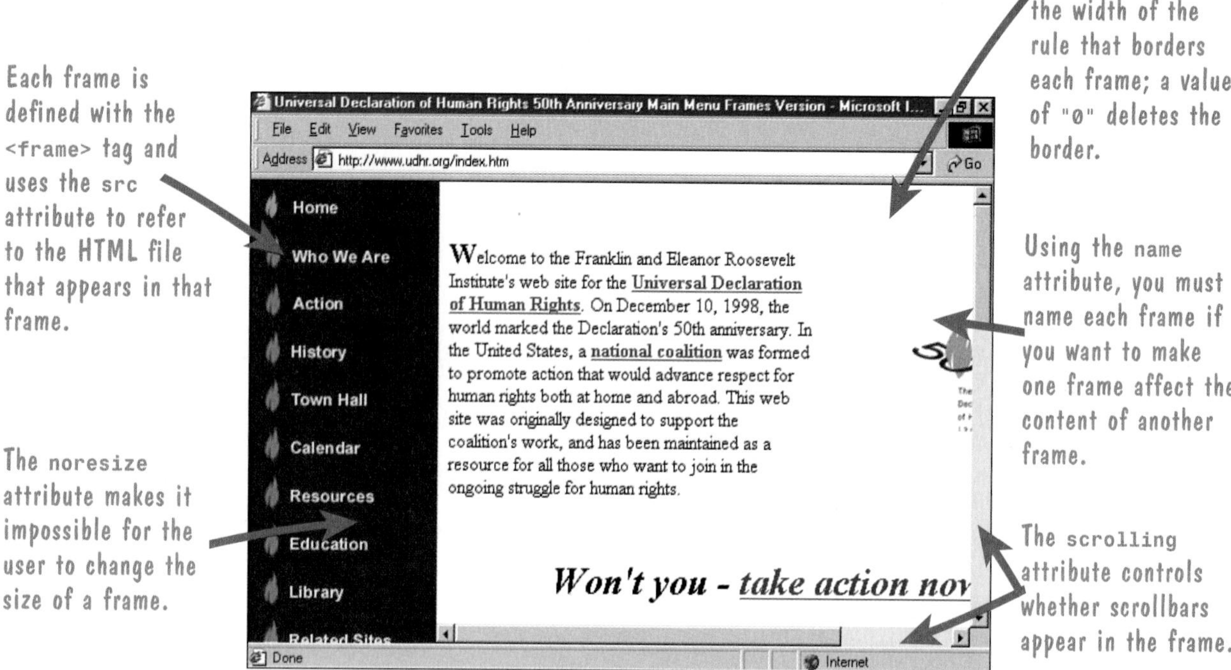

Six Pages to Create One?

Actually, you need seven pages to fill the frameset defined in the last task: You need one page to act as the frameset. You created that page in the last task. Then you need another page for every frame. Because our example has two rows and three columns, you'll need six pages to fill all those slots. That's a total of seven HTML documents. Don't worry though; it's not really seven times the work of a non-framed page. First of all, remember that some frames will be static, so you'll have to create those frames only once. Only the dynamic frames require you to create new content. Also, although this example uses two rows and three columns, it is quite unusual to have that many frames in one frameset. In fact, the frameset I've constructed here works for demonstration purposes, but is not very realistic at all. Task 4, "How to Create More Complex Frame Arrangements," shows you how to make a more typical (and more complicated) frameset.

1 Create the HTML Documents

Each frame you've specified in your frameset will hold a different HTML document. Therefore, you must create a new document for each frame—six in our sample frameset. Actually, there's no reason that two frames couldn't hold the same HTML document if the situation called for it. Create the six documents that will fill the sample frameset. They don't have to be fancy, just different. For illustration purposes, give each document a different-colored background.

```
<html>
<head>
<title>Frameset Test, Page Two</title>
</head>
<body bgcolor="#96c0f30">
<h2>Here is the Header Frame</h2>
</body>
</html>
```

2 Specify the Frames

Use the **<frame>** tag to specify the frames of the frameset. You specify frames one row at a time, starting at the top row, moving from left to right, and then moving down to the next row, and so on. Use the **src** attribute to assign one of the HTML documents you created in Step 1 to each frame. Define the **src** attribute with the pathname of the file you want to assign to that frame.

```
<html>
<head>
<title> My First Frameset </title>
</head>
<frameset rows="250, *"
cols="175, 35%, *">
<frame src="frame1.html" />
<frame src="frame2.html" />
<frame src="frame3.html" />
<frame src="frame4.html" />
<frame src="frame5.html" />
<frame src="frame6.html" />
</frameset>
</html>
```

3 Specify Frame Attributes

The **<frame>** tag has several useful attributes. Use **frameborder="0"** to delete the default border between frames. Use **noresize** to make sure that the user can't drag the border of a frame to change its size. Use **scrolling="auto"** to include scrollbars when the content is longer than the frame (this is the default), **scrolling="no"** to disable scrollbars (content that is too long for the frame will not be readable), and **scrolling="yes"** (scrollbars are on regardless of whether they're needed).

```
<html>
<head>
<title> My First Frameset </title>
</head>
<frameset rows="250, *" cols="175, 35%, *">
<frame src="frame1.html"
noresize frameborder="0" scrolling="yes" />
</frameset>
</html>
```

4 Name the Frame

One additional attribute of the **<frame>** tag deserves special mention. Use the **name** attribute to give each frame a name. This name will be used in Tasks 5 and 6 when we talk about coding one frame to affect another. The only way you can change the document in a frame to a different one is to refer to the frame by the name you give it here. Make the names easy to remember...and to type!

```
<html>
<head>
<title> My First Frameset </title>
</head>
<frameset rows="250, *" cols="175, 35%, *">
<frame name="navbar" src="frame1.html"
noresize frameborder="0" scrolling="yes" />
</frameset>
</html>
```

End

TASK 4 How to Create More Complex Frame Arrangements

In Task 2, you learned how to structure a frameset. The example given is a very basic arrangement: It has two rows, and each row has three columns. But what if you want a layout with two rows, one of which has one column, and the other with three columns? Layouts like these are much more common. For example, a navigation frame might be alone in the top row, whereas the row beneath it might contain two or three columns. Such arrangements require a little more effort, and things do get a little more complicated. This task shows you how to construct somewhat more complex frame arrangements.

Keep It Simple

Although you certainly can create very complex frame structures and pages with frame after frame after frame, think twice before getting too carried away with frames. An overly complex frame structure can be difficult to work with, and maintaining your site can be very time-consuming. Besides that, if the reason you're using frames is to make it easier for your visitors to navigate through your site, the last thing you want to do is to present them with some complicated hodge-podge of frames that they have to figure out before they get anything out of your site. Keep your structure simple. Three or four frames should really be enough if your page is well designed. Take a critical look at your layout and ask yourself whether every frame is necessary. Doing so now will make your job easier, and will probably make your visitors' surfing experience more enjoyable.

1 Consult Your Sketch

Look at the sketch you made in Task 2 and determine the number of rows and columns you're going to need. For this example, assume that you want a page with three frames. The first is a column on the left edge of the page that stretches from the top of the browser window to the bottom. The second column is split into two rows.

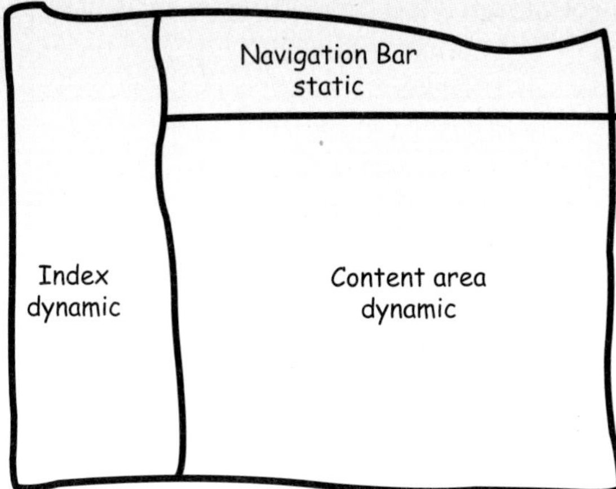

2 Create a Frameset to Define the Rows

In a complex layout, you'll have to deal with things in pieces. In this case, we'll take the second column (which has two rows) first. Create a frameset that defines the two rows in column 2. Use the same techniques you learned in Task 2 to define these rows. If you view this frameset in your browser, you will see a page with two frames (one above the other) that stretch the entire width of the browser window.

```
<html>
<head>
<title>A More Complex Layout</title>
</head>
<frameset rows="20%, *">
<frame src="frame2.html" noresize />
<frame src="frame3.html" noresize />
</frameset>
</html>
```

3 Define Another Frameset

To create two columns, each of which contains a different number of rows (as does this example), create a new frameset that encompasses the frameset you built in Step 2. Type **<frameset cols="175, *">** just before the **<frameset rows="20%, *">** tag. Type the closing **</frameset>** tag just after the closing tag for the frameset that defines the rows. You now have one frameset (defining the rows) nested within another (defining the columns).

```
<html>
<head>
<title>A More Complex Layout</title>
</head>
<frameset cols="175, *">
<frameset rows="20%, *">
<frame src="frame2.html" noresize />
<frame src="frame3.html" noresize />
</frameset>
</frameset>
</html>
```

4 Add the Missing Column

The columns frameset calls for two columns. The rows frameset (which is nested within the columns frameset) acts as one column. Add the second column by referencing an HTML document in the normal way. Add **<frame src="frame1.html" noresize scrolling="yes">** between the two **<frameset>** tags. This makes the first column frame hold the document **"frame1.html"**; the second column holds the rows frameset that consists of two rows (**"frame2.html"** and **"frame3.html"**).

```
<frameset cols="175, *">
<frame src="frame1.html" noresize
scrolling="yes">
<frameset rows="20%, *">
<frame src="frame2.html" noresize />
<frame src="frame3.html" noresize />
</frameset>
</frameset>
```

End

TASK 5

How to Make One Frame Affect Another

You can make one frame on your page react when the user clicks a link in a different frame. This is the whole idea behind using frames for enhanced navigational tools. In this situation, frames allow you to build a list of links that appear in the navigational frame; click a link and have the page that link points to open in your content frame (leaving the original navigational frame unchanged). This is the way frames are typically used; if you decide to create a framed site, you will use this technique over and again.

A Couple of Old Friends

To accomplish the technique of clicking a link in one frame to affect the content in a different frame, we'll call on a few familiar tools. Recall that you used the **name** attribute to identify form controls in Part 7, "Building Forms." You'll use that attribute again here as a critical part of navigating between frames. You also learned about the **target** attribute back in Part 4, Task 3, "How to Link to a Page on a Different Web Site," when we explored creating remote hyperlinks. You'll learn about another use for the **target** tag here. And of course, you'll need the anchor tag that you also learned about in Part 4 to create the link. That means that you already know most of what you need to know to make a link in one frame affect the content in another frame. Basically, you create a link in one frame and use the name of another frame as the target of that link. Instead of opening the HTML document in a new browser window (as we did in Part 4), you open the document in a different frame.

1 Give Your Frames a Name

Use the **name** attribute to give each frame a name. This attribute is critical if you are going to open a new page in that frame when you click a hyperlink in another frame. Type **<frame src="frame1.html" name="frame1" />**. Give a name to all the frames in your frameset.

```
<html>
<head>
<title>Interaction Between Frames</title>
</head>
<frameset cols="175, *">
<frame src="frame1.html" name="frame1">
<frameset rows="20%, *">
<frame src="frame2.html" name="frame2" />
<frame src="frame3.html" name="frame3" />
</frameset>
</frameset>
</html>
```

2 Create a Hyperlink in Frame 1

Suppose that frame 1 is our navigation bar. It will hold the hyperlinks. In the **frame1.html** document, create a hyperlink.

```
<html>
<head>
<title>Frameset Test, Page One</title>
</head>
<body bgcolor="#ff0000">
<h2>Here is Frame 1</h2>
<p>Here is a link to page
  <a>frame4.html</a>.</p>
</body>
</html>
```

3 Specify the Page You Want

Use **"frame4.html"** as the value for the **href** attribute in the anchor tag you created in the last step. So far, this hyperlink is no different from any other hyperlink you have ever created. If you click the link now, page **frame4.html** would open in the frame that holds the page with the link. This is not exactly the result you want.

```
<html>
<head>
<title>Frameset Test, Page One</title>
</head>
<body bgcolor="#ff0000">
<h2>Here is Frame 1</h2>
<p>Here is a link to page
<a href="frame4.html">
frame4.html</a>.</p>
</body>
</html>
```

4 Specify the Target Frame

To specify the target frame, add the **target** attribute to the anchor tag. For the value of the **target** attribute, specify the name you gave to frame 3 (**frame3**) in Step 1. Because you want the new page to open in frame 3, type **target="frame3"**. Now when you click the link on the page in frame 1, the page **frame4.html** opens in frame 3.

```
<html>
<head>
<title>Frameset Test, Page One</title>
</head>
<body bgcolor="#ff0000">
<h2>Here is Frame 1</h2>
<p>Here is a link to page
<a href="frame4.html"
target="frame3">
frame4.html</a>.
It will open into frame #3.</p>
</body>
</html>
```

End

TASK 6 How to Create a Persistent Navigation Bar

The argument I hear most often in defense of frames is that they allow you to create a better navigational scheme for your site. This is made possible by the techniques outlined in Task 5 for opening an HTML document in one frame when you click a link in a different frame. You can see that the frame holding the links would act as a good navigation bar, especially because you can make that frame persistent, so that no matter where on your site the visitor goes, the navigation bar is always there.

The navigation bar is a common reason to use frames: Click a link here, browse to other areas in the site, and always have the navigational panel as a guide to the site.

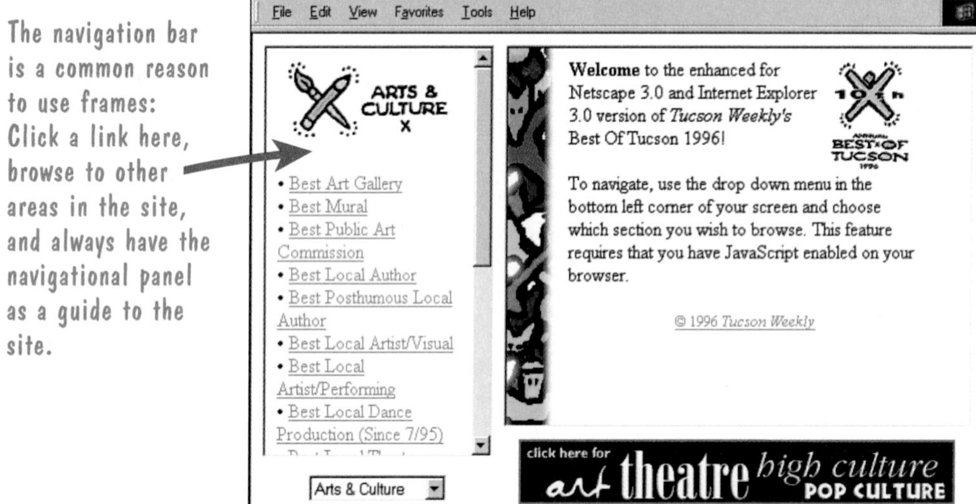

If Not with Frames, Then How?

As I've mentioned, one of the strong points of frames is their capability to create sophisticated navigational tools. What's the alternative to frames? There are a couple of ways to create a "persistent" navigation bar without frames. First, you could use graphics that appear in the same spot on every page of your site. Remember that after the graphic is downloaded on the first page, it loads faster on subsequent pages and can therefore serve well as a persistent navigation tool. Another idea is to use a page as a *template* for all new pages. This template would have your navigation links in it, and you would replace only the content of the page, leaving the table cell holding the navigation links the same for each page.

Although I think these are viable alternatives, if what you've seen of frames excites you, I urge you to look more deeply into using them. If frames help you make a better Web site, use them!

1 Create the Frameset

Using the techniques you've learned so far in this part, create a frameset that defines the layout of your page. Don't forget to give a name to any frame that will eventually be the target of a hyperlink.

```
<html>
<head>
<title>A More Complex Layout</title>
</head>
<frameset cols="175, *">
<frame src="frame1.html" noresize
scrolling="yes">
<frameset rows="20%, *">
<frame src="frame2.html" noresize />
<frame src="frame3.html"
name="frame3" />
</frameset>
</frameset>
</html>
```

2 Set a Default Target

Typically, most pages in a framed site consistently open in one frame. You can set the default target so that you don't have to specify it for each individual anchor tag. If you want, you can override the default target by including the **target** attribute in a particular anchor tag. To specify **frame3** as the default target for every link on the document that makes up the navigation frame, type **<base target="frame3" />** within the head tag pair on the page that contains the links.

```
<html>
<head>
<title>A More Complex Layout</title>
<base target="frame3" />
</head>
<frameset cols="175, *">
    .
    .
    .
</frameset>
</html>
```

3 Create the Links

In the document that acts as the navigation frame, create the hyperlinks you need. Use either text or graphical links. All the links will open their respective documents in whatever frame you specified in the **<base>** tag in Step 2. Use the **target** attribute of the **<a>** tag to override the default specified with the **<base>** tag.

```
<head>
<title>Frameset Test, Page One</title>
<base target="frame3" />
</head>
<body bgcolor="#ff0000">
<p><a href="frame4.html">News</a><br />
<a href="frame5.html">Products</a><br />
<a href="frame6.html">Archives</a><br />
<a href="frame7.html">About Us</a><br />
<a href="frame8.html">Contact Us</a><br />
<a href="frame9.html"
target="frame2">Employment</a></p>
</body>
```

4 Test Your Links

Open the frameset in your browser. If you coded everything correctly, frame 1 holds the list of links you created in Step 3. When you click any of these links, the new HTML documents open in frame 3 because that has been defined as the default target.

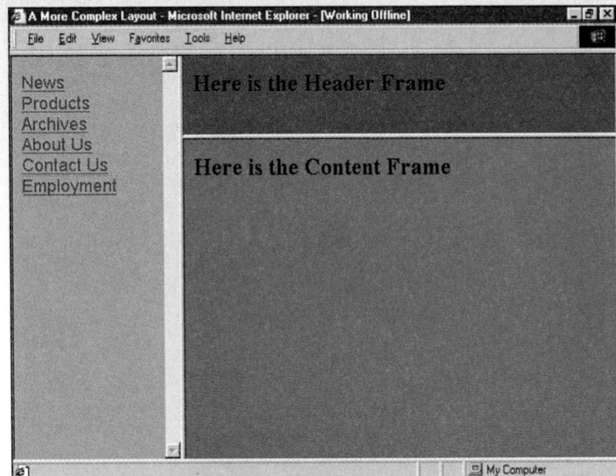

Task

PART 9

Working with the Layout of Your Web Pages

Okay, I admit it. This part doesn't have anything in particular to do with learning HTML. You won't learn anything more than perhaps the odd tag here or miscellaneous attribute there. But what this part will do is help you make HTML pages that are easy to read, that communicate effectively, and that just plain look nice.

One of the biggest mistakes I see HTML authors make (and I'm not just talking about beginners) is falling under the spell of an ill that I've already mentioned several times in earlier parts of this book. I'm referring, of course, to the dreaded "I'm gonna do this just because I know how to" affliction. You see signs of this everywhere you look on the Web.

Unless I miss my guess, the reason you are here right now is that you don't want to be like those authors who know the technology but haven't a clue how to use it to present a page that *invites* people to stop and read. Hopefully, you want to create Web pages that get a message that's important to you across to someone you think will be interested. If the message is important, and you let technology get in the way of it, you fail in your mission.

At the same time, I'm not trying to kid anyone...your visitors probably won't be all that impressed with your clever graphic design, either. What they will be impressed with is the *content* of your site. In my opinion, the perfect Web page is one that—although it uses the technology and solid graphic design—gets noticed for the quality of its content. Technology and graphic design have one purpose on my pages, and that is to help me effectively convey my message without getting in the way. I'm not a technical wizard; nor am I an amazing graphic designer. That's how I know that if the technology and design are noticed, they're probably getting in the way!

I'm not trying to squelch your enthusiasm, but if you keep one thing in the back of your mind while you design your pages, you'll be on the right track. You've heard it before: Just because you can, doesn't mean you should!

TASK 1 How to Make It Easy to View Your Pages

Reading your HTML pages shouldn't be a chore for Web surfers. It should be fun. Or it should be functional. Or why not both? There are a number of design tricks you can use to help the reader absorb the information on your page without undue effort. You make it easy to view your pages by making things as clear as possible. Text that stands out against the background. Images that relate logically to the text. Elements that are consistent from one paragraph to the next, and from one page to the next. These are the things that aid readability.

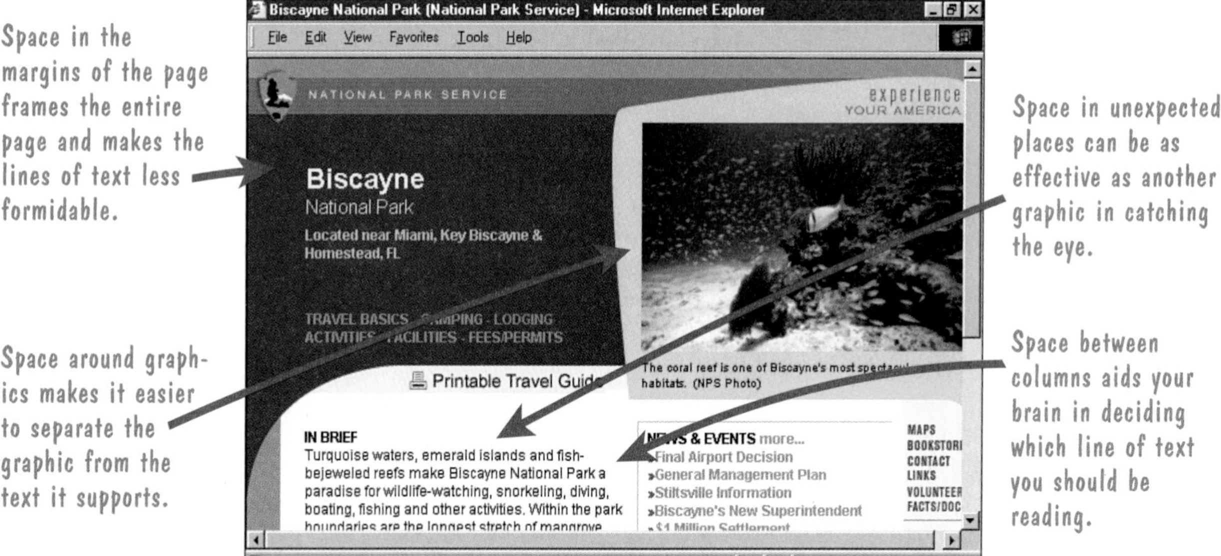

White Space Is Your Friend

White space is any spot on your page that doesn't contain text, images, or graphical elements. Whether or not the space is actually white, the point is that you can't cover every pixel of your page with graphics or text, or it would be a mess. Look at the individual letters of a word. These letters are made up of a combination of black ink and white paper. What would the letter *O* be without white space? Nothing but a black blob. The white spaces in each letter have as much to do with defining the letter as the black ink does. The same holds true for your pages. The space you give your reader to "breathe," the relief you provide for the reader's eyes, has as much to do with the readability of your pages as the words and graphics you put on them. A page without white space is as bad as a conversation without silence. You need the silence to understand the spoken words. You need the white space to understand the written words.

1 Put Space in the Margins

White space around the edges of your page helps frame the page and makes the text lines seem more manageable to the reader. Long lines of text are difficult to read, and lines that reach the edges of the browser window look longer than they are. Leave a fair amount of white space at all borders of your page. I usually leave up to 30 pixels of white space all around the page.

Pele's Faces

The big island of Hawaii offers an incredible range of unmatched diversity in its lush forests, humbling volcanoes, towering mountain peaks, breathtaking waterfalls, beautiful beaches, stark deserts, and of course miles and miles of ocean in every direction. In Hawaiian legend, this is the home of Pele, the great goddess of fire who is said to have created the Hawaiian Islands. Chased from island to island by the god of the sea, who destroyed her home on each island, Pele finally came to settle on the island of Hawaii, where she still lives today.

A week is not nearly enough to see everything the big island has to offer. Day trips from a base in Kona on the windward shore, or Hilo on the leeward shore, offer so many options that you'll find great difficulty in deciding how to spend your all-to-limited time.

Awe-inspiring sunrises greet you in the morning, as the early winds sweep in from mysterious ocean origins. Breath-taking sunsets tuck you in at night as the relentless crash of the ocean pounds the shore, the rhythm of the sea soothing your soul, and singing you to sleep.

No need to look further. Your paradise adventure starts here on the "Big Island". Hawaii!

Done My Computer

2 Put Space Around Graphics

Another important area in which you can add a bit of white space is around the edges of your images. It is much easier to read the text when there is a buffer between it and the image next to it. You can use the **hspace** and **vspace** attributes of the **<img>** tag you learned about in Part 5, "Implementing Web Graphics," to "push" the text away from the edges of the image. Try between 5 and 15 pixels for starters. I tend to settle at around 10 for my images.

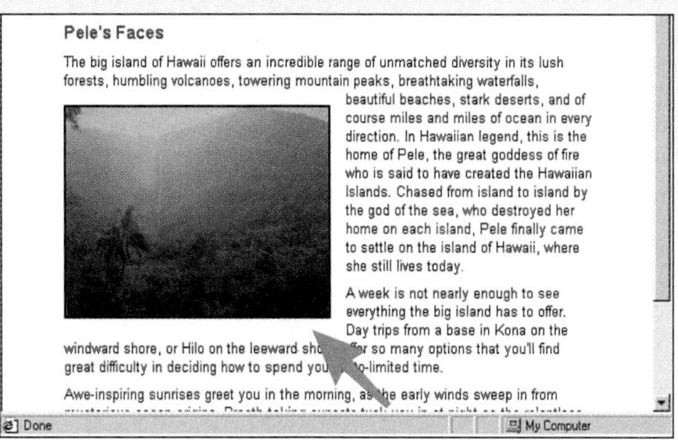

3 Put Space Between Columns

If you have more than one column of text on your page, make sure that you include adequate space between the columns. This space is the visual clue the eye needs to send the signal to the brain to stop reading one line and move to the next one down. If adequate space does not exist between columns, it takes the eye and brain longer to figure out which line of text you should currently be reading. Again, around 10 pixels of space is a good place to start.

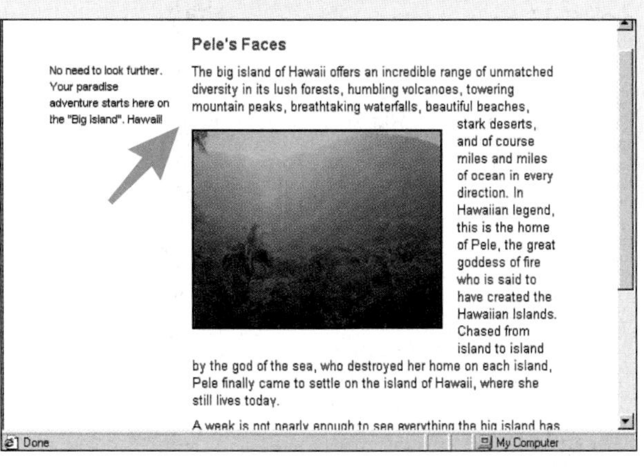

4 Put Space in Unexpected Places

Sometimes it works to put space where you wouldn't normally expect it. For instance, when you include an image with the text, it might be an interesting effect to have the text start about a quarter of the way down the side of the image, instead of even with the top. This approach leaves the top of the image "sticking up" above the text, with a large area of white space above the text. Experiment!

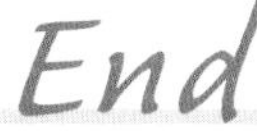

TASK 2 How to Choose a Background

Despite all my pleading and opinionated ranting, some of you are going to want a background on your pages. As usual, I do have a strong opinion about backgrounds, but I'm willing to concede that you might have a legitimate reason to use some sort of background image. Therefore, this task gives you a few guidelines for choosing a background.

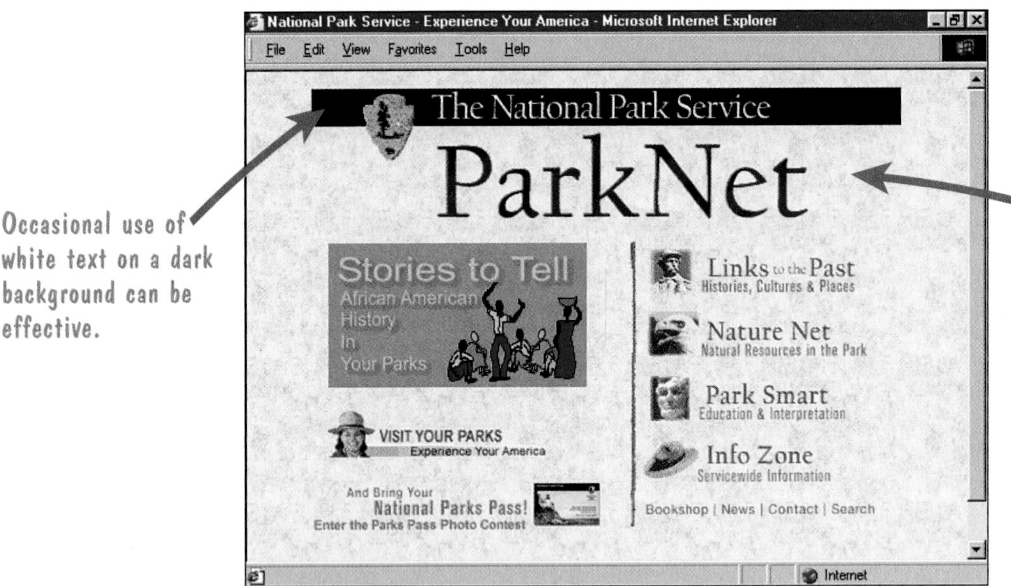

Occasional use of white text on a dark background can be effective.

Use a solid color, or at least a very light pattern for your background so that text maintains its legibility.

White Space Killers

Backgrounds are perhaps the most common stumbling blocks to effective graphic design I see on the Web. Who told all those Web designers that backgrounds are a good idea? You just spent an entire task learning how to add white space to your page. Now please don't fill all that hard-earned white space with some goofy background image! Rarely, if ever—heck, I'll go so far as to use the word *never*—have I seen a background on a Web page that I actually thought helped the page communicate more effectively. And nothing falls more squarely into the "I did it because I can" category than backgrounds. They do not help the reader. Instead, they hurt readability because the background constantly competes with the text for the eye's attention. And if the page element isn't helping the reader, what's the point of including it?

1 Choose a Background Color

Generally speaking, dark text on a light background is easier to read than light text on a dark background. This is especially true when there is a lot of text on the page. You can sometimes get away with a large headline or subheading in a light color on a dark background, but it's too much to expect that readers will be happy about reading an entire page of regular-sized white text on a black background.

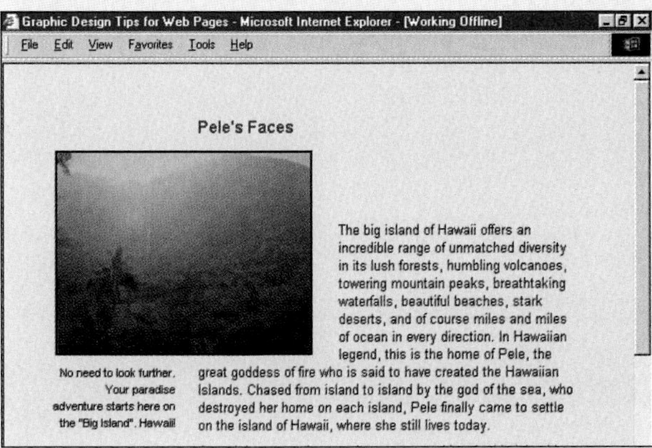

2 Use a Solid Color

Think twice before using a blend or a gradient for a background. One of the keys to high readability is uniformity. When we read, we often read as much by the shape of the word as by the shape of the letter. A gradient background makes it harder for the eye to recognize shapes, thus making the text harder to read.

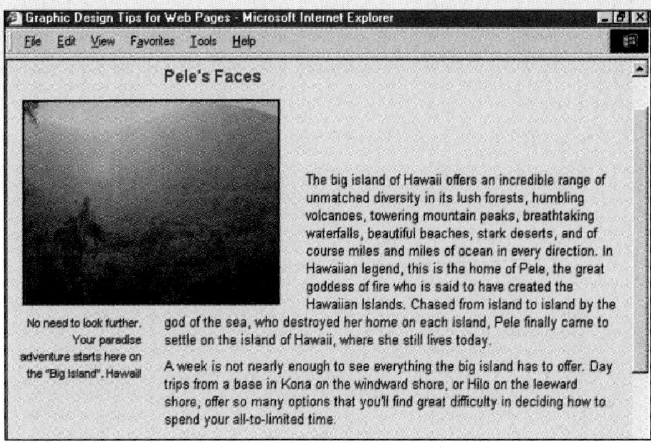

3 Choose a Subtle Image

If you must use an image as a background, make the image subtle. You'll have a tough job ahead of you to find an image that does not interfere with the text on the page. Is your text black? Does the background image have any areas of black or other dark colors in it? If so, that image will make it difficult to read the black text that prints over it. The busier the background on the page, the tougher the job of reading the text on the page.

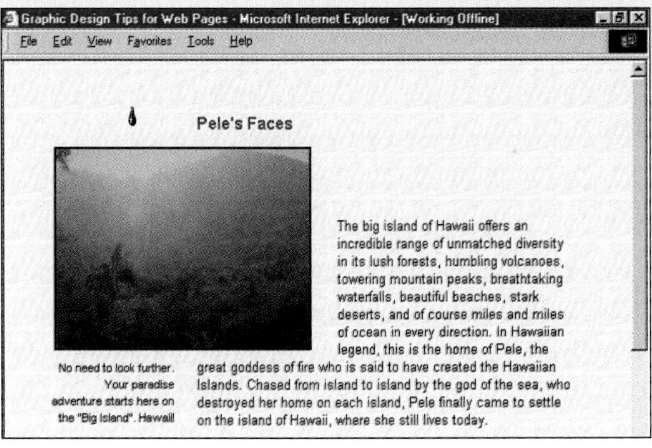

4 Try a Partial Background

You might be able to have the best of both worlds if you use a partial background. This type of background might show an image or color behind large text (such as a headline) or behind navigation buttons, but leaves blank the area behind the body text so that readability is not affected. But be careful: Even a partial background can be distracting.

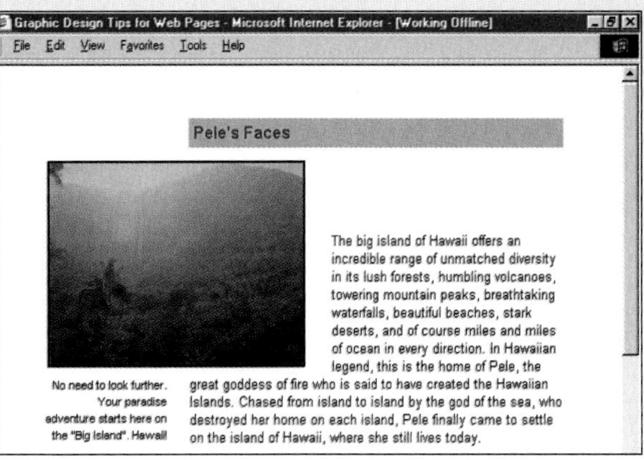

TASK 3 How to Create an Orderly Look

Graphic design is the art of bringing order to the various elements included on the page. Even elements that are not necessarily vital can be included in your page as long as there is some order to it all. It is this order that helps the reader digest the information you are presenting. Part of building order is using white space wisely as discussed in Task 1. This task gives you some pointers for creating order in your Web pages.

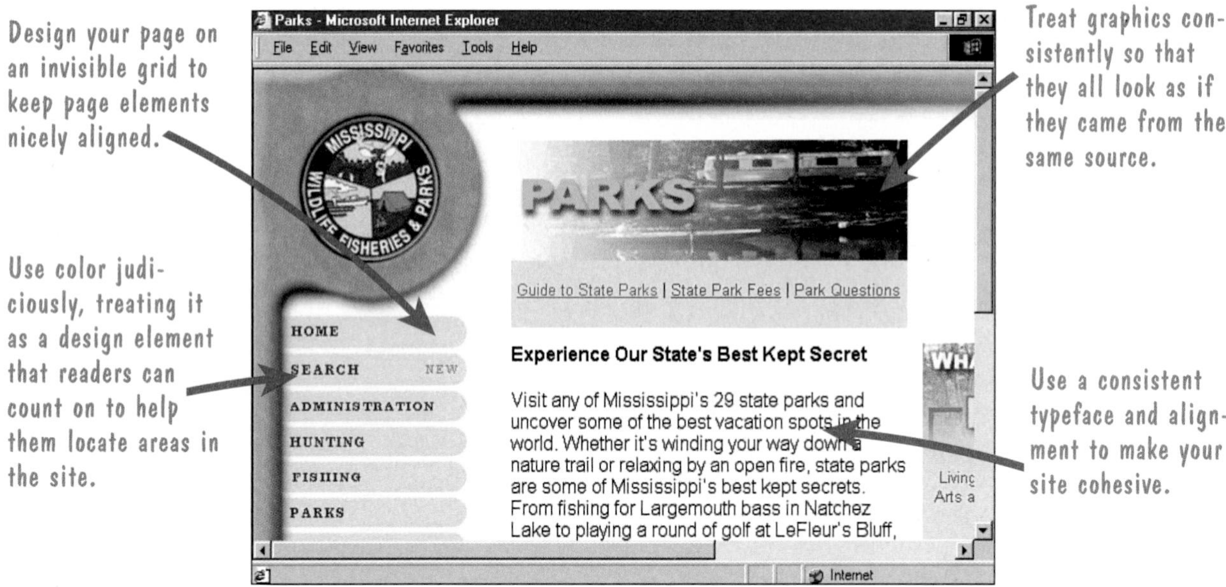

Rules Are Meant to Be Broken

Although order definitely helps in graphic design, so does the occasional disorder. A headline that hangs over into the margin...a photo that you rotate slightly in your image editor before adding to your Web page...a set of columns, one of which is shorter than the others...these are the kinds of exceptions to the rules that can make your designs interesting. But you must start with order and depart from there. And be careful not to stray so far that you lose the order you started with. Don't kid yourself into thinking that you can start freeform with no sense of order and make things work. You'll end up with what you start with—chaos. When you're first starting out, it might be best to design your entire page in strict order. Then, after that's done, take an element and see what it looks like a little off kilter. If you don't like it, put it back and try something else.

1 Design to a Grid

One of the oldest graphic design tricks in the book is to design over an invisible grid. The grid helps you keep things lined up and straight. The grid can have virtually any configuration you want it to have, as long as it has perfectly horizontal and vertical lines. For instance, maybe your grid has two columns of equal width and a third half as wide; the grid might also have two rows. Define a grid and design to it.

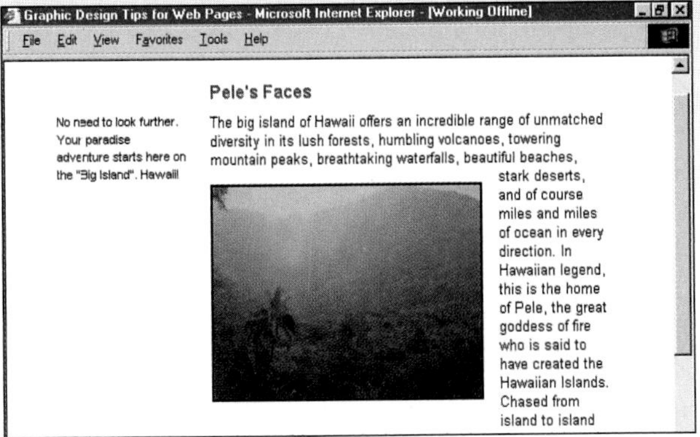

2 Be Consistent

Nothing destroys a sense of order faster than inconsistency. You should strive for consistency on the page, as well as across the Web site. If you present information consistently (using a consistent typeface and a consistent justification), you help the reader develop a feeling of familiarity. After a while, the reader knows what to expect and where to look for certain elements on your pages. If every page is a hunting expedition for readers, they'll soon leave your site.

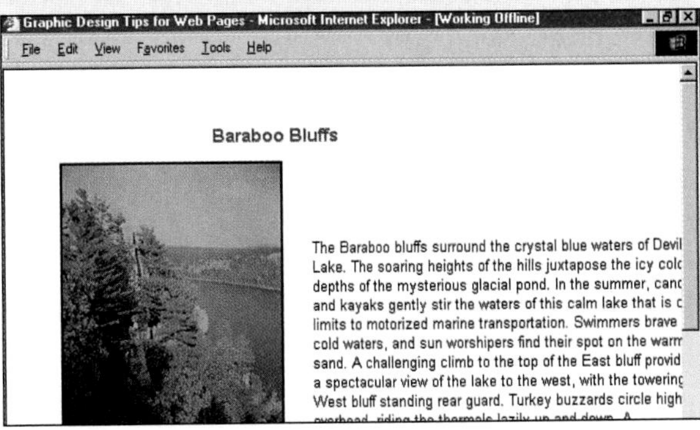

3 Use Color Prudently

It's fun to make things different colors, and by all means, color can be a very effective communication tool. But don't get carried away. If you use too many different colors on your pages (more than three or four), you destroy the sense of order that comes from assigning a color to mean a specific thing. For instance, if all your headings are dark blue, they're easy to recognize. If they are all different colors, the reader can't rely on color to find important sections in the page.

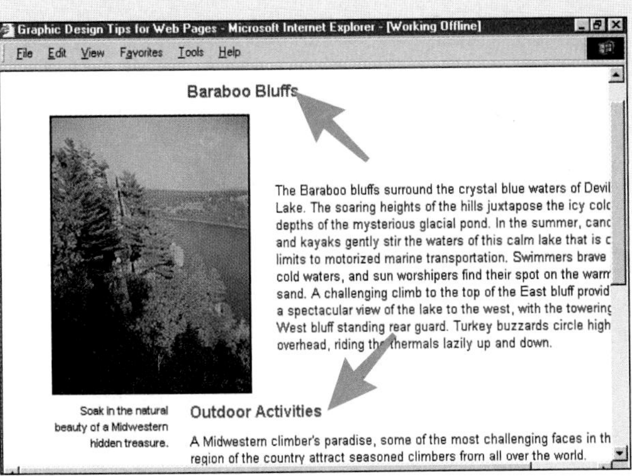

4 Treat Graphics Similarly

Make sure that you are consistent in your treatment of your Web graphics. For instance, if you have a photo at the top of the page, and you put a border around it, you should put a border around the image at the bottom of the page, too. It might also be a good idea to size the images equally, although this rule is less rigid.

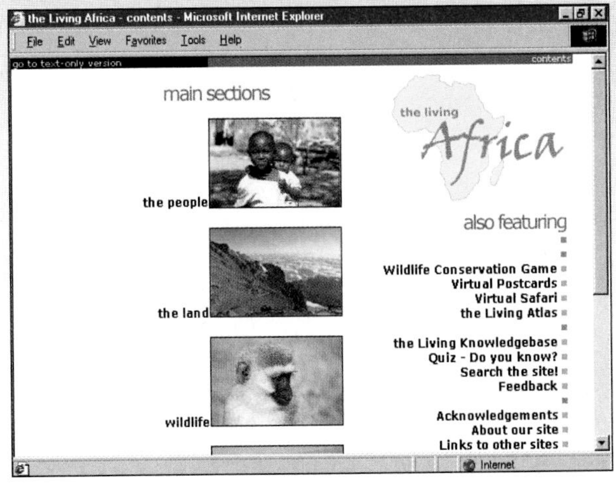

End

TASK 4

How to Present Text

Believe it or not, there's an art to presenting text. There are thousands of type styles and fonts available, and I know designers who labor over the placement and spacing between every letter in their headings. Although HTML doesn't give you easy control over things like the space between letters or lines of text, there are a few basic rules you can follow to make your text more readable. This task explores some of the techniques you can employ to increase the chances that the text you've worked so hard to write is actually read.

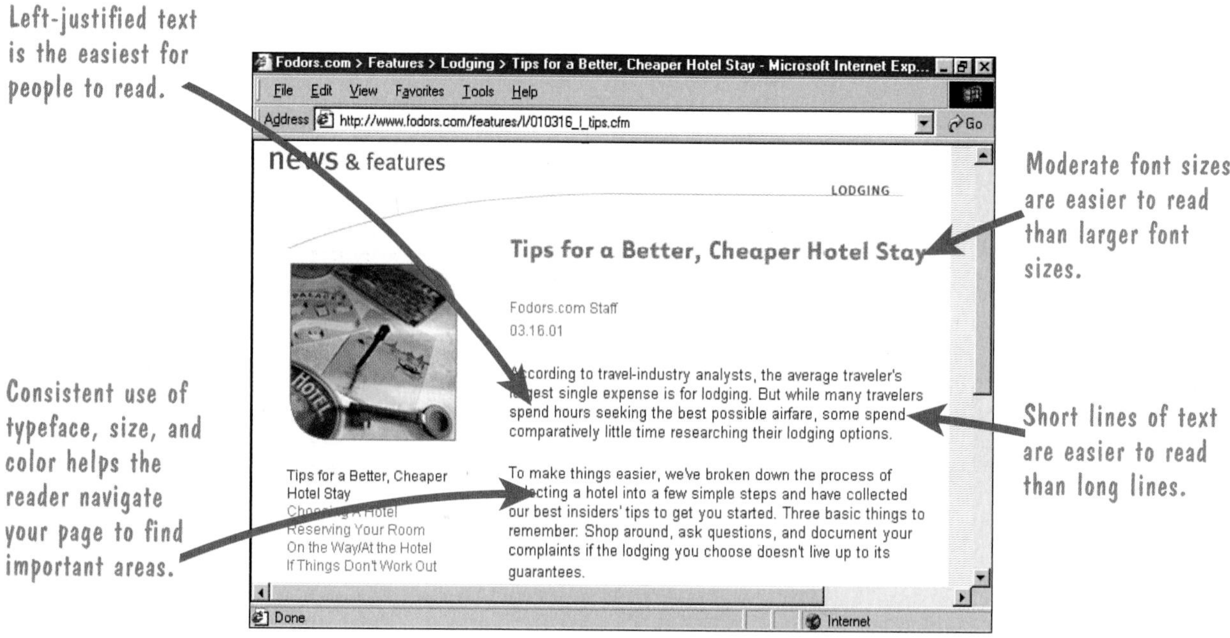

It's Only Words

Sure, it's only text. And text is text, right? You should be able to simply put it on the page, and people will read it. Oh, if only it were that easy! You have to invite people to read the text you place on the page. You have to make it easy for them to read it. If you don't, someone else will, and you'll lose your visitors faster than you can say, "cover your left eye and read the bottom three lines." Take into consideration things such as line length and text color. Text size and type style are also important to keep in mind. Of course, background images and colors also play a role in making your text legible, as mentioned in Task 2. And as you learned in Task 1, white space is critical. Sometimes it seems that even the phase of the moon has something to do with the readability of text on an HTML page. Luckily, there are some helpful guidelines you can follow to improve the odds that the text on your page will actually be read.

1 Be Consistent

Pick two or three font sizes (for example, one for headlines, one for body copy, and one for photo captions), and stick with them. Don't use more than a couple different font colors. Use the bold (<b>) tag sparingly so that you don't dilute its significance. Large blocks of bold or italic text are almost always a bad idea because they become difficult to read—especially on the computer screen of a Web surfer.

2 Choose a Justification

And stick with it. The easiest text to read is text that is left justified (the left edge is straight) with the right edge jagged. Sometimes you'll want to justify things differently. Just be consistent. Don't left-justify one paragraph, center another paragraph, and right-justify the third paragraph. I suggest that you try the default left-justified text before experimenting with other options.

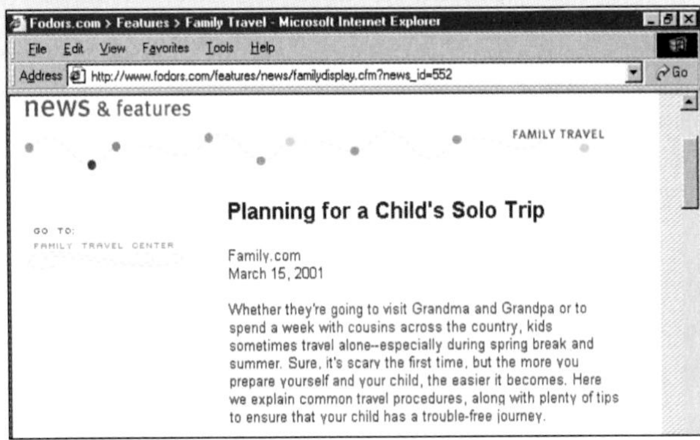

3 Shorter Line Lengths

The Web is full of pages with lines of text that are just too long to be read comfortably. Keep your line lengths relatively short. A good goal is less than a dozen words or so per line. Breaking the text lines up with photographs or graphics is a great way to provide relief to the reader and to help keep line lengths down. Keep the length of your paragraphs on the short side, too.

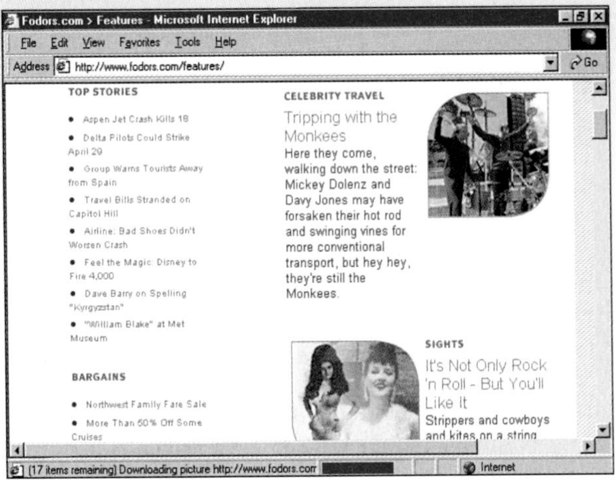

4 Use Moderate Font Size

It's common for inexperienced designers to think that all they have to do to make their text more readable is to make it bigger. This is not so! Just as too small is a problem, too large a font size makes reading more difficult. I usually set my body font size to `"2"` and my headlines perhaps a size larger. Sometimes I'll even use `size="1"` (although that's getting pretty small for some eyes).

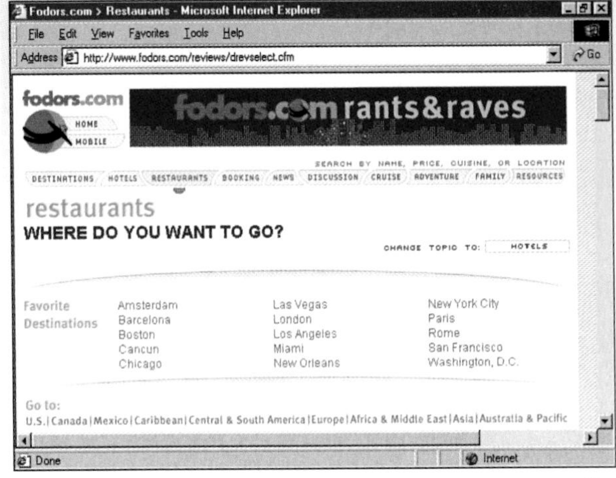

End

TASK 5 How to Decide When to Use Animations

There are a couple basic types of animations on the Web these days. The first is the animated GIF files discussed in Part 5, Task 11, "How to Create Animated GIF Files." An entirely different world of animations is created in Macromedia Flash. It's pretty easy to create animated GIF files. Flash animations require more work and specific knowledge of the software.

Regardless of how the animations are physically created, the question we're currently concerned with is when you should use animations. There are a lot of situations when an animation might help make your point. There are a lot of times when it won't. This task helps you sort it out a bit.

Still images and plain old text might be your best choices if file size and download times are a concern.

Animations can add interest to a page, but unless that movement focuses the visitor's attention where you want it, the animation might not be effective.

The Animation Trap

Why don't I like animations? Well, in addition to the fact that they increase the download time of Web pages, I *do* have other reasons. Animations are deceptive. They seem so cute or so cool. But it's surprising how quickly "cute" and "cool" turn to just plain annoying. Hot debate rages over how well animations serve their purpose of drawing attention. More importantly, it's not at all clear whether the attention they draw is more positive or negative. There are certainly good uses for animations on Web pages, but there is even more certainly a definite skill in choosing or creating an animation that works for you instead of against you. Be careful with animated GIF files. It's easy to fall into the "animation trap" and start throwing animations at your pages like darts at the bull's-eye. Unfortunately, like those darts aimed so carefully, no matter how hard you try, you usually come closer to hitting the wall than the target.

1 Consider a Text Alternative

Many animations on the Web could effectively be replaced by simple text. A perfect example is an animated mailbox image. A simple link to an e-mail address serves the purpose just as effectively as an annoying animation. In fact, a large number of animations could just be eliminated and not replaced by anything because they serve no apparent purpose anyway. Never be guilty of that sin!

2 Create a Static Image First

You have to create a static image anyway because an animated GIF file is really nothing more than a series of static images played in succession. Give honest effort to creating a static image that adequately conveys your message. Careful consideration of to a static image will more times than not make the crutch of an animated file unnecessary. After creating this image, evaluate it honestly to decide whether you need to go farther.

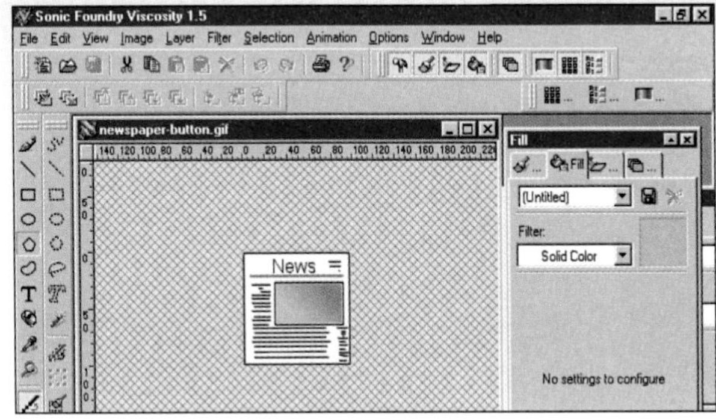

3 Create the Animation

If you determine that the static image just doesn't do the job, create your animated GIF file. The fewer frames you can use, the better off you'll be in terms of file size and download times (you don't want to annoy your readers with long download times that don't deliver something worthwhile). On the other hand, the more frames you use, the smoother and more expressive your animation will be. Careful planning can help you strike a balance.

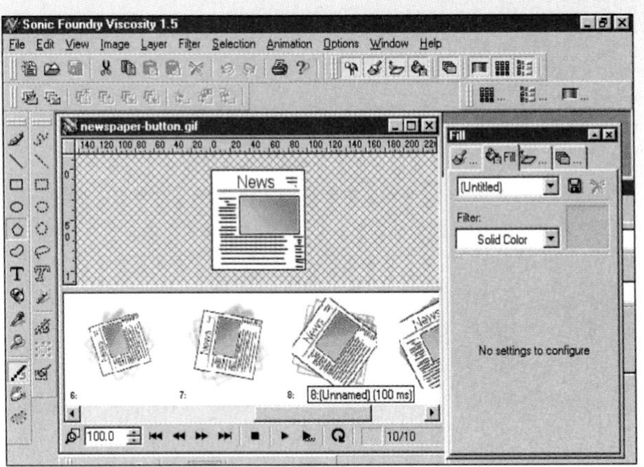

4 Evaluate the Animation

Now add the animation to your page. Does it add anything to the page? Does it make the page clearer or more functional? Don't place it there just because you think it'll look neat. Does it actually serve a legitimate purpose? List the pros and cons and compare the good against the bad. If the good outweighs the bad, use the animation. If not, reevaluate the alternatives.

End

TASK 6

How to Use Tables as a Layout Tool

The graphic design capabilities of HTML are weak at best. HTML was originally intended for use in formatting technical documents, so graphics were a minimal consideration. But as the Web booms, people want greater control over layout, and tables have become the workhorses in this field. Purists say that page layout is an unacceptable use of tables, but until a better solution is widely supported by browsers, tables will rule. That better solution is the subject of Part 10 of this book, "XHTML and Cascading Style Sheets." Unfortunately, current support for XHTML and CSS is inexcusably poor, so we'll continue to rely on tables for some time to come.

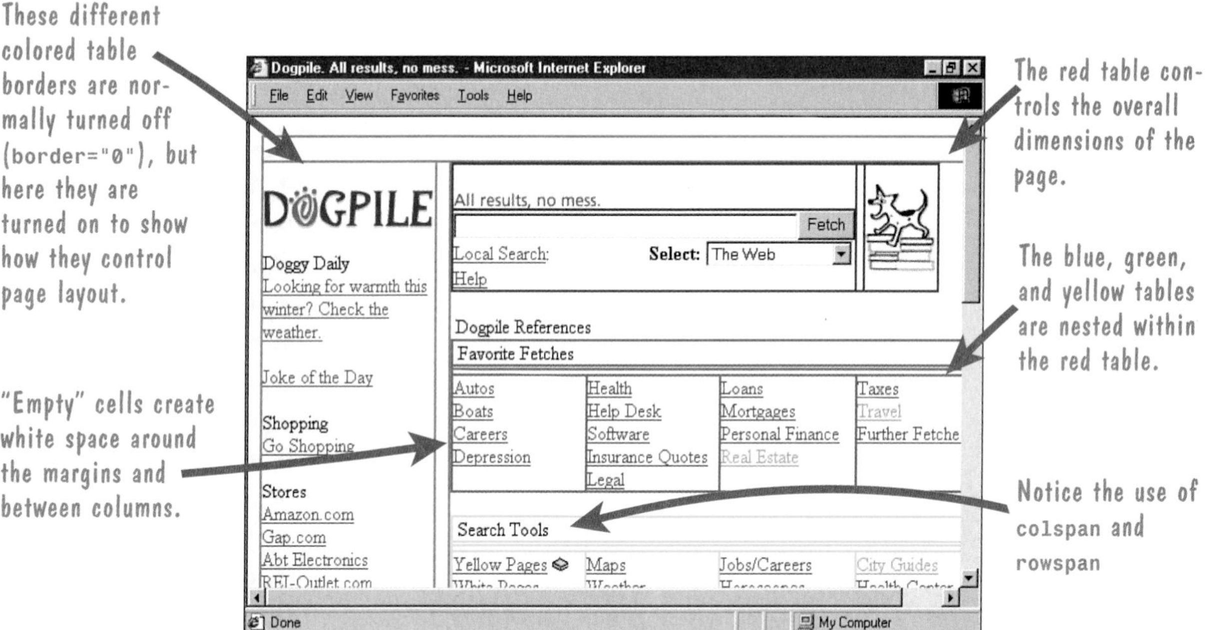

Grid Construction Kit

In Task 3, "How to Create an Orderly Look," I talked about designing to a grid. One of the reasons tables have come to play such a prominent role in Web page design is that they allow you to construct the grid on which you want to base your page layout. Tables are perfect for this because you can use them to divide the page into nice, neat rows and columns. Granted, tables can get complicated, and they have other limitations. Still, they force you to design to a grid. And if you want to break the grid, tables force you to think twice about doing it because it can be quite a task to figure out how to step outside the boundaries of rows and columns. When you decide to break those boundaries, you'll make use of the **rowspan** and **colspan** attributes. Constructing a table that results in the page layout you're after can be a fun challenge.

1 Plan Your Page Layout

It's a good idea to plan your page layout on paper before you try to build it in HTML. Remember that when you're coding in HTML, you can't see what the page is really going to look like until you check it in a browser. So, having something visual on paper while you type out tags and attributes can be an invaluable construction aid.

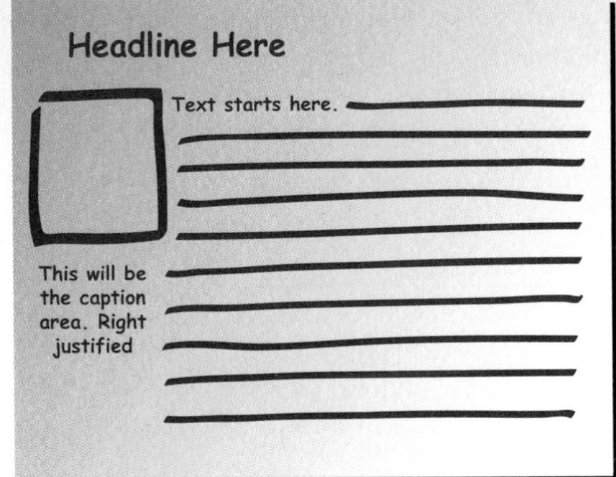

2 Plan Your Table Layout

After you have the overall look of the page sketched out, use a different-colored pencil to sketch in the table skeleton that is needed to translate the design from paper to an HTML page. Make note of where the **colspan** and **rowspan** attributes are necessary. Draw in any nested tables that are needed. To the side, write out your preliminary impressions of what HTML code you'll need.

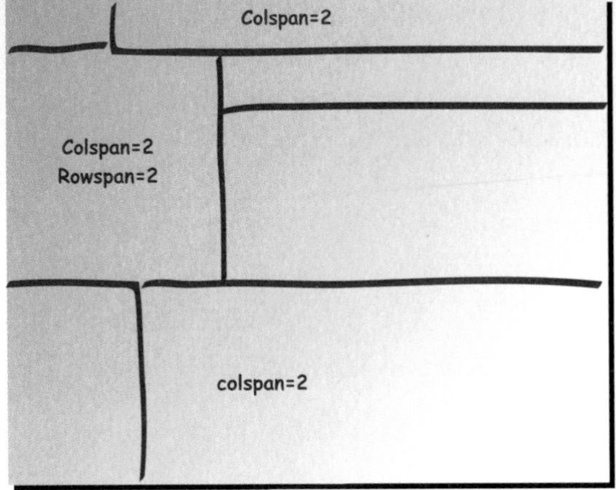

3 Construct Your HTML Table

Using the sketches and notes you made in the last two steps, start coding. Remember that it will make things a lot easier if you use borders on your tables during development. This is especially important when you have nested tables, or cells devoted to white space. You might have to do some image splicing to achieve the desired effects with images. You have a deep bag of tricks already. Reach in there and see what you can pull out!

```
<table border="1">
<tr>
<td>1...</td>
<td colspan="2">2...</td>
</tr>
<tr>
<td colspan="2" rowspan="2">3...</td>
<td>4...</td>
</tr>
</table>
```

4 Add White Space

Task 1, "How to Make It Easy to View Your Pages," talked about the value of white space; tables give you a great way of adding it to your pages. You can use **cellpadding** or **cellspacing**, or you can create "empty" table cells. It's not a good idea to leave a table cell completely blank. Instead, use the nonbreaking space escape code (** **) to put something invisible into the cell. This technique helps you build white space and preserve order.

```
<table border="1">
<tr>
<td>1...</td>
<td colspan="2">2...</td>
</tr>
<tr>
<td colspan="2" rowspan="2">3...</td>
<td> </td>
</tr>
</table>
```

End

TASK 7

How to Create Indents and Custom Spacing

You have a few options when creating indents and custom spacing. You can use the invisible one-pixel image trick (described in the hint) to push text around, or you can construct a table that structures the page so that you achieve the spacing and indentations you want. Here I present a few basic ideas. Most of them are not very practical in a real-world situation, but the ideas might spark better ideas for your page design dilemmas. I hope they help you think creatively, while at the same time helping you recognize some of the limitations of graphic design using HTML.

You can use the one-pixel GIF trick to space out the letters in a heading. You use the hspace attribute of the <img> tag to specify the space.

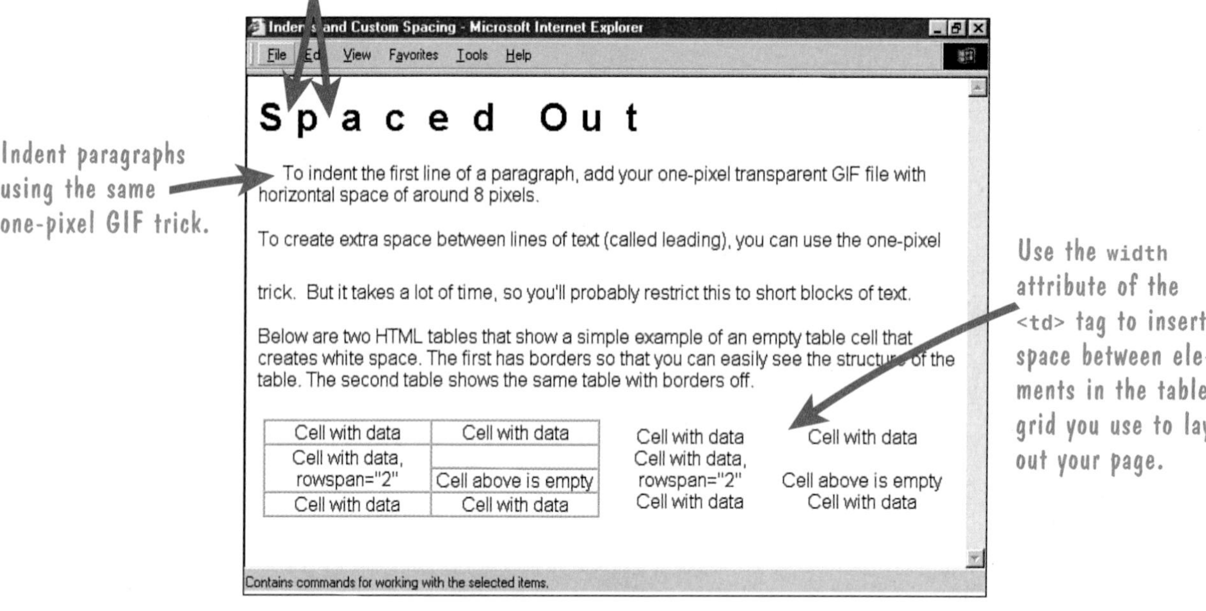

Indent paragraphs using the same one-pixel GIF trick.

Use the width attribute of the <td> tag to insert space between elements in the table grid you use to lay out your page.

Special Cases and Rare Instances

In the one-pixel transparent GIF technique, you create a transparent GIF square, insert it into your text, and use the **hspace** attribute to push the words that follow it horizontally, or the **vspace** attribute to push the lines that come above and below it vertically. Because some of these techniques for creating custom spaces and indents are so cumbersome, their practical applications are fairly limited. There certainly comes a point at which the effort it takes to make the spacing work out a certain way is just not worth the payoff received. You might have to accept the fact that your page just won't look exactly the way you want it to. Before you spend too much time trying to manipulate these spaces, try building the page without them; see whether you can design an effective layout that doesn't require such time-consuming design tricks as those described here.

1 Create Space Between Letters

In some very special cases, you might want to include a large amount of space between two letters. For instance, you might want to create a special treatment for a headline in which you insert space between every pair of letters. Type **<img src="1pix.gif" hspace="5" />** after each letter to accomplish this. Here, **1pix.gif** is the name of the one-pixel transparent GIF file. You can see how specialized this case would be!

```
<font face="arial">
<h1>S<img src="1pix.gif" hspace="5" />p
<img src="1pix.gif" hspace="5" />a
<img src="1pix.gif" hspace="5" />c
<img src="1pix.gif" hspace="5" />e
<img src="1pix.gif" hspace="5" />d
<img src="1pix.gif" hspace="10" />O
<img src="1pix.gif" hspace="5" />u
<img src="1pix.gif" hspace="5" />t
</h1></font>
```

2 Indent Paragraphs

To create an indent for the first line of a paragraph, start off the line with **<img src= "1pix.gif" hspace="5" />**. Although this is easy enough to implement for a single line, you can imagine that this technique is very difficult to maintain throughout an entire Web site. This trick will slow you down tremendously as you put your pages together, so give serious thought to the technique before you decide to begin using it.

```
<font face="arial"><p>
<img src="1pix.gif" hspace="10" />To indent
the first line of a paragraph, add your
one-pixel transparent GIF file with
horizontal space of around 8 pixels.</p>
</font>
```

3 Create Space Between Lines

Even more tedious is the technique of using the one-pixel transparent image along with the **vspace** attribute to control the space between lines of text (referred to as leading). To create extra leading, insert **<img src="1pix.gif" vspace="x"** where **"x"** is the desired space measured in pixels. To make this work, you'll have to insert this command on every line of the text! Reserve this trick for very special cases because it is impractical to implement to a wide extent.

```
<p>To create<img src="1pix.gif"
vspace="20" /> extra space between lines
of text (called leading), you can use the
one-pixel trick. <img src="1pix.gif"
vspace="20" /> But it takes a lot of
time,<img src="1pix.gif" vspace="20" />
so restrict its use to short blocks of
text.
</p>
```

4 Create Space Between Elements

A much more common technique is to use "empty" table cells to create space between page elements. But because table cells should never actually be left empty, use the nonbreaking space escape code as an invisible placeholder. Then use the **width** or **height** attribute of the **<td>** tag to specify the amount of space between two elements. For example, type **<td width="5">** to add a five-pixel-wide space.

```
<table border="1">
<tr>
<td>1...</td>
<td colspan="2">2...</td>
</tr>
<tr>
<td colspan="2" rowspan="2">3...</td>
<td> </td>
</tr></table>
```

End

TASK 8

How to Learn More About Graphic Design

The crash course I've given you in this part is really just enough to help you avoid some common graphic design pitfalls. There is so much more to know about the art of laying out pages and presenting material in a clear and effective manner. There are books, Web resources, videos, classes, seminars, and more that can help. This task tries to point you in the right direction if you want to learn more about graphic design, both in general and in relation to Web pages.

You can find many resources for learning more about graphic design.

One Person's Pain Is Another's Pleasure

Graphic design is very much a matter of opinion. You might not agree with everything I've said here. Still, there are common conventions that form the basis of good design, and until you become more experienced with this art form, I suggest that you don't stray too far from them. It is these guidelines that I've tried to present here. As you gain experience, you might find a way to break every rule I've laid out and still create an interesting, pleasing, and effective design. I don't want your pages to look just like mine. That might be flattering, but it would also make for a very boring Web. I hope you take what I've taught you here and expand it, bend it, break it, twist it, and turn it upside down and inside out. As long as you have a solid base from which to start, you should be able to manipulate the page-layout rules and still maintain good graphic design!

1 Search the Web for Resources

A fun place to start is **http://dir.yahoo.com/Arts/Design_Arts/Graphic_Design/Web_Page_Design_and_Layout/Bad_Style/**. This collection of Web resources approaches the subject of good design from the back door. You can learn all kinds of things about good design by these tongue-in-cheek looks at bad design.

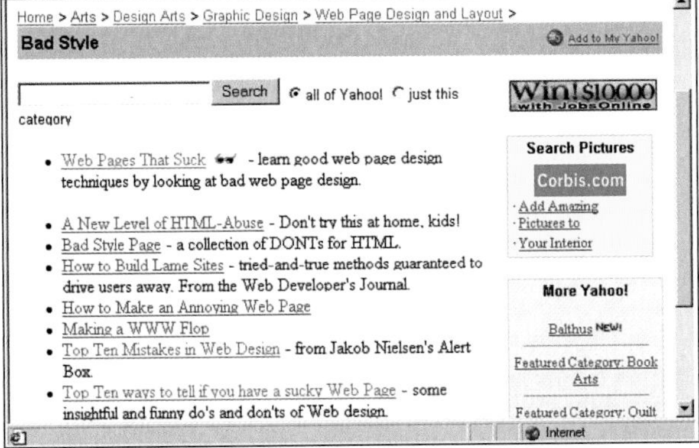

2 Read a Good Book

There are countless books on the subject of Web development and design. Jakob Nielsen and Vincent Flanders are popular authors, and generally have smart things to say. Visit your favorite bookstore, and you'll find a number of good books on the subject of graphic and Web design.

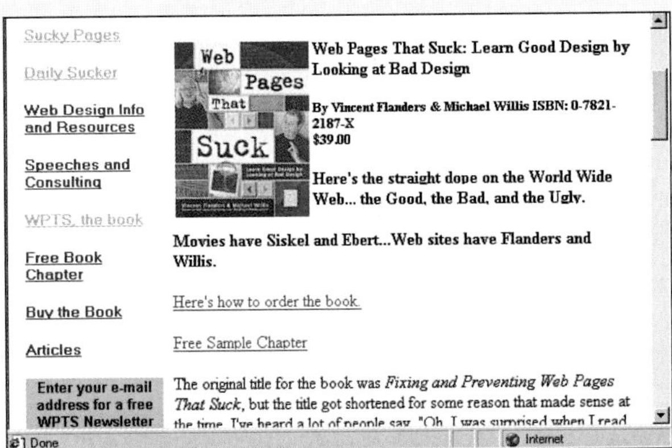

3 Take a Seminar

There are many classes and seminars related to the Web, HTML, and graphic design. My search on AltaVista.com turned up a long list of resources. You should be able to find something in your area. Also check with local groups and clubs (most cities have some sort of graphic designers' club). Attend one of their meetings and ask for some of the resources available for you to check into.

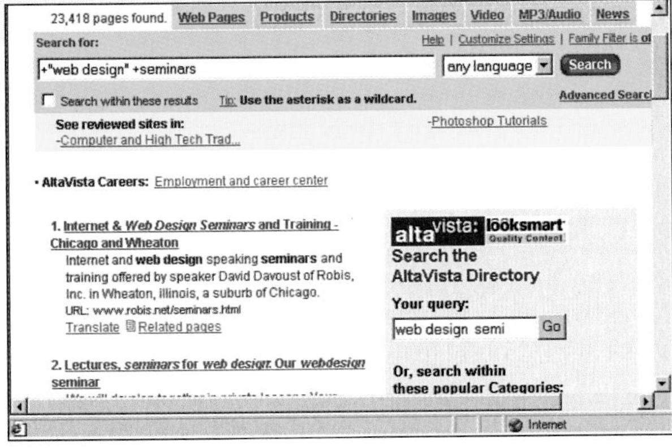

4 Learn by Doing

Even after all the books, all the videos, and all the seminars, there's nothing like the School of Hard Knocks to teach you your lessons. The best way to learn is to go out and start creating Web pages. Then compare them to other pages you like. Be objective and honest. If you don't like something about your pages, change it. Accept criticism from friends and colleagues. You can learn a lot that way!

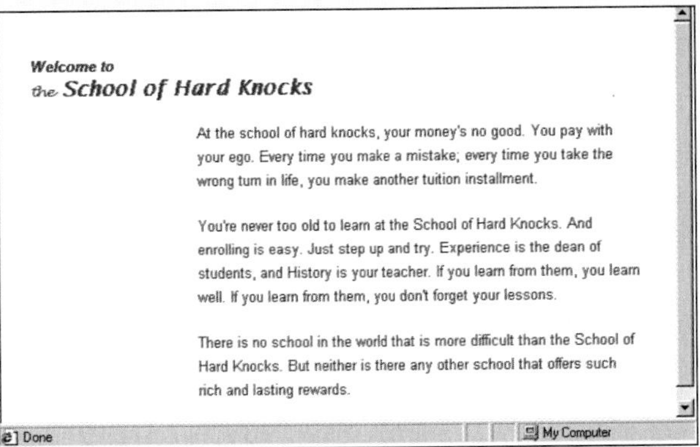

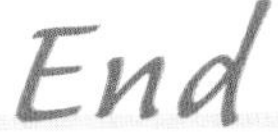

Task

PART 10

XHTML and Cascading Style Sheets

There is a brighter future ahead for anyone who's ever struggled with the layout of a Web page. That brighter future is Extensible Hypertext Markup Language (XHTML) and Cascading Style Sheets (CSS). In a simplistic sense, XHTML can be viewed as essentially the next step beyond HTML 4.0. Because it represents a significant shift in the approach to coding pages, instead of calling it HTML 5.0, the W3C has called it XHTML 1.0.

This "significant shift" is represented by the *X* in *XHTML*. The *X* stands for *eXtensible*. Extensible means that authors can customize their code by creating specialized tags and attributes to accomplish their goals. The tool for creating these custom elements is the technology known as Cascading Style Sheets (CSS). To use CSS, you build your page using most of the standard HTML tags you've learned so far, but instead of using attributes to define those tags, you use style sheets to modify the look, size, color, position, and more.

One reason that CSS technology is so powerful is that it creates an invisible object box out of every element in your page. For example, each **<p>** is treated as an object box, as is each **<h1>** and even the **<body>** tag. And if you want a custom object box, you can create it. Unlike the elements in HTML 4.0, these object boxes can be manipulated in many flexible ways. They can be positioned anywhere on the page regardless of their original position in the code. One object can even be positioned over the top of another object to create layers (known as positioning in the "z" dimension). Whereas tables have been indispensable for controlling page layout, they provide nothing like the possibilities available using CSS.

You might wonder why, if XHTML and CSS technology is so wonderful, did we spend so much time learning about HTML. Don't worry; your time and energy has not been wasted. True, CSS does make obsolete some of the HTML tags you've learned. The W3C has designated these tags as *deprecated* meaning that the W3C suggests that you use CSS to accomplish what these tags achieve. Still, it'll be some time before you can code strictly with CSS because too many Web surfers don't use browsers capable of understanding the code. For a while longer, you'll have to create your pages the HTML way. But learning the XHTML and CSS technologies will put you ahead of the curve. ●

TASK 1

How to Use the <!doctype> Identifier

Remember that all HTML pages start with a few standard tags such as **<html>**, **<head>**, and **<body>**. XHTML pages require these tags, but they also require one more: the **<!doctype>** tag. There are three types of XHTML pages that you can write: strict, transitional, and frameset. You must identify which type of page you are writing, and you do so with the **<!doctype>** tag. This task shows you how to use this tag for each of the three page types. In truth, the W3C also includes the **<!doctype>** tag (with specific attributes) in the specification for properly coded HTML, but it is rarely used in practice. Therefore, I delayed mentioning it until now.

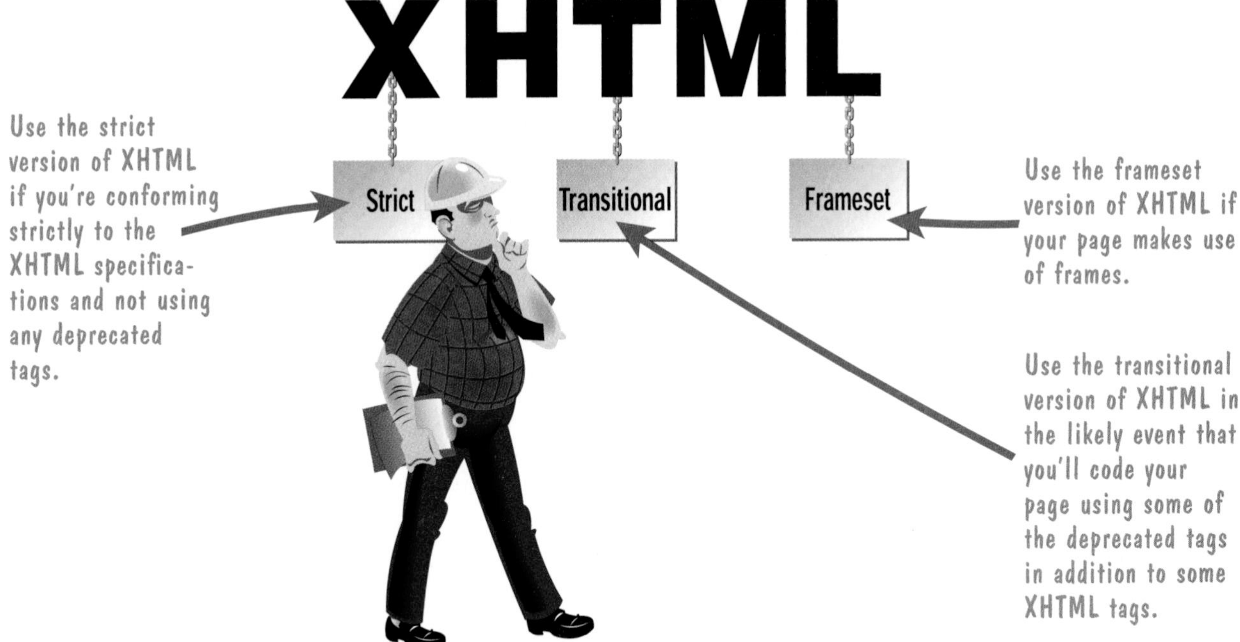

XHTML
Strict
Transitional
Frameset
Use the strict version of XHTML if you're conforming strictly to the XHTML specifications and not using any deprecated tags.
Use the frameset version of XHTML if your page makes use of frames.
Use the transitional version of XHTML in the likely event that you'll code your page using some of the deprecated tags in addition to some XHTML tags.

Not Quite There Yet

As you'll discover throughout this part, XHTML and Cascading Style Sheets make the job of page layout much more intuitive, flexible, and easy. Web designers are looking excitedly toward the day when Cascading Style Sheets can be used exclusively to control the graphic design of Web pages. Unfortunately, that day is still off in the future because browser manufacturers cannot (or will not) get in line with the technologies; implementation and support for CSS and XHTML are sadly inconsistent among browsers (and older browsers don't recognize or support them at all). That being the case (along with the fact that most sites are not built using frames), the XHTML pages you'll most often be creating in the near future will likely be transitional. *Transitional pages* allow you to use the parts of XHMTL that are well supported in your target browser, and to use traditional HTML for everything else.

1 Add the <!doctype> Tag

To identify the version of XHTML you are using, add the **<!doctype>** tag. Within this tag, you define the type of XHTML page you are writing, and the version of XHTML you are using. Add the tag to your page in front of the **<html>** tag. Type **<!doctype html public "-//w3c//dtd xhtml 1.0 version//en" "http://www.w3.org/tr/xhtml1/dtd/version.dtd" />**. The next steps explain what to type in place of **version**.

```
<!doctype html public "-//w3c//dtd xhtml 1.0
version//en"
"http://www.w3.org/tr/xhtml1/dtd/
version.dtd" />
<html>
</html>
```

2 When to Use the Strict Version

Use the strict version of XHTML only when you use CSS to perform *all* formatting operations on the page. You'd only do this if you are sure that your audience will be viewing your pages in a browser that properly supports XHTML and CSS. Because this is a fairly unlikely condition, you will probably not use the strict version very often (at least for a while). But in the event that you use it, type **<!doctype html public "-//w3c//dtd xhtml 1.0 strict//en" "http://www.w3.org/tr/xhtml1/dtd/strict.dtd" />**.

```
<!doctype html public "-//w3c//dtd xhtml 1.0
strict//en"
"http://www.w3.org/tr/xhtml1/dtd/
strict.dtd" />
<html>
</html>
```

3 When to Use the Transitional Version

A more likely scenario is that you'll use CSS to specify some of the formatting for your page and use regular (including deprecated) HTML tags for other formatting. Deprecated tags are those that have been identified as obsolete by the W3C. These are the tags that the more powerful techniques of CSS have displaced. In this case, use the transitional version, and type **<!doctype html public "-//w3c//dtd xhtml 1.0 transitional//en" "http://www.w3.org/tr/xhtml1/dtd/transitional.dtd" />**.

```
<!doctype html public "-//w3w//dtd xhtml 1.0
transitional//en"
"http://www.w3.org/tr/xhtml1/dtd/
transitional.dtd" />
<html>
</html>
```

4 When to Use the Frameset Version

For those of you who decide to use frames on your pages, you must use the frameset version of XHTML. Type **<!doctype html public "-//w3c//dtd xhtml 1.0 frameset//en" "http://www.w3.org/tr/xhtml1/dtd/frameset.dtd" />**.

```
<!doctype html public "-//w3c//dtd xhtml 1.0
frameset//en"
"http://www.w3.org/tr/xhtml1/dtd/
frameset.dtd" />
<html>
</html>
```

End

TASK 2

How to Write Properly Formatted XHTML

Throughout this book, I've presented HTML tags in the format you need to use for XHTML. Remember that although HTML can be somewhat forgiving when it comes to your coding habits (you can use uppercase or lowercase letters, omit some closing tags, and so on), XHTML demands precision.

Hopefully, good XHTML coding practices are already part of your coding technique, so it will be easy for you to make the transition from HTML to XHTML. This task summarizes and reviews the important requirements of coding XHTML.

Why Bother?

Right about now you might be thinking, "Now wait. First you tell me that HTML isn't very picky about how I code. Then you tell me XHTML is. On top of that, you tell me I can't realistically use much XHTML right now because of poor browser support. My point is, why worry about whether my code is solid for XHTML? I can't use it anyhow!"

Well, the point *really* is that XHTML is the future. You know enough about HTML now to go make countless pages. But XHTML is taking over, and we don't really know when the takeover will be complete. Sooner or later, there will be a revolution in the way we view the Web, and my money is on XHTML as a part of that revolution. I don't know about you, but when it happens, I'm going to be very glad that I don't have to update any sloppy old HTML pages so that an XHTML-only browser can see them.

1 Use All Lowercase Letters

HTML doesn't care if you use uppercase, lowercase, or mixed-case letters in your tags and attributes. You can mix them up to your heart's content. But XHTML is more strict. To conform to XHTML, you must type all your tags and attributes in lowercase letters.

```
<!doctype html public "-//w3c//dtd xhtml 1.0
transitional//en" "http://www.w3.org/tr/
xhtml1/dtd/transitional.dtd" />
<html>
<head>
<title>My XHTML Page</title>
</head>
<body>
</body>
</html>
```

2 Enclose All Attribute Values in Quotes

In HTML, there are times when the quotation marks around your attributes are optional. This gets tricky because there are other times when they are not optional. So, the wise HTML author uses quotation marks all the time just to be safe. That's a good practice because the transition to XHTML will be easier. XHTML requires quotation marks around all attribute values without exception.

```
<!doctype html public "-//w3c//dtd xhtml 1.0
transitional//en" "http://www.w3.org/tr/
xhtml1/dtd/transitional.dtd" />
<html>
<head>
<title>My XHTML Page</title>
</head>
<body><img
src="../images/bluffs.jpg"></body>
</html>
```

3 Close All Tags

In XHTML, you must make sure to close every tag. As you've seen, for those HTML tags that don't have a closing tag, you add the forward slash (/) just before the end bracket of the tag. You might have noticed in the code example for the previous step that the **<img>** tag is not closed. In the example for this step, the closing slash has been added.

```
<!doctype html public "-//w3c//dtd xhtml 1.0
transitional//en" "http://www.w3.org/tr/
xhtml1/dtd/transitional.dtd" />
<html>
<head>
<title>My XHTML Page</title>
</head>
<body><img src="../images/bluffs.jpg" />
</body>
</html>
```

4 Always Nest Tags Properly

With HTML, you could improperly nest a couple of tag pairs and be no worse for the wear. This is sloppy code writing even in HTML, but you could sometimes get lucky and get away with it. Not so with XHTML. Make sure that all your tag pairs are nested properly—the first one in is the last one out.

```
<!doctype html public "-//w3c//dtd xhtml 1.0
transitional//en" "http://www.w3.org/tr/
xhtml1/dtd/transitional.dtd">
<html>
<head>
<title>My XHTML Page<title>
</head>
<body><p>Make sure to <b>properly
 <i>nest</i> tags</b>!</p></body>
</html>
```

End

TASK 3 How to Use Cascading Style Sheets

You're almost ready to start learning the details of how to control your page layout using CSS. But first, it will help to get to know a little bit more about the technology and what you can do with it. This task presents some of the main uses for CSS in broad strokes. It will give you the framework you need to understand why you're learning the techniques explained in subsequent tasks. As you work through this task, let your mind run with these ideas, and try to see the possibilities as they relate to your own Web pages.

After you become familiar with CSS, you'll find countless uses for the technology.

Familiar, But Different

Style sheets will feel somewhat familiar to you. You'll recognize tag names from HTML, as well as some of the same attribute names and values. Specifying colors in a style sheet is just the same as it is in HTML, and you can use either specific color names, or more properly, hex color values. All this makes perfect sense because, ultimately, all you're doing is using a style sheet to define tags instead of using the attributes of the tag itself, as you do in HTML. Some tags have been made obsolete by style sheets. These are the ones that have been marked as *deprecated* by the W3C. When you're working with style sheets, you'll have a few new techniques to get used to, and there are a lot of details, but overall, style sheets are pretty easy to understand. And they're well worth the effort it takes to learn them. After you see how they work, you'll wish that browsers properly supported them right now.

1 Make Your Pages Easily Updateable

Cascading Style Sheets make it possible to update the look of your entire page—indeed, your entire Web site—quickly and painlessly. For example, with HTML, to change the font face of all of the body text in your Web site, you'd have to embark on an arduous seek-and-destroy mission to find every **<font>** tag and change its **face** attribute. With CSS, you change one command, save the document, and your entire site is updated. Take the rest of the day off!

2 Position Objects on the Page

Although tables have been the best layout tool to date, CSS gives you much more control when you're placing items on the page. Tables can get complex very quickly, and often your layout is dictated by the limitations of tables. CSS allows you to position items on your page *exactly* where you want them. After you learn the techniques, doing so is a much less complex and time-consuming task than building tables.

3 Layer Objects on the Page

Since graphic designers began getting involved with laying out Web pages, they have complained about the lack of ability to layer objects on the page. CSS gives them that ability by allowing positioning of objects in three dimensions (x, y, and z). You have to be careful with this technique, using it only for occasional special effects, but when you decide you have a use for layered objects, CSS is your only option. HTML provides no way to accomplish this objective.

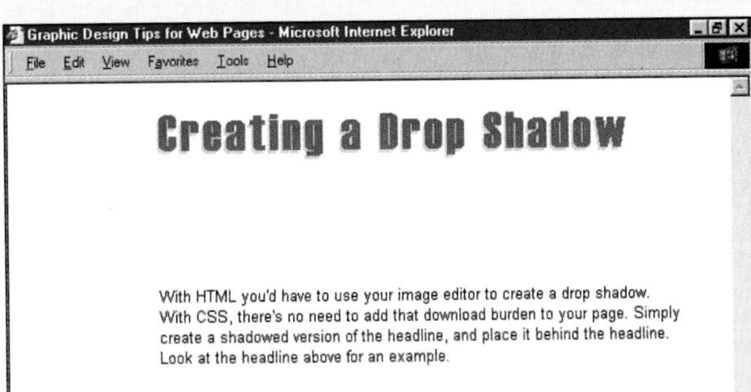

4 Create Custom Tags

Use CSS to create custom tags that allow you to achieve specialized objectives. For example, instead of defining all your paragraphs with the **<p>** tag, you might create a new tag to use for paragraphs that you want to treat somehow differently than the main paragraphs. You can create a tag to span a number of different elements, and treat them all according to the tag you define. This ability really makes the possibilities endless!

End

TASK 4 How to Apply External Style Sheets

External style sheets are the most global of the three kinds of style sheets because you can apply the same one to an unlimited number of pages. An external style sheet is a great way to develop a consistent style across pages. It also allows you to easily change the look of your entire Web site. Simply make the change to the external style sheet, and every page that calls on that style sheet is instantly updated the next time it is viewed in a browser (you might have to click the **Refresh** or **Reload** button to see the change). Imagine: You can change the color of every headline in your Web site with one simple operation!

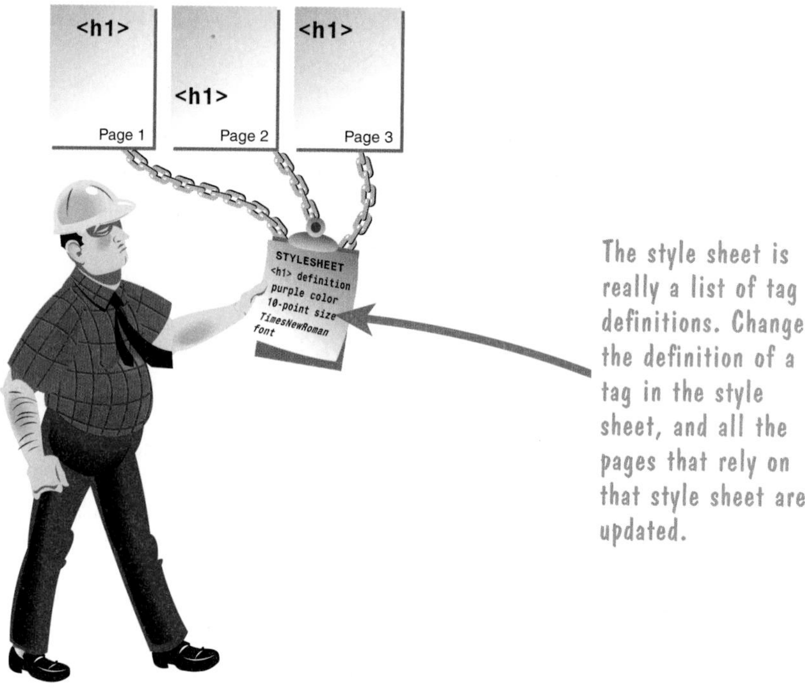

The style sheet is really a list of tag definitions. Change the definition of a tag in the style sheet, and all the pages that rely on that style sheet are updated.

Get It Now?

Picture this: You've created a 50-page Web site for your best client. It's taken you a great deal of work to put it all together; you've labored over every **<p>** tag and **src** attribute until you've created exactly what the client wants. Moments before you're scheduled to go live with the site, his 13-year-old daughter walks in, smirks at you with that "I'm way smarter than you" grin, and says, "Daddy, don't you know that the first line of every paragraph should be indented five spaces?" As the father of a 13-year-old, I know that Daddy instantly says, "Of course I do, Honey!" Then he turns to you and whispers, "That's not hard to change, is it?" So, what do you say? The traditional HTML answer is to scream as you jump out the window. The CSS answer is, "Heck no, by the time you're done signing that paycheck, it'll be fixed. What a darling child...." (Flip to Task 12, "How to Align Text with CSS," to learn how this is done.)

1 Create the Style Sheet

Like an HTML page, an external style sheet is simply an ASCII text document you can create in a basic text editor such as Notepad or Simple Text. We'll talk more about the specifics of specifying styles in later tasks. For now, create a new text document and assume that we've finished specifying the styles.

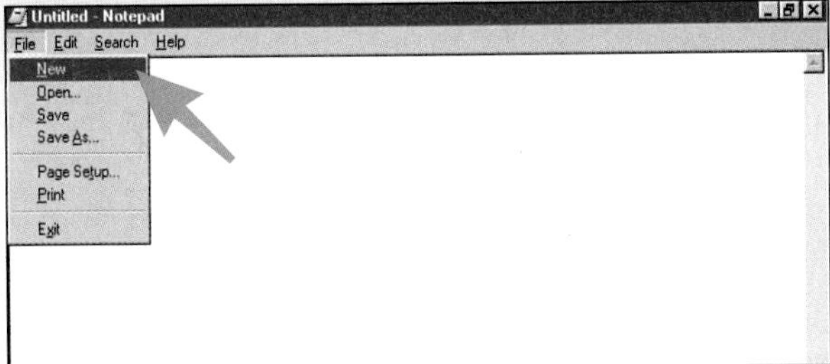

2 Save the Document as a Style Sheet

Now save the document. Instead of using the **.htm** or **.html** file extension you've been using throughout this book, you use the file extension **.css** for this document to identify it as an external style sheet. Give it a filename such as **externalstyle**. In the File Name field of the Save As dialog box in your text editor, type **externalstyle.css**.

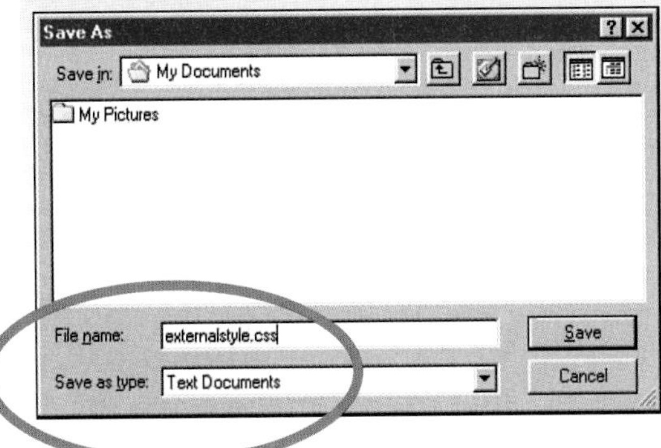

3 Attach the Style Sheet to a Web Page

Use the **<link>** tag to attach the style sheet to as many Web pages as you want. Within the head tag pair of the HTML page, type **<link rel="stylesheet" href="externalstyle.css">**. You are familiar with the **href** attribute from using it with the anchor tag. This pathname assumes that the style sheet document is in the same folder as the Web page. The **rel** attribute defines the style sheet as *persistent*, which means that it cannot be overridden by browser settings.

```
<head>
<title>Using Cascading Style Sheets</title>
<link rel="stylesheet"
href="externalstyle.css" />
</head>
```

4 Test the Page

After attaching the style sheet to the HTML document, open the page in your test browser to make sure that the browser is interpreting the style sheet the way it should be. If you're not happy with the way the page looks, go back to the style sheet document and make the desired changes. Save the changes, and refresh your browser. The changes are instantly reflected in the Web page.

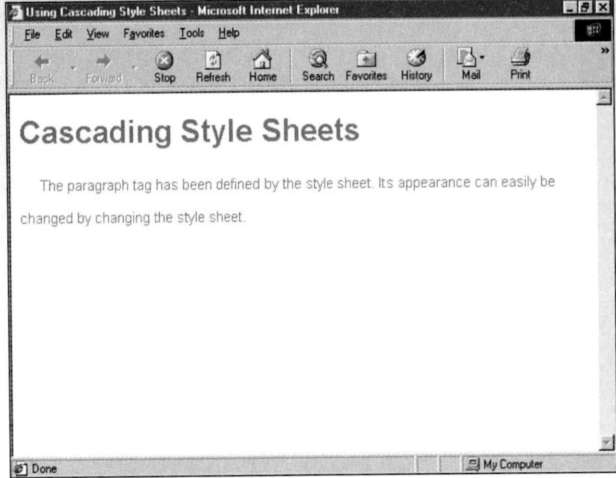

TASK 5

How to Create Embedded Style Sheets

The second method available for using style sheets is to embed the styles directly into the head tag pair of the Web page in which you want to use them. An *embedded style sheet* comes in handy when you have a page on your Web site that you want to present in a different style from all other pages. For instance, perhaps you are running a special promotion and have developed a page especially for advertising the promotion. You want that page to be noticeably different from the rest of your site, so you embed style sheet information directly into it. Embedded style sheets override external style sheets.

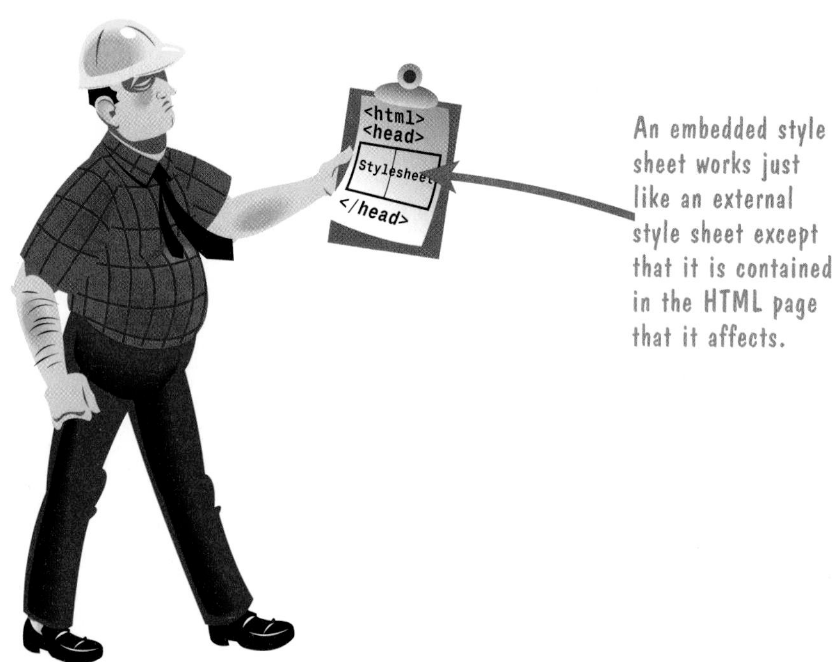

An embedded style sheet works just like an external style sheet except that it is contained in the HTML page that it affects.

Couldn't I Just Use Another External Style Sheet?

Sure, you could use another external style sheet to control the look of the page instead of embedding a style sheet in the page. Even though right now you have only one special page, you might save yourself some work by using an external style sheet instead of embedding the style sheet within the individual HTML page. For example, if you decide later that you need two special promotion pages, you'll have to embed the same style sheet into the second page to make it match the first. If you then decide to change something about the look of the promotional pages, you'll have two pages to change. If you had used an external style sheet, you'd have to change just the one style sheet document to make the change in both promotion pages. However, it might be better to use embedded style sheets in certain instances. For example, if you want to change something about a particular page temporarily, embed the style sheet and override the external style sheet. Later, you can remove the embedded style sheet, and the external style sheet will then take over again.

1 Create the HTML Page

Begin your HTML page as normal (with the addition of the **<!doctype>** tag information that identifies it as an XHTML page). Use the standard HTML tags for everything on the page except those things that you want Cascading Style Sheets to influence. For instance, CSS is good at controlling font styles, so leave out the **<font>** tag (which has been deprecated). You'll have to include the **<p>** tag to add new paragraphs, but leave out the **align** attribute; you'll control alignment with CSS.

```
<!doctype html public "-//w3x//dtd xhtml 1.0
transitional//en" "http://www.w3.org/TR/
xhtml1/dtd/transitional.dtd">
<html>
<head>
<title>Using Cascading Style Sheets</title>
</head>
<body>
</body>
</html>
```

2 Identify the Style Definition Area

Within the **<head>** tag pair, add the **<style>** tag pair. Include the **type** attribute to alert the browser that this page uses an embedded text style sheet. Type **<style type="text/css">**...**</style>**. With CSS2, you'll eventually be able to specify types other than text, such as audio style sheets for the visually impaired. For now, you're limited to text as the style type.

```
<head>
<title>Using Cascading Style Sheets</title>
<style type="text/css">
</style>
</head>
```

3 Add Comment Tags

Whenever you embed style sheets into your HTML pages, make sure that you enclose the style definitions within comment tags. This prevents browsers that don't support style sheets from seeing—and becoming confused by—the definitions. Type **<!--**...**-->** within the **<style>** tag pair.

```
<head>
<title>Using Cascading Style Sheets</title>
<style type="text/css">
<!--
-->
</style>
</head>
```

4 Choose the Selector

Style sheets are made up of a series of what are called *rules*. The rules are simply a way of saying, "Present this element this way." The first part of the rule is called the *selector*. It specifies (or selects) the item you are defining. Selectors are really just HTML tags. For example, the selector is **p** if you want to define the **<p>** tag. Type **p { }** to start your new rule.

```
<style>
<!--
p { }
-->
</style>
</head>
<body>
</body>
```

Continues

5 Specify the Property

The second part of the rule is called the *declaration*. The declaration has two parts: The first of these parts is the *property*. You can specify a number of different properties in each rule. For instance, to change the color of the text within your paragraph tag pairs, use the **color** property. Type **p { color: }** to declare **color** as the property you want to define. Notice that the property is separated from the value (discussed in the next step) by a colon (**:**).

```
<style>
<!--
p { color: }
-->
</style>
</head>
<body>
</body>
```

6 Specify the Value

The second part of the declaration is the value. In the case of the **color** property, the value is the specific color in which you want the text in each paragraph to print. To define the color, you use the same hexadecimal color model used in standard HTML. To specify dark-blue text, type **p { color:#3333ff }**. Notice that, just as in HTML, the hex color recipe must be preceded by the hash mark (**#**), but it is not enclosed in quotation marks. Now the text in every paragraph on this page will print in the color you specified.

```
<style>
<!--
p { color:#3333ff }
-->
</style>
</head>
<body>
</body>
```

7 Separate Two Declarations

You can specify more than one declaration for an element at a time. For example, so far we've changed the color of the text in our paragraphs. We could also specify a font to use. To do so, first type a semicolon to separate the two declarations. Type **p { color:#3333ff; }**.

```
<style>
<!--
p { color:#3333ff; }
-->
</style>
</head>
<body>
</body>
```

8 Type the Next Property

To specify the font to use for your paragraphs, use the **font** property. Don't forget to follow it with a colon. Type **p { color:#3333ff; font: }**.

```
<style>
<!--
p { color:#3333ff; font: }
-->
</style>
</head>
<body>
</body>
```

9 Type the Value

Finally, fill in the value that specifies the type font to use. Notice that the font name is an exception to using quotation marks for declaration values; enclose the type font name in quotations. Type **p { color:#3333ff; font:"arial" }**

```
<style>
<!--
p { color:#3333ff; font:"arial" }
-
</style>
</head>
<body>
</body>
```

10 Specify Another Rule

You can add as many rules as you need to the style sheet. Start a new rule after the closing bracket of the previous rule. You'll probably find it helps to put each rule on a separate line so that it is easy to distinguish one from the next. To add a rule to define the **<h1>** tag in addition to the rule you already created, type **h1 { color:#993300; font:"arial" }** on the next line.

```
<style>
<!--
p { color:#3333ff; font:"arial" }
h1 { color:#993300; font:"arial" }
-->
</style>
</head>
<body>
</body>
```

11 Add the Page Content

Now you can create the content of your page. Although this step is listed here towards the end of the task, you could really have done this much earlier if you wanted. Use all your HTML skills to build your page, except don't use the **<font>** tag. It is no longer needed, because the style rules you wrote will do the work for you.

```
<style>
<!--
p { color:#3333ff; font:"arial" }
h1 { color:#993300; font:"arial" }
-->
</style>
</head>
<body>
<h1>Heading Defined by A Style Rule</h1>
<p>The attributes of this paragraph will be
defined by the style sheet.</p>
<p>Notice that this new paragraph is also
defined by the same style sheet.</p>
</body>
```

12 Test Your Page

That's it. Test your page in your browser. Notice that any additional paragraphs are affected by the style rule. Because you created a rule for the paragraph tag, each paragraph tag follows the rule. Therein lies the power of style sheets. If you now decide that you don't want all your paragraphs to contain blue text, simply change the color in the style sheet, and all paragraphs change with it.

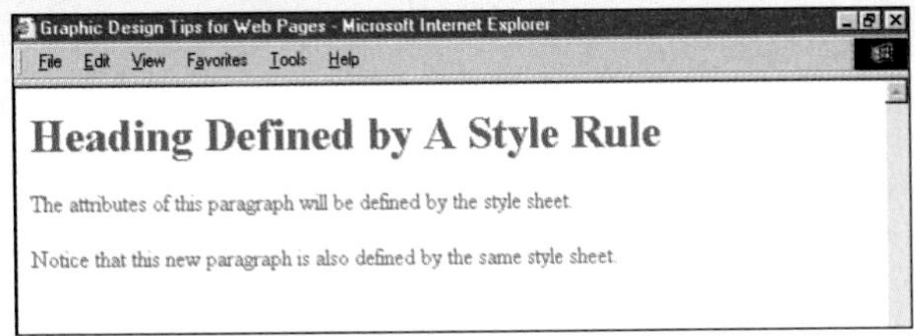

End

TASK 6 How to Create Inline Style Sheets

The final of the three types of style sheets is inline styles. *Inline style sheets* are added just as any other inline tag in your HTML page. They are perfect for making isolated changes (particularly positioning) to a headline, paragraph, picture, or other page element. Inline style sheets override both embedded and external style sheets. They are the least flexible type of style sheet because they are not at all global in nature. In that respect, they're not much different than specifying an HTML tag. But inline style sheets are like HTML tags in that respect only; they are much more powerful than HTML tags alone.

<p style="style definition">
Here's a paragraph
<p class="classname">
Here's another paragraph
Use inline styles much the same as HTML tags; they override both external and embedded style sheets.

That's Where "Cascading" Comes From

Inline style sheets override the settings you make on the same element in your embedded style sheets, which in turn override any external style sheets. That's what "cascading" means. The cascading aspect of style sheets is what makes it practical to make temporary changes to just one page out of a group that's affected by an external style sheet, or a single element out of a group that's affected by an embedded style sheet. This adds an extra dimension of flexibility and usefulness to style sheets. It's easy to see why the style sheet approach to page layout and design is so exciting to Web designers who have been frustrated by the graphic design limitations of HTML. Style sheets are flexible, logical, and comprehensive.

1 Create the HTML Page

Even more than the other two methods of applying style sheets, you'll have to create your HTML page before applying inline style sheets. After you have the HTML in place, you can add the inline style sheet in the appropriate place. For instance, instead of changing font size with the inline **<font>** tag pair, you can add an inline style sheet to accomplish the task and take advantage of the additional functionality of CSS, such as repositioning the text and exercising much greater control over text size.

```
<body>
<h1>How to Use Inline Style Sheets</h1>
<p>To use inline style sheets, first create
the HTML page as you normally would.</p>
</body>
```

2 Define a Paragraph Style

Use the techniques you learned earlier in this part to create an embedded style rule that defines the look of your **<p>** tags. For example, type **p { font:12pt/15pt "arial"; color:#08215A }** to make all your paragraphs print in dark blue, 12-point, Arial text with a line height of 15 points. Don't forget to put the rule within the style tag pair and enclose it in comments to hide it from browsers that don't support CSS.

```
<head>
<style>
<!--
body { margin:30px }
p { font:12pt/15pt "arial"; color:#08215A }
-->
</style>
</head>
<body>
</body>
```

3 Add Two Paragraphs to Your Page

Type two paragraphs into your HTML page. Remember to enclose both of them in their own paragraph tag pair, and place them within the body tag pair.

```
<body>
<p>Here is the first paragraph. It conforms
to the rule you specified in the style tag
pair. It remains unaffected by the inline
style rule you create in the next step.
</p>
<p>Here is the second paragraph. An inline
style rule was added to the style attri-
ubte, and a value was added to make the
text print in red.</p>
</body>
```

4 Test Your Progress

When you're done adding the paragraphs, take a second to save your page and test it in your browser. Notice that both paragraphs share the style you defined in the style rule you constructed in Step 2.

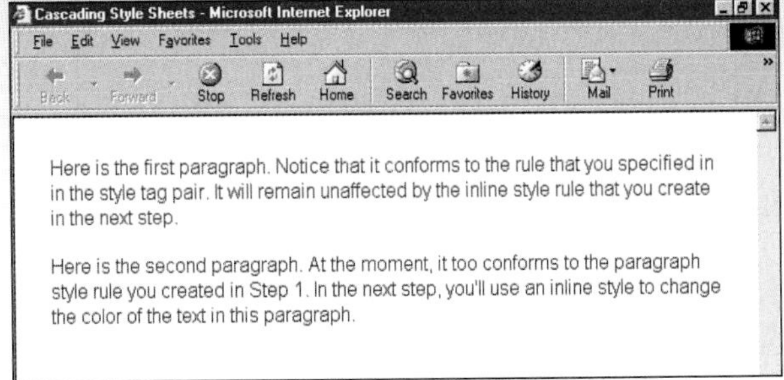

Continues

5 Choose Between a Style or Class Approach

You can use the **style** attribute with almost any HTML tag as one approach to using inline style sheets. This attribute is good for isolated cases. Another approach is to create a new class to refer to an embedded style sheet on the page. This allows you more flexibility to change the class quickly in the future.

6 Add the Inline Style

In the `<p>` tag for the second paragraph, add the **`style`** attribute. For the value of the attribute, define a new style rule that creates dark-red text instead of dark-blue text: Type **`<p style="color:#630000">`** to effect this change. Notice that the **`style`** attribute is defined just the same as any other attribute in that it is enclosed in quotation marks. The rule itself is built just the same as any other style rule you've learned to construct.

```
<body>
<p>Here is the first paragraph. It conforms
to the rule you specified in the style tag
pair. It remains unaffected by the inline
style rule you create in the next step.
</p>
<p style="color:#630000">Here is the second
paragraph. An inline style rule was added
to the style attriubte, and a value was
added to make the text print in red.</p>
</body>
```

7 Test the Page

Save the HTML document and test the page in your browser. Notice that the second paragraph is now in red, and that the first paragraph remains unaffected. Also notice that the second paragraph still prints in Arial. Because you didn't specify a new font face, the inline style rule did not override the **`font-family`** portion of the embedded style rule. Only the color is specified in the inline rule, so only the color is affected.

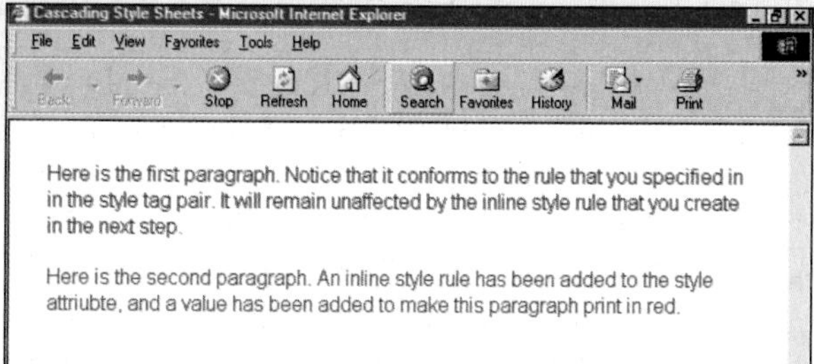

8 Define a New Class

To define a new class, type the tag name, followed by a period, followed by the class name. Then use the normal techniques to define the style rule for that new class. For example, type **`p.othercolor { font:12pt/15pt "arial"; color:#630000 }`** to create a new paragraph class called **`othercolor`**. If you're using an HTML document that employs the inline **`style`** attribute to make changes to individual paragraphs, don't forget to remove the **`style`** attributes.

```
<style>
<!--
body { margin:30px }
p { font:12pt/15pt "arial"; color:#08215A }
p.othercolor { font:12pt/15pt "arial";
color:#630000 }
-->
</style>
```

9 Apply the New Class

In the `<p>` tag for the paragraph you want to affect with the formatting defined by the **othercolor** class, add the **class** attribute. For the value, use the class name you specified in Step 8. Type `<p class="othercolor">` to call the **othercolor** class for a particular paragraph. Save your page and test it in your browser. The second paragraph now refers to the **p.otherclass** style rule, and therefore prints in red.

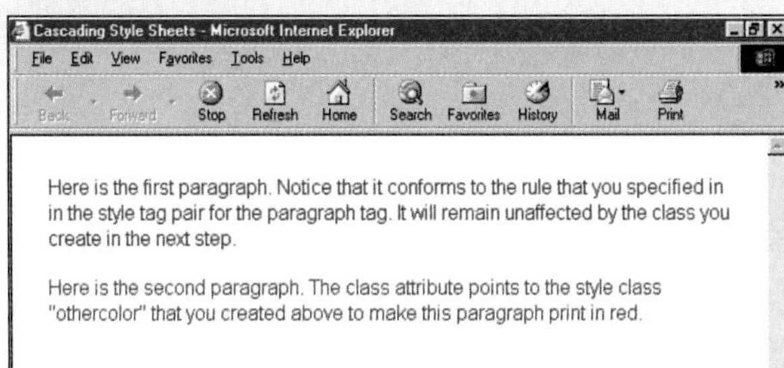

10 Change the Class Rule

Now suppose that you want green paragraphs instead of red paragraphs. You can easily accomplish this change by changing the style rule you created for the **othercolor** class of the `<p>` tag. Type **p.othercolor { font:12pt/15pt arial; color:#299c39 }** to change the color of the **othercolor** class to green.

```
<style>
<!--
body { margin:30px }
p { font:12pt/15pt "arial"; color:#08215A }
p.othercolor { font:12pt/15pt arial;
color:#299c39 }
-->
</style>
</head>
```

11 Test Your Results

Save your page and view the results in your test browser. Notice that by simply changing the color in the **p.othercolor** class rule, you have changed the color of every paragraph that uses the **othercolor** attribute. Any paragraph that uses the regular **p** style rule is unaffected by changes to the **p.othercolor** rule.

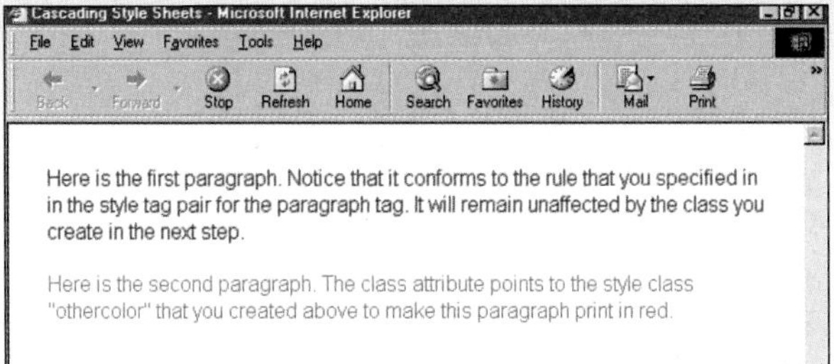

12 Create Custom Tags

You can use the **<span>** and **<div>** tag pairs of HTML along with style sheets to create your own homemade HTML tags. The **<span>** attribute allows you to make custom inline tags; the **<div>** tag allows you to create custom block-level tags. Task 13, "How to Create Custom Inline Tags," and Task 14, "How to Create Custom Block-Level Tags," go into these techniques more completely.

```
<body>
<h3><span class="classname">H</span>ow to
Use Inline Style Sheets</h3>
<p>To use inline style sheets, first create
the HTML page as you normally would.</p>
</body>
```

End

TASK 7 How to Control the Background with CSS

Now that you know how to create style sheet rules, the rest is simply a matter of knowing the selectors, declarations, and properties with which you can work. Although I don't have the space to go over all of them in this book, I'll give you a sampling of some of the most common ones. Although you know how I feel about backgrounds, if you're going to use them, you might as well know how to do it with style sheets. That way, you can remove them quickly and easily when you finally get them out of your system!

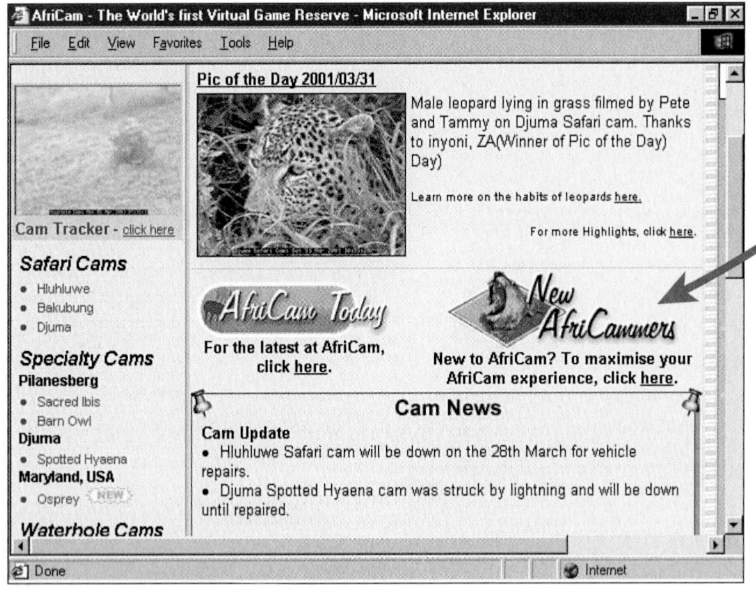

Use style sheets to specify a background color or background image for the body of all pages in your site. Change only the style sheet to change the background in all your pages.

Oh Great...

Just when I've convinced you not to use backgrounds, along come style sheets to allow you to add backgrounds not only to the whole page, but to virtually any item on the page. For instance, if for some sick reason you wanted to put a red background behind the paragraphs that you colored blue in the last task, you can do it. As long as you're at it, why not put a yellow background on the whole page? And then you could add a header with a green background. You always wanted a Web page that looks like a big stop-and-go light, didn't you? Alright, I'll get serious. There might be times when you want to put a light background behind a paragraph or two that you are treating as a sidebar on your page, and this can easily be done to nice effect with style sheets. You'll probably think of other legitimate uses for partial backgrounds. Style sheets make it easy to create them.

1 Start a New Rule

First, let's change the background of the page to a light gray. You can use almost any HTML tag as the selector in your rule, including the **<body>** tag. To start this new rule in the style sheet you began in Task 3, just add it before the paragraph rule you created. The order of your rules doesn't matter for anything other than helping you keep them straight. I like my body rule first. Type **body { }** to begin defining the rule.

```
<head>
<style>
<!--
body { }
p { color:#3333ff }
-->
</style></head>
<body>
<p>The attributes of this paragraph will be
defined by the style sheet.</p>
</body>
```

2 Add the Background Property

Next add the background property to the rule. Remember that although we are using the **body** selector in this example, we could define rules for many other tags (**<p>**, **<h1-6>**, **<ul>**, and so on), and give them a background in the same way that we are using here. Type **body { background }** to add the background property to the **body** rule.

```
<style>
<!--
body { background }
p { color:#3333ff }
-->
</style></head>
<body>
<p>The attributes of this paragraph will be
defined by the style sheet.</p>
</body>
```

3 Specify a Background Color

Like many other properties, the **background** property has several subproperties you can define. For instance, you can specify the background color, the background image, the background position, and more. To specify which subproperty you are setting, separate the property from the subproperty with a hyphen. For example, type **body { background-color:#cccccc }** to specify a gray background color.

```
<style>
<!--
body { background-color:#cccccc }
p { color:#3333ff }
-->
</style></head>
<body>
<p>The attributes of this paragraph will be
defined by the style sheet.</p>
</body>
```

4 Specify a Background Image

Specifying a background image is just slightly different than defining most other values because you must include the pathname to the image you want to use. In this example, assume that the background image is stored in the same folder as the page you're working on, so the pathname is simply the name of the background image. (You can obviously specify more complicated pathnames.) Type **body { background-image:url (background.jpg) }** to define the background image used for the page.

```
<style>
<!--
body { background-image:url(background.jpg)
}
p { color:#3333ff }
-->
</style></head>
<body>
</body>
```

End

TASK 8 How to Create Margins and Padding on a Page

Whenever you create a rule for an HTML tag, the rule is applied every time you use that tag. Each occurrence of the tag actually creates a new "box" that holds the object to which the rule is applied. Three more properties you can define for object boxes are margins, padding, and borders. Every box has a border (whether visible or not). *Padding* is the space between the contents of the box and its border. The *margin* is the space between the border and other object boxes. This task discusses margins and padding; the next task explains borders.

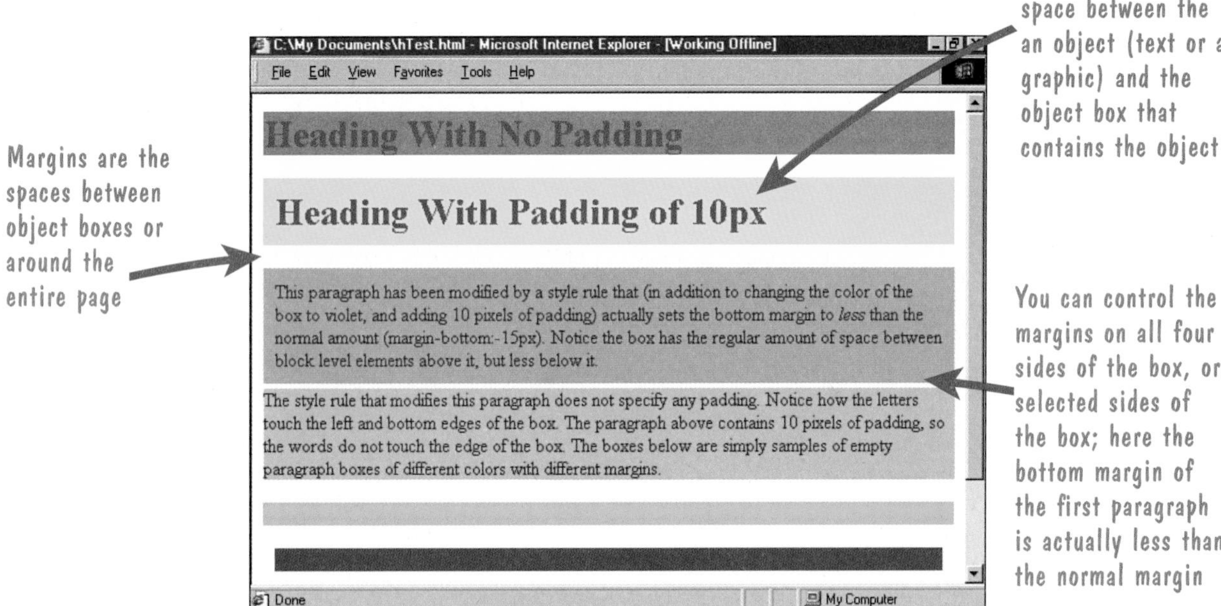

All Boxed In

It helps quite a bit to think of style sheets in terms of the boxes that your rules create around the elements defined by HMTL tags. Even if you choose not to show the border of the object boxes, remember that it is there. You can add margins and padding to create and control the white space between page elements. You can also position these boxes precisely (as you'll learn in Task 10, "How to Control Layout with Style Sheets") for extremely fine layout control (which authors using tables for layout can only dream about. To visualize this, imagine that you created a rule that applied a black border to the paragraph tag. Because the rule creates a new box around each element defined by the **<p>** tag on your page, if you have three paragraphs, you would see three distinct boxes, each holding one of the paragraphs. Adding a margin value in the rule defining the **<p>** tag allows you to control the space between paragraphs.

1 Create Page Margins

When you create a rule for the **<body>** tag, an object box is established around the entire page (although in this case you *can't* add a border to it). Use the **margin** property to define your page margins. The **margin** property has four subproperties (**top**, **right**, **bottom**, and **left**) that can be set individually for different margins on different sides. Type **body { margin:30px }** to set all the margins on the page to 30 pixels.

```
<head>
<style>
<!--
body { margin:30px }
-->
</style>
</head>
```

2 Specify Multiple Properties

You can use the subproperties of the **margin** property to specify margins of different widths for an object. This is a good technique for adding space around three sides of an image. Type **img { margin-top:10; margin-right:15; margin-bottom:10 }** to specify the top, right, and bottom margins for all images on the page. Notice that when you add several properties to one rule, you separate the properties with a semicolon. Some rules can actually get quite long as you add more properties.

```
<head>
<style>
<!--
body { margin:30px }
img { margin-top:10px; margin-right:15px;
margin-left:10px }
-->
</style>
</head>
```

3 Add Padding

Sometimes, you'll want to add space between the object and its border. For instance, you might have a headline that you want to print inside a bar of solid color. You'll want to put a little padding between the text and the edge of the box that contains the headline. Type **h2 { padding:4px }** to specify a padding of four pixels for all **<h2>** headings.

```
<head>
<style>
<!--
body { margin:30 }
h2 { background-color:#30f300;
padding:14px; color:#3333ff }
-->
</style>
</head>
```

4 Add Different Padding to Each Side

As does the **margin** property, the **padding** property has four subproperties: **top**, **right**, **bottom**, and **left**. Type **h2 { padding-top:4px; padding-right:6px; padding-bottom:6px; padding-left:8px }** to specify different padding for each side of the headline. Remember that if you don't specify a side, its padding remains set to **0** pixels.

```
<head>
<style>
<!--
body { margin:30 }
h2 { padding-top:4px; padding-right:6px;
padding-bottom:6px; padding-left:8px }
-->
</style>
</head>
```

End

TASK 9 How to Apply Borders to Page Elements

In this task, you'll learn how to manipulate the borders around the object boxes on your page. Applying borders with style sheets can be a very efficient way to maintain a consistent look for your site (as you learned was so important back in Part 9, "Working with the Layout of Your Web Pages"). A great example is creating a rule that adds a border to the image tag. When you specify this property in a style sheet, the style sheet surrounds all images on the page with the same border. If you later decide to remove the borders from your images, just remove the border declaration from the style sheet rule, and all your images will be borderless.

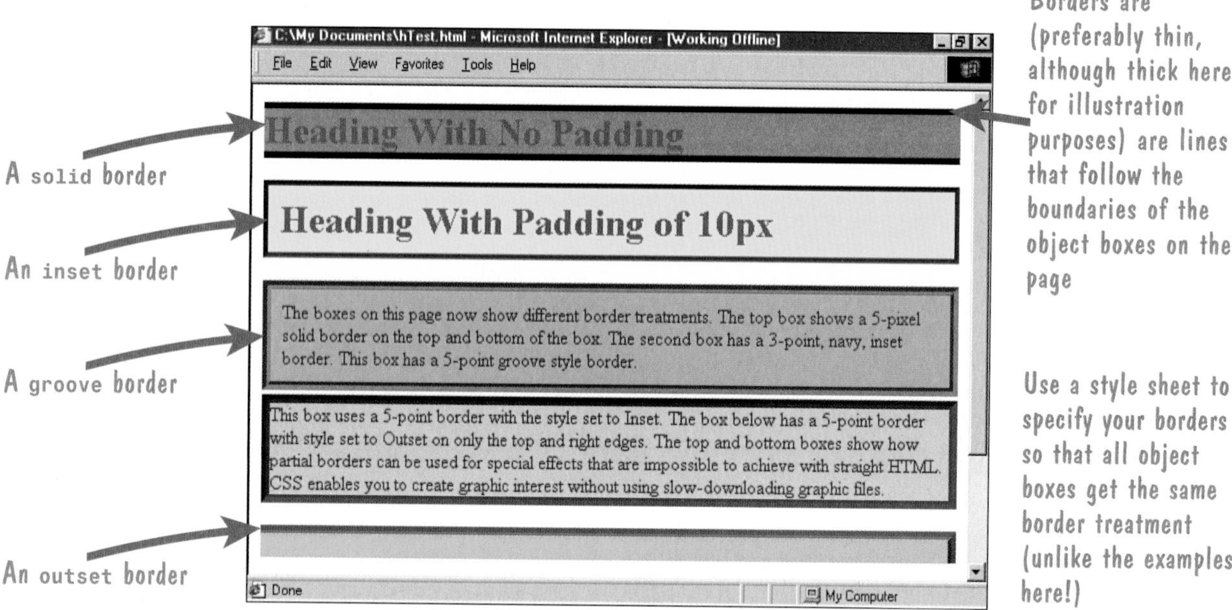

Getting Creative

In Part 6, "Working with Tables," I mentioned that I usually turn off the borders for the tables I use on my pages. Style sheets give you so much more flexibility with borders that I can find a lot more reasons to use them than when I'm stuck using tables. In a table, you can't turn borders on for one cell without turning them on for all the other cells. But style sheets allow you to be more creative. As you'll see, you can turn on the right border for an object box without turning on any of the other borders. In this way, you can create single horizontal and vertical lines to separate parts of your page. If you give the arrangement of elements on the page just a little thought, you can use the borders of the object boxes in creative ways.

1 Define the Border Style

Use the **border-style** property to set all four sides of the border to the same style. Use **border-left-style**, **border-top-style**, **border-right-style**, and **border-bottom-style** to specify different borders for each side of the object box. The style values you can assign to the **border** property are **inset**, **outset**, **solid**, **dotted**, **dashed**, **double**, **groove**, **ridge**, and **none**. For example, type **img { border-style:inset }** to add an inset border around all the images on your page.

```
<head>
<style>
<! –
body { margin:30 }
img {border-style:inset }
– >
</style>
</head>
```

2 Define the Border Color

You can also define the color of the border. Use the **border-color** property to define the color of all four sides of the box. Use **border-color-left**, **border-color-top**, **border-color-right**, and **border-color-bottom** to define different colors for the various sides of the object box. Type **img { border-color:#000000 }** to use a black border around all your images.

```
<head>
<style>
<! –
body { margin:30 }
img {border-style:inset;
border-color:#000000 }
– >
</style>
</head>
```

3 Define the Border Width

Use the **border-width** property to set the width of all sides of the border at once. Use **border-width-left**, **border-width-top**, **border-width-right**, and **border-width-bottom** to set the border of individual sides separately. You can specify the border value as **thin**, **medium**, **thick**, or in pixels. Type **img { border-width:2px }** to specify a two-pixel-wide border for all images.

```
<head>
<style>
<! –
body { margin:30 }
img {border-style:inset;
border-color:#000000; border-width:2px }
– >
</style>
</head>
```

4 Set All Three with One Property

The **border** property has a shortcut method of setting all three of the previous properties at one time. To use it, add the **border** declaration as normal to the rule and then specify the width, style, and color values one after the next separated by a space. For instance, type **img { border:thin black solid }** to create a thin, black, solid border around all your images.

```
<head>
<style>
<! –
body { margin:30 }
img { border:thin black solid }
– >
</style>
</head>
```

End

TASK 10 How to Control Layout with Style Sheets

For anyone who's ever struggled to make their HTML pages look nice by creating tables to force a layout, style sheets are a true blessing. In addition to the **`background`**, **`border`**, and other properties you've learned about in the last several tasks, style sheets provide a number of other powerful layout tools that allow you to put items essentially anywhere on your page. You can even overlap items—another thing you can't do in HTML. This task explores some of the powerful layout tools that style sheets give you.

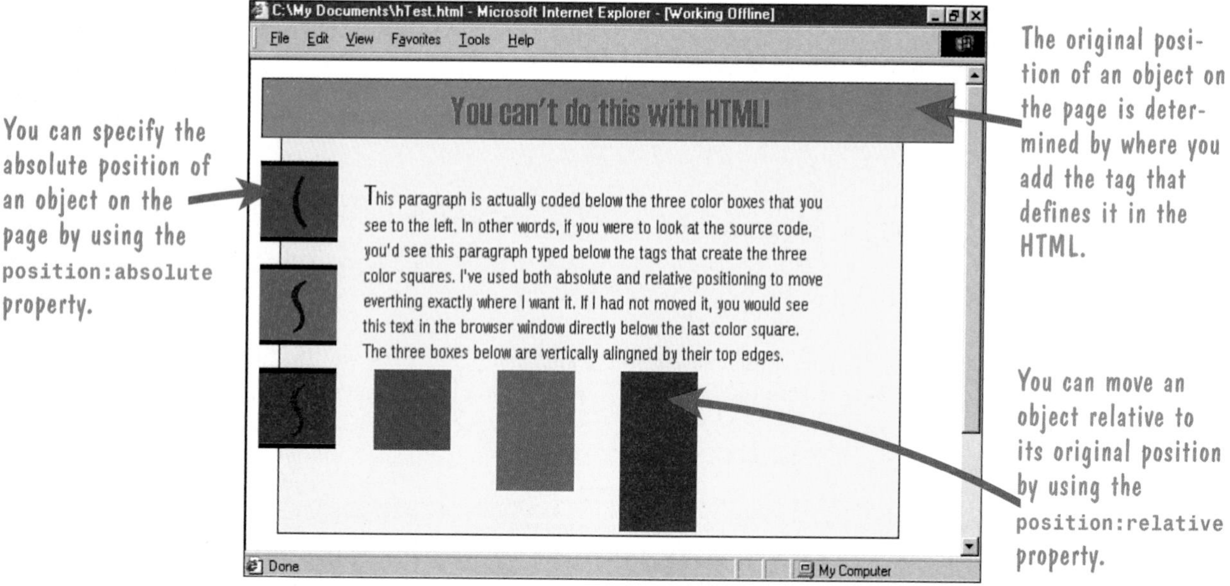

You Say You Want a Revolution

The layout capabilities style sheets bring to Web site design are truly revolutionary. They free the Web designer from the shackles of forced and unnatural page layout inherent in HTML. I don't mean to abandon trusty old tables as soon as something better comes along, but when something *this* much better is available.... As you work with style sheets, it won't take you long to realize how much more powerful and useful they are for layout purposes than HTML tables. Style sheets allow you to position objects precisely where you want them. They let you create layers of objects. They allow you to control the space between objects. In short, they give you real layout tools instead of workarounds, and they allow you to present your pages without excuses or compromise.

1 Position Objects

You can place items exactly where you want them on your page. With the **position** property, you can specify the position of an object relative to its normal position on the page, or you can specify an absolute position for the object. To position an image 50 pixels to the left and 10 pixels below its original position, type **img { position:relative;left:-50px;top:10px }**. To position the image at an absolute location of 50 pixels down, 20 pixels right of the top-left corner of the page (position 0,0), type **img {position:absolute;top:50px;left:20px }**.

```
<head>
<style>
<!--
body { margin:30 }
img {position:absolute;top:50px;left:20px }
-->
</style>
</head>
```

2 Control Text Wrap

Just as in regular HTML, an image appears on the page in line with the text around it by default. As you learned back in Part 5, "Implementing Web Graphics," Task 6, "How to Wrap Text Around a Graphic," it looks nice if you flow text around the side of an image. To specify how text wraps around an image, add the **float** property to the image rule. Type **img { float:left }** to wrap text around the right edge of graphics.

```
<head>
<style>
<!--
body { margin:30 }
img { float:left }
-->
</style>
</head>
```

3 Set Height and Width

Style sheets give you precise control over the dimensions of object boxes. Use the **width** and **height** properties in the rule to specify these measurements in pixels. Most text-related tags (such as **<p>** and **<h1-6>**) don't support the **width** property. To control the width of those elements, enclose them in a **<div>** tag pair, as discussed in Task 14, "How to Create Custom Block-Level Tags," and specify the width for that. For images, including these dimensions helps the browser load the page. Type **img { width:550; height:320 }** to specify dimensions.

```
<head>
<style>
<!--
body { margin:30px }
img { width:550; height:320 }
-->
</style>
</head>
```

4 Set Vertical Alignment

Use the **vertical-align** property to align one or more object boxes on the page. The three most logical properties (and the ones I use most often) are **top** (to align the top edges of the objects), **bottom** (to align the bottom edges), and **middle** to align them by the midpoints of the objects. For example, type **img { vertical-align: top }** to align the top edges of the image objects on the page.

```
<head>
<style>
<!--
body { margin:30px }
img { vertical-align:top }
-->
</style>
</head>
```

End

TASK 11 How to Define Font Appearance and Style

One of the most significant tags to be deprecated in favor of CSS is the `<font>` tag. The **font** properties of style sheets give you great power to present your text in exactly the way you want. You typically add the **font** properties to the rules you develop for presenting paragraphs and headers, although you may often use the technique of defining fonts in your `<span>` and `<div>` tags, too. You'll learn how to use those tags in Task 13, "How to Create Custom Inline Tags," and Task 14, "How to Create Custom Block-Level Tags."

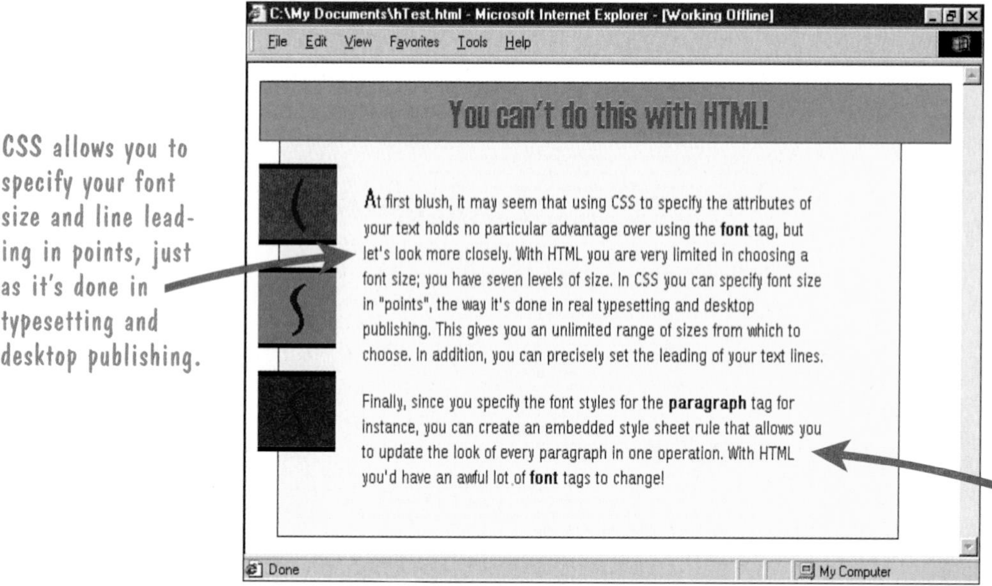

C:\My Documents\hTest.html - Microsoft Internet Explorer - [Working Offline]
File Edit View Favorites Tools Help
You can't do this with HTML!
At first blush, it may seem that using CSS to specify the attributes of your text holds no particular advantage over using the font tag, but let's look more closely. With HTML you are very limited in choosing a font size; you have seven levels of size. In CSS you can specify font size in "points", the way it's done in real typesetting and desktop publishing. This gives you an unlimited range of sizes from which to choose. In addition, you can precisely set the leading of your text lines.
Finally, since you specify the font styles for the paragraph tag for instance, you can create an embedded style sheet rule that allows you to update the look of every paragraph in one operation. With HTML you'd have an awful lot of font tags to change!
Done
My Computer

CSS allows you to specify your font size and line leading in points, just as it's done in typesetting and desktop publishing.

Text font and size can be tied to elements such as paragraphs with style sheets. This makes it infinitely more practical to change fonts or size for an entire Web site.

<font> or font?

It can be a little confusing; in CSS, the HTML `<font>` *tag* has been replaced mostly by **font** *properties*. Using style sheets, you'll no longer use the deprecated `<font>` tag to specify the face, size, or color of your text. Instead you'll use the various font-related properties presented in this task to accomplish those things and more. As you'll see, these properties can be added to the rules you define for text-related tags such as the paragraph tag and the various heading tags. Using style sheets allows you to set these values globally so that you can change them easily if you decide to change the look of your page later. You can also add these font properties to the `<div>` and `<span>` tags you'll learn more about in Tasks 13 and 14.

1 Specify Typeface

Use the **font-family** property to specify the typeface you want to use. Just as you can with HTML, you can use style sheets to specify whatever font you like on your pages. However, it is still the best policy to stick with Times and Arial (and Helvetica for the Macintosh) because those fonts are typically installed on every computer. For example, type **h3 { font-family:"arial" }** to specify the **Arial** typeface for all your **<h3>** tags.

```
<head>
<style>
<!--
body { margin:30px }
h3 { font-family:"arial" }
-->
</style>
</head>
```

2 Specify Type Size and Color

Use the **font-size** property to specify the size of your text in points (the standard measurement for fonts, which is much more flexible than the HTML system); use the **color** property to specify the color of the text. Note that the **color** property is not related to the **font** properties and can be used independently. To make your **<h3>** tags create dark red, 16-point text, type **h3 { font-size:16pt; color:#630000 }** within the style tags.

```
<head>
<style>
<!--
body { margin:30px }
h3 { font-family:"arial";
font-size:16pt; color:#630000 }
-->
</style>
</head>
```

3 Specify Type Style and Weight

Use the **font-style** property to define your text with the **normal**, **italic**, and **oblique** values (often it is difficult to distinguish between italic and oblique text). Use the **font-weight** property to define your text with the **normal**, **lighter**, **bold**, or **bolder** values. For example, to make your **<h3>** tags create bolder-than-normal and italic headings, type **h3 { font-weight: bolder; font-style:italic }** within the style tags.

```
<head>
<style>
<!--
body { margin:30px }
h3 { font-family:"arial";
font-weight:bolder; font-style:italic }
-->
</style>
</head>
```

4 Specify Several Properties at Once

The preceding steps explained how to specify font properties one at a time. Sometimes it's easier to specify all the properties at once. Use the **font** property to do so: Type **h3 { font:italic bolder 16pt "arial"; color:#630000 }** to set the style, weight, size, and typeface for all **<h3>** tags. Note that there are no commas (just spaces) between the values, and that the order of the values must be exactly as they are listed here (style, weight, size, family), although only the size and family values are required. The **color** property must still be specified separately.

```
<head>
<style>
<!--
body { margin:30px }
h3 { font:italic bolder 16pt/24pt "arial";
color:#630000 } -->
</style>
</head>
```

End

TASK 12 How to Align Text with CSS

Style sheets have revolutionized Web page layout and design. At least they will when browsers finally support them properly. With style sheets, you can easily accomplish tasks that HTML authors can only dream about or achieve through awkward workarounds. Now, controlling the space between letters (known as *tracking* when applied over entire blocks of text or *kerning* when applied to two adjacent letters) is easy. Adjusting the *leading* (the space between lines of text) is a snap. Indenting the first line of each paragraph is a breeze. This task explores some of the most useful style sheet techniques for working with the text in paragraph and heading tags.

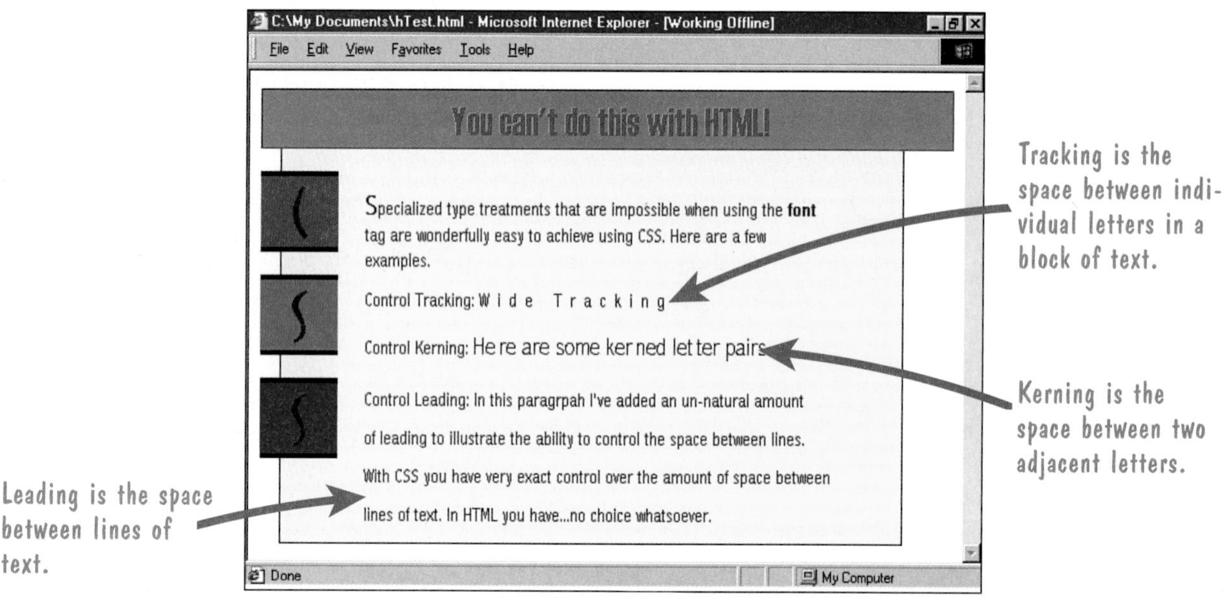

With Power Comes Responsibility

Style sheets are a wonderful advancement in Web technology. They are powerful, flexible, and easy to use. They give you all kinds of new ability to present page elements in creative ways. So, what could possibly be the problem with that? Well, I don't call it a problem exactly, but a caveat. Now more than ever you must keep in mind that "just because you can, doesn't mean you should." With the flexibility of style sheets comes the increased probability that we'll soon see all kinds of new and—shall we say, "interesting"—graphic design decisions on the Web. It's more important than ever for you to develop a solid base of graphic design skills so that you can put the power of CSS to work *for* you instead of *against* you. Style sheets allow you to massage your pages into effective communicators. They also open the door wide for graphic design atrocities. Which way will you go?

1 Control the Space Between Letters

You can create more space between the letters on your page with the **letter-spacing** property. Adjusting the tracking for the letters in a block of text can be useful for special design effects, as well as for making some typefaces easier to read (especially at smaller font sizes). However, beware that too much space between letters makes your text *more* difficult to read, so use this technique judiciously. For example, type **h3 { letter-spacing:20px }** to add 20 pixels of space between each pair of letters in your level-three headlines. To subtract space, use a negative value.

```
<head>
<style>
<!--
body { margin:30px }
h3 { letter-spacing:20pt }
-->
</style>
</head>
```

2 Control the Space Between Lines

The **line-height** property enables you to create interesting graphic effects as well as affect the readability of your text. Use it to specify the space between lines (called *leading*). For example, type **h3 { line-height: 20pt }** to make the line height 20 points. You can also define line height in the **font** property, as discussed in Step 4 of Task 11, "How to Define Font Appearance and Style." To do so, tack the line height value onto the type size value: **h3 {font: 16pt/20pt "arial" }**.

```
<head>
<style>
<!--
body { margin:30px }
h3 { line-height:20pt }
-->
</style>
</head>
```

3 Underline and Strike Through Text

With the **text-decoration** property, you can use the values **underline** (to underline text), **line-through** (to run a line through—or strike through—text), or **overline** (to put a line above text). For example, type **h3 { text-decoration:underline }** to underline your level-three headings.

```
<head>
<style>
<!--
body { margin:30px }
h3 { text-decoration:underline }
-->
</style>
</head>
```

4 Indent and Align Text

You use the **text-align** property to specify the alignment of your text with the **left**, **right**, and **center** values. Remember that left-aligned text is generally the easiest to read, but the other types of alignment can be used for occasional special design effects. Type **p { text-align:right }** to align the text in your paragraphs to the right. Use the **text-indent** property to indent the first line of your paragraphs by an absolute value. Type **p { text-indent:20px }** to indent the first line 20 pixels.

```
<head>
<style>
<!--
body { margin:30px }
p { text-indent:20px }
-->
</style>
</head>
```

End

TASK 13

How to Create Custom Inline Tags

Another of the features that really makes CSS a treasure for Web designers is that you can use it to make "homemade" tags. For instance, if you have several sections in your Web site, and you give the introduction of each section the same graphic treatment, you can create a custom tag and use it to define the style for all the section introductions. Two HTML tags—**<span>** and **<div>**—make creating custom tags possible. The first of these, the **<span>** tag pair, enables you to create custom inline tags. This task shows you how to use the **<span>** tag pair to create a common graphic design element: a stylized initial-cap letter. In Task 14, you'll learn how to use the **<div>** tag.

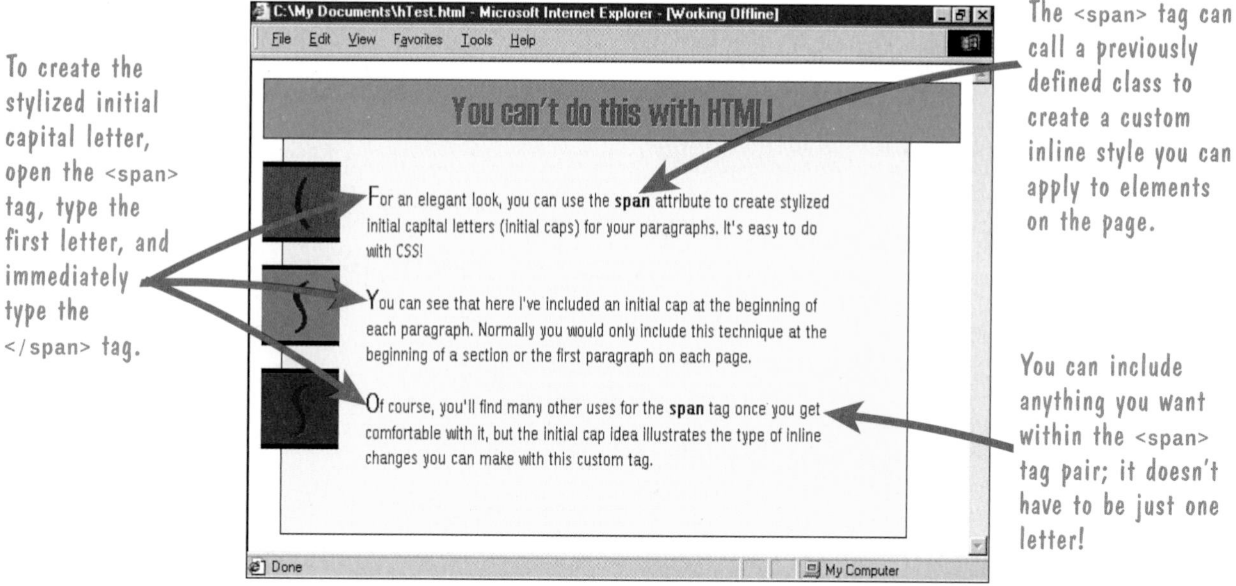

Have Some Class

The key to successfully using the **<span>** tag and the **<div>** tag (discussed in the following task) is to remember that they both rely on the **class** attribute technique discussed in Task 6, "How to Create Inline Style Sheets." Although these tags are both part of the HTML 4 definition, they don't do anything on their own. You must write a style sheet rule that can be referenced by the **class** attribute of these two tags. Their beauty lies in the fact that they are not related to, or based on, any other tag. They are truly freelance tags you can use in any way to define a style rule. They work just like any other HTML tag. You add one to your page (don't forget the **class** attribute!), type the appropriate definition information, and then type the closing tag. I'll give you an example of how to use each, but you'll surely think of many others as you become more familiar with the technique.

1 Create a New Class

With the techniques you learned in Task 6, create a new class of the **<span>** tag. This class will allow you to quickly and consistently create a stylized initial capital letter for any paragraph to which you apply the class. Type **span.initialcap { }** to set up a new class of the **<span>** tag called **initialcap**. Add any other style rules you need to create the look you want on your page.

```
<style>
<!--
body { margin:30px }
p { font:12pt/15pt "arial"; color:#08215A }
span.initialcap { }
-->
</style>
```

2 Write the Rule

To create a stylized initial capital letter, write a rule that specifies a different font size and typeface than what is used by the paragraph in which you intend to insert the initial cap. You might also want to specify a complementary color to use for the initial cap.

```
<style>
<!--
body { margin:30px }
p { font:12pt/15pt "arial"; color:#08215A }
span.initialcap { font:bold 18pt/15pt
"Lucida Handwriting"; color:#630000 }
-->
</style>
```

3 Apply the Style

Now type your paragraph. At the very beginning of the paragraph (after the **<p>** tag and before the first letter) type **<span class="initialcap">**. Then type the first letter of the paragraph. Finally, type **</span>** to close the initial cap treatment and continue typing the rest of the paragraph.

```
<body>
<p><span class="initialcap">A</span>dding
the initial cap to your paragraph is now
simply a matter of using the span tag and
calling the initialcap class. Don't forget
to close the span tag.</p>
</body>
```

4 Test the Page

Save your page and open it in your test browser. The first letter of the paragraph is now stylized. Note that you could include as many letters or words within the span tag pair as you want. Maybe you want the entire first word to be stylized, or the entire first line. Just move the closing **</span>** tag to include as much text as you want.

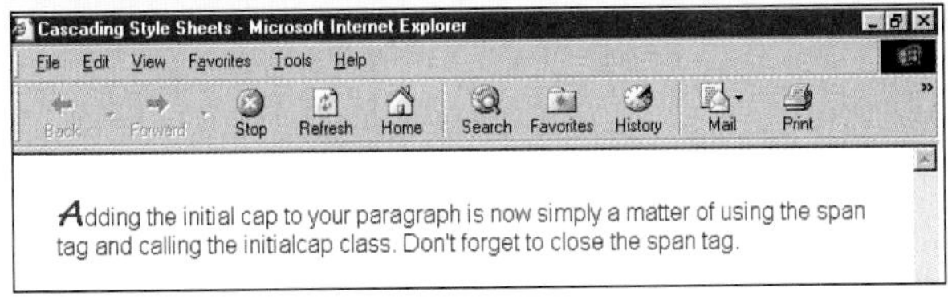

End

TASK 14

How to Create Custom Block-Level Tags

The **<div>** tag allows you to create custom block elements. For instance, you might want to create sidebars in which both the header and the paragraph text are right aligned, but are in every other way the same as all other headers and paragraphs. You could create special classes of the **<p>** and **<h3>** tags to specify the right alignment, but it might be easier to define a new **<div>** tag class to do it. Then enclose the header and paragraph within the div tag pair to apply the treatment. This task shows you how.

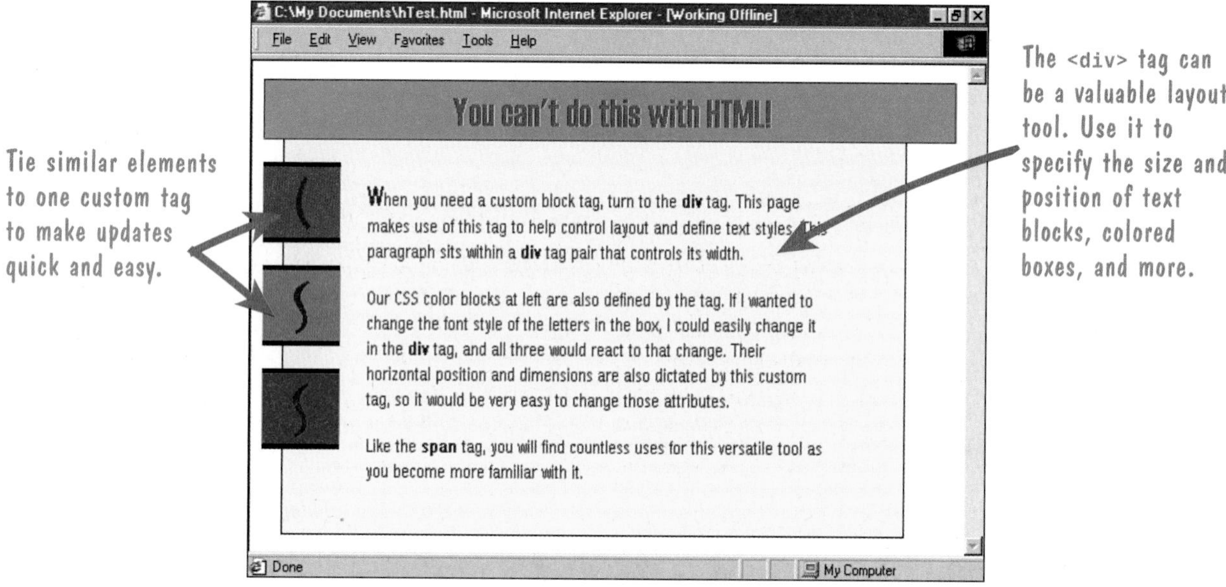

Powerful Tools

The **<span>** and **<div>** tags (and their corresponding closing tags) are two of your most powerful Web design tools. Because they have no default function, you can do pretty much whatever you want with them. Your ability to create custom tags with them expands the control you have over your pages light years beyond where HTML alone could take you.

<div> or <span>? Name Your Poison

It can be difficult at first to keep these two tags straight. The key difference is that the **<div>** tag is a block element. Therefore, every time you use it, it creates a paragraph break. The **<span>** tag is an inline element; it does not create a paragraph break.

1 Create a New Class

You create a new class of the **<div>** tag just as you have created other classes previously. Type **div.sidebar { }** to declare a class called **sidebar**. Add any other style rules that you need for your page.

```
<style>
<!--
body { margin:30px }
h3 { font:16pt/20pt "arial"; color:#630000 }
p { font:12pt/15pt "arial"; color:#08215A }
div.sidebar { }
-->
</style>
```

2 Write the Rule

To the **sidebar** class declaration, add the rule that will define the look of your right-aligned sidebar. Use the **text-align** property, the **background-color** property, and the **border-width** property to give the sidebar its unique look.

```
<style>
<!--
body { margin:30px }
h3 { font:16pt/20pt "arial"; color:#630000 }
p { font:12pt/15pt "arial"; color:#08215A }
div.sidebar { margin-right:30px;
position:relative; top:0; left:0;
float:left; padding:15px;
text-align:right;
background-color:#94d6e7; width:200px;
border: solid thin #000000 }
-->
</style>
```

3 Apply the Style

To apply the style to a paragraph and its heading, enclose the paragraph and heading within the div tag pair. In the opening **<div>** tag, use the **class** attribute with **sidebar** as the attribute value to apply the sidebar style. Type **<div class="sidebar">...</div>** to do so.

```
<div class="sidebar">
<h3>Right-Aligned Text Made Easy</h3>
<p>By including this paragraph and heading
within the div tag pair, you can use the
class attribute to refer back to the
sidebar class. If you decide to change
the treatment, you can change the style rule
applied to the sidebar class.</p>
</div>
<h3>A Regular Header and Paragraph</h3>
<p>Notice that this paragraph maintains its
regular properties because it is not
surrounded by the div tag pair. The text
enclosed within the div tag pair appears as
a sidebar on the left edge of the page.
This text flows to the right.</p>
```

4 Test the Page

Save your page and view it in your test browser. The heading and paragraph you enclosed within the div tag pair appear at the left edge of the page in a light blue box with a thin black border. These elements also appear right aligned. The heading and paragraph you added after the **</div>** tag appear to the right using the paragraph and heading styles defined by the style sheets. They are unaffected by the **sidebar** class.

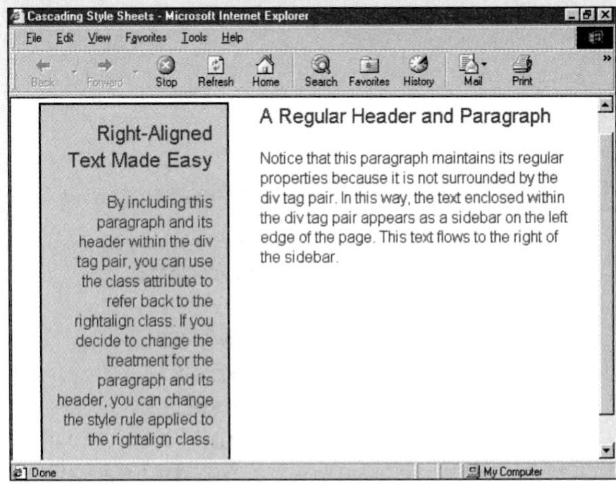

End

TASK 15 How to Learn More About CSS

Although you now know enough about Cascading Style Sheets to get started controlling the layout of your pages with them, there is much more that I was not able to cover here. I urge you to find out as much as you can about CSS. Sooner or later, we will all be using style sheets much more than is currently practical. You can turn to a number of resources to learn more about the technology. This task gives you a few ideas.

You can learn more about CSS from reference books and Web sites.

Learn from Others

Because many style sheets are embedded into the pages that they control, you can see what other people are doing by reading the source code of pages that have been created using style sheets. (Remember that, to view the source code, you right-click the Web page and choose your browser's equivalent of **View Source** from the pop-up menu.) It might be difficult to identify pages that use embedded style sheets, but after you get used to the limitations of graphic layouts created with HTML, you might be able to recognize when a page looks like it steps beyond those limitations. If you come across a page with a layout that looks too complicated for HTML, take a quick peek at the source code. Even if the author doesn't use style sheets, you should be able to learn something from the code! (Unfortunately, you won't be able to view the code of external style sheet documents.)

1 Read a Good Book

A number of good books are available to help you learn more about Cascading Style Sheets. Visit Amazon.com and search for **`Style Sheets`**. You'll find a number of excellent titles from several authors. Your local bookseller will doubtless have many other options as well.

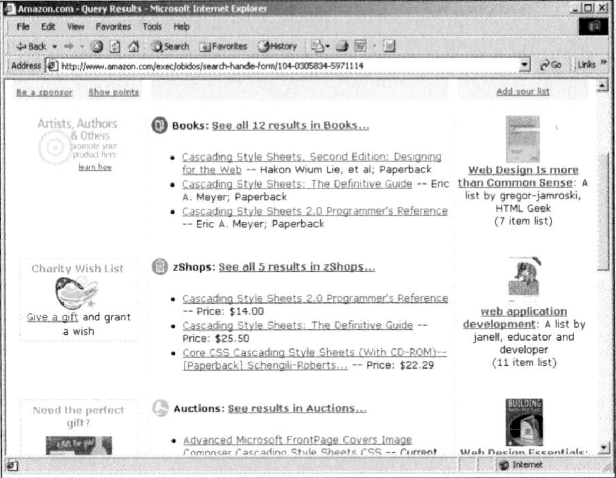

2 Explore Online Resources

You can find a wealth of information on the subject of Cascading Style Sheets on the Web. A great place to start looking is the W3C Cascading Style Sheets home page. There is a ton of useful information there, and you can follow countless links to other resources. Alternatively, go to your favorite search site and run a search on **`Style Sheets`**. You'll find all kinds of helpful sites. To visit the W3C Cascading Style Sheets home page, go to **`http://www.w3.org/Style/CSS/`**.

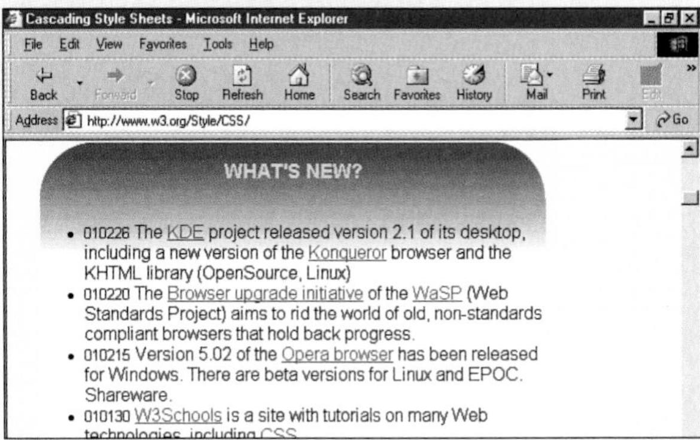

3 Attend a Seminar

You should be able to find good seminars and conferences in your area on the subject of Cascading Style Sheets. Check with your local community or technical college. These institutions often offer useful courses. Check the Web for programs coming to your area. My search for **`Style Sheets Seminar`** on **`www.Google.com`** netted several possibilities.

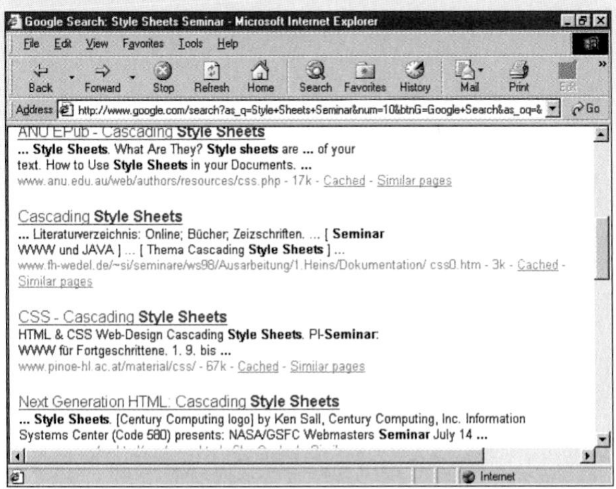

4 Learn by Doing

Nothing beats experience! The more you work with style sheets, the more you'll grow to understand them. As your understanding grows, you'll begin to use more and more sophisticated techniques.

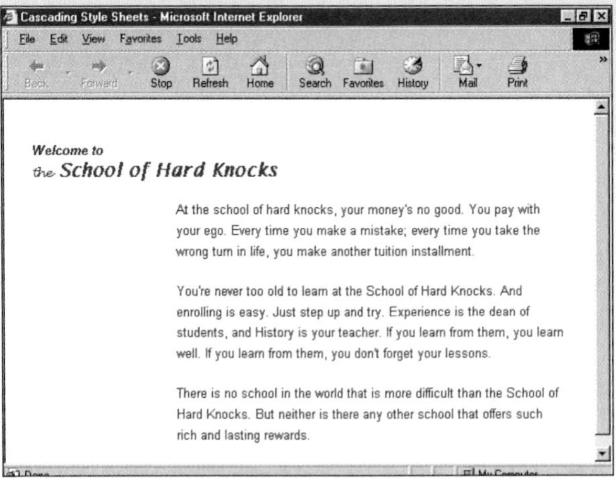

End

Task

PART 11

Incorporating Multimedia

Ah, multimedia! The gem of the Web...The darling of the Internet...The promise of Shangri-La...An unending repository of sight and sound, all waiting for your whims and desires. You can see anything, you can hear anything. And it all looks and sounds impeccable.

Ah, reality. I won't call multimedia on the Web a disappointment, but its great promise is certainly as yet unrealized. Probably the biggest obstacle to realizing the promise of rich multimedia experience on the Web is that of limited bandwidth. Most of us are still simply connecting to the Internet at modem speeds that are too slow to support the delivery of sight and sound at the quality we are used to with our televisions and compact disc players.

Disappointing, yes. A lost cause, absolutely not! Just because we're not all the way there yet doesn't mean there aren't a lot of good things happening in the multimedia area of the Web. You *can* see just about anything—it just won't look like the DVD movie you rented last night. And you *can* hear just about anything—you just won't get the CD-quality surround sound that shakes the plaster off the downstairs neighbor's ceiling.

Things are getting better. Huge steps have been made with audio over the Internet. Witness the MP3 craze—highly compressed audio files that impressively reduce file size while maintaining equally impressive sound quality. As MP3 continues to grow in popularity, other technologies such as Microsoft's Windows Media Audio, RealNetworks' RealMedia, Liquid Audio, OggVorbis, and a host of other audio formats continue to improve in an attempt to win the hearts of the Web-listening audience. (See the Glossary for quick definitions of these formats.)

Video is coming along, too, although the huge processing demands of video make progress here lag behind that of the audio technologies. RealNetworks, Apple, and Microsoft have all developed ways to deliver video over the Internet in formats known as *streaming video* that allow you to begin viewing a file without waiting for the entire file to download.

There's just no way we can thoroughly cover this whole issue in one part of an introductory HTML book. But, at the very least, you'll become familiar with some basic concepts, as well as come away with a few solutions and techniques for including multimedia in your pages. There's a lot to learn in this area, and hopefully this quick overview will at least get you speaking the language of multimedia over the Web.

TASK 1

How to Determine What Multimedia to Include

Multimedia is such a broad area it's sometimes difficult to decide where best to start. You're probably getting used to my style by now, so you might have figured that my first suggestion involves a little bit of planning. This task explores some of the issues to think about when you're deciding what type of multimedia to add to your page—or even whether you should add multimedia at all. It isn't always necessary to add audio and video; you must decide whether adding multimedia is worth the time that it takes to do so.

Use sound as your first option for multimedia because sound file sizes are usually smaller than those for video—especially for MIDI.
Use video only when necessary; the large file sizes and long download times might be more than your visitors are willing to suffer through to view what you want to show them.
Page Plan
Video?
Audio?

What Gives You the Right?

Keep in mind that it's easy to run afoul of the law in the area of multimedia. Although you might think it's innocent to tape something funny on TV and post it up to your Web site so that your visitors can share the joke, the owners of the copyrights for that TV program won't look at it that way. You might think you're not really hurting anyone if you use your favorite song as background music for your home page, but the owners of the copyrights for that music won't agree. If you created the video or audio, you have the right to post it to your Web site. If you didn't, don't use it without written permission from the copyright owner. What difference does it make to anyone? It means money. And money is a great motivator. If someone thinks they're losing an opportunity to make money because you're using their work without permission, they might be motivated to call their attorney. Are you prepared to call yours?

1 Evaluate the Message

Take a good look at the message you are trying to convey on your page. If you can convey that message adequately without multimedia, it might be a good idea to do so. Delivering text only, or even text and graphics, requires much less bandwidth than delivering multimedia. It also takes much less time to prepare text and graphics than it does to prepare multimedia.

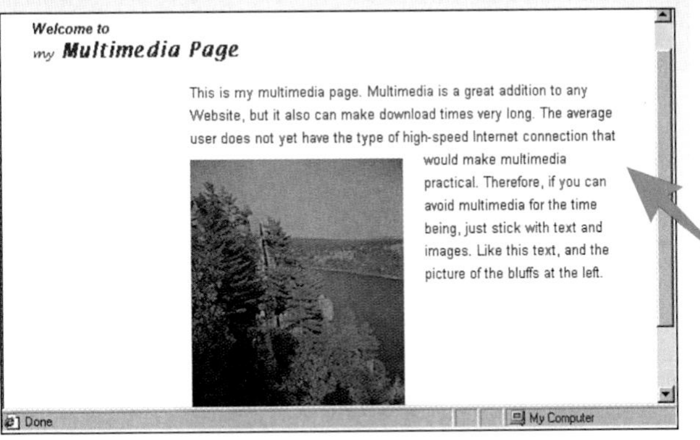

2 Choose an Audio Message

If you've determined that text and graphics just aren't enough, decide whether you can get by with just an audio message. For instance, if you make music that you want to share with your site's visitors, a bit of text, a graphic or two, and a few audio samples might be enough to give your visitors an idea of what they'll be getting if they buy your CD.

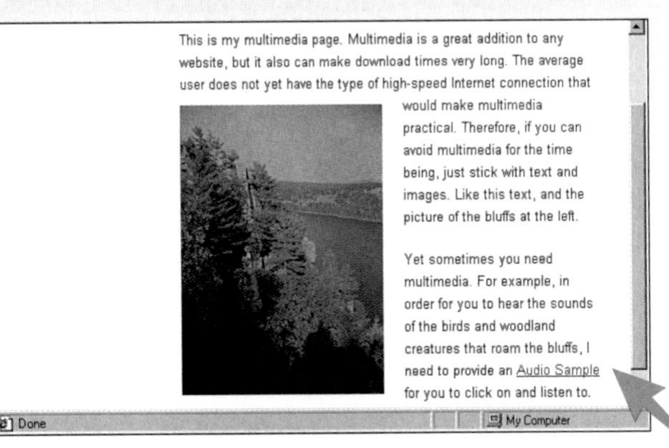

3 Choose a Video Message

Maybe text, graphics, and audio still aren't enough. For example, if you're trying to promote your first music video, both the audio and video portions are important for giving your visitors the complete experience of your work. Or perhaps you've been asked to deliver the contents of the company meeting to your salespeople out in the field. If photos and a transcript of the meeting won't cut it, you might have to include the entire video.

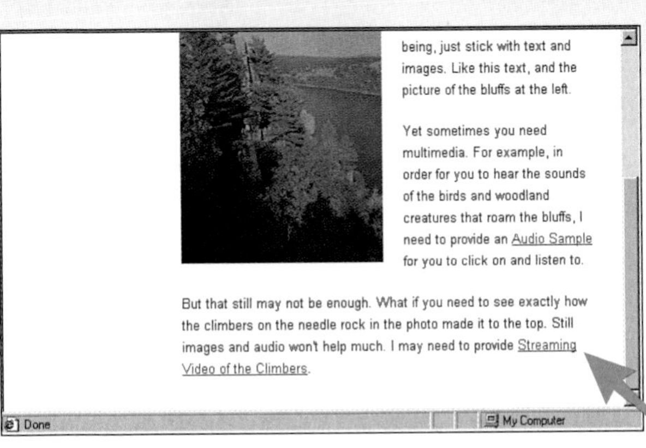

4 Choose an Animated Message

Other times, animation might be the way you've decided to convey your message. An obvious example is if you are an animator, and you want to showcase your work. Or maybe you've developed a new piece of equipment, and you want to use an animation to present it to your investors. There are countless situations in which animation might be the technique you decide to use.

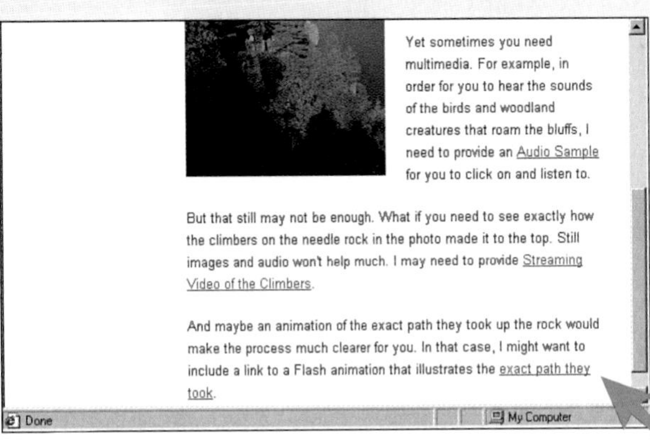

End

TASK 2 How to Link to Multimedia Files

The most straightforward and easiest way to provide multimedia on your Web pages is to create a link directly to the movie or audio file. Your visitors can then choose whether they want to experience your multimedia offering. If so, they can click the link. If not, they can move on. Links are a good way to provide the multimedia experience not only because it is easy to do, but also because it puts the power in the hands of your visitors to decide whether they want to wait through the download necessary to play the file.

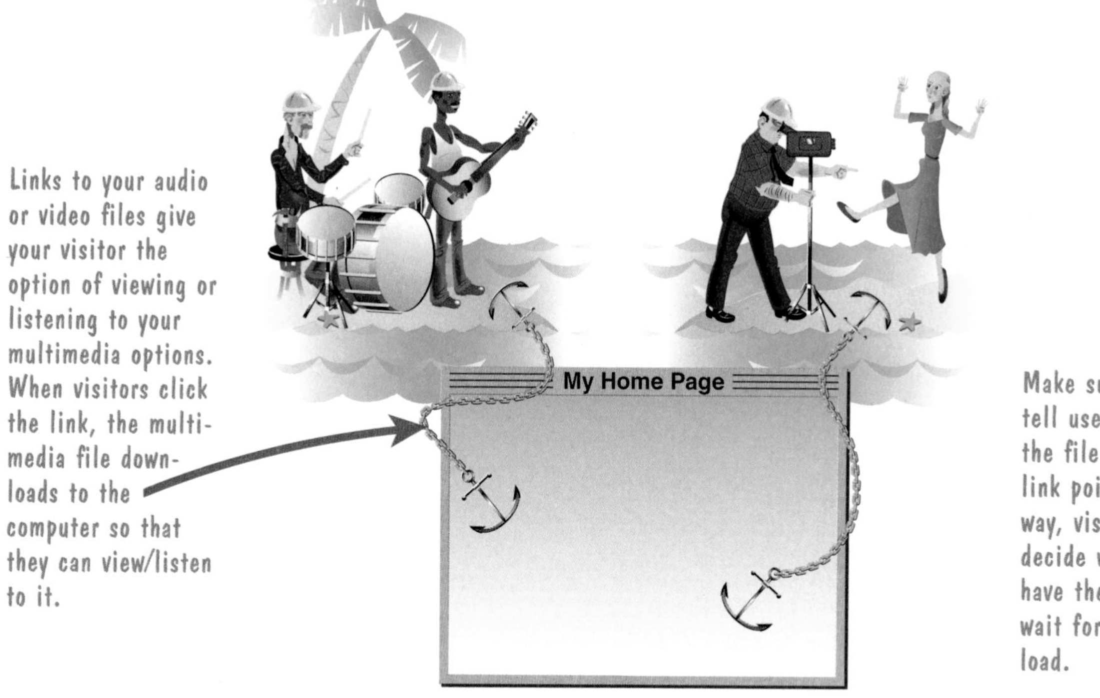

Links to your audio or video files give your visitor the option of viewing or listening to your multimedia options. When visitors click the link, the multimedia file downloads to the computer so that they can view/listen to it.

Make sure that you tell users how big the file is that the link points to. That way, visitors can decide whether they have the time to wait for it to download.

What Happens When You Click?

When your visitor clicks the link to your multimedia file, a couple possible outcomes exist. For some files (such as **.wav** audio files and **.avi** video files on the Windows operating system), both Netscape Navigator and Internet Explorer launch a player, download the multimedia file to a temporary directory, and play the file. Other times, the browser might not recognize the file type and will open a dialog box to ask whether you want to specify a player to use or to save the file to your hard disk. Obviously, depending on your choice, a player will open, download the file to a temporary directory, and play the file, or the file will be downloaded to a location you specify so that you can play it later. Keep in mind that by right-clicking the link you provide, visitors can download the multimedia file to their computer. If you don't want people to copy your file, don't provide a link to it!

1 Create the Anchor Tag

Just as you do with any other link you build on your page, to link to a multimedia file, you insert an anchor tag onto your page. Type **`<a href="url">hear my great new song</a>`** where **"url"** is the pathname of the file to which you are linking.

```
<html>
<head>
<title>Working with Multimedia</title>
</head>
<body>
<p>
If you like music, <a href="url">hear
my great new song</a>!
</p>
</body>
</html>
```

2 Link to an Audio File

Fill in the **href "url"** attribute value with the pathname of the file to which you want to link. The pathname should look just like any of the other paths you built earlier in this book. Pay special attention to the file extension of the file to which you are linking. For instance, to link to a WAV audio file called **mysong.wav**, type **`<a href="../multimedia/mysong.wav">hear my great new song</a>`**.

```
<html>
<head>
<title>Working with Multimedia</title>
</head>
<body>
<p>
If you like music, <a href="../multimedia/
mysong.wav">hear my great new song</a>!
</p>
</body>
</html>
```

3 Link to a Video File

Linking to a video file is exactly the same as linking to an audio file. The only difference lies in the file extension of the file to which you are linking. For example, to link to an AVI video file, type **`<a href="../multimedia/mymovie.avi">see my great new movie</a>`**.

```
<html>
<head>
<title>Working with Multimedia</title>
</head>
<body>
<p>
If you like music, <a href="mysong.wav">
hear my great new song</a>!<br />
If you like movies, <a href="myvideo.avi">
watch my great new movie</a>!
</p>
</body>
</html>
```

4 Test Your Links

Save your page and open it in your test browser. Click each link to verify that each link works as expected.

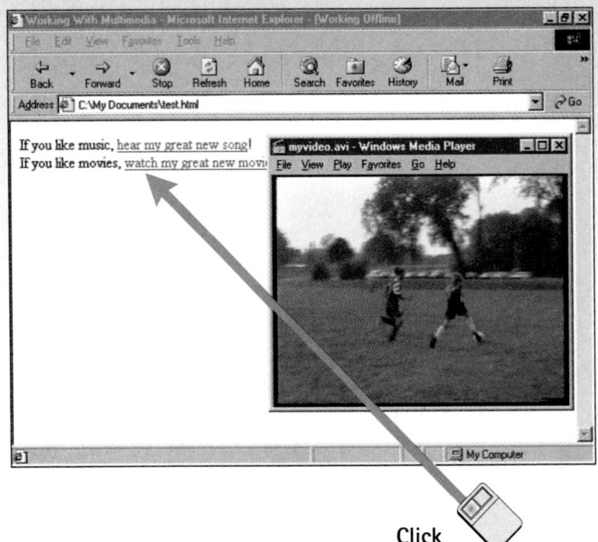

TASK 3 How to Embed Multimedia Files

Another way to include multimedia is to embed the files right into the pages themselves. Embedding a file allows you to provide a multimedia player on the page from which the visitor can control the playback of the audio or video. This arrangement can make for a nice, clean, compact presentation; some people feel that it looks more professional and sophisticated than simply supplying a link to a file. This task explores the basic issues involved with embedding multimedia into your Web pages.

The embedded player appears as part of the page.

Reasonable types of multimedia files to embed in your page include audio files that play background sounds after the page loads and animation files.

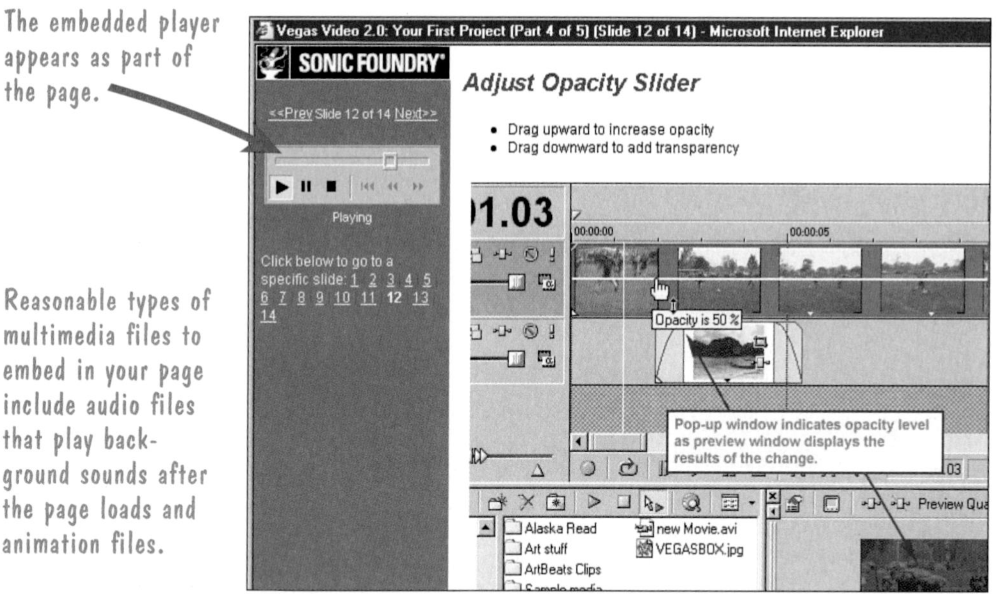

The HTML 4.0 specification includes the <object> tag, but support for this tag from the major browsers has been sketchy.

Good in Theory

In theory, embedding multimedia in your pages makes a good deal of sense. It's compact, clean, and easy. The reality is, unfortunately, far from any of those adjectives. The W3C has specified that the **<object>** tag be used for the purposes of embedding multimedia. But in their infinite wisdom, the two major browser manufacturers have apparently decided that they know better, and neither supports the **<object>** tag exactly as the W3C has specified. Internet Explorer does a better job than Netscape Navigator, which doesn't handle it well at all. Instead, Navigator relies on a tag that is not even part of the HTML 4 specification, the **<embed>** tag. In the end, you're forced to use a combination of the two. Confused? So are a lot of other people. Annoyed? You're not alone. Frankly, to me it's not worth the trouble. I'd rather provide links, or use a streaming format, which you'll learn to do in Tasks 7, 8, and 9.

1 Add the Object Tag

The first step in embedding multimedia files in your page is to add the object tag pair. Internet Explorer uses this tag to play the multimedia file. Add this tag pair within the body of your document, just as you would add any other tag. Type **<object>...</object>**.

```
<html>
<head>
<title>Working with Multimedia</title>
</head>
<body>
<p>
The following is an
embedded video file:<br />
<object>...</object>
</p>
</body>
</html>
```

2 Specify the Desired File

Use the **data** attribute to specify the file you want to embed in the page. For the attribute value, type the pathname that leads to the file.

```
<body>
<p>
The following is an
embedded video file:<br />
<object data="../multimedia/myvideo.avi">
</object>
</p>
</body>
```

3 Add the Embed Tag

Now that you've covered Internet Explorer with the **<object>** tag, you'll use the **<embed />** tag to tell Netscape Navigator to look for the multimedia file. Type **<embed />** (notice that you close this tag as you do the **
** and several other tags). Notice also that the **<embed />** tag is nested within the **<object>** tag pair.

```
<body>
<p>
The following is an
embedded video file:<br />
<object data="../multimedia/myvideo.avi">
<embed />
</object>
</p>
</body>
```

4 Specify the Multimedia File

Use the **src** attribute to specify the file you want to embed in your page. You are familiar with this attribute from adding images to your page. For the value of the attribute, type the pathname that points to the file you want to embed.

```
<body>
<p>
The following is an
embedded video file:<br />
<object data="../multimedia/myvideo.avi">
<embed src="../multimedia/myvideo.avi" />
</object>
</p>
</body>
```

End

TASK 4

How to Decide Which Audio Format to Use

There are many different audio formats—far too many to talk about here. The most common full-quality formats are WAV for Windows machines and AIFF for Macintosh machines. There are also compressed formats, the most famous of which is MP3. WMA files and RM files are the most popular formats for "streaming" audio from your Web site (as described in Task 9, "How to Stream Media from Your Site"). This task explores these file formats and helps you decide which one is the right one for your Web page.

The WAV/AIFF formats are capable of higher-than-CD quality. The file size is typically too large for Web delivery.
WAV/AIFF
MIDI is a way to send data instructions that play synthesized music.
MIDI
MP3
STREAMING
The MP3 file format greatly compresses the file size of an audio file while maintaining relatively high quality.
Streaming audio allows your visitors to begin listening to the audio before it fully downloads.

There Is No "Right One"

The truth is, you'll probably want to give your visitors many options as far as file types go. For instance, Macs use the full-quality AIFF file format but Windows machines use the WAV format. Because some of your visitors will be using Macintoshes and others will be using Windows PCs, you should probably include both formats if you want to supply your visitors with the highest-quality audio file possible. In general, both platforms can play either file format these days, but it doesn't hurt to supply both formats. Later on, we'll talk about MP3 and streaming formats. Here again you might want to include a number of formats. For instance, if you provide an MP3 file, you might also want to include a full-quality version such as WAV or AIFF—or both. Of course, if you provide too many options, you might end up confusing your visitors, so be careful that way, too!

1 Provide Full-Quality Files

The audio in WAV and AIFF files is uncompressed and so contains all the originally recorded audio quality. A professionally recorded WAV or AIFF file sounds as good as a CD. Obviously, more quality is better, but it comes at a price—large file sizes.

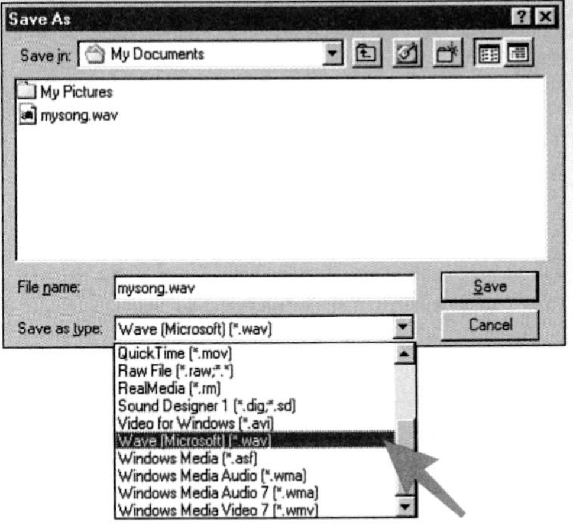

2 Provide an MP3 File

MP3 is probably the hottest audio format on the Web today. This compressed file format allows you to create files with sizes roughly 10 times smaller than a WAV or AIFF file of the same material. When you use MP3, however, you pay the price in reduced audio quality. Still, MP3 files are popular because they retain an impressive amount of quality given the rate of file compression.

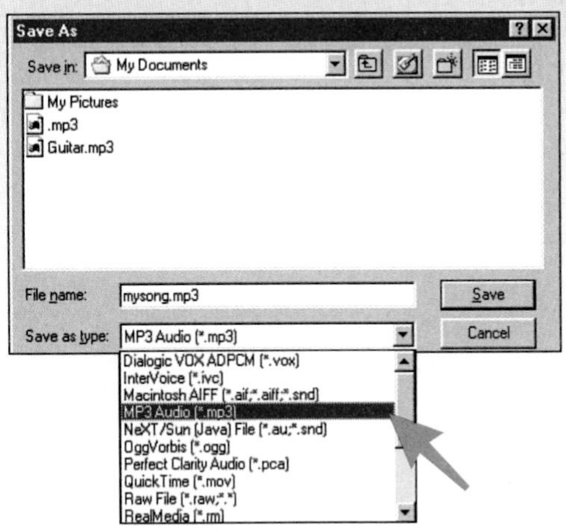

3 Provide a MIDI File

MIDI files contain a set of instructions that your visitor's computer interprets and plays back as music. Because a MIDI file contains digital instructions instead of audio, the file sizes are extremely small, and download times are cut dramatically. The downside is that the musical quality might not thrill you. You cannot use the MIDI format to supply acoustic sounds (such as speech or other "real-world" sounds).

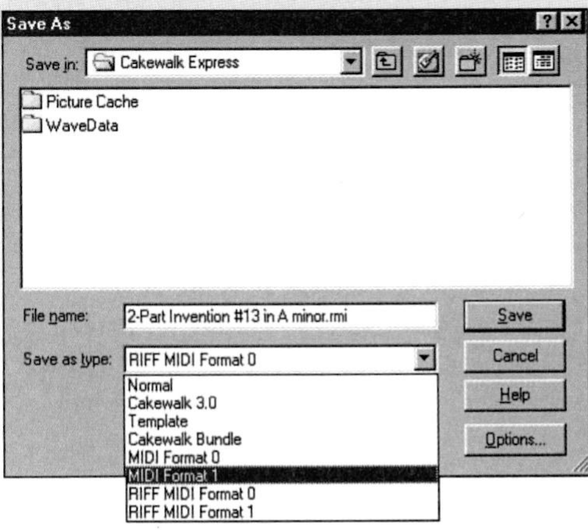

4 Provide Streaming Audio

The process of *streaming* (typically with Windows Media Audio and RealMedia formats) is one in which the audio is downloaded to the visitor's machine even as he or she listens to the file. You can typically provide fair quality audio with this method. Streaming audio is an excellent choice when you want to avoid long downloads. Later tasks explore this technique in more detail.

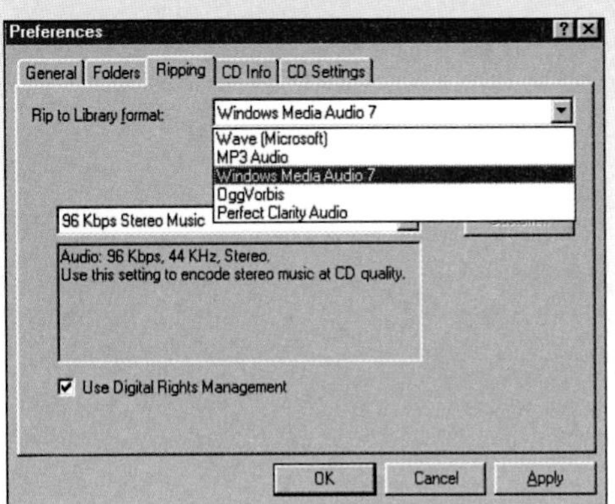

TASK 5

How to Create MP3 Audio Files

As mentioned earlier, the MP3 audio craze has made that format the hottest topic on the Web. You know something's big when it replaces the word *sex* as the most frequently entered word at search sites! It's easy to see why when you can include an MP3 file on your page that most people would say sounds almost as good as the full-quality version, yet is roughly one-tenth the file size. This task shows you how to create MP3 files using Siren XPress, a free tool from Sonic Foundry, but you can use any number of software tools to get the job done.

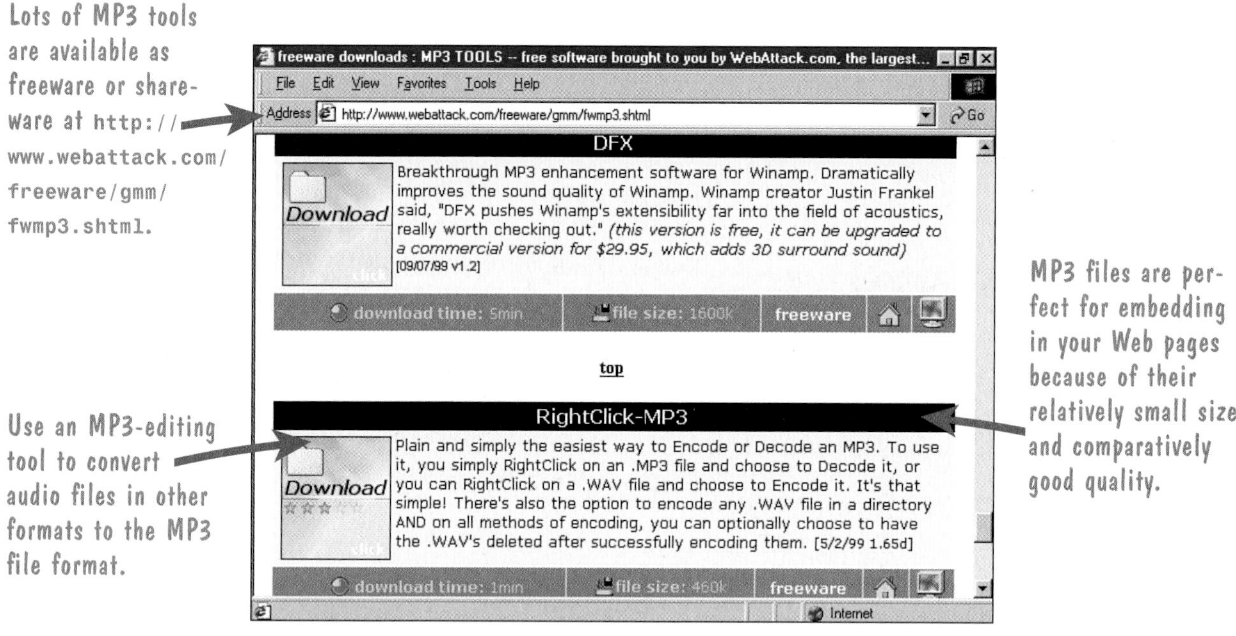

Lots of MP3 Tools

I use Siren XPress in this task for several reasons. First, because my job is to train people how to use Sonic Foundry software (including Siren XPress), I'm obviously very familiar with this program. In addition, it's one of the most versatile pieces of software available for working with your music collection. And the full version of the software does even more than the free, limited version available for download. Still, because MP3 is so popular, it should come as no shock that there are a number of companies that offer excellent software tools you can use to create MP3 files. Some of them are free consumer applications, and some are quite expensive pro-level programs. Some devote themselves strictly to MP3s, and others provide full-featured music management. Search for **"MP3 Creation Tools"** (or similar phrases) at your favorite search site. You can download Siren XPress free from the Sonic Foundry Web site at **www.sonicfoundry.com**.

1 Locate the Original File

Click the **Explore Files** tab in the **Media Manager** panel. This action brings up a Windows Explorer–type window that allows you to navigate the folder structure of your computer to find the file you want to convert to MP3. Typically, this file will be a WAV file, but it can be in any of a number of other formats that Siren XPress recognizes. Click the filename to select it.

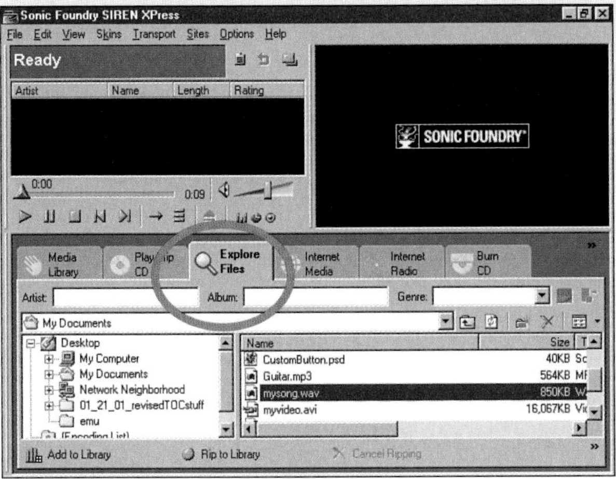

2 Choose Your Ripping Options

Siren XPress calls the process of converting a file to MP3 "ripping to the Media Library." First, set your ripping options: Choose **Options, Preferences** and click the **Ripping** tab. In the **Rip to Library format** drop-down list, choose **MP3 Audio**. Then choose your desired quality from the drop-down list that contains the choices and descriptions. For quick downloading over the Web, the **64 Kbps FM Radio Quality Audio** option is best. Click **OK** to finalize your settings.

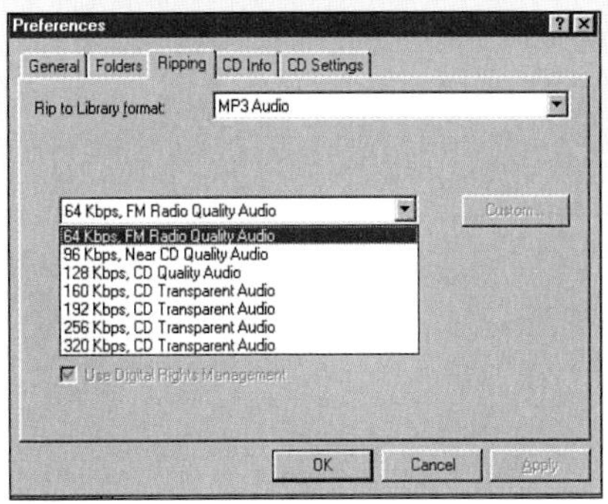

3 Rip to the Media Library

Click the **Rip to Library** button at the bottom of the Siren XPress window. Dismiss the next dialog box and sit back; Siren XPress is doing its thing!

Click

4 Play Your New MP3 File

Click the **Media Library** tab to view the contents of your Media Library. By default, the Media Library is stored in a folder on your C drive called **`My Music`**. From the **Media Library**, click the name of the MP3 file to select it, and then click the **Play** button to listen to your new MP3.

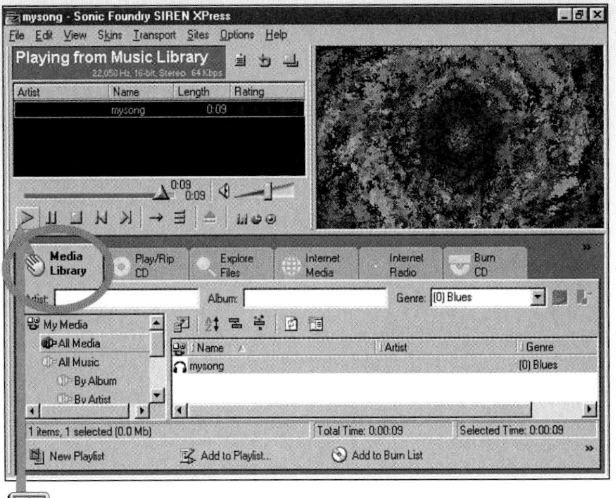

Click

End

TASK 6 How to Prepare Video for the Web

The incredibly high processing demands of video make its delivery over the Web a challenging area indeed. In reality, you currently have only one choice, and that is to "stream" your video. I introduced the concept of streaming audio in Step 4 of Task 4, "How to Decide Which Audio Format to Use," and the idea is the same for video. The way you prepare the video plays a huge roll in the results you achieve. This task presents some of the issues to keep in mind when preparing your video for streaming. This isn't all you need to know, but the tips in this task will get you started.

When preparing and shooting video for the Web, simplify the background as much as possible.
DIRECTOR
SCRIPT
Keep your video edits simple. Use jump cuts instead of fades or other transitions. Use stationary shots instead of zoom and pan techniques.
Minimize the amount of motion in the clip to reduce the file size of the clip (think talking head).

Wanna Be Frustrated?

If you like frustration, you've come to the right place! Video on the Web is full of challenges. There are so many variables and so much to think about that even people who have been involved with the technologies for a long time find themselves scratching their heads trying to find a better way. But video on the Web also holds out one of the juiciest carrots to Web pioneers. The prize that awaits the first one to figure out how to deliver high-quality, full-motion video to the masses over the Web is sweet. Rest assured that, sooner or later, someone will figure it out. A new technology will be born. Or a breakthrough improvement on current technology will open the floodgates. However it happens, and whenever it happens, there is likely to be an explosion of video across the Internet. If video is your game, it's an exciting time to be involved.

1 Keep It Simple

The biggest mistake people make with streaming videos is to make the video too complex. You'd better get out of your MTV editor role right away, especially when targeting visitors who connect with a 56Kbps modem. Keep things as simple as possible. Instead of shooting the video with a backdrop of a beautiful lake and waving willows, shoot against a blank wall.

2 Keep Motion to a Minimum

Part of keeping things simple is to hold motion down to a minimum. If you're shooting a person giving a lecture, don't let the person wander back and forth on stage. One reason not to shoot in front of those wonderful waving willows is that all that motion puts too many demands on the equipment.

3 Crop Out Unnecessary Content

Another enemy of video streaming is unnecessary content. All those little extras that make a video interesting on TV—such as the gentle waving of shadows in the background, or cars driving by behind the focal point to set the scene, only spell trouble for streaming video. The best streaming video is a "talking head" in which you shoot a virtually motionless speaker from about mid-chest up. Crop out everything you can that isn't critical to the message.

4 Edit for the Web

When you edit the video clip you have made, edit with the Web in mind. Avoid fancy video filters such as noise generators and wave filters. Instead of using complex transitions or crossfades from scene to scene, use simple jump cuts. Avoid compositing techniques such as picture-in-picture and other methods of showing more than one video clip on the screen simultaneously. Basically, all the things that make video editing fun are danger signs in the streaming world. Sorry!

End

TASK 7

How to Encode Streaming Audio

In this task, I'll show you how to convert a WAV file into a Windows Media Audio (WMA) file—a process known as *encoding*—so that you can stream it to your Web visitors and save them a long download wait. You can use Siren XPress to accomplish the task. WMA is Microsoft's streaming file format for audio. In this capacity, the format competes mainly with Real Media (RM) files from RealNetworks.

Obviously, audio is hard to portray in print media, but with streaming audio, you can play a portion of a sound track while the rest of the sound track is downloading; the sound "streams" as it plays.

Media players do not depend on the Web browser (although they may be embedded into the Web page), so any streaming format can play on any machine, as long as the visitor has a media player that supports the format. Most major media players support all the major streaming formats.

To play streaming audio files, visitors need a media player; most computers come with audio and video players such as Windows Media Player or RealPlayer, but you can direct your visitors to `www.download.com` to look for a particular free player.

This figure shows a streaming audio file playing in Siren Xpress.

Sometimes Free Matters

This task talks about creating a streaming file in Microsoft's WMA format. RealNetworks offers RealSystem Producer Basic free. You can download it from **`http://www.realnetworks.com/products/producer/index.html?src=pddwnld`** (say that three times fast!) Many programs will create files of both types. But I wanted to give you free alternatives in this book so that you can easily test the concepts, and then decide whether or not you should spend the money on a for-sale product. These days, any audio editing software that's worth its salt should be able to save both WMA and RM files. Sonic Foundry Sound Forge XP Studio is a great audio editor that you can purchase for less than $50. (It is also bundled free with many different software and hardware packages, so you might already own it!) Sound Forge XP Studio allows you to create streaming audio files in both formats.

1 Find the Desired File

In Siren XPress, click the **Explore Files** tab. Navigate through your local or network drives to the location of the file you want to encode. Click the file and then click the **Play** button to listen to it and verify that it is the correct one. If you have more than one file to encode, select them all now (press **Ctrl** as you click to select the various files).

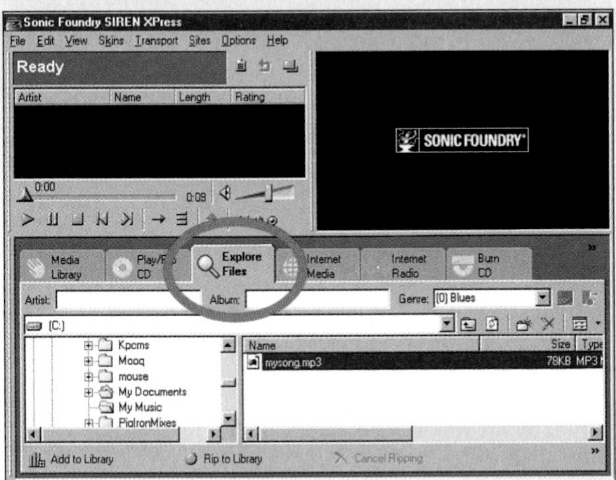

2 Set the Ripping Preferences

In Siren XPress, choose **Options, Preferences**; click the **Ripping** tab. From the **Rip to Library format** drop-down list, choose **Windows Media Audio 7**. Choose an encoding quality from the next drop-down list that is equal to or less than the connection speed of your typical visitor. For instance, if your visitors connect with 56Kbps modems, you won't have much luck trying to stream a file encoded with the **128Kbps CD Transparency Audio** option.

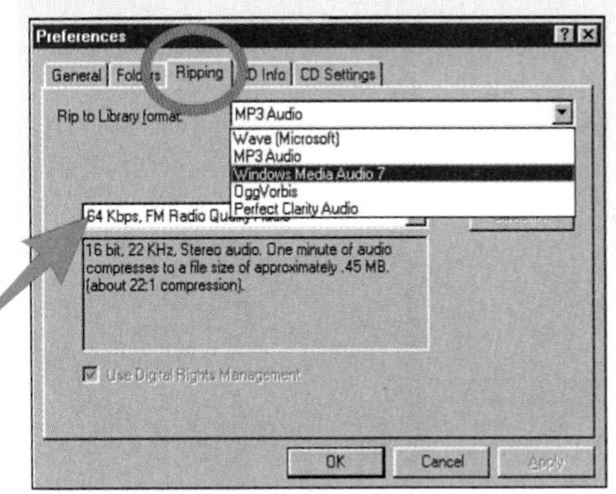

3 Rip to WMA

After you dismiss the **Preferences** dialog box, click the **Rip to Library** button. Siren XPress encodes each selected file to the WMA file format and places the encoded files in your **Media Library**. By default, the Media Library is the **My Music** folder on your C drive.

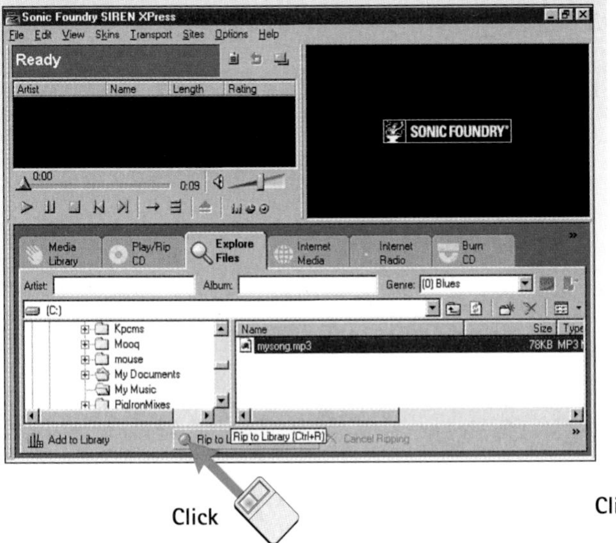

4 Test Your WMA File

Click the **Media Library** tab. You should see the WMA file or files that you encoded in the previous three steps. Click to select the file and then click the **Play** button to evaluate the results of the encoding process you just went through.

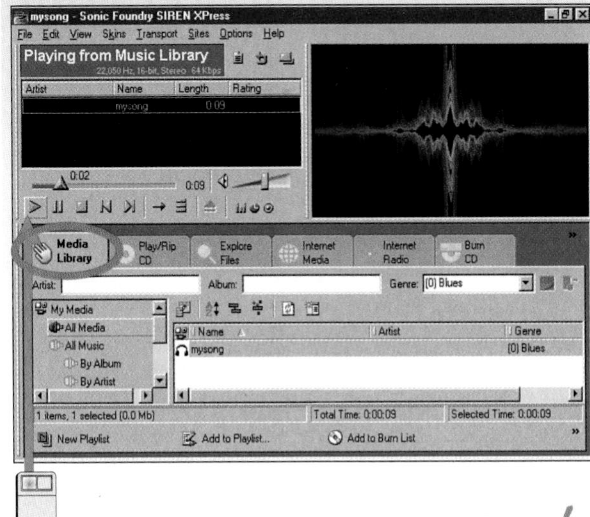

End

TASK 8 How to Encode Streaming Video

Encoding streaming video is not much more complicated than encoding streaming audio. I've already talked about the art of preparing a video to be streamed. Now it's time to talk about encoding (that is, converting) the video file you created into a streaming format. This task walks you through the process of encoding a video file into an ASF file, which can then be posted to your Web site and streamed to your visitors.

Like streaming audio, streaming video makes it possible to play a portion of a video while the rest of the movie clip is downloading; the clip "streams" as it plays.

To play streaming video files, visitors will need a player; most of the media players that can play the streaming audio you created in Task 7 can also play streaming video files.

What's ASF?

Yep, I've tossed a new file format into the mix. ASF stands for Active Streaming Format (or File, depending on who you ask). Microsoft developed this file format as their entry into the streaming video field. The format has since been replaced by Windows Media Video (WMV), but is still supported by the major streaming media players. The reason I'm using ASF for this task is that, as I mentioned, I want to give you free tools you can use to get your feet wet. The free tool I know about is called On-Demand Producer. You can download it free from the Microsoft Web site at **`www.microsoft.com`**. If you're interested in a more full-featured version of On-Demand Producer, check the Sonic Foundry Web site at **`www.sonicfoundry.com`** for Stream Anywhere. This big brother of On-Demand Producer allows you to save ASF, WMV, and RM streaming video files. Almost all video-editing software can save video in these three formats.

1 Open the Video File

In On-Demand Producer (ODP), choose **File, Open/Add.** In the **Open/Add Files** dialog box, navigate to the AVI file or files that you want to encode. ODP allows you to open more than one movie file at a time so that you can set the encoding parameters once, and encode all the files in the project list in a batch. Click the **Open** button to add the files to your project.

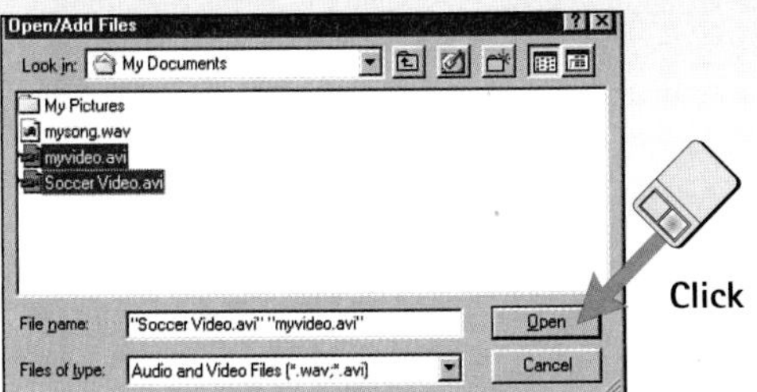

2 Prepare the Video For Encoding

You can do several things to enhance your streaming video. Click the **Summary** tab to add information about your movie such as title, author, and copyright. Click the **Process** tab and adjust the brightness of the movie. At the bottom of the window, add markers and commands that can be used by the media player to perform operations (such as opening a new Web page) at specific points in the video.

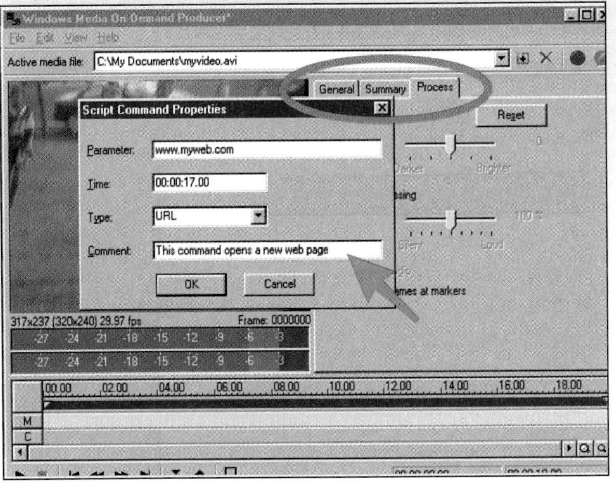

3 Encode the File

Choose **File, Save as Windows Media.** Follow the steps in the **Save as Windows Media Wizard.** In the various wizard windows, you make decisions about what target connection speed you are encoding for, add summary information, specify a save location for the new ASF file, and so on. On the last screen of the wizard, click the **Finish** button. You will see the encoding process with the original file on the left, and the encoded file on the right.

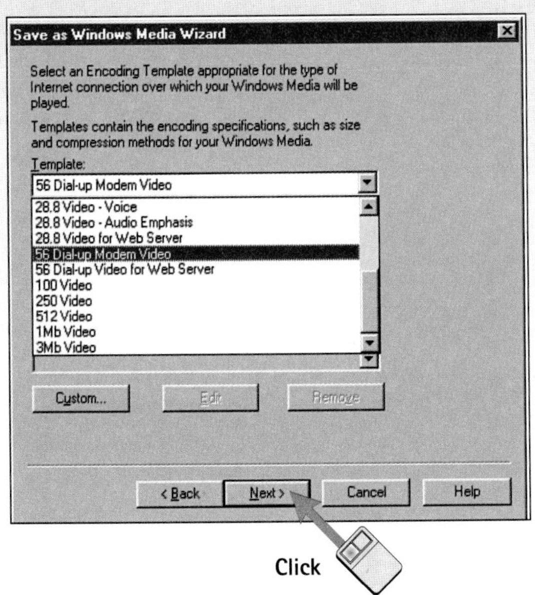

4 Publish the Streaming File

Choose **File, Publish Windows Media** to launch the **Publish Windows Media Wizard.** In this wizard, you specify names and locations for the *redirector* file (details about this file type are provided in the next task), and the HTML file. The wizard writes the HTML needed to embed the encoded file onto a Web page. When you're finished, your file is encoded and ready to stream over the Internet.

End

TASK 9 How to Stream Media from Your Site

After you have encoded your streaming media (as described in the preceding two tasks), you have to set up your Web site so that you can stream the media to your visitors. Streaming media requires some different techniques than simply embedding files into your HTML pages. This task explores the basic concepts of streaming media from your Web site so that you'll at least have an idea of the issues you have to investigate further if you decide to include streaming media on your site.

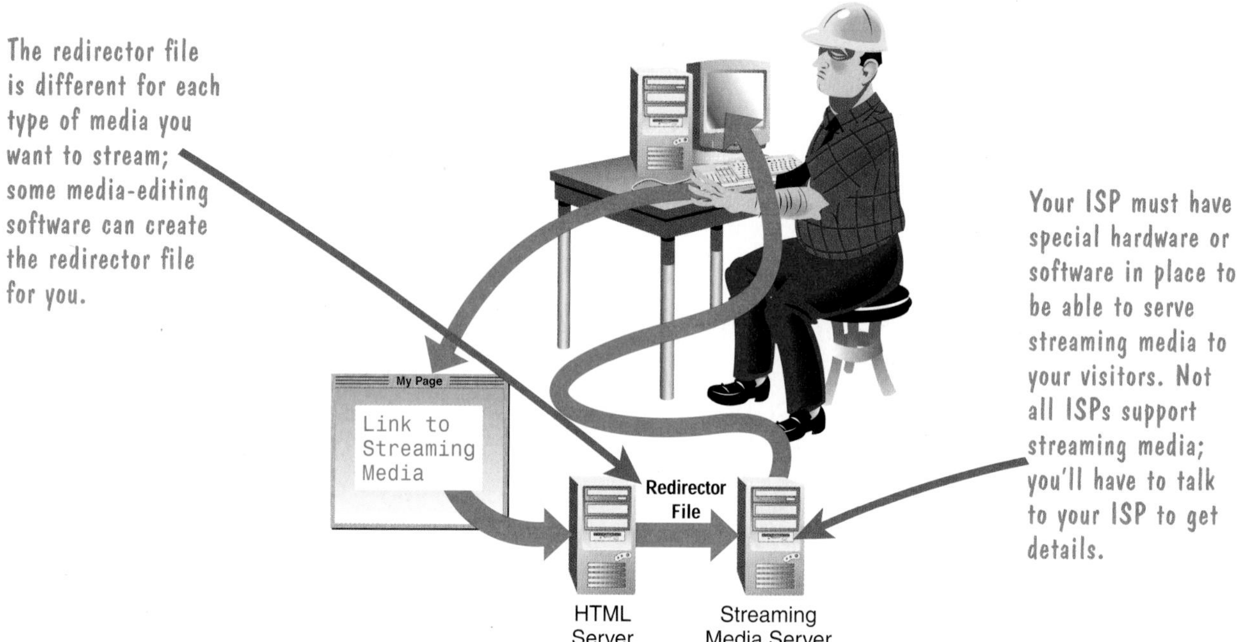

The redirector file is different for each type of media you want to stream; some media-editing software can create the redirector file for you.
My Page
Link to Streaming Media
Redirector File
HTML Server
Streaming Media Server
Your ISP must have special hardware or software in place to be able to serve streaming media to your visitors. Not all ISPs support streaming media; you'll have to talk to your ISP to get details.

Help from the Experts

Streaming the media can get somewhat complicated and can be demanding on your server resources. In all likelihood, you will have to work with an Internet Service Provider (ISP) that provides streaming as part of its services. You might have to look around a little to find an ISP willing and able to do so. Sometimes you can stream right off your regular HTML server, but this is a very limited way to do the job and will not support multiple requests from visitors for the same piece of streaming media. If you are going to stream media from your Web site, you really should find an ISP that not only provides the service but can also help you through the process of setting it up. As I said, making streaming media available for your visitors can get complicated; you might need more help from your ISP than you typically need when serving up regular HTML pages.

1 Create the Streaming Media

Tasks 7 and 8 showed you how to encode your audio and video files so that they can be streamed from your Web site. Follow the steps in one or the other of those tasks (depending on whether you're encoding audio or video) to create the streaming media file you need.

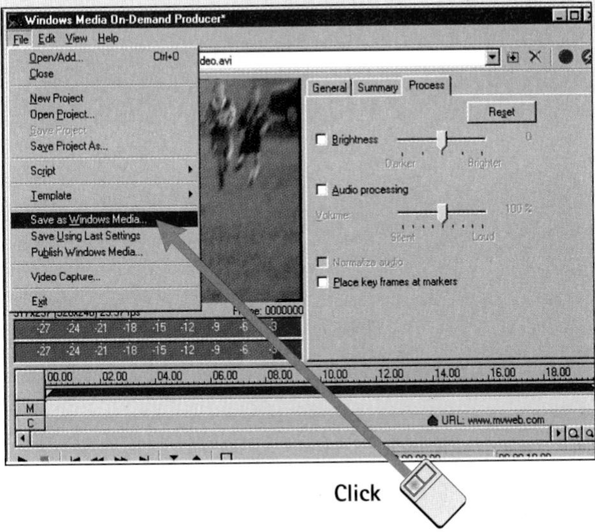

2 Set Up a Streaming Server

Because of the data requirements of streaming media, you'll have to serve the media from a different Web server than your regular HTML pages. This "other server" can be a completely different computer or it can be different server software on the same machine that serves your HTML pages. Check with your ISP to make sure that it supports streaming media. If not, find another ISP that supports the technology.

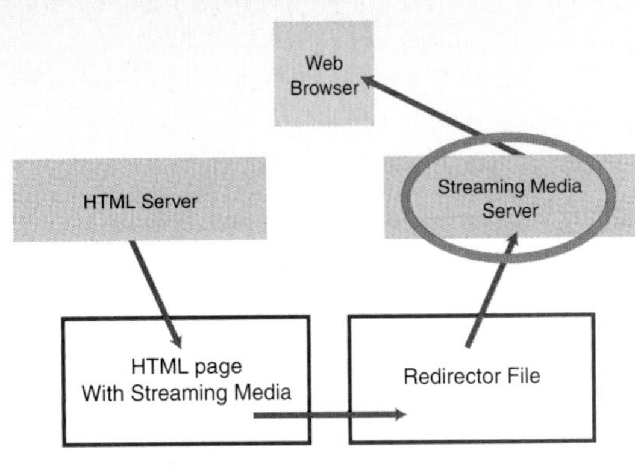

3 Add a Redirector File

Because the media you are streaming does not reside on your HTML server, you must create a *redirector file*. The HTML in your page calls the redirector file, which in turn calls the streaming media on your streaming server. On-Demand Producer creates the redirector file for you; alternatively, you can talk to your ISP about what you have to do to create the proper file. You need different redirector files for the different streaming formats.

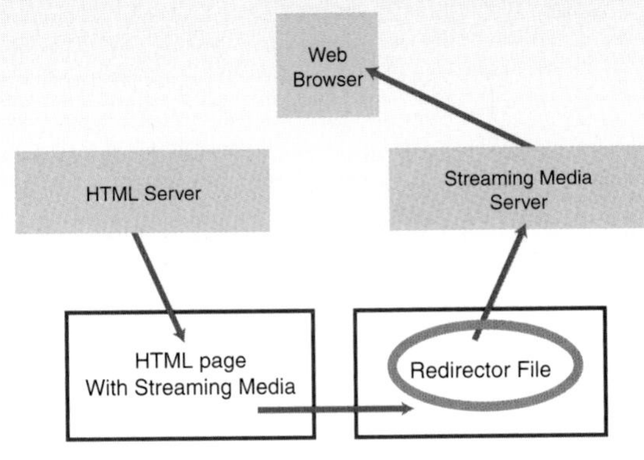

4 Link to the Redirector File

On your HTML page, include a link to the redirector file. It's also a nice courtesy to include a link to a location at which your visitors can download the media player they need to play your streaming file in case they don't already have the player installed on their computers.

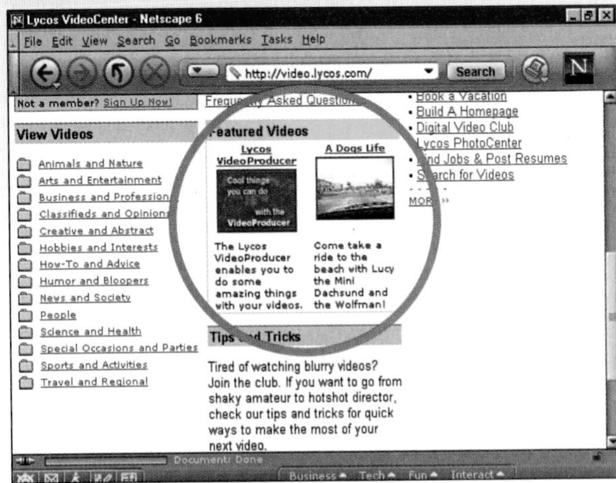

End

TASK 10

How to Create Flash Animations

One of the most exciting Web technologies is a program called Flash from Macromedia. This sleek software package allows you to create complex animation sequences that can then be included on your Web pages. The beauty of Flash is that it creates what are called *vector graphics*. These animations are lean and efficient, and therefore work extremely well on the Web. So well, in fact, that entire Web sites are being built based on Flash technology. This task introduces some of the very basic concepts of creating Flash animations for your Web site.

Visitors will need a special Flash player to view Flash animations. Provide a non-Flash alternative page that contains a link visitors can follow to download the player if they don't have it. More information can be found at www.macromedia.com.

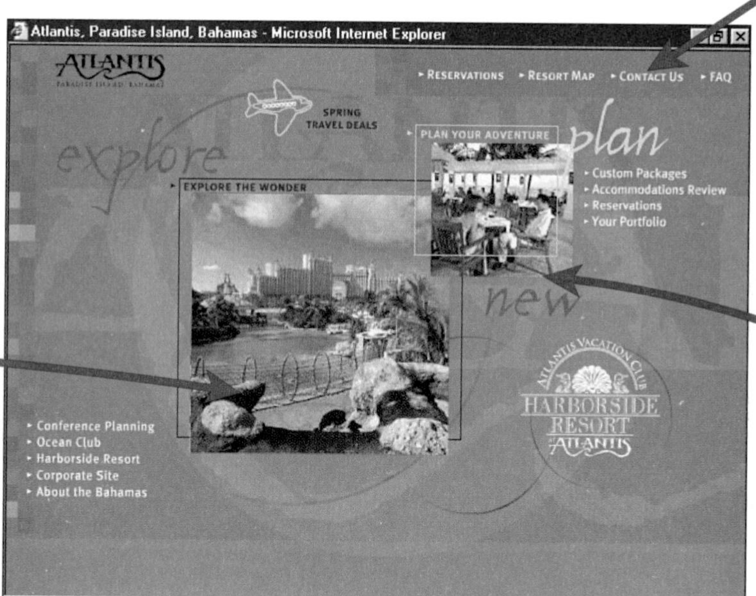

Animated navigation buttons are easy to create in Flash, allowing you to give your visitors an enhanced Web experience.

Flash creates lean animation files that you can then embed into your pages using the usual techniques.

Shameless Self-Promotion

The subject of Flash animations is yet another topic about which I could write an entire book. As a matter of fact, along with my friend Denise Tyler, I've done just that. *How to Use Macromedia Flash 5* (published by Sams Publishing) is available from your favorite bookseller. In the easy-to-use style of the *How to Use* series, Denise and I walk you through the steps involved in creating sophisticated animations for use in your own Web projects. The topics discussed in this task merely scratch the surface of what this program can help you accomplish. But if this task sparks your interest, check out *How to Use Macromedia Flash 5*. I recommend it highly—it's by one of my very favorite authors!

1 Create Your Artwork

Flash provides a number of easy-to-learn and easy-to-use drawing tools. From simple shapes to complex artwork, the Flash drawing tools make it easy to create the graphics you want. You can also import art, video, and sounds into your Flash project. Scale, rotate, and otherwise alter the shape of objects; add text blocks. Use multiple layers to keep your artwork organized and easy to edit.

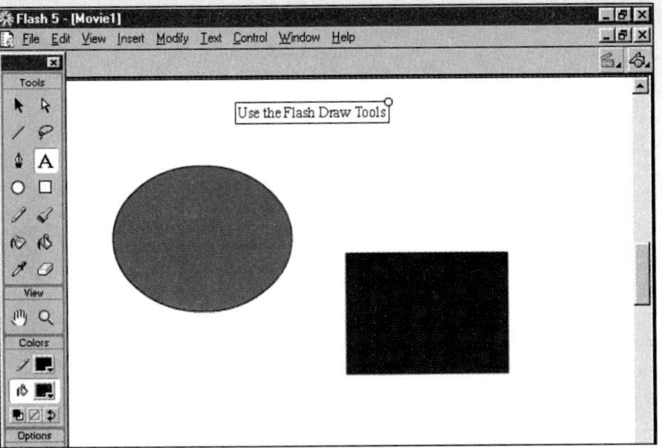

2 Create Motion

Flash provides a couple of different techniques for creating animation sequences. First, using handy "onion skin" techniques that allow you to view the progress of an object across the stage, you can create intricate frame-by-frame sequences that emulate traditional animation. You also can use a method called *tweening*, in which you supply the first and last frames of the sequence and let Flash create the intermediate steps.

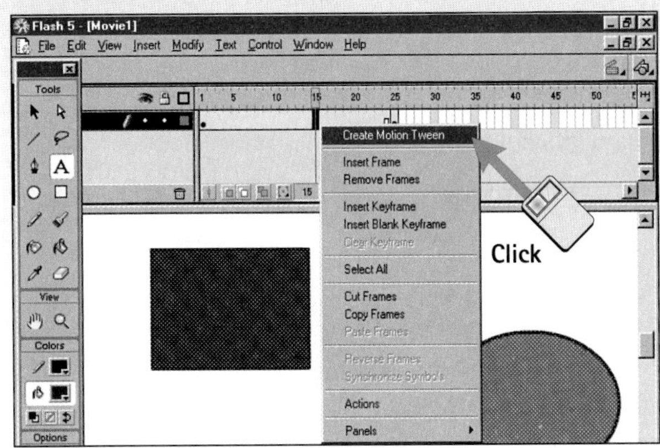

3 Create Navigation Buttons

Use a combination of the techniques in Step 1 and Step 2 to create animated navigation buttons. Use Flash's scripting capabilities to build functionality into your buttons. Create buttons that play videos, play music, start and stop animations, jump to different scenes of the video, or link to other Web pages. This button capability enables you to base your entire site on Flash.

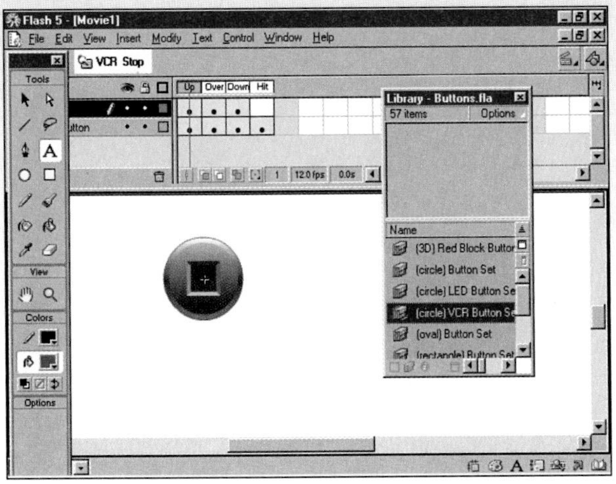

4 Test Download Performance

Test the download performance of your movie at various target connection speeds. Doing so allows you to identify potential problem areas in your animation. You can choose to show streaming progress to determine whether or not the animation will download fast enough to keep pace with playback. You can then go back and simplify the areas in which performance bogs down. When the animation passes your tests, you are ready to add it to your HTML page, as described in the next task.

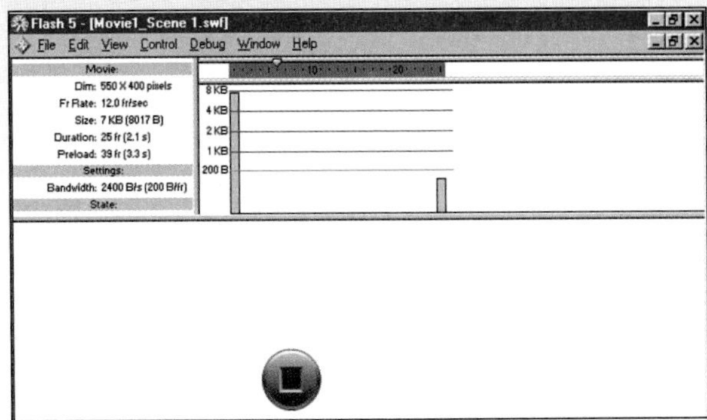

End

TASK 11 How to Embed Flash Animations

Embedding Flash animations into your HTML documents is easy—because Flash does most of the work for you! Using the Flash **Publish** commands, you need only indicate your publishing preferences and click the proper buttons. Flash then writes the appropriate HTML for you—and it does a nice job of it at that. You can then copy the code and paste it into another HTML document if you want. This task gives you a taste of how easy it is to use the Flash **Publish** commands to add animations to a Web page.

Flash can actually create the HTML that embeds the animation file in an HTML page for you.

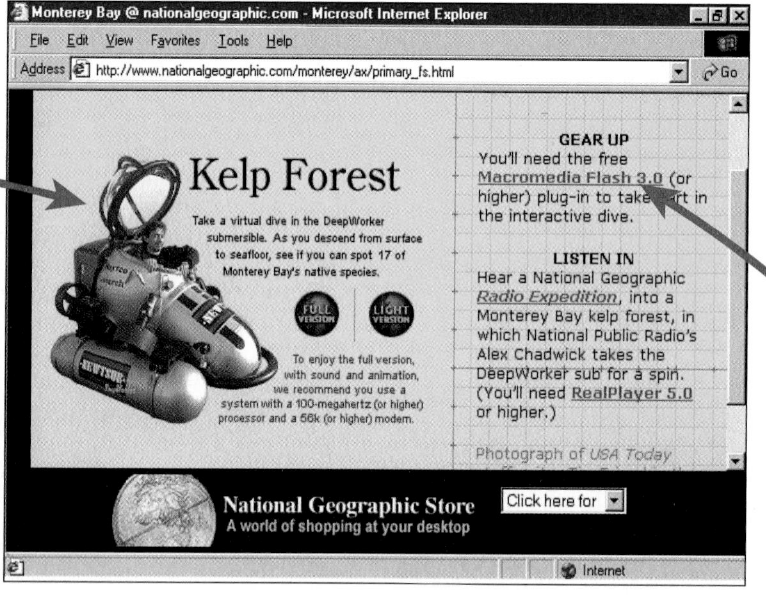

The Flash Publish options let you control the size of the video window, the quality of the video, and the number of times the animation plays.

Don't Want to Take the Easy Way?

Concerned about letting Flash publish your animations to HTML? You can do it yourself. After all, if you took my advice way back in Part 1, you don't like to rely on software to do the work for you. Well, this is one instance when you have my blessings to break that rule. Flash does a good job writing the code you need. But, because you're still adamant about writing the code yourself, you can use the combination `<object>`/`<embed>` method explained in Task 3, "How to Embed Multimedia Files." You'll have to know a little more about these tags than what I was able to cover there, but at least you're familiar with the basic tools. One good way to learn exactly what you need is to use the Flash **Publish** tools and then explore the source code that Flash writes. Then you'll know what you have to write the next time you want to do it yourself.

1 Choose a Template

In Flash, choose **File, Publish Settings** to open the **Publish Settings** dialog box. Click the **HTML** tab to access the HTML publish settings. From the **Template** drop-down list, choose the template that best matches how you want to present your animation. Specify the dimensions of the movie. Choose **Match Movie** to create a Flash movie in your HTML page that displays at the same size as your Flash movie project.

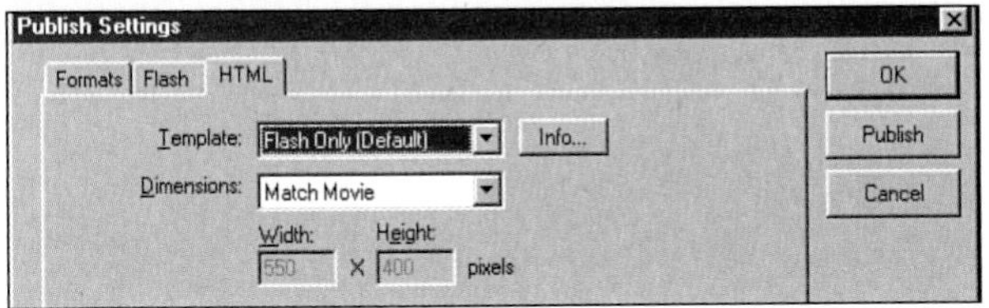

2 Choose Playback Options

The **Playback** section of the dialog box provides options that control how the user interacts with the movie. You can decide whether the movie starts as soon as the page loads or waits for the user to click on it. You can also specify whether you want the movie to play once and then stop or to continue in an endless loop.

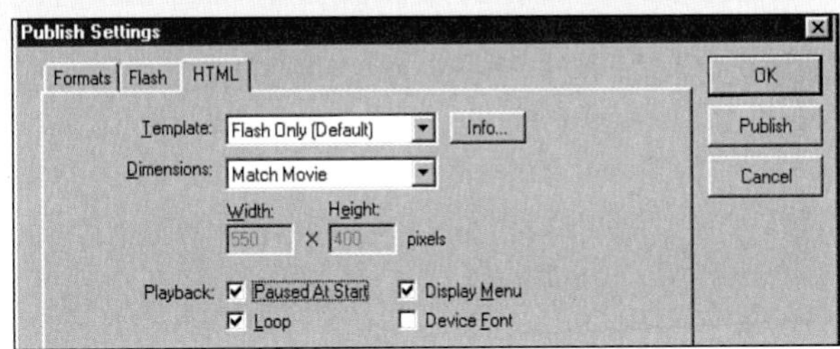

3 Select Movie Quality

The **Quality** drop-down list box enables you to choose a movie quality at which to publish your movie. You can choose options that concentrate on playback speed at the expense of image quality, or options that do just the opposite. These options give you the flexibility to decide what is more important and to publish your animated Flash movies accordingly.

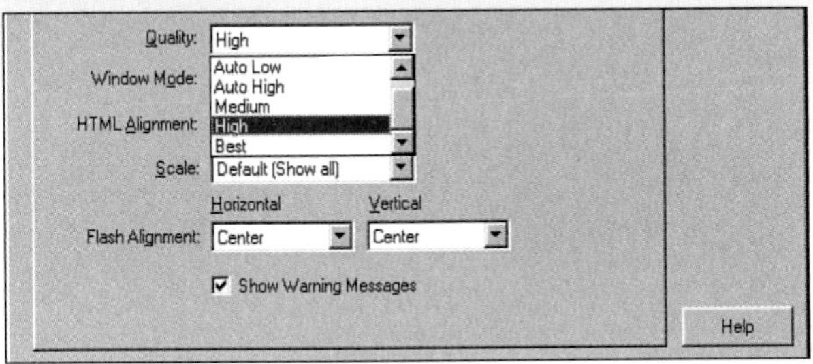

4 Set Alignment and Scale

You can control how the movie is aligned on your HTML page with the options in the **HTML Alignment** drop-down list. Align the movie to the top, bottom, left, or right edges of the page. With the **Scale** drop-down list, you determine how the embedded Flash movie reacts when the browser window is resized. When you have made all your choices, click the **Publish** button; Flash does the rest. Test your page to see how you like it!

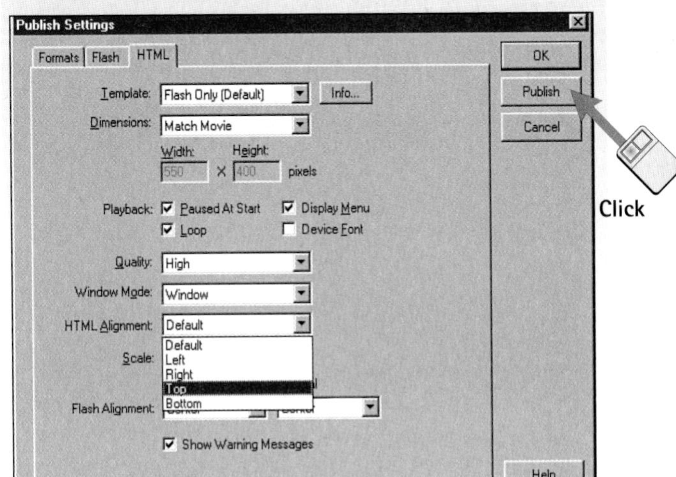

TASK 12

How to Learn More About Incorporating Multimedia

We've hardly made a dent in what you need to know to create quality multimedia and include it on your Web pages. But hopefully you've gotten enough information from the tasks in this part to both spark your interest and help you begin to ask the right questions. Obviously, if you're going to get serious about multimedia on your Web site, you'll have to learn more about all these issues. This task gives you some ideas on where to look for more information.

Learning from Others

Remember that you can always look at the source code of any Web page you come across that uses multimedia in a way you like. That's how I first discovered the **<embed>** tag. You'll see a lot of attributes in the **<object>** and **<embed>** tags that I didn't have room to talk about here. Make note of them and use the resources in these steps to figure out exactly what they all mean. Not that every bit of code you read will be written correctly, but the more code you look at, the more familiar you will become with the techniques. Soon you'll find yourself critiquing code and saying things like, "They should know better than that." When you reach this point, sit back, close your eyes, take a deep breath, and simply accept the fact that you've become a computer geek! Don't worry though...it happens to the best of us.

1 Read a Good Book

There are several good books available for teaching you how to prepare multimedia for the Web. I've already mentioned *How to Use Macromedia Flash 5.0* (published by Sams Publishing). There are also books dedicated to both audio (such as *Audio on the Web: The Official IUMA Guide*, by Jeff Patterson and Marjorie Baer) and video (such as *e-Video: Producing Internet Video as Broadband Technologies Converge*, by H. Peter Alesso). Your local bookseller carries other titles.

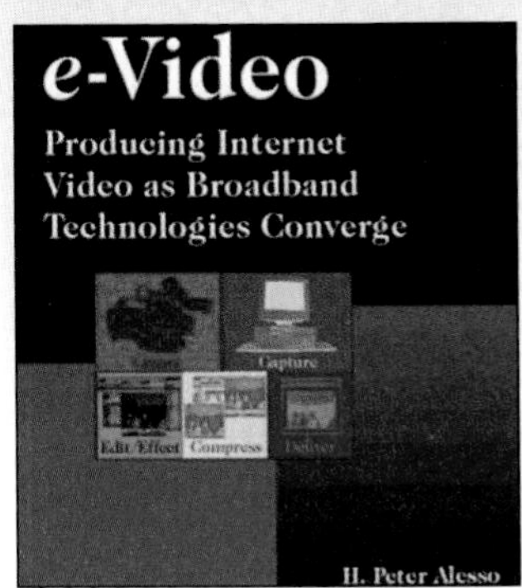

2 Online Resources

A great place to turn for help is **`http://www.webdeveloper.com/`** on the Web. My search on this site for **"web multimedia"** turned up 1,140 pages. The page also has links to other Web resources. You'll find articles, question and answer pages, and a multimedia forum.

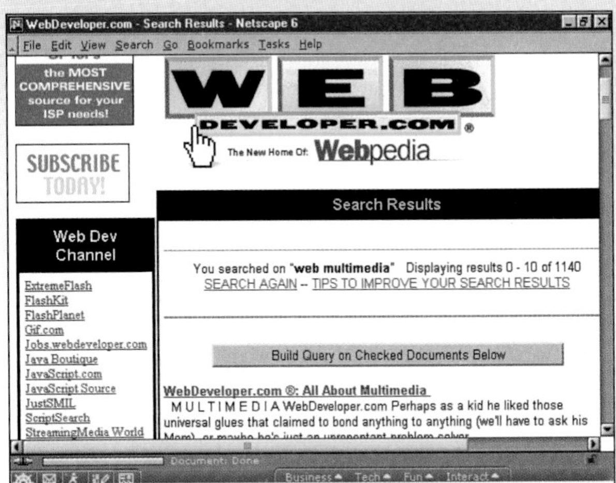

3 Attend a Training Seminar

You can more than likely find a training seminar focusing on multimedia somewhere near you. Also check with your local community college and technical college. These institutions often offer courses on multimedia-related topics. My search on Google.com for **`"web multimedia seminars"`** turned up thousands of related pages.

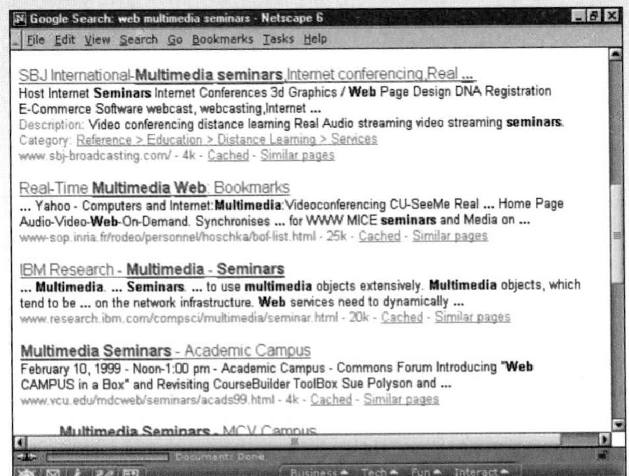

4 Learn by Doing

By now you know that I'm a big advocate of the learn-by-doing method. The more multimedia you include on your pages, the more the tricks and techniques will become part of your skill set. Don't worry about making mistakes. The good thing about developing Web pages is that you don't have to publish them until they work properly, so who's going to know?

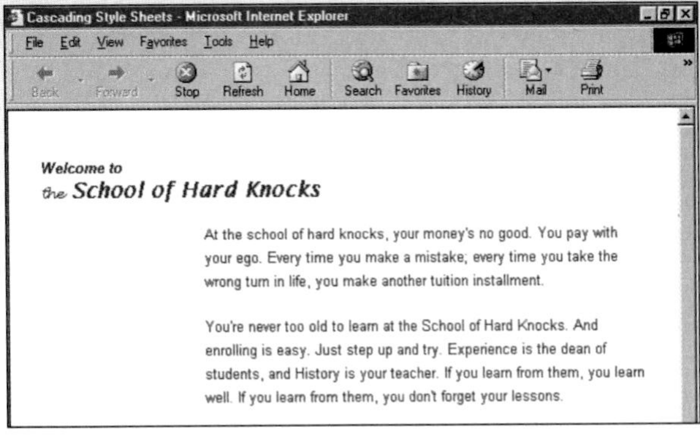

End

Task

Part 12

Letting the World See Your Work

You've come a long way! You now have the basic tools you need to build your Web site. You've also been introduced to some advanced topics that you might want to learn more about to take your Web development skills to a higher level. But whether learning HTML is the end of your Web development education or just the beginning, whether you want to post a simple HTML-based Web site for fun or a sophisticated e-business Web site using all the latest technologies, there's no reason not to use what you already know to get your pages "out there" for the whole world to see right now.

That's what this part is all about. We'll talk about how to choose an Internet Service Provider (ISP) so that you can establish your connection to the World Wide Web. You'll learn how to transfer your Web site files to the ISP's server so that you can finally "go live" with your Web site. For those brave souls who are interested in setting up their own Web server, I'll provide a few basic pointers to get you started. Finally, we'll look at some of the things you can do to make it easier for search engines to find your pages.

The tasks in this part of the book really serve as the most basic of introductions. There isn't space to explore these areas fully, but I think it's important to introduce you to some of the issues and terminology you'll need to move fully into this stage of developing your Web site.

I hope you've enjoyed learning about HTML and the other Web-related technologies we've talked about in this book. I also hope you've found this book to be helpful and enjoyable. I've tried to give you the knowledge you need to make Web pages, while at the same time giving you my take on Web site design considerations. I know that not every opinion I've presented is shared by everyone who has read them—or even by other Web and design professionals. They are, after all, *my* opinions. But I do hope that they serve to help you form your own style for the work you are about to undertake. If nothing else, I hope that my ideas have at least made you aware of some of the considerations you need to keep in mind when creating your HTML pages.

In any event, give yourself a pat on the back. You've come a long way and have worked hard. You now know HTML, a valuable and marketable skill. Thanks for reading. Now go out and make great Web pages!

TASK 1 How to Choose an ISP

Your choice of an ISP is important. Your ISP is the critical link between you and the visitors to your Web pages. You need a reliable source from which to serve your Web pages. There are hundreds, if not thousands, of ISPs out there, all ready to take your business. But before you choose the cheapest one, give some consideration to a number of important issues. This task helps you identify and understand some of those issues so that you'll know the right questions to ask when interviewing ISPs.

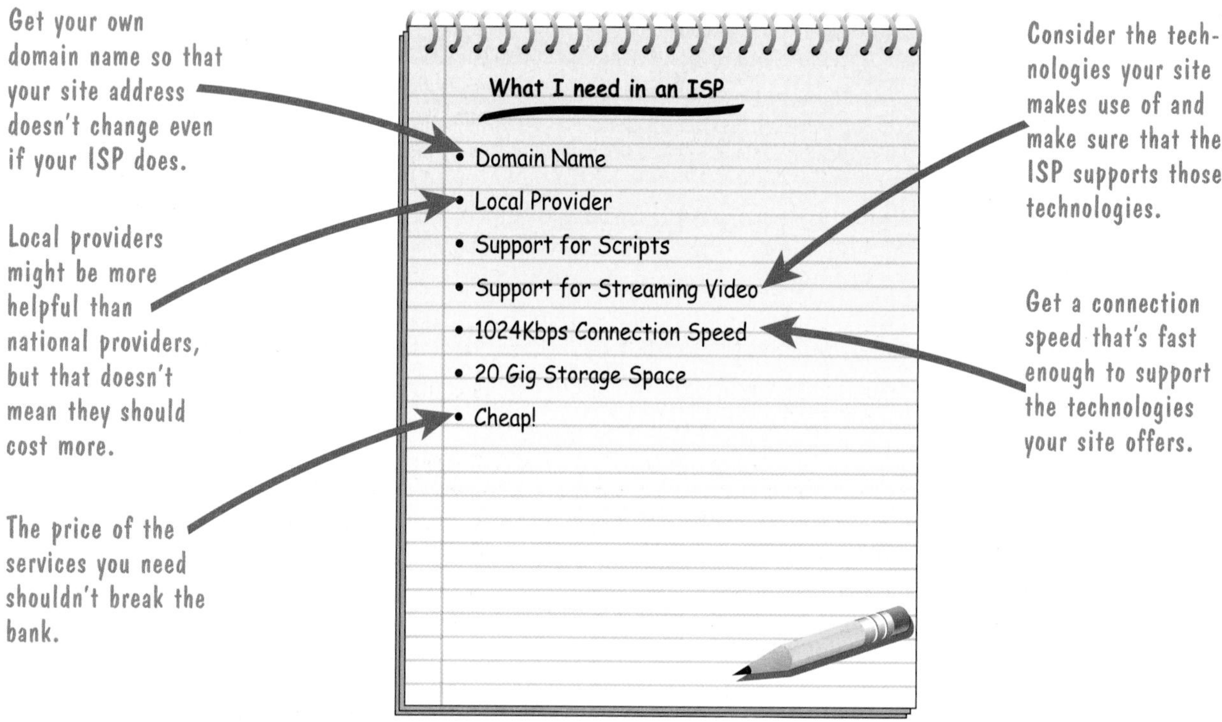

Get your own domain name so that your site address doesn't change even if your ISP does.
Local providers might be more helpful than national providers, but that doesn't mean they should cost more.
The price of the services you need shouldn't break the bank.
What I need in an ISP
• Domain Name
• Local Provider
• Support for Scripts
• Support for Streaming Video
• 1024Kbps Connection Speed
• 20 Gig Storage Space
• Cheap!
Consider the technologies your site makes use of and make sure that the ISP supports those technologies.
Get a connection speed that's fast enough to support the technologies your site offers.

Your Domain Name

The address to your site includes the name of your ISP. This is because your ISP has its own *domain name*, that is, the name it uses to identify its server on the Web. Because you're renting space on your ISP's server, you inherit the ISP's domain name as part of the address to your Web site. However, you can establish your own domain name. This is a good idea for several reasons. One is that if you change ISPs, you can take your domain name with you so that your Web address won't change. Of course—for better or worse—this is capitalism, and you'll have to pay for your own domain name. It costs about $70 to register it and about $35 annually to renew it. Talk to your ISP for details on setting up your own domain name. But remember, they're capitalists, too, and they'll probably charge you $25 or $30 to help you set one up.

1 Look Locally

I suggest that you work with a local ISP so that you can more easily keep tabs on what's going on with its operation. Look in the Yellow Pages under **Internet Service Providers** for ISPs in your area. If you prefer to cast your net wider, let the Internet help. Go to **`http://www.thelist.com`** for a master list of ISPs you can search by services, location, and name.

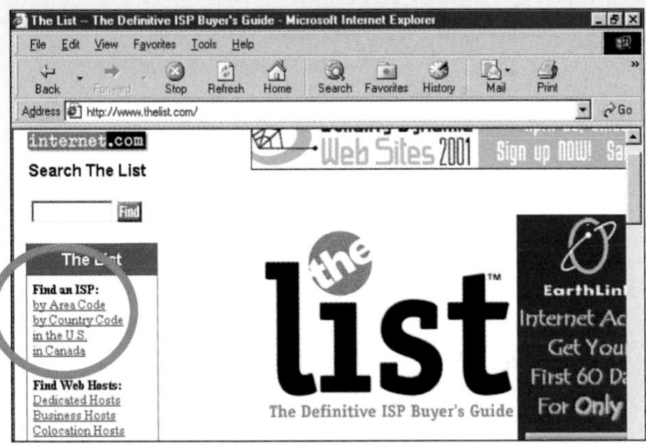

2 Identify the ISP's Offerings

You might think that all ISPs are the same, but that's not so. Before you sign up for a service, make sure that you know exactly what you're signing up for. Do you need to serve strictly HTML pages? Or do you need to support CGI scripts or Active Server Pages? Do you intend to stream audio or video from your site? Look at your requirements and then make sure that the ISP supplies these services...*before* you sign the contract!

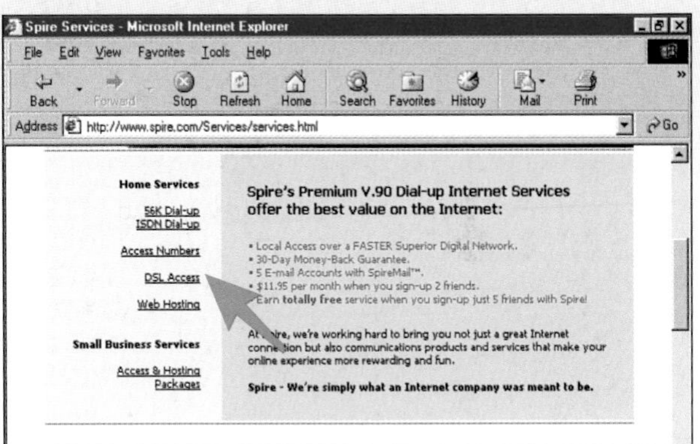

3 Connection Speed, Redundancy, and Space

HTML files don't take much space, but image and multimedia files can. Will the ISP give you enough space for all your current content with room to grow? You're paying for continuous service; does the ISP have redundant (that is, backup) servers to seamlessly take over when its main server crashes? Finally, a 56Kbps connection might be okay for your HTML pages, but is your ISP's connection fast enough to serve images, multimedia, and streaming media?

4 Identify the Charges for Service

Notice that price is *not* the first consideration on my list! Of course, price is important, but surely someone along the way has mentioned that you get what you pay for. This is not to say that you shouldn't find the lowest price you can, but make sure that you're not sacrificing services—including access to all-important technical support. An ISP should give great service (for basic needs) for about $20 per month. If not, look elsewhere.

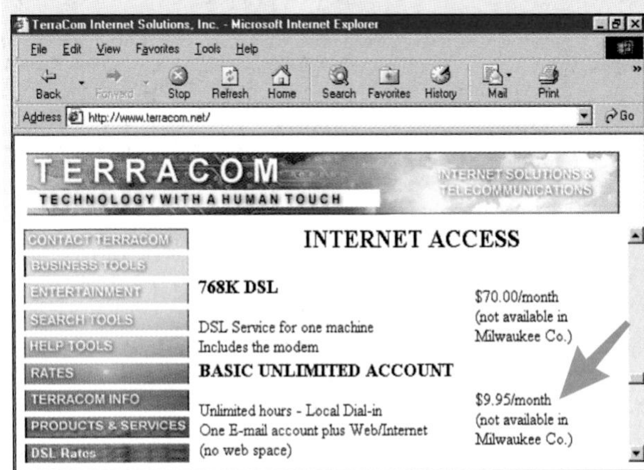

End

TASK 2

How to Transfer Files to Your ISP's Server

Well, you've got your pages and your ISP. Now's the moment you've been working toward this whole time: It's time to transfer the pages from your development machine to your ISP's Web server. Although the Web is part of the Internet, it's not the whole Internet. Normally, you'll use another aspect of the Internet called File Transfer Protocol (FTP) to copy the files from your computer across the Internet to your ISP's server. Your ISP's technical support department can help you through this process. If they can't, you might want to reread the previous task!

FTP is the protocol you use to get your HTML files from your computer to your ISP's server.

Cute

In this task, I'll show you how to transfer your files using a nifty shareware program called CuteFTP. You can download CuteFTP from **`http://www.globalscape.com/`**. You can use any FTP program you want (a popular one for Mac users is called Fetch), and there are many from which to choose. If you don't have an FTP program already, go to your favorite search site and run a search on **FTP** or **File Transfer Protocol**. You should be able to find a number of options. You can also run a search on **Shareware** or **Freeware** to find sites that list these types of software programs. Then look under the FTP section (or search the site for **FTP**). You shouldn't have any trouble finding an FTP program that you like. Check with your ISP to find out whether it has a preferred method of transferring files to its server.

1 Create an FTP Folder

When you first launch CuteFTP, the **FTP Site Manager** window opens. Click the **Add Folder** button to create a new folder in which you'll store your Web site documents locally before you upload them to your ISP's server. Move your files to that folder. Make sure that the folder you just created is highlighted and click the **Add Site** button. This action opens the **Add Host** dialog box.

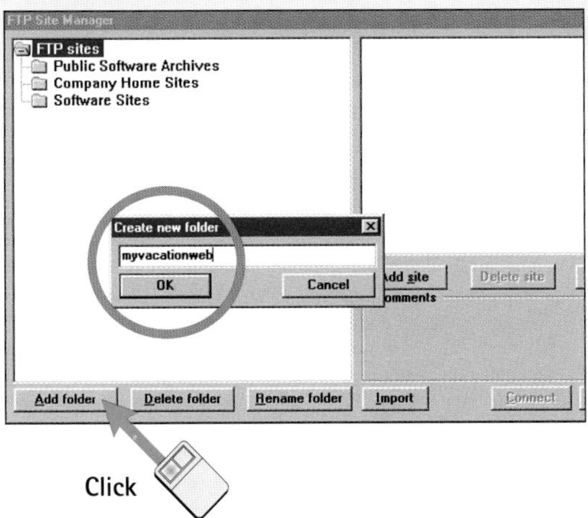

2 Identify Yourself

In the **Add Host** dialog box, there are four important fields to fill in. The **Site Label** field lets you give your site a name so that you can find it later; enter whatever name you want. In the **Host Address** field, type the FTP address for your ISP's FTP server. Enter your **User ID** and **Password** in the appropriate fields. You'll have to talk to your ISP for the information you must enter in the last three fields mentioned here.

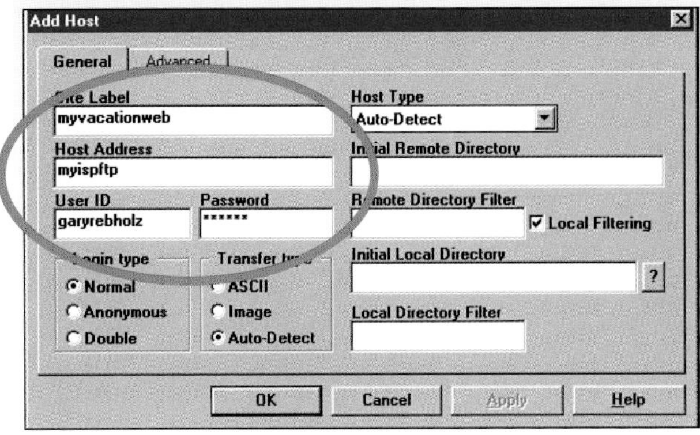

3 Connect to Your ISP

Click the **OK** button; you return to the **FTP Site Manager** window. In the right pane, highlight the name of the site you just created and click the **Connect** button to connect to your ISP's FTP server (the address you entered in Step 2). The file structure on your computer shows up in the left pane. The file structure of your Web site on the ISP's server shows up in the right pane (it might be relatively blank if this is your first time uploading files).

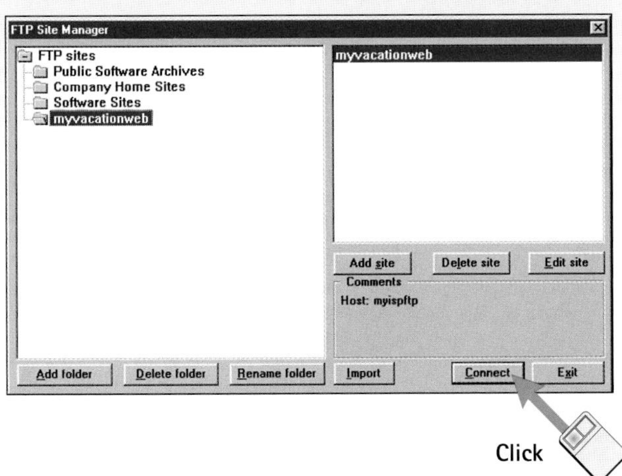

4 Transfer the Files

Now it's just a matter of copying files from one place to another. Navigate to the files on your hard drive using the folder structure in CuteFTP's left pane. Drag the files you want to transfer to your ISP to the location of your ISP in the right pane. That's all there is to it! As mentioned, you should be able to get help for this process from your ISP.

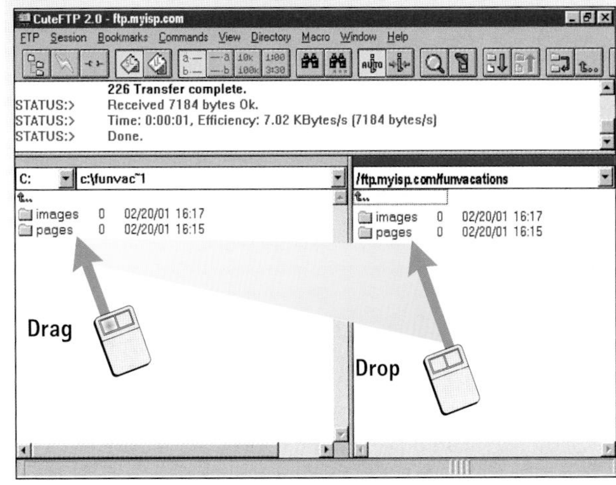

End

TASK 3

How to Set Up Your Own Web Server

I see you're one of the brave souls! It is possible to set up your own Web server, although you'll have a whole new set of issues to deal with if you choose to go this route. Not only issues of setting up the server, but all the issues involved with maintaining it, keeping it up and running, and solving software and hardware problems and issues. All that on top of your duties as the Web page designer and author. It's not for everyone, but it certainly gives you more control over the operation of your Web site.

Your server needs a hard disk that's big enough to store all the multimedia files, graphics files, and HTML files used by your pages.
Don't forget that the hard disk also has to store the server software—the programs that tell the computer how to be a Web server.
Your server's connection to the Internet should be, at a minimum, a dedicated phone line. If possible, get a cable connection or a T1 line.
FIXING & REPAIRING PCs
The maintenance of your server is up to you, so bone up now on how you'll fix it when it crashes.

The Ultimate Flexibility

There is a lot to be said for running your own Web server. It takes more patience and technical know-how than most of us have. But if you're the technical type, and you like solving computer-related problems, you might really enjoy the challenges waiting for you in this area. When you run your own server, *you* get to make the decisions. You get to decide what technologies you support. You get to decide how you are going to support them. You have total flexibility to change your Web site. Want to serve streaming media? Want to include forms on your site so that you can gather information? Want a dynamic site that accesses a database through CGI or ASP technologies to serve custom pages depending on user input? Although you can find an ISP that supports these technologies, when you run your own server, you get to do whatever you want, whenever you want. You'll just need the time to make it all happen....

1 Get a Dedicated Computer

A Web server is really nothing more than a computer that serves Web pages. Depending on the type of technology you're serving, it doesn't even have to be a super-powerful computer (although it wouldn't hurt). But the computer should be dedicated to the task of serving up Web pages. Depending on the size of your site and the types of files on it, you might need a relatively large hard drive.

2 Load the Server Software

What makes a computer a Web server? The server software. You can set up a server on virtually any platform including Windows, Macintosh, and Unix. My favorite underdog server is the Apache server software, an interesting open source project that I encourage you to learn more about at **`http://httpd.apache.org/`**. I suggest that you use whatever platform you are most comfortable with. You can find server software on the Web or at your local software reseller.

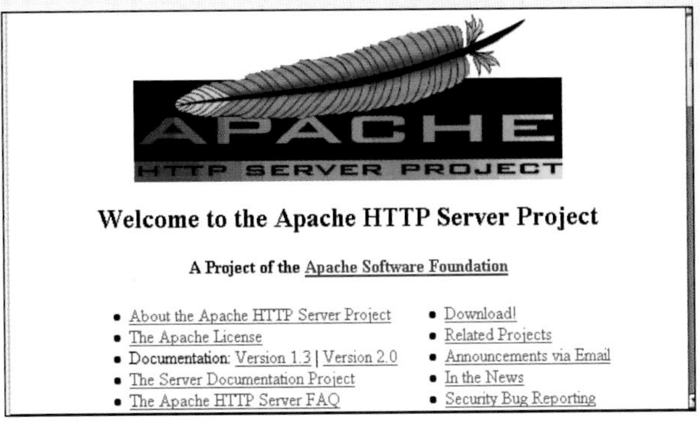

Welcome to the Apache HTTP Server Project

A Project of the Apache Software Foundation

- About the Apache HTTP Server Project
- The Apache License
- Documentation: Version 1.3 | Version 2.0
- The Server Documentation Project
- The Apache HTTP Server FAQ
- Download!
- Related Projects
- Announcements via Email
- In the News
- Security Bug Reporting

3 Make an Internet Connection

Naturally, you need a dedicated phone line or another connection to the Internet like a T1 line, cable modem, or a high-speed DSL connection. If you're using a phone line, you'll be connecting no faster than what a 56Kbps modem can muster; depending on the content you're serving, that might not be fast enough. If your site is going to be available 24 hours a day, you'll need a dedicated phone line. You'll still have to talk to an ISP to set up the actual connection to the Internet.

4 Keep on Top of It

This has been the scantest of outlines, but hopefully you get the idea that it's not so mysterious to set up your own server. If you decide to set up your own server, you'll have a lot to learn, and a lot of work ahead of you. Most of all, you'll have to be on the job all the time, especially if your site is intended for commerce. A downed server can cost you business!

End

TASK 4

How to Help (or Hinder) the Search Process

If you're like me, when you want to find information on the Web, the first thing you do is type in the address of your favorite search site. My favorite search engine keeps changing—AltaVista today, Google.com yesterday, Lycos last week, Yahoo! tomorrow. Wouldn't it be nice if your pages came up at the top of the results list when someone runs a search for the stuff your Web site offers? There are a few things you can do climb the search-results charts. This task gives you some tips on how to make your page more (or less) "findable" by any of the popular search engines.

The title of your page should contain words that people will likely type in a search site to find your page.
Keywords are like extensions to the title; include other words that people might search for but that don't fit nicely into your page's title.
Summaries are included in the results of a search; here's your opportunity to summarize your site succinctly (25 words or less).

Your Marketing Plan

If your site is designed to conduct business, it should play a prominent role in your business's marketing plan. It's not enough to be good at what you do, you have to let people know you're good. You can be the best in the industry at what you do, but you'll still go hungry if you can't properly market your services. Don't skimp on the marketing. Give it the attention it needs. If you can't, pry that wallet open and pay someone else to do it. Done properly, it'll pay for itself many times over.

Search Engines

How do search engines work anyway? Basically, a search site is a great big index of Web pages. When you enter a topic and click the **Search** button, the search engine scours the index to try and find all the pages that might relate to your search entry. These indexes are constantly updated, and new pages are added all the time. Some pages are added when people submit them manually, and some are added by automatic *robots* or *spiders* that constantly crawl around on the Internet looking for new pages to add.

1 Pick the Right Title

Way back in Part 1, "Getting Started," Task 6, "How to Give Your Page a Title," you learned how to add a title to your page. One of the most important functions of the title relates to search engines. In general, the closer your title matches the words entered in a search on a search site, the closer to the top of the list your page will appear. Make sure that your page title includes words that people will enter to find your site.

```
<head>
<title>Fun Vacations</title>
</head>
```

2 Include Keywords

Use the **<meta>** tag with the **name** and **content** attributes to include keywords in your page's header area. Search engines look for these keywords, so use words that you think are likely to be entered in searches on search sites. For example, for a vacation Web site, you might type **<meta name="keywords" content= "vacation, trip, getaway, fun, cruise, resort, relax" />** You might even want to include common misspellings so that even I can find your page!

```
<head>
<title>Fun Vacations</title>
<meta name="keywords"
content="vacation, trip, getaway, fun,
cruise, resort, relax" />
</head>
```

3 Include a Summary

When your page does show up in the results of a search, the search site generally provides a short summary of the contents of the page. If you don't supply a content summary, the search site uses the first few words of your page as the summary. Either make those first few words descriptive or (better yet) use the **<meta>** tag to supply a summary. Type **<meta name="description" content="complete vacation resources" />** to summarize your site in as few words as possible.

```
<head>
<title>Fun Vacations</title>
<meta name="description"
content="complete vacation resources" />
</head>
```

4 Stay Away!

Search sites employ *robots* or *spiders* to search the Internet for pages they don't already know about. When they find one, they index it and follow its links in search of other pages. What if you *don't* want search sites to list your page? (For instance, you might not want a search site to list a personal page intended for your family or for a specific client only.) Type **<meta name="robots" content="noindex, nofollow" />** to prevent a robot or spider from indexing your page or following any of its links.

```
<head>
<title>Fun Vacations</title>
<meta name="robots"
content="noindex, nofollow" />
</head>
```

End

TASK 5 How to Register with Directories

Well, your Web site is live! Sit back and let the world come see it. You wish. Unfortunately your work isn't finished just yet. You'll have to let people know that your site is available. One of the best ways is to have your page come up when someone instigates a search. You can sit back and hope that your page is found by a search site's robot or spider, or you can take matters into your own hands. This task shows how to register with search sites to increase your chances of being found in a search.

Register with as many search sites as you can. Start with the ones you think your audience is most likely to use.
Many specialized search sites exist. Find out whether there is a search site devoted to the subject of your Web site or to a related subject.
Dear Search Site,
We are here!
My web address
is www...
If it's important for your page to be found in Internet searches, take matters into your own hands and register with search sites. Don't wait for them to find you...they have millions of Web pages to read!

It Never Hurts

Even if you register with several search sites, it is difficult to register with them all. Some search sites request that you register only one of your pages; the sites then promise that they will use a robot or spider to follow your links and to find the rest of your pages. For those reasons, it's a good idea to create a page full of links to other pages on your site and submit that to the search engines. Some people call this a *crawler page*. You can use the **Favorites** tools in Internet Explorer and the **Bookmark** tools in Netscape Navigator to help you create a crawler page quickly. Add all the important pages from your site as bookmarks or favorites. Then use Explorer's **File, Export** command or Navigator's **File, Save As** command to save those favorites as an HTML file. Submit that page to the directories.

1 Call Up the Search Site

Unfortunately, registering your site with search sites is a one-by-one process. There is no way to submit to every search engine simultaneously. (They are all in competition with each other!) Start with the search site that you think is most likely to be used by potential visitors to your site. Navigate to the site.

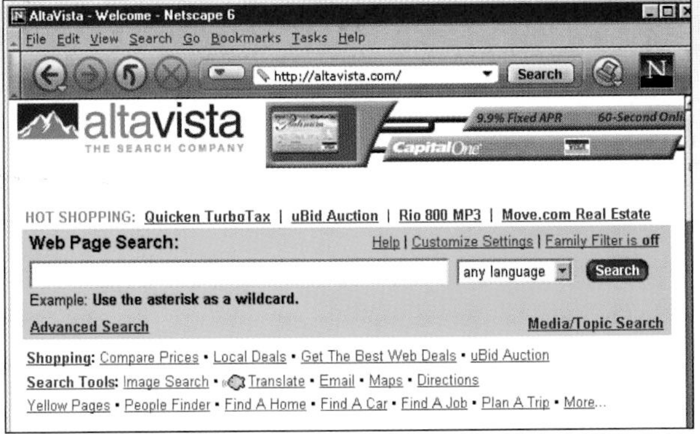

2 Go to the Submission Page

Most search sites have a page that allows you to submit or add your page to their search database. You can usually find a link to this page pretty quickly from the home page of the site. Click the link to navigate to the submission page.

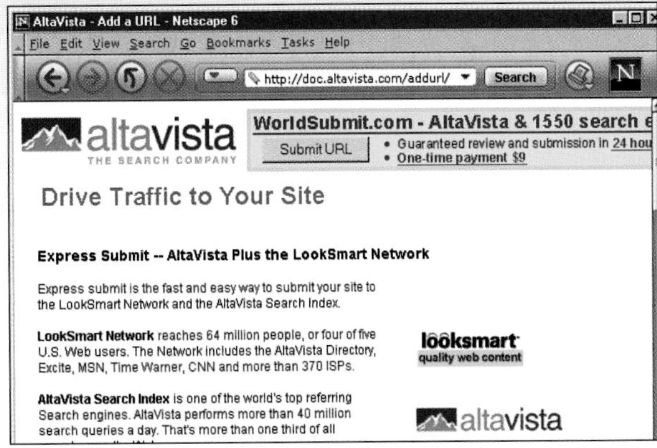

3 Fill In the Information

Follow the instructions on the submission page. Make sure that you enter all the required information. Type the address of the page you are submitting (your crawler page, if you created one). When you are finished entering the appropriate information, click the **Submit** button (or whatever the appropriate button on the search site is called).

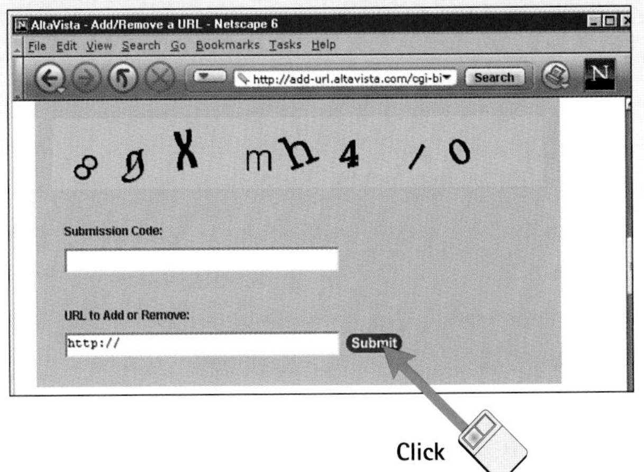

4 Check Back

Give the search site a couple weeks to get to your request, and then go back and run a search related to the subject of your pages. Hopefully, the search will yield the results you want...your page at the very top! If you're not at the top, you might want to adjust your **`<title>`** or **`<meta>`** tags as described in Task 4, "How to Help (or Hinder) the Search Process." If your page doesn't show up at all in the search results, resubmit your page to the site.

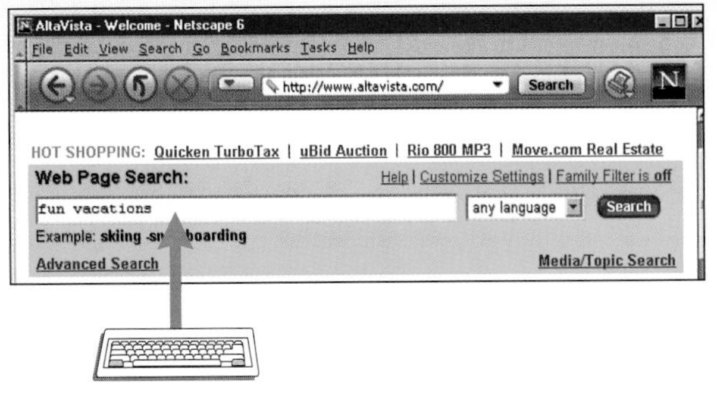

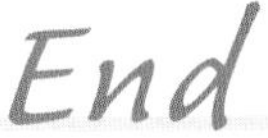

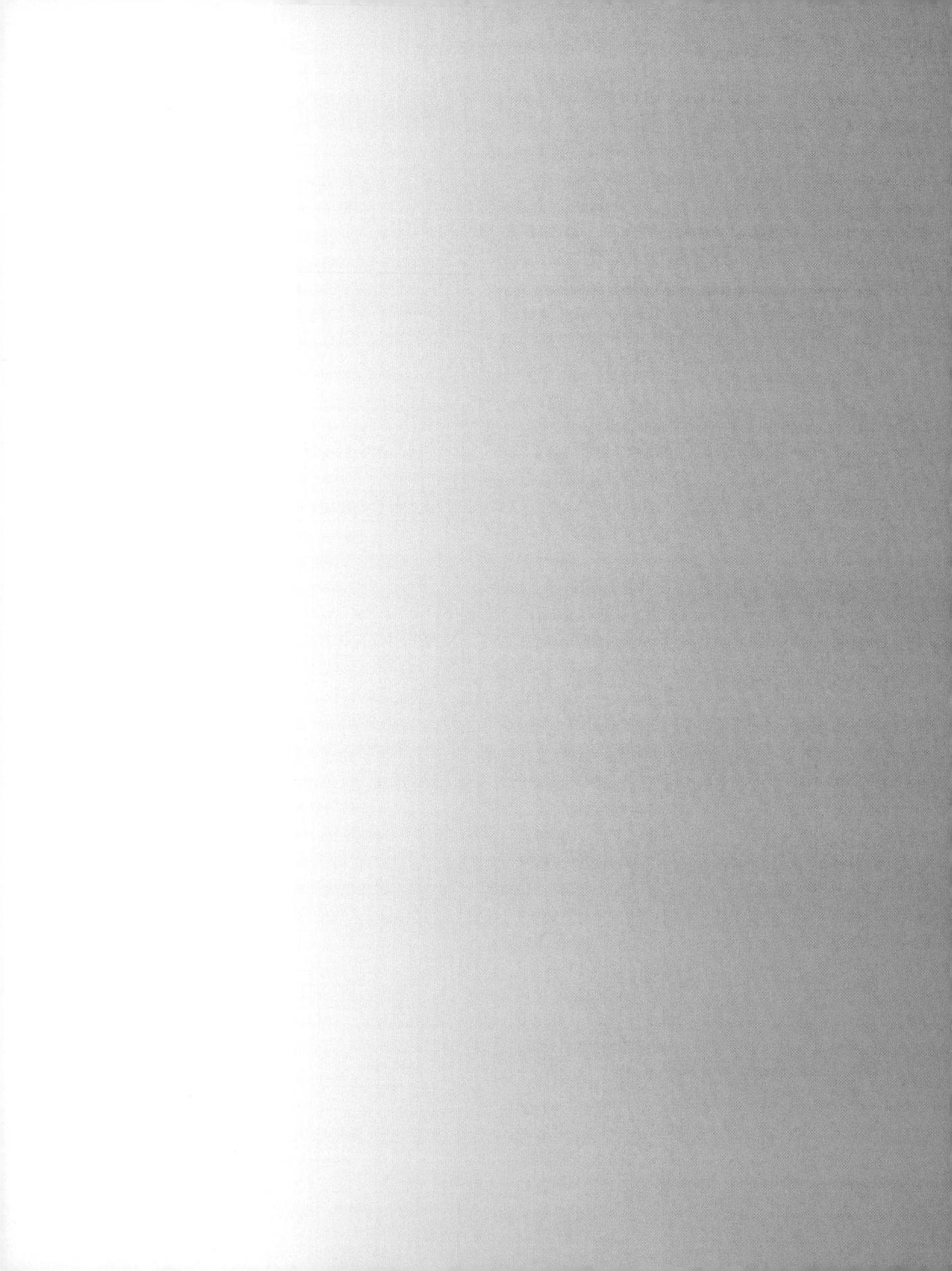

Appendix

Colors and Hex Equivalents

This chart shows the hexadecimal (hex) codes for the 216 "browser-safe" colors. To use a color in your HTML document, use the hex code that appears in this chart above the color you want. To mix custom colors, change the code using any combination of numbers **1** through **9**, and letters **a** through **f**. Always remember to precede the number with the crosshatch symbol (**#**).

Because the colors shown in the following chart are printed, they will appear different than the actual colors you see on your computer monitor. In general, the colors you see on your computer will be lighter than those shown in this chart. Use the chart as a quick reference to get you close to the color you want, then make adjustments to your hex code to fine-tune your color selection. ●

#ffffff	#ccffff	#99ffff	#66ffff	#33ffff	#00ffff	#ff99ff	#cc99ff	#9999ff
#ffffcc	#ccffcc	#99ffcc	#66ffcc	#33ffcc	#00ffcc	#ff99cc	#cc99cc	#9999cc
#ffff99	#ccff99	#99ff99	#66ff99	#33ff99	#00ff99	#ff9999	#cc9999	#999999
#ffff66	#ccff66	#99cc66	#66ff66	#33ff66	#00ff66	#ff9966	#cc9966	#999966
#ffff33	#ccff33	#99ff33	#66ff33	#33ff33	#00ff33	#ff9933	#cc9933	#999933
#ffff00	#ccff00	#99ff00	#66ff00	#33ff00	#00ff00	#ff9900	#cc9900	#999900
#ffccff	#ccccff	#99ccff	#66ccff	#33ccff	#00ccff	#ff66ff	#cc66ff	#9966ff
#ffcccc	#cccccc	#99cccc	#66cccc	#33cccc	#00cccc	#ff66cc	#cc66cc	#9966cc
#ffcc99	#cccc99	#99cc99	#66cc99	#33cc99	#00cc99	#ff6699	#cc6699	#996699
#ffcc66	#cccc66	#99cc66	#66cc66	#33cc66	#00cc66	#ff6666	#cc6666	#996666
#ffcc33	#cccc33	#99cc33	#66cc33	#33cc33	#00cc33	#ff6633	#cc6633	#996633
#ffcc00	#cccc00	#99cc00	#66cc00	#33cc00	#00cc00	#ff6600	#cc6600	#996600

#6699ff	#3399ff	#0099ff	#ff33ff	#cc33ff	#9933ff	#6633ff	#3333ff	#0033ff
#6699cc	#3399cc	#0099cc	#ff33cc	#cc33cc	#9933cc	#6633cc	#3333cc	#0033cc
#669999	#339999	#009999	#ff3399	#cc3399	#993399	#663399	#333399	#003399
#669966	#339966	#009966	#ff3366	#cc3366	#993366	#663366	#333366	#003366
#669933	#339933	#009933	#ff3333	#cc3333	#993333	#663333	#333333	#003333
#669900	#339900	#009900	#ff3300	#cc3300	#993300	#663300	#333300	#003300
#6666ff	#3366ff	#0066ff	#ff00ff	#cc00ff	#9900ff	#6600ff	#3300ff	#0000ff
#6666cc	#3366cc	#0066cc	#ff00cc	#cc00cc	#9900cc	#6600cc	#3300cc	#0000cc
#666699	#336699	#006699	#ff0099	#cc0099	#990099	#660099	#330099	#000099
#666666	#336666	#006666	#ff0066	#cc0066	#990066	#660066	#330066	#000066
#666633	#336633	#006633	#ff0033	#cc0033	#990033	#660033	#330033	#000033
#666600	#336600	#006600	#ff0000	#cc0000	#990000	#660000	#330000	#000000

Glossary

A

absolute path A directory path that starts at the top level of your computer filing system. For example, `<a href="/c:/vacweb/pages/past/vacations.html">` specifies a link using an absolute path to the the file `vacations.html`. In the anchor tag, absolute pathnames always start with a forward slash. They give you the advantage of not having to know the location of the page you're linking to in relation to the page you're linking from. However, they're somewhat risky because they'll instantly break if you change the name of any folder along the path.

absolute size The specified size of text. Text can be assigned a size from 1 to 7. The default base font size is 3. Specifying `size="4"` increases the font size from the default size.

action The attribute of an HTML form that dictates what happens when the user submits the form. Normally, the action references a script on the Web server that processes the information gathered by the form.

Active Server Format (`.asf`) Microsoft's original file format developed for streaming audio and video over the Web. It is still useable, but has been replaced by Windows Media Audio (`.wma`) and Windows Media Video (`.wmv`).

AIFF An uncompressed audio file format capable of better-than-CD-quality audio. AIFF files are used mainly on Macintosh systems.

animated GIF A GIF file made up of several individual frames that you create with image-editing software. Each frame is slightly different from the others; when the frames are played in succession by the browser, movement is implied. Animated GIF files play continuously while the page is open in the browser.

ASCII text The format in which all HTML documents must be saved in order for them to be read by the browsers that display the documents as pages.

attribute A modifier of a basic HTML command (called a tag). For example, if you are defining something called Gary with the basic tag `<gary>`, a version of the command that includes some attributes might be `<gary height="tall" coloring="dark" appearance="handsome">`. Sounds like someone worth knowing!

AVI A video format capable of high-quality video with varying levels of video compression. AVI files are the standard for Windows machines.

B

base font The size and face of the default text used on the page. You can change the look of the base font with the `<basefont>` tag.

block elements Tags that create a paragraph break in addition to their main function. Tags such as the paragraph tag, the list tag, and the six heading tags all qualify as block elements.

body The area of the page where all the real action takes place! The information you type between the `<body>` tag and the `</body>` tag appears on your Web page when it is viewed in a browser. You'll write most of your HTML within the `<body>` tag pair.

browser The application that can read the HTML file you have created and interpret the code to display the Web page as you intended it to look. Some browsers can display text, graphics, and frames; other browsers can display only text. Specialized browsers exist for the vision impaired. Commonly available browsers include Internet Explorer, Netscape Navigator, and Opera. Note that just becuase your Web page displays properly in one browser does not mean that it will display properly in every other broswer. You should test your pages in as many browsers—and in as many versions of each browser—as practical.

browser-safe colors The 216 colors that you can be sure will show up properly in a browser running on an 8-bit (low-resolution) monitor. If such a browser is forced to read an image with more than 216 colors, it replaces non-safe colors with ones from the browser-safe palette. In hex, browser-safe colors use combinations of these hex pairs: `00`, `33`, `66`, `99`, `cc`, and `ff`. In RGB, the numbers are 0 and multiples of `51`.

bulleted list *See* unordered list.

C

cell padding The space between the contents of the cell and the edge of the cell or the cell's border, if you're using a border. Define cell padding with the `cellpadding` attribute of the `<table>` tag.

cell spacing The space between one cell and the next cell in a table. Define cell spacing with the `cellspacing` attribute of the `<table>` tag.

check box list A list of items on a form, each of which is preceded or followed by a check box. The user makes selections from the list by clicking the appropriate check boxes.

closing tag The second of a tag pair that repeats the opening tag and is prefaced by a forward slash (/). For example, in the tag pair `<html> </html>`, the second tag, `</html>`, is the closing tag. The opening tag begins the formatting, and the closing tag ends the formatting. Closing tags are required in XHTML.

comments Text included in an HTML document that appears only in the text file; it cannot be seen in the browser view of the page. Comments help organize the document and make it much easier to understand what was written and to remember why it was written when you (or others) work with the HTML document in the future.

HTML comments are defined by the **<!--** and **-->** tags. Anything appearing between these tags is recognized by the browser as a comment and will not be displayed in the browser window.

controls The fields, boxes, and buttons you include on an HTML form to gather information.

crawler page A page that contains hyperlinks to all the pages in your site. When you register your page with a search site, register the crawler page. The site's robot will then follow all the links on your crawler page and add the linked pages to the database. This is a good way to make sure that all the pages in your site wind up in the search index.

crop To physically cut away portions of an image that are not central to the theme or focus of the image.

CSS (Cascading Style Sheets) A technology used as part of XHTML to define the elements used to create the page. Style sheets are used, for example, to control the font used in paragraphs, set the leading, and position the paragraph on the page. They allow for much greater control over page layout because you can specify exact locations of objects, even overlapping objects if desired. Cascading refers to the level of precedence that exists between various types of style sheets. For example, you can add a reference to an external style sheet document to define your elements. If you add an embedded style sheet to an individual page, the embedded style overrides the settings of the external style sheet when the two conflict. Finally, you can add an inline style sheet that overrides any conflicting style from an embedded or an external style sheet.

D

database-driven Web site A sophisticated method of creating a Web site that is linked to a database of information with a server-side script. The script can populate data to, and read data from, the database and then act on that data. Using this technology, you can write scripts that can automatically serve custom Web pages and dynamically interact with the visitor.

declaration When working with style sheet rules, the declaration defines the rule for the selector (the item being defined). The declaration has two parts: the property and the value.

dedicated phone line A telephone line that does nothing but maintain an open connection between your computer and the Internet. Alternatives to a dedicated phone line include cable modems, T1 lines, ISDN lines, and DSL.

definition list A type of list that gives you a good way to present terms and their definitions. You might use a definition list to create a glossary of terms used on your Web site. Definition lists contain a term to be defined and a block of explanatory text. The **<dl>**...**</dl>** tag pair defines a definition list.

deprecated tag A tag designated as obsolete by the W3C. The W3C intends for you to use CSS instead of deprecated tags. Deprecated tags remain in popular use, however, and are likely to remain in use for some time to come.

digitization The process of getting an image from a canvas, a piece of paper, or some other tangible form onto your computer in digital form.

document An electronic computer file that contains the information necessary to create a particular entity. For example, the HTML code that you write for a Web page might be stored as a Notepad text document, but the graphic that you want to appear on the Web page might be created as a Microsoft Paint graphics document.

domain name An Internet address for a site, such as **yoursite.com**. The first part of the address usually identifies a particular computer. The second part indicates what kind of organization is in charge: Commercial sites use **.com** or **.net** (for networks); not-for-profit organizations use **.org**; schools use **.edu**; and the U.S. military uses **.mil**. Sites not based in the United States typically use an extension that identifies their country of origin. For example, a German site might be **www.deutschweb.de**.

drop-down list A form control that, when you click the arrow at the right-end of the field, drops down a menu of options from which you can choose a single option or multiple options. A variation of this type of list displays multiple list items in a "permanently open" window. You also have the option of creating a scrollable list.

E

embedded style sheet Tag definitions that are included in the **<head>** tag pair for the page. Like an external style sheet, an embedded style sheet controls the appearance of page elements that use tags defined by the style sheet. An embedded style sheet controls only the page in which the style sheet is embedded; embedded style sheets override any external style sheets applied to the page. *See also* external style sheet *and* inline style sheet.

encode To transform a file from a full-quality format (such as AVI, WAV, or AIFF) to a streaming format (such as ASF, WMA, WMV, or RM).

exclusive list *See* radio button list.

external style sheet A separate text document that contains the definitions of all the tags used in the XHTML page (or multiple pages) that references the style sheet. By changing the definition or attributes of the tag in the style sheet, you effectively change every tag in every page that relies on the style sheet. *See also* embedded style sheet *and* inline style sheet.

F

face The name of the font style you use for your text. For example, Helvetica and Times Roman are font faces; when you combine a font face with a font size, you have a font.

font The style of text you use on your page. Although the word "font" is frequently misused for "face," this book uses the word "font" to refer to the combination of font size and font face.

form A section of an HTML document that resembles paper forms you're used to filling out with a pen. The purpose of the form is to gather information from your Web site visitors and return that data to you. Use the `<form>`...`</form>` tag pair to define a form. *See also* server-side scripting.

frame A simple Web page that displays as part of a larger, more complex page called a frameset. Typically, a page that uses frames displays two or more frames, each of which acts independently of the other frames on the page (for example, each frame can have its own content and scrollbars).

frameset The group of multiple frames that have been associated to create a single Web page.

frameset XHTML version The XHTML you are writing when you develop framed pages using CSS.

G–H

GIF A graphics file format suitable for computer-generated images such as logos that have blocks of solid color. The GIF format makes use of lossless compression techniques, which means that image quality doesn't degrade when you compress the file.

glossary list *See* definition list.

head area The location in the HTML file that contains information such as your page title, indexing information, expiration and creation dates, and author information. For pages that use scripting technologies such as JavaScript, the head area might contain scripting information. With the exception of the page title, the information that appears between the `<head>` and `</head>` tags cannot be seen in the browser.

hexadecimal The base-16 system used in many aspects of computer programming. Hex values consist of the numbers 0 through 9 plus the letters a, b, c, d, e, and f. For example, the hex value `0` means 0; the value `f` means 16. The HTML `<color>` tag (along with a few others) uses a hex value to specify a specific color (such as 000000, which is pure black).

host *See* Web server.

hotspot On an imagemap, a particular area that, when clicked, links to another Web page. For example, on an imagemap graphic that shows the United States, the area occupied by the State of Wisconsin can be defined as a hotspot; click the Wisconsin hotspot to link to a page about the wonders of cheese.

HTML (HyperText Markup Language) The computer language (or code) used to create documents published as Web pages to the Internet, and for many other purposes. HTML uses a system of indentifiers called tags to identify specific elements of a document.

hyperlink The simple name for the technology that allows a visitor to your page to click a word or picture and jump to another Web page that exists either on your site or on any other site in existence. The `<a>`...`</a>` tag pair defines a hyperlink.

I

image editor A software program that allows you to manipulate images. Sometimes referred to as "paint" programs, image editors are used to prepare graphics for the Web. The most popular program in this area is Adobe Photoshop. Another popular program is Macromedia Fireworks. For the examples in this book, I've used both Adobe Photoshop and Sonic Foundry Viscosity.

image slicing The process of breaking up a large image into several smaller pieces, and then using an HTML table to reassemble the image in the browser. Image slicing is one way to create the illusion that the page is loading faster than it is. You might also slice an image when you have a graphic that is the same on several pages except for one portion: You slice the image to isolate the changing portion, download the nonchanging portion, and then have to download only the changing portion the next time that image is used.

imagemap A set of defined areas that correspond to portions of a graphic. Each defined area can link to a different location. For example, an imagemap can be applied to a photograph of a desktop cluttered with office supplies. The imagemap can link to the various areas of an online office-supply catalog: Click a pencil to see a list of the writing implements in the catalog; click the paper to see a list of paper supplies, and so on. *See also* hotspot.

inline elements Tags incorporated into a line of text without causing the text to break into a new paragraph. Tags such as font, bold, and italic simply tell the browser to make the text that falls between the opening and closing tags look a certain way.

inline style sheet Style definitions that are added in the same way as any other inline tag in your HTML page. Inline style sheets are perfect for making isolated changes to a headline, paragraph, picture, or other page element. Inline style sheets override both embedded and external style sheets. *See also* embedded style sheet *and* external style sheet.

ISP (Internet Service Provider) A company that provides access to the Internet. Most ISPs can also host Web sites on their Web servers, of which they usually have more than one. A good ISP will also provide technical support and will be happy to answer questions you have when trying to set up your Web site. An ISP might provide a range of other Web-related services in addition to hosting your Web site. These services might include support for server-side scripting and database technologies, Web site design, site statistics compilation, and much more.

J

JPEG A compressed graphics file format suitable for continuous-tone images such as photographs. The JPEG format makes use of lossy compression techniques, which means that image quality is degraded when you compress the file.

jukebox Software that allows you to manage and listen to the music on your computer's hard drive. Some jukeboxes also allow you to listen to and view streaming audio and video, translate files from one format (such as **.mp3**) to another (for example, **.wma**), rip songs from a compact disc, and burn songs to recordable compact discs.

K-L

kerning Controlling the space between two adjacent letters. *See also* tracking.

leading (Pronounced *led-ing*, rhymes with *letting*). The space between lines of text in a paragraph or a group of paragraphs.

link *See* hyperlink.

Liquid Audio A compressed audio file format suitable for delivering high-quality audio files by downloading them over the Web.

local link A link to another page on the same Web site (on the same Web server as the page containing the link). Local links provide a great way for you to build cross-references into your Web site. *See also* remote link.

logical tag A text-formatting tag that tells the browser of your intended use for the text, but that leaves it to the browser to decide how to display it. For instance, the `<em>` tag tells the browser that you're using this text for emphasis. Most browsers translate this tag to italics, but you can't count on that treatment from all browsers. *See also* physical tag.

lossless compression A type of file compression that makes the file size smaller, but does not damage the quality of the image. In the audio world, Sonic Foundry Perfect Clarity Audio is a lossless compression format. In the graphics world, the GIF format is a lossless format.

lossy compression A type of file compression that makes the file size smaller by degrading the quality of the file. In the audio world, MP3 is a lossy format. In the graphics world, JPEG is a lossy format. You have to find a comfortable trade-off between file size and image quality.

M

mailto link A link that, when clicked, launches the user's default e-mail message window so that the user can compose an e-mail message. The link fills in the **To:** field automatically based on how you code the link. For instance, the link `<a href="mailto:gary@garyisp.com">` will automatically fill the **To:** field with **gary@garyisp.com**.

margin The space between the contents of a page and the edges of that page. In CSS, *margin* also refers to the space between the edges of adjacent object boxes.

MP3 A compressed audio file format suitable for downloading high-quality audio files from the Web. This has become a wildly popular format. MP3 is a lossy compression technology.

N

nested tag A tag, or tag pair, included within another tag pair is said to be nested. The tag pair `<b>...</b>` is nested within the tag pair `<i>...</i>` in this example: `<i><b>...</b></i>`.

nesting The process of putting one element inside another element. For example, you might put a table of data within a table that defines the layout of your page. In this case, the table of data is said to be nested within the table that defines the page layout.

numbered list *See* ordered list.

O

object box The rectangular area in which text or graphics modified by CSS are contained on the page. Each paragraph on a page, for example, is contained in a separate object box. Style sheets can manipulate the properties for each object box as a group or separately.

OggVorbis A compressed audio file format suitable for delivering high-quality audio files by downloading them over the Web. OggVorbis was developed as an open source alternative to the MP3 format. It is a lossy compression technology.

One-Pixel GIF Trick A technique that enables you to insert a specific amount of space on your HTML page. Create an image that's one pixel wide and one pixel tall. Make it a one-color image and specify that color as transparent when you save the file as a GIF. Now add that invisible image to your page and use the **hspace** or **vspace** attribute of the `<img />` tag to create extra space around the image, thus adding space on your page.

You can use this trick to indent the first line of a paragraph, add space between letters, and so on. Remember that in HTML, you can't just press the Tab key.

ordered list A type of list used when the list items have an order of importance. For instance, you'd use an ordered list to display the numbered steps of a recipe or your top five favorite vacation attractions. An ordered list supplies numbers (Arabic numerals or uppercase or lowercase Roman numerals) in front of each list entry. The `<ol>...</ol>` tag pair defines an ordered list.

P

padding The space between the text or image contained in an object box created by CSS and the border of the box.

page *See* Web page.

password field A form control that is similar to the text field but that displays asterisks (*) instead of the actual characters that the user types. The password field provides no real security for the information typed into it. It merely prevents someone who might be looking over your shoulder from reading what you type.

persistent style sheet A style sheet that cannot be overridden by browser settings. You make a style sheet persistent by using the `rel="stylesheet"` attribute of the `<link>` tag.

physical tag A text-formatting tag that tells the browser exactly how to format the text. For instance, the `<i>` tag tells the browser to format the text as italic. *See also* logical tag.

property When working with style sheet rules, the property is the specific aspect of the selector you want to define. You can specify a number of different properties in each rule. For instance, to change the color of the text within your paragraph tag pairs, use the `color` property. Type `p { color: }` to declare `color` as the property you want to define.

pull-down menu *See* drop-down list.

push button A special form control that allows you to create a button to which you can assign a custom action. These buttons normally reference a server-side script (such as a JavaScript).

Q - R

QuickTime A video format capable of rendering high-quality video with varying levels of video compression. QuickTime is the format developed by Apple for the Macintosh. The QuickTime format can also be used as a streaming format.

radio button list A list of items on a form, each of which is preceded by a selection circle. The user can select only one of the options in the group of options presented at a time; this type of list is called an exclusive list.

RealMedia by RealNetworks (`.rm`) The RealNetworks format developed for streaming audio and video over the Web.

redirector file A file that is called by the HTML in your page, which in turn calls the streaming media on your streaming server. The On-Demand Producer program creates the redirector file for you; you might want to talk to your ISP about what you have to do to create the proper redirector file.

relative path A directory path that starts in the current file and "backs up" or "goes forward" in the filing system to the target file. For example, if you want to create a relative link from `c:/pages/past/current.html` to `c:/pages/future/target.html`, type `<a href="../future/target.html">`. Relative pathnames are preferred over absolute pathnames because they are harder to break. You can change the name of the `pages` and `past` folders without breaking this link. For this reason, relative paths make your pages easier to move to your Web server.

relative size The specified size of text relative to the size of the base font. You can change the size of the font from the default of 3 to 5 by using `size="+2"`.

remote link A link to a page that exists on a site somewhere on the Web (that is, on a site other than the local site). Remote links are what make the Web interesting. *See also* local link.

RGB (Red, Green, Blue) A model used to specify a particular color by defining a combination of red, green, and blue light. In the RGB model, every color is defined by its RGB "recipe," that is, by the amounts of red, green, and blue light that are combined to make the color. Each color can have a possible value ranging from 0 to 255 units (a total of 256 possible levels per color). In this model, the color black is represented as `0, 0, 0` (that is, no light at all); white is `255, 255, 255` (the maximum of all three color lights); red is `255, 0, 0`; green is `0, 255, 0`; blue is `0, 0, 255`; and yellow is `255, 255, 0`.

robot A technology used by search engines and indexing sites to add more Web pages to their databases. The robot roams the Web, searching for hyperlinks. It follows the links and logs the new pages. It then follows the links on the new page, and continues on.

S

script A miniprogram that performs a designated set of actions. The actions of a script can be predetermined, or can depend in part on input from the Web visitor. Scripts can run locally (on the client side, scripts are usually written in JavaScript) or remotely (on the server side, scripts are usually written in PERL or VBScript).

search engine A Web tool that compiles an index of existing sites. When you "search the Web" for a term or phrase, the search engine refers to its index and posts results from that index. Different search engines have different methods of creating their indexes, so searches for the same term will turn up different results on different engines. Some popular search engines are **www.yahoo.com**, **www.google.com**, **www.bigfoot.com**, **www.altavista.com**, **www.lycos.com**, **www.askjeeves.com**, **www.bomis.com**, **www.alltheweb.com**, and **www.dogpile.com**. There are also specialized search engines that focus on a particular area of interest.

selector When working with style sheet rules, the selector specifies (or selects) the item to be defined. Selectors are really just HTML tags. For example, the selector is p if you want to define the **<p>** tag. *See also* declaration.

server-side scripting The process of creating a script, or a miniprogram (usually in Perl script or VBScript), that runs on the Web server to process the information gathered by a form on a Web page. *See also* form.

site *See* Web site.

size The size of the text you place on your page. In HTML, size can be one of only several values: 1 through 7. Depending on the browser, a font size of 3 might appear to be different heights.

spider *See* robot.

streaming media (audio and video) A technique for transferring data from a server to a Web browser so that the data can be processed as a steady stream. The technology allows the visitor to listen to or view the media even as it continues to download. This allows Web sites to provide video and audio media that would take too long to download in the traditional way. This technology has become important because most people still do not have fast enough connections to the Internet to download large multimedia files.

strict XHTML version The XHTML you are writing when you use CSS to control all your formatting. In strict XHTML, you do not use any deprecated HTML tags.

T

table An organized structure of rows and columns used for presenting data in a logical format. Tables are also used extensively for controlling page layout in HTML. Use the <table>...</table> tag pair to define an HTML table.

table headings Special cells in an HTML table that are treated differently than regular table cells. Most browsers show the text in table headings as bold and centered. Use the **<th>**...**</th>** tag pair to define a table heading cell.

tag The most basic element of HTML code. A tag begins with a left angle bracket (<) and ends with a right angle bracket (>). The tag name that appears between the brackets defines the HTML command. Modifiers to the basic command (called attributes) are also included between the brackets. Learning how to use tags and attributes is the key to learning HTML.

tag pair The set of two tags that together constitute the complete tag. Although HTML lets you omit the closing tag in some cases, XHTML does not. For example, the tag pair **<html>**...**</html>** identifies every HTML page that you create; all other tags are nested between the opening and closing **<html>** tags.

text area A form control that enables the user to input large amounts of text.

text editor A program that lets you type text characters and save the document file as a simple ASCII text file. To work, an HTML document must be saved as an ASCII text file. Examples of basic text editors are Notepad, Wordpad, and Simple Text.

text field A form control that accepts a few short words of text from the user.

thumbnail A small image that appears on the page to represent a larger, more detailed image. The thumbnail image can be formatted as a link, so that when the visitor clicks the thumbnail, the larger, more detailed image file loads.

title area The location in the HTML file that contains text that will appear in the title bar at the top of most browsers. This is the text that also appears on someone's bookmark or favorites list if they choose to add your page to their list of favorite sites; many search engines use the title information you provide here to identify your page. The title information is defined by the **<title>** tag pair, which is nested within the **<head>** tag pair.

tracking Controlling the space between letters in a block of text. *See also* kerning.

transitional XHTML version The XHTML you are writing when you mix CSS with deprecated tags to control the formatting of your pages.

tweening A process of creating an animation in which you supply the first and last frames of the animation sequence and let another entity (such as the Macromedia Flash program) create the intermediate steps in the sequence.

U-V

unordered list A type of list that allows you to present a list of items that don't necessarily have a particular order. For instance, you might use an unordered list to list your favorite foods or to list the places you've visited on vacation. Unordered lists use bullet points (•) in front of each list entry; the look of these bullet points can be changed. The <ul>...</ul> tag pair defines an unordered list.

unvisited link A link on which the visitor has not yet clicked. By default, these links are usually blue underlined text.

vector graphics A way of creating graphics that relies on vectors rather than on actual bitmapped lines and fills. Macromedia's Flash program uses vector graphics to create animation files that are lean and efficient and that therefore work extremely well on the Web.

W

W3C (World Wide Web Consortium) According to the W3C Web site at **`www.w3c.org`**, "The World Wide Web Consortium (W3C) develops interoperable technologies (specifications, guidelines, software, and tools) to lead the Web to its full potential as a forum for information, commerce, communication, and collective understanding." The W3C strives to develop `open standards` so that the Web evolves in a single direction. This is the organization that tries to keep browser manufacturers honest!

WAV An uncompressed audio file format capable of better-than-CD-quality audio. WAV files are used mainly on Windows-based systems.

Web page An HTML document that is usually one of many related documents that are published to the Internet as a group and that are available for anyone to view with the proper browser software.

Web server The computer that serves the contents of a Web site to visitors to that site. Normally, you'll rent space on a Web server (frequently simply called a server) from an ISP, but you can also learn to set up and maintain your own server.

Web site A group of related HTML documents (or Web pages) that are published to the Internet and that are available for anyone to view with the proper browser software.

Web-safe colors *See* browser-safe colors.

white space Any spot on a page that doesn't contain text, images, or graphical elements. Proper placement and use of white space is as important as the proper placement of page elements in effective graphic design.

Windows Media Audio (`.wma`) The Microsoft format developed for streaming audio over the Web.

Windows Media Video (`.wmv`) The Microsoft format developed for streaming video over the Web.

WYSIWYG (What You See Is What You Get) editor A type of Web page development program that enables you to drag and drop objects on the screen to create the kind of layout you want your Web page to have. The editor itself writes the HTML code to display what you have designed. Because these types of editors can create document files that contain unnecessary and redundant HTML code, the pages they create might take longer to download. Therefore, using these types of editors might not be the best way to create an efficient Web page.

X-Y-Z

XHTML (eXtensible HyperText Markup Language) According to the W3C, XHTML is "a reformulation of HTML 4.0 as an application of the Extensible Markup Language (XML)." XML is a structured set of rules for defining any kind of data to be shared on the Web. Extensible means that you can invent your own markup tags for a particular purpose. This is where Web development is headed in the future. In a way, you can think of XHTML as HTML 5.0 because it is considered the next step after HTML 4.0. There will never be an actual HTML 5.0. The baton has been passed to XHTML 1.0. XHTML enables the page author to define new elements (tags and attributes) to control the structure of the Web page. You use Cascading Style Sheets to accomplish this task.

Index

Symbols

A

B

C

D

E

F

G

H

I

Q-R

S

T

U

V

W-Z